WAR *and* RESISTANCE *in the* PHILIPPINES, 1942–1944

WAR *and* RESISTANCE
in the
PHILIPPINES, 1942–1944

JAMES KELLY MORNINGSTAR

Naval Institute Press
Annapolis, Maryland

Naval Institute Press
291 Wood Road
Annapolis, MD 21402

© 2021 by James Morningstar

All rights reserved. No part of this book may be reproduced or utilized in any form or by any means, electronic or mechanical, including photocopying and recording, or by any information storage and retrieval system, without permission in writing from the publisher.

First Naval Institute Press paperback edition published in 2024.
ISBN: 978-1-55750-171-4 (paperback)
ISBN: 978-1-68247-629-1 (eBook)

The Library of Congress has catalogued the hardcover edition as follows:
Names: Morningstar, James Kelly, author.
Title: War and resistance in the Philippines, 1942–1944 / James Kelly Morningstar.
Description: Annapolis, Maryland : Naval Institute Press, [2021] | Includes bibliographical references and index.
Identifiers: LCCN 2020050510 (print) | LCCN 2020050511 (ebook) | ISBN 9781682475690 (hardcover) | ISBN 9781682476291 (ebook) | ISBN 9781682476291 (pdf)
Subjects: LCSH: World War, 1939–1945—Underground movements—Philippines. | Guerrillas—Philippines. | Philippines—History—Japanese occupation, 1942–1945.
Classification: LCC D802.P5 M67 2021 (print) | LCC D802.P5 (ebook) | DDC 940.53/599—dc23
LC record available at https://lccn.loc.gov/2020050510
LC ebook record available at https://lccn.loc.gov/2020050511

♾ Print editions meet the requirements of ANSI/NISO z39.48-1992 (Permanence of Paper).
Printed in the United States of America.

9 8 7 6 5 4 3 2 1

Maps drawn by Chris Robinson.

To Jon Tetsuro Sumida

"The last great gentleman among military historians"

Contents

List of Maps   ix

Preface   xi

1. Introduction: Three Roads to War   1
2. A Time to Die: December 1941–March 1942   11
3. The Death March: March–May 1942   42
4. Alone: May–August 1942   68
5. Islands at War: August 1942–January 1943   99
6. The Aid: January–May 1943   133
7. Divisions: May–October 1943   168
8. A Dangerous Game: October 1943–May 1944   202
9. The Return: May 1944–August 1945   235
10. Conclusion: Legacies   272

Notes   277

Selected Bibliography   345

Index   357

Maps

1.1	The Philippine Islands and major ethnic groups	2
2.1	Japanese invasion landings in the Philippines, December 1941	13
3.1	Situation, 8 May 1942	64
6.1	Major guerrilla units tracked by SWPA G-2, 1943–1944	136
6.2	Military districts and SWPA-appointed commanders, 13 February 1943	143
6.3	AIB missions to the Philippines, December 1942–July 1943	165
7.1	Philippine regional section missions, October 1943–October 1944	172
9.1	Intelligence coverage in the Philippines, 27 May 1944	243

Preface

In the two-and-a-half years between the Japanese conquest of the Philippines in 1942 and Gen. Douglas MacArthur's return in October 1944, some 260,000 guerrillas in the Philippines waged an epic campaign against imperial subjugation. Their fight inspired resistance by the general population on a national level, obstructed Japanese efforts to economically exploit the islands, and set the conditions for eventual liberation by U.S. forces. Their campaign gave critical weight to MacArthur's argument for returning to the Philippines and thereby altered the course of the Pacific War. Moreover, the guerrillas' struggle for power significantly defined the social and political aspects of the postwar Philippine nation. Their story, however, has never been fully told. There is no comprehensive official or scholarly account or assessment of their struggle. As a result, evaluations of the geographic, cultural, social, political, and economic dynamics of the war remain incomplete.

Drawing from considerable though narrowly focused literature, memoirs, and archival material, reinforced with a multidisciplinary academic approach, this book is an attempt to fill this historiographical void by providing a comprehensive narrative of the military and nonmilitary interactions between the Japanese, the Americans, and—above all—the Filipinos during the period of occupation. No one work, of course, can hope to capture the entirety of such an epic story. Rather, it is the intention of this book to provide a basis for a fuller discussion of resistance during war as experienced in the Philippines during World War II. As such, it is necessary to first provide historical context to the war.

1

Introduction

Three Roads to War

In many ways, World War II in the Philippines was the culmination of imperial conflict dating back to 1541 when a Spanish adventurer arbitrarily grouped 7,100 Southwest Pacific islands, with more than one hundred diverse tribes, and named them in honor of his king (see map 1.1).[1] For the next three hundred years Spanish administrators used military force to economically exploit the Philippines while assisting the Catholic church in pacifying the natives. Their subjects increasingly relied on "kinship networks" to maintain native social power.[2] An average family could count 825 members along paternal and maternal lines, with marriage doubling that number.[3] The Spanish colonizers therefore sought alliances through miscegenation with powerful native clans, resulting in an elite mestizo class of landowners connected to Spain through trade. Over time, Philippine society stratified into an uneasy hierarchy of Spanish and mestizo *hacienderos* (landowners), native noncultivating tenants, and sharecropper peasants.[4]

Generations of Filipino elites sent their children to European universities, and by the early nineteenth century they brought back radical democratic notions that climaxed with the failed Katipunan revolution of 1896–97. The American victory in the Spanish-American War in 1898, however, quickly rekindled Filipino hopes for independence. The U.S. Navy returned the revolutionary leader Emilio Aguinaldo from exile in Hong Kong to help secure the islands. Believing other powers—particularly Japan—were waiting to pounce, President William McKinley decided to retain the Philippines as a protectorate until they could govern and defend themselves. Aguinaldo felt betrayed by this decision and led

MAP 1.1 The Philippine Islands and major ethnic groups

a new insurrection that lasted until his defeat in 1902 at the hands of the Americans and their Filipino allies.

As McKinley suspected, U.S. control of the Philippines thwarted Japan's imperialist ambitions. In 1893 the Overseas Development Society in Tokyo delineated the empire's regional interests: "Men in the north, materials in the south."[5] Japan's seizure of Taiwan two years later reduced its distance to the Philippines from 1,500 to a mere 200 miles, and the Society cast its eyes on Philippine resources.[6] Tokyo offered to buy the islands from Spain before the Spanish-American War and immediately afterward proposed to occupy them with, or in lieu of, the United States.[7] As Japan's population exploded to more than 64 million people in the 1920s, officials there worried they were outgrowing the resource capacity of their national territory.[8] (The Philippines, roughly the same size as Japan, held fewer than 14 million people.) Tokyo responded with policies to encourage migration, and over the next ten years 510,000 Japanese moved to foreign countries.[9] As many as 20,000 Japanese moved to the Philippines, mostly to Davao, Mindanao.[10]

With domestic resources plentiful and population growth manageable in the Philippines, the Americans proved to be disinterested imperialists. They opted not to adequately invest in defenses for the Philippines, which U.S. military experts deemed fundamentally indefensible anyway. They pursued a native "attraction policy" that—despite its notable racism—seemed to placate most Filipinos with improved government, education, hospitals, sanitation, and other reforms.[11] This policy, however, did little to curb rising social antagonisms between Filipino underclasses and elites.

U.S.-guaranteed rights moved the Philippine class struggle into a new phase. Newly legal workers' and peasants' unions and political parties attracted international attention. In 1922 American communist William Janequette (alias Harrison George) invited labor leaders Jacinto Manahan, Domingo Ponce, and Crisanto Evangelista to the first congress of the Oriental Transportation Workers in Canton, China.[12] They returned to organize a secretariat "under the direction of the Third International of Moscow."[13] Subsequent trips to Canton, Shanghai, and Moscow led Manahan to establish the Communist Party in 1930 dedicated to independence, social revolution, and the overthrow of the Philippine government.[14] Meanwhile, Pedro Abad Santos founded the Socialist Party and the General Workers' Union (*Aguman ding Malding Talapagobra* [AMT]), with Luis Taruc as both Socialist Party general secretary and AMT political director.[15] When the Philippine supreme court outlawed the Communist Party in 1932, many party leaders fell in with the Socialists. Others seeking political participation and national independence joined the Sakdal political party of peasants organized the next year by Benigno Ramos.[16]

The rising Philippine political movements pushed the United States to honor its pledge to grant independence. In 1935 Congress responded with the Tydings-McDuffie Act that promised Philippine independence after a ten-year period intended to allow for the organization of a new government and military defenses. When Manuel Quezon became the country's first president, Franklin Roosevelt warned him that "the American military force in the Islands is too small to protect the Philippines against foreign invasion," and he deemed it "impossible to induce Congress to appropriate the necessary funds for the military defense of the Islands and the maintenance of an army of sufficient size to keep any enemy at bay."[17] Roosevelt granted Quezon's request to send his old friend Gen. Douglas MacArthur to be his military advisor and serve as the islands' first field marshal.

At the same time, the Tydings-McDuffie Act irritated Tokyo. Japan had recently invested millions of pesos both to build corporations in the Philippines and to help 775 Japanese-owned small stores in the islands compete with 13,818 rival Chinese shops.[18] Moreover, the United States was setting a precedent by being the first imperial nation to voluntarily free a colony. This not only undermined imperial systems, it also threatened Japan's interests by creating a new nationalistic Philippine government bent on restricting immigration and foreign economic exploitation. When Japan invaded China in 1937, it warily noted a protest boycott of Japanese products initiated by the Chinese community in the Philippines that monopolized 80 percent of the country's retail.

In July 1940 the Imperial Japanese Army general staff and the military affairs section of the war ministry reacted to the fall of France by issuing the "Principles to Cope with the Changing World's Situation." It argued that Japan's economy would suffer unless it "decided immediately to take the initiative in laying the groundwork in the south."[19] Japan then occupied northern French Indochina in September, although it would return portions of it to Vichy France. The second Fumimaro Konoe cabinet also considered striking British and U.S. possessions in the Pacific, leading the Japanese general staff to envision a new "self-supply area" between Manchuria, Australia, India, and the Pacific Islands—centered on the Philippines.[20]

To accomplish these aims, the Japanese army general staff first section research group issued "Proposals for the Governance of Occupied Territories in the Southern Area of Operations" that broadly described "destroying American strongholds" while cautioning that the "extraction of Philippine natural resources should not be looked upon as urgent."[21] The proposals stressed: "In any and all cases, our military forces are not to become involved in the direct governance of the country, except for the purpose of attaining our military mission or providing assistance to the Philippine government for the establishment of a new domestic economy."[22]

Forty-eight hours after the Germans crossed the Russian border on 22 June 1941, the Konoe cabinet pursued an unequal military alliance with Vichy French Indochina in hopes of isolating China. On 2 July a liaison conference of government and imperial general headquarters officials called for southern and eastern expansion of "the Greater East Asia Co-Prosperity Sphere"—an evolving concept of an economically self-sufficient Asian bloc free from Western influence.[23]

On 24 July, as Roosevelt offered to recognize French Indochina as a neutral country, Japanese troops disembarked at Cam Rahn Bay in southern French Indochina.[24] Twenty-four hours later, the U.S. president froze Japanese assets in the United States (and the Philippines), increased lend-lease shipments to China, and recalled MacArthur to active duty to command the single U.S. infantry division in the Philippines and nine native reserve divisions in a new command, the United States Army Forces, Far East (USAFFE). Roosevelt promised MacArthur an annual $6 million budget; in comparison, that month alone the United States sent $240 million in military aid to China.[25] MacArthur expected a similar investment in his force and began to plan accordingly. In the meantime, U.S. planners moved B-17 bombers to Manila in the belief they could deter the Japanese, whose cities were vulnerable to incendiary bombs.[26]

When Tokyo announced a French-Japanese joint defense pact on 29 July, the president of the prime minister's planning board, Teiichi Suzuki, delivered his confidential estimate that Japan possessed a two-month reserve of nickel, four months' worth of manganese, and one month's worth of Manila hemp—much-needed war resources that were available in the Philippines.[27] The imperial staff warned of "the inevitable and natural deterioration of relations with the United States" and ambiguously stated that Japan would "solve the southern area problem by taking advantage of opportunities."[28] Suzuki proposed four options for seizing the Philippines, each requiring the destruction of U.S. forces.[29] When Roosevelt declared an embargo of oil to Japan on 1 August, Japan held estimated reserves for "a one-and-a-half year supply at stable consumption rates."[30] War, of course, would increase consumption rates. There were vulnerable oil fields in the Dutch East Indies, but the U.S.-controlled Philippines stood in the way.

On 10 August the imperial army headquarters summoned the Catholic archbishop of Tokyo, Tatsuo Doi, and the bishop of Osaka, Yoshigoro Taguchi. Taguchi arrived the next day with Tatsuo's representative, Father Tatsuya Shimura, to be told that war was imminent. The army asked the prelates for 50 clergy and 150 laity for religious propaganda work in the Philippines.³¹ With more than 12 million Catholics in the islands, this request would secure one Japanese priest for every 240,000 Filipino faithful. Father Shimura gave Major Yokoyama of the general staff the names of three priests, five seminarians, and eight laity who would report to the army in November.

On 19 August Quezon announced: "Should the United States enter the war, the Philippines will follow her and fight by her side. . . . America's fight is our own fight."³² MacArthur, however, lacked the logistics to mobilize USAFFE's nine reserve divisions of Filipinos, and his one U.S. division was without one of its four authorized brigades and much of its equipment.³³ Nevertheless, he scheduled a gradual call-up of 120,000 Philippine army reservists to commence 1 September.

A liaison conference in Tokyo issued a national policy statement on 5 September: "The Empire, determined to face a war against the United States, Britain, and the Netherlands for the sake of self-existence and self-defense, will complete preparations for war with early October as the approximate deadline."³⁴ Until then, Japan would pursue negotiations.³⁵ Preparations seemed impeded by an air of fatalism hanging over Japan's decisionmakers. "The government has decided," said chief of the naval staff Osami Nagano, "that if there is no war, the fate of the nation is sealed. Even if there is war, the country may be ruined."³⁶ From 10 to 13 September the imperial navy's combined fleet assembled "all commanding officers and staff officers of the Fleet" at the naval staff college in Tokyo to war-game the seizure of the southern area and an attack on Hawaii.³⁷

Meanwhile, MacArthur drew up plans to use his 30,000 U.S. regulars and Philippine Scouts augmented by the 120,000 Filipino reservists to repel 50,000 invaders sometime in 1942. The first of three reserve regiments in each reserve division reported as ordered on 1 September; the second three would come at the end of October and the third toward the end of December.³⁸ Equipment shortages, obsolete weapons, ill-prepared leaders, and a pervasive lack of discipline would hamper their training.

The U.S. Army advertised for officers to command its new Philippine units. After a twenty-three-day voyage from San Francisco, signal corps Lt. Donald Blackburn reported in October to the 12th Infantry Regiment of Igorot reservists, who did not speak English.³⁹ "How do we train these people?" 2nd Lt. Charlie Youngblood asked him. Blackburn answered, "We're just going to have to draw pictures, I guess."⁴⁰

Infantry Capt. Russell Volckmann became the executive officer of the new 11th Infantry Regiment near Baguio. He recalled, "Officers, non-coms, and privates all had practically no knowledge of basic military tactics and techniques. What little they did know was in most cases either wrong or obsolete."[41] On paper the regiment had 1,850 soldiers; in reality it contained a smaller number of civilians in uniform. Moreover, President Quezon wanted to use the call-up to build better citizens. White House advisor Fred Howe toured MacArthur's command and witnessed the new soldiers training "in hygiene, in agriculture, in handicraft, and in making them ready to take up homesteads and establish themselves as self-respecting citizens."[42]

Curiously, neither MacArthur nor the Japanese considered unconventional warfare. The Japanese had seen pervasive guerrilla war in China. As a young officer, MacArthur fought Philippine guerrillas. In March 1933, when MacArthur was the Army chief of staff, Brig. Gen. C. E. Kilbourne of the war plans division informed him that the Philippines could not be defended and advised, "Let the department commander utilize his mobile troops as the nucleus of a large number of volunteer bands to conduct guerrilla warfare. The conquest of those islands could, in that way, be made very expensive and the forts could put up a defense that would be lastingly creditable to our flag."[43] Both MacArthur and the Japanese must have known the Filipino citizen-soldiers lacked the equipment, training, and cohesion to fight conventional battles. Even Quezon, a veteran guerrilla who served under Aguinaldo, never seemed to consider unconventional resistance against a Japanese invasion. Some others, however, did prepare for just such an option: in October, the communist leaders of the AMT party in Manila issued orders for "all cell groups to prepare for guerrilla warfare."[44]

Meanwhile, the Japanese military fretted. On 7 October Nagano warned chief of the army general staff General Hajime Sugiyama, "The undue extension of the time limit for the purpose of continuing negotiations will deprive us of the opportunity of taking the initiative in war and, in consequence, will make the carrying out of future operations more difficult."[45] The premier and foreign minister clashed with the war minister, while the navy minister remained indecisive. "Accordingly," an official later recalled, "Imperial General Headquarters pressed the Government to clarify its attitude on the issue of peace or war, but the Government was unable to give a definite answer."[46] Frustrated, the third Konoe cabinet resigned on 16 October.

The new prime minister, General Hideki Tojo, convened a liaison conference from 23 to 30 October under the assumption that war would begin in March 1942. The president of the planning board warned that Japan would have to occupy the oil fields in the southern areas four or five months before continuing fighting.[47] He also cautioned: "As time passes, the ratio of military strength between Japan and the United States will be more and more to Japan's disadvantage."⁴⁸ Another liaison conference convened with the emperor in the imperial court room on 5 November.⁴⁹ The prime minister, foreign minister, planning board president, finance minister, and military chiefs of staff briefed their plans for war. Under the assumption that the Philippines added four thousand soldiers each month, they decided to go to war in early December.

The chief of the army general staff predicted a fifty-day campaign to conquer the Philippines.⁵⁰ To seize the islands, he augmented the Fourteenth Army with the 16th Division, 48th Division, and two tank regiments.⁵¹ The 11th Air Fleet would fly support. The plan included detailed air raids and amphibious assaults, along with vague "mopping-up operations."⁵² There was no consideration of guerrilla resistance.

To command the Fourteenth Army, the imperial headquarters selected General Masaharu Homma, a thirty-four-year army veteran known for "a taste for good paintings and furniture, a modest talent for verse, a flair for Western languages."⁵³ On 10 November Homma reported to the chief of the general staff, the war minister, and the commander in chief of the Southern Army. They instructed that the Philippines' "existing administrative structures were to be utilized as much as possible and racial customs were to be respected."⁵⁴ Homma was to maintain foreign trade, national currency, and civil order, but he was told: "The people of the occupied countries were to be warned that they would have to face some deprivation as it would be necessary for the occupation forces to acquire certain defense materials."⁵⁵ The central authorities and the planning board in Tokyo would oversee the economic exploitation of the islands while Homma maintained order through the existing government.⁵⁶

Another liaison conference on 13 November approved a "Plan to Speedily Conclude Hostilities against the United States, Great Britain, and the Netherlands and the Chiang Regime."⁵⁷ It directed the military to establish "public peace, assist in the rapid acquisition of national defense resources and to help maintain the forces engaged in the operations."⁵⁸ No one seemed concerned about the numerous assumptions in the Japanese plans: MacArthur's defense would not last beyond fifty days; the Philippine government would remain an effective body under the Japanese; there would be no significant guerrilla resistance; and invasion would not cause unbearable hardship on Filipinos. They drafted no contingencies should any of those assumptions prove invalid.

The commanders of Japan's 3rd Fleet, 11th Air Fleet, and 5th Air Group met with the Southern Army on 14 and 15 November to prepare for operations in the Philippines.⁵⁹ Advance detachments would capture Batan Island, Vigan, Laoag, and Aparri and construct supporting airfields.

The 48th Division would land in the Lingayen Gulf, sweep central Luzon, and occupy half of Manila. The 16th Division would land in Lamon Bay, sweep southern Luzon, and occupy the rest of Manila. After a decisive battle for the Philippine capital, several detachments would seize Legaspi, Davao, and Jolo and secure naval bases in Subic Bay and Olongapo.[60]

The imperial general staff established the "restoration of law and order, immediate extraction of defense-related resources, and Occupation Force self-sufficiency, as the three cardinal rules of occupation."[61] They set targets for acquiring 50,000 tons of manganese, 50,000 tons of chrome, 100,000 tons of copper, and 300,000 tons of iron ore from the Philippines in the first year.[62] The head of the department of industries, Michizo Yamagoshi, prioritized assignments for Japanese industries: three copper mines at Mankayan, Hixbar (Rapurapu), and Antique; the chrome mine at Zambalese (Masinloc); two manganese mines at Bohol (Gundorman) and Busuanga; and, the iron mine at Kalambayangan.[63] The general staff also reiterated instructions for using "existing governmental institutions, protecting and respecting existing religious institutions, and the inevitability of burdening the livelihood of citizens in order to obtain defense resources and achieve self-sufficiency for the Occupation force."[64]

The Southern Army Group and Fourteenth Army completed their plans under the assumption that they would attack sometime in the new year.[65] On 26 November the Japanese representatives met once more with U.S. secretary of state Cordell Hull, who again demanded that Japan withdraw from China and Manchuria. The next day Tojo convened another liaison conference. On 29 November the senior Japanese leaders met with the emperor to confirm their belief that war was now inevitable.[66] Tojo recalled: "Japan desired an early decisive battle, but in war there was always the other side so there would always be times when the situation would not develop as expected or desired. Therefore, we must be prepared for a prolonged war."[67] He was thinking in terms of the larger war, not the Philippine campaign. Tojo addressed concerns about "unrest of the people at large," meaning Japanese citizens, not occupied populations.[68] He also admitted that "there was no definite plan as to the means by which the war would be terminated."[69]

Japanese government officials prepared an "Outline of Information and Propaganda Policies for the War between Japan and the Anglo-American Powers" to be issued in conjunction with the opening of hostilities. The outline denied Japan was declaring war against white people (so as not to offend their Axis allies) and said their cause was a moral one for a "new world order" that "enabled all nations and races to assume their proper place in the world, and all peoples to be at peace in their own sphere."[70] They believed this appeal would attract the cooperation of occupied peoples.

The next day at 1500 hours, Tojo met with the emperor, who noted that the navy was still against going to war. The prime minister argued they had no choice. The emperor authorized an imperial conference on 1 December with all the ministers to announce that negotiations had failed and the nation was going to war.

The Philippines, Japan, and the United States had arrived at the brink of war from three different margins of imperialism. The moment had caught the withdrawing Americans unprepared to safeguard their protectorate. The aggressive Japanese, however, were too late to thoroughly prepare their military for conquest and too optimistic that their promised "new world order" would pacify their conquered subjects. The Filipinos, attempting to create a new independent nation despite boiling social unrest, were caught on the field of battle between these imperial forces. Through the exchanges that followed, each side would learn the interconnected limits of their powers and vulnerabilities.

2

A Time to Die
December 1941–March 1942

MANILA, D1/R-1,048 (DAY 1 OF OCCUPATION/1,048 DAYS UNTIL MACARTHUR'S RETURN)

It was 8 December in the Philippines when the Japanese attacked Pearl Harbor. Isabel "Lita" Yumol, the nine-year-old daughter of a Manila attorney, first heard the news from a neighbor, followed by stories of attacks on Malaya, Thailand, Singapore, Guam, Hong Kong, and Wake Island. That night Lita asked her father if the Japanese would attack their home. He explained, "The Philippines is a commonwealth of the United States and we're friends, and so the Japanese will think of us as enemies."[1] Many Filipinos shared the same thought.

Japanese troops had in fact already seized the little island of Batan, 150 miles north of Luzon, and had begun building an airfield. General MacArthur had been caught with his underequipped U.S. division and nine partially mobilized Philippine divisions in USAFFE. Only days earlier, MacArthur had assigned four divisions with one cavalry regiment to Maj. Gen. Jonathan Wainwright to defend three likely invasion points on Luzon: the Lingayen Gulf, the Zambales coast, and the Bataan Peninsula.[2] He told Wainwright that there would be "no withdrawal from the beach positions," which were to be held "at all costs."[3] Ten hours after Pearl Harbor, however, Japanese warplanes struck the U.S. air base at Clark Field north of Manila and crippled General MacArthur's Far East Air Force.[4] Later that night, the U.S. Navy's Asiatic Fleet Task Force 5 abandoned Luzon for Australia.

Early on 9 December Japanese aircraft struck Nichols Field south of Manila. That evening, planes appeared over the capital. Manila resident Adalia Marquez recalled, "Utter confusion seized our whole neighborhood."[5] Helen Lawson Cutting, a member of the advertising staff at the *Philippines Herald*, asked editor Carlos Romulo, "Why aren't we fighting them? Where are our planes?"[6] He had no answer. Romulo was about to return to active military duty as an aide to MacArthur. Reporter Yay Panlilio, single mother of three, joined others from the paper walking to USAFFE headquarters to see the assistant chief of intelligence at Fort Santiago. Captain Ralph Keeler swore her in as a U.S. intelligence agent, badge number sixty-seven, with instructions to report anything important.

Japanese air attacks the next day destroyed U.S. Navy facilities at Cavite, putting around five thousand Filipinos out of work.[7] That morning, the Tanaka detachment landed on Luzon's north coast at Aparri while the Kano detachment came ashore on the northwest coast at Vigan. These were part of six Japanese advance landings that MacArthur dismissed as diversions.[8] He confided to reporters: "The basic principle of handling my troops is to hold them intact until the enemy commits himself in force. These small landings are being made to tempt me to spread out and weaken our defenses."[9] Against the Japanese incursions (see map 2.1), USAFFE defenses melted. A U.S. commander recalled that "when the Japs fired on the Filipinos, the noise would scare these guys more than anything else, and that they would often break and run."[10]

In the face of the invasion, most Filipinos clung to their way of life, the fields and paddies that provided their livelihoods. "They were poor people who had nothing to do with this new war and little knowledge of the events that brought it upon them," Lt. Ed Ramsey remembered.[11] Many Filipinas began cutting their prized long hair and dressing like men in hopes of avoiding Japanese attention. As Marquez explained, "We had heard about the sex atrocities the Japanese had committed in China."[12]

MacArthur began shifting forces and equipment across Manila Bay to the Bataan Peninsula and the island fortress of Corregidor. Thirty-nine-year-old Chick Parsons, a recently recalled U.S. Navy lieutenant, junior grade, supervised the fueling and supply of ships in Manila's port. Short and dark complexioned, Parsons had spent twenty years in the islands.[13] The first three years he served as a secretary for retired Gen. Leonard Wood and former governor-general W. Cameron Forbes, sailing the islands aboard the yacht *Apo* to investigate the readiness of the Philippines for independence. He later studied at the University of the Philippines and worked with several local companies before accepting a commission in

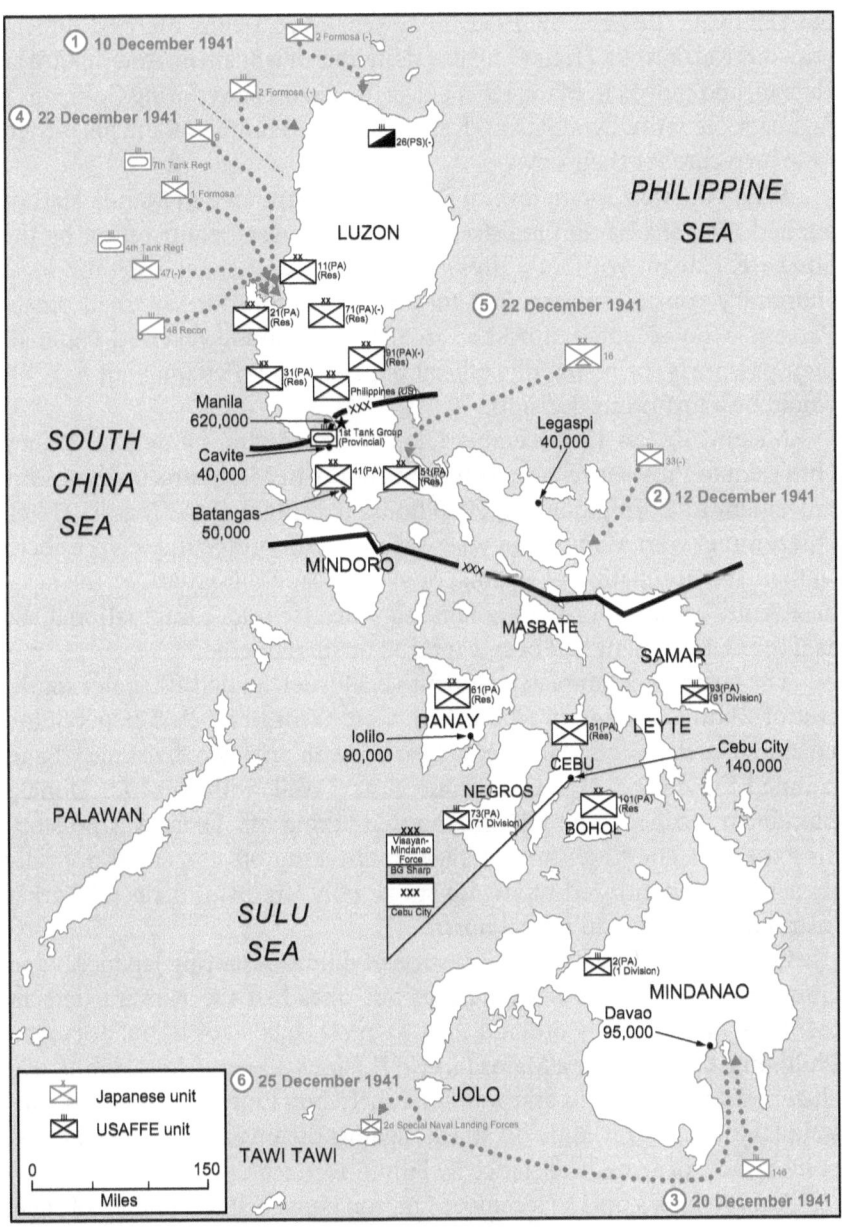

MAP 2.1 Japanese invasion landings in the Philippines, December 1941

the U.S. Navy Reserve. In 1932 thirty-year-old Parsons married fifteen-year-old Katraushka "Katsy" Jurika, daughter of a Spanish-American War veteran, and moved to Manila to manage the Luzon Stevedoring Company's tugboats. He retired young, and Katsy's widowed mother, Blanche, moved in to help care for their boys.

When the war began, several Danish ships stranded in Manila Harbor applied for Panamanian registration so as to escape confiscation by the Japanese. Caught without a diplomat in Manila, Panama sought a local "honorary consul" to carry out the transfer. Authorities reached out to Parsons, who accepted almost as an afterthought and received Panamanian passports for his family, official papers, and a Panamanian flag.[14] It would be a fortuitous decision.

Meanwhile, on 12 December General MacArthur's aide Col. Sidney Huff went to President Manuel Quezon's house in Mariquina to discuss his movement to Corregidor.[15] At 2000 hours that night at the Manila Hotel, Quezon met with MacArthur, who was intent on protecting the president so that "the occupation of Manila, or even of the Philippines, by the Japanese Army would not have the same significance under international law as if the Government had been captured or surrendered."[16]

The Japanese Kimura detachment's 2,500 men landed 200 miles southeast of Manila at Lagaspi where Maj. Gen. George M. Parker Jr.'s South Luzon Force defended 250 miles of beaches with only two divisions.[17] Sand jammed the defenders' few machine guns. "Well, with this," Lt. Donald Blackburn recalled, "the Filipinos started taking off. There was no stopping them."[18] The English- and Tagalog-speaking officers could not rally their untrained enlisted men who spoke only the Bicol dialect.[19] Parker instructed his forces to retreat north.

Officials in Manila received reports of Filipinos looting Japanese- and Chinese-owned stores in Camarines Sur ahead of the Kimura detachment's advance.[20] They ordered the provincial inspector of the Sorsogon Philippine Constabulary, Major Licerio P. Lapus, to move Legaspi's 40,000 citizens into nearby hills and wait for aid. To buy time, Lapus led his constabulary in small hit-and-run attacks against the invaders—likely the first of many acts of armed resistance by Filipino citizens.

At 1100 hours on 13 December Quezon convened his council of state, with vice president Sergio Osmeña, speaker of the national assembly Jose Yulo, chief justice Jose Abad Santos, and secretary of justice Jose P. Laurel among those in attendance. As liaison to MacArthur, senator Manuel Roxas wore his U.S. Army major's uniform.[21] Major General Basilio Valdes reviewed the call-up of 80,000 Filipino reserves, and Brigadier General Guillermo Francisco reported that his 6,000 constabulary men had "orders to round up all the Japanese and to take them to internment camps."[22] Interestingly, former guerrilla Quezon still did not consider irregular resistance.[23]

SOUTHERN LUZON, D7/R-1,042

As the Japanese advanced on Camarines Sur, assemblyman Mariano Villafuerte appealed to local governor Ramon Imperial to stop hiding and restore order in the provincial capital of Naga.[24] The governor instead deputized Villafuerte to act in his place. Villafuerte went to Naga, rallied the police, and got the government operating well enough to satisfy both the province and the commonwealth government.

At 0800 hours on 14 December the Japanese entered Naga. Residents had to decide to fight, flee, or cooperate. After sending the governor's brother, senator Domingo Imperial, to meet the invaders, Villafuerte left for his home in Sipocot. Japanese commander Denzo Kuriyama called for the governor, the former governor, assemblyman Ramon Felipe, and Villafuerte. "That early," Jose V. Barrameda Jr. wrote, "their policy apparently was to get the political big guns to serve in the government a-forming under the control of the Japanese military."[25]

For two days Kuriyama met with Villafuerte, both Imperial brothers, bishop Pedro P. Santos, and American judge Robert E. Manley, whose mansion had become the Japanese military police headquarters. It fell to Villafuerte to organize the province's thirty-two municipalities for occupation. With the provincial treasury's 600,000 pesos (P) frozen in the Philippine national bank, he needed a loan of P500,000 but found no source of funds. On 16 December Kuriyama released P3,000 to the province.[26]

Other Filipinos chose to fight. In Legaspi, Camarines Norte, recently elected congressman and Philippine army reserve lieutenant Wenceslao Q. Vinzons, assisted by Francisco "Turko" Boayes, organized several hundred men into Vinzons' Traveling Guerrillas (VTG).[27] They impounded a mill from Chinese merchant Dy Hian Sian and stashed its stockpiles of rice.[28] Vinzons then moved his provincial government from Legaspi to the remote town of Tuláy na Lupà.

Negritos from Labo came to Vinzons to complain of Japanese pillaging and raping.[29] He advised them to fight back with their bows and poison arrows. Several days later, incredible reports circulated of sixty Negritos destroying a column of two thousand Japanese on the Manila South road.[30] The diminutive dark-skinned tribesmen were natural guerrillas. The same could be said of the "pygmy-sized, bushy-haired, extremely dark skinned" Igorots, who dressed in loincloths and carried bolo knives and bows and arrows.[31] Army Cpl. Bob Stahl witnessed their lethality against a target one hundred feet distant: "Three arrows in not more than ten seconds, all without the attention-gathering noise of rifle fire, and if there had been a six-inch-diameter bull's eye on that tree, all three arrows would have been in it!"[32]

Barrameda reported: "During the first days, the invaders treated the civilians generally with almost exemplary courtesy, partly because most of the Japanese troops were being thrown northwards in a savage drive to bring MacArthur and his stubbornly heroic Filipino-American soldiers to their knees according to a timetable."[33] Vinzons set out to disrupt that timetable. At 0430 hours on 18 December the VTG attacked Japanese troops at Laniton bridge in Basud and killed five soldiers.[34] Six hours later, 120 Japanese soldiers arrived to clear out Daet. Vinzons fled with his men back to Tuláy na Lupà.

Near Iriga about halfway between Vinzons and Villafuerte, Philippine Constabulary sergeant Faustino Flor and municipal counselor Teofilo Padua organized the Camp Isarog guerrillas.[35] The group named Flor their captain with Padua as his first lieutenant and executive officer. Like most other rising guerrilla bands, they had more volunteers than weapons.

Almost all Filipinos carried knives with blades that varied by tribe: wavy *kris*, thick elliptical *barong*, curved *campilan*, and angled *kukri*. Guns were harder to find. Some gathered Springfield and Enfield rifles from abandoned USAFFE barracks or battlefields. Others created weapons such as the crude *baltik (or paltik)* made from sliding sections of a three-quarter-inch pipe, a nail, a wooden stock, and two-gauge shotgun shells.[36] It was not a long-range weapon. "Nor was the baltik accurate," Bob Stahl reported, "for without a rifle's bore to send it point-first on a direct course, the slug, *if* it hit its target, often hit broadside, with very effective results. Crude as it was, the baltik had killing power, and that was what mattered."[37]

To resist the advancing enemy columns, the Philippine government called up the country's militia, which also had more guts than guns. One U.S. officer observed, "Most had never seen a rifle and few possessed even uniforms."[38] Even junior and senior Reserve Officers' Training Corps (ROTC) cadets received orders to report to USAFFE. Instructors sent freshman and sophomore cadets home, however, though many would not stay there.

USAFFE hastily shuffled units to the front. Lieutenant Ed Ramsey had joined the 26th U.S. Cavalry at Fort Stotsenburg in June only to spend "every spare minute" preparing for a match against the Manila Polo Club. Meanwhile, he remembered, "reports of Japanese over-flights became so frequent that we scarcely took notice of them."[39] Now he had orders to take twenty-seven Filipino cavalrymen on horseback along with a staff car, a radio, two machine guns, and local constabulary troops, and defend the east coast from

Dingalen to Baler. Traveling across the area by car took more than three hours. "It was a forlorn hope," Ramsey recalled. "I knew it as I set out."[40]

DAVAO, MINDANAO, D13/R-1,036

Word of attacks by Filipinos on Japanese residents caused Homma to divert a battle group under Lieutenant Colonel Toshio Miura from Palau to Davao on 20 December.[41] The next morning, USAFFE chief of staff Richard Sutherland dictated a message to Washington: "Enemy attacking Davao with land forces from four transports. Engaged by advance elements of the 101st Division. If more than predatory effort I plan to launch guerrilla warfare throughout Mindanao with Mohammedan population."[42] In fact, he had no such plans.

After securing Davao, Miura released his 56th Brigade for Jolo Island and the Netherlands Indies. He then augmented his remaining battalion with local constabulary forces and tried to advance into Digos, Augusan, and Zamboanga. A few skirmishes later, he decided to remain around Davao.[43] The U.S. commander on Mindanao, Gen. William F. Sharp, thought it best not to attack Miura.[44]

CENTRAL LUZON, D15/R-1,034

Late on 22 December eighty Japanese ships dodged 155mm artillery fire and entered the Lingayen Gulf north of Manila. The next morning they landed six regiments of the 48th Division and threatened to cut off the 11th Philippine Regiment at the southern tip of the bay at Daguban. Major Russell Volckmann, a thirty-year-old West Pointer from Iowa, had just assumed command of the regiment.[45] His men scavenged shovels to prepare positions before receiving orders to retreat without ever having seen the enemy.

The commander of Camp John Hay at Baguio, Lt. Col. John P. Horan, tried to organize units retreating from the Lingayen Gulf. Regimental commanders Col. Donald Bonnett, Maj. Max Ganahl, Lt. Col. Martin Moses, and Lt. Col. Arthur Noble met with him to discuss waging guerrilla warfare from the area's many mines. Blackburn recalled, "Most of the mines, as the story went, had about six months to a year's supply of food, and quantities of weapons, and a lot of the miners were [in the] Reserves."[46] Horan radioed to MacArthur's headquarters 130 miles to the south. Most of the units, however, had no radios.[47]

With the Japanese cutting between Baguio and Manila, MacArthur authorized Horan to save the units.[48] Horan gathered his forces and retreated to Caranglan but turned back to Kiangan as the Japanese cut him off at Balete Pass. On Christmas Eve, Horan radioed: "My right hand is in a vise, my nose in an inverted funnel, constipated my bowels. Open my south paw."[49] USAFFE replied, "Save your command."[50] Horan destroyed his vehicles and equipment, dissolved his force, and authorized his men to either head for Bataan, surrender, or fight on as guerrillas. Filipino soldiers could go to their homes.[51]

As for himself, Horan opted to fight on as a guerrilla. Volckmann wrote: "As a result of this order, sparks of resistance spread to every corner of North Luzon, and from these sparks a flame sprang that burned throughout the dark days of the Japanese occupation."[52] Volckmann was clearly unaware that Lapus, Vinzons, and many other Filipinos had already begun guerrilla warfare against the Japanese.

SOUTHERN LUZON, D16/R-1,033

MacArthur left Bicol undefended. Lieutenant Colonel Montano Zabat of Albay, Sorsogon Province governor Salvador C. Escudero, and Gregorio Espinas in Sorsogon City filled the vacuum. Zabat led the strongest group with nearly four hundred armed men in Camarines Norte.[53] Escudero enjoyed powerful family and political connections in Sorsogon but inspired challenges from others—especially Lapus, who maintained a base near Manito in Albay on the remote Bulusan volcano slopes. The groups began competing for scarce support, leading the U.S. Army to report: "Fighting between units over matters of area command almost exceeds any fighting against the Japanese."[54]

Constabulary academy graduate Lieutenant Ernesto S. Mata led another one hundred armed men along the coast of Camarines Norte. Damaso O. Dianela, who claimed to be a U.S. Army captain, raised the Camp Tinawagan guerrillas in Camaroan. Major Francisco Sandico, senior constabulary in Bicol, and Lieutenant Julio Llanrezas raised other groups in Albay, and twenty-one-year-old Lieutenant Salvador Rudolfo led guerrillas on Cantanduanes. Captain Eustacio D. Orobia, a Philippine division air officer, would assume the title of "general" and organize two hundred men at the Bagong Katipunan around Jovellar.[55] Major Aguilar reportedly formed a band around Tiwi. Zabat, Lapus, and Padua competed for a small group under a Captain Tacerua on Burias Island.

NORTH AND CENTRAL LUZON, D17/R-1,032

In Pangasinan Province, Jose de Guzman led guerrilla attacks in Umingan, San Nicolas, Asingan, San Quentin, and Tying.[56] Closer to Manila,

Pacifico Cabreras led forty men in operations near Baliuag. Cagayan Province governor Marcelo Adduru moved his government from Tuguegarao to the inland town of Tuao on the Chico River. A reserve major in the Philippine army, Adduru had spent the past five months training his constabulary in guerrilla tactics.[57] He organized two companies, augmented by USAFFE stragglers under U.S. Capt. Ralph Praeger, into the Cagayan Guerrilla Force.

Praeger's C Troop of the 26th Cavalry had attempted to delay the invaders from Aparri in the Cagayan Valley until the enemy from the Lingayen Gulf cut them off. Praeger withdrew toward Ilocos Sur until receiving orders to disperse his force. He took what remained of C Troop back northwest and picked up a number of Filipino soldiers from disbanded units.[58] Praeger arrived at Adduru's headquarters with Lt. Francis Camp and three other American officers from Horan's command.

Lacking food, radios, sleep, and guidance, USAFFE units became increasingly frustrated as men stumbled past their limits of endurance.[59] Seeing his friend Cliff Hardwick shot through the head, Ramsey recalled, "I brooded over it all day until I felt I might be going mad."[60] Only the promise of reinforcements coming soon from the United States kept them going. Leaders in Washington, however, knew the bitter truth. In conversation with prime minister Winston Churchill, President Roosevelt confessed that the Philippines were lost, and Secretary of War Henry L. Stimson added: "There are times when men have to die."[61]

Early on Christmas Eve the Japanese 16th Division landed at Lamon Bay at the waist of Luzon. At 0900 hours Colonel Huff went back to Malacañang Palace to inform Quezon that it was time to move. That afternoon, Quezon departed with his family and staff for SS *Mayon* anchored about a mile out in the bay.[62] U.S. high commissioner to the Philippines Francis Bowes Sayre and his family and staff joined them.[63] Finally, at 1700 hours MacArthur followed them to Corregidor. Major General Francisco stayed behind to maintain law and order along with MacArthur's deputy chief of staff, Brig. Gen. Richard J. Marshall, who commanded the rear guard. Quezon left Laurel and Vargas with instructions: "You two will . . . deal with the Japanese."[64]

Homma approached the capital on Christmas Day, but he was already behind schedule. The next day MacArthur declared Manila an open city, denying the Japanese their decisive battle. He urged the 684,000 residents to leave the city, and about 400,000 would comply.[65] The Yumol family joined the exodus in an overloaded Packard headed for Bataan, but many relatives remained in Manila saying, "This is our home—we were born and grew up here; we built up this town. We would never abandon it; we need to keep it going."[66]

Looters broke into several storehouses along the harbor. Journalist Pacita Pestano-Jacinto of the *Manila Tribune* observed, "A horde of men, women and children clawing at each other to get in. The looted stores belong to the American companies. It is a shame."[67]

MacArthur's men withdrew to the Bataan Peninsula. On 27 December near Bayambang, Volckmann received orders to move his 11th Regiment another fifty miles to Bataan. He commandeered all the vehicles he could find and headed south. Bado Dangwa, who ran a transportation company in Mountain Province, turned over 130 buses and vehicles to USAFFE. When the Japanese arrived, he headed into the hills.

Japanese soldiers entered the home of twenty-five-year-old Japanese mestizo Cecile Okubo Afable, an editor for the *Baguio Midland Courier*. They executed her pacifist Japanese father and seized his house for use as a brothel because it had a grand piano.[68] About a hundred women were brought to the house as sex slaves for the soldiers. A number would be killed to prevent their escape or testimony after the war.

On 28 December Filipinos listened to President Roosevelt on the radio: "I give to the people of the Philippines my solemn pledge that their freedom will be redeemed and their independence established and protected. The entire resources, in men and material, of the United States stand behind that pledge. It is not for me or for the people of this country to tell you where your duty lies. We are engaged in a great and common cause. I count on every Philippine man, woman, and child to do his duty. We will do ours."[69] Quezon later said, "On reading the message I was instantly electrified and thrilled."[70] News correspondent Hernando J. Abaya, however, recalled thinking, "Our freedom would be *redeemed*! This meant the battle of the Philippines was already lost."[71] Captain Jesus Villamor, serving as an aide to Quezon, realized, "Clearly no American warships were on the way. There would be no victory dinner at the Manila Hotel on New Year's Day."[72]

Reelected as president in November, Quezon insisted on demonstrating a functioning government with an inauguration ceremony on Corregidor on 30 December. His staff scrambled to find a radio to "communicate with the outside world."[73] For the ceremony, Sayre and MacArthur flanked Quezon as chief justice Jose Abad Santos gave the oath. Quezon then spoke: "At the present time we have but one task—to fight with America for America and the Philippines. . . . We are fighting for human liberty and justice, for those principles of individual freedom which we all cherish and without which life would not be worth living."[74] Privately, however, Quezon expressed doubts about Roosevelt. "It seems that Washington does not fully realize our situation," he mused, "nor the feelings which the apparent neglect of our safety and welfare have engendered in the hearts of the people here."[75] He considered avenues to independence and neutrality.

In Manila, activist members of the leftist democratic Philippine Civil Liberties Union feared the Japanese.[76] Antonio Bautista hosted a secret meeting to organize an underground he called "the group."[77] Eventually, the organization became better known as the Free Philippines and would place agents throughout the collaborationist government and Japanese headquarters. For the time being, they agreed to send communist leader Vincente Lava "out to the province to help set up an underground movement."[78]

SOUTH CENTRAL LUZON, D21/R-1,028

The Chinese community also feared Japanese occupation.[79] The Philippine Chinese United Workers' Union, dramatic clubs, cultural association, and salvation association combined to form the Chinese Anti-Japanese Guerrilla Force (*Feilubin huaqiao kangri zhidui*, or Hua Zhi) in Bataan with later cells in Laguna, Tayabas, Tarlac, Nueva Ecija, Pampanga, Bulacan, Rizal, and Batangas. They provided communications and assisted people in escaping the Japanese while spreading propaganda and encouraging loyalty to the United States, the Philippines, and the Kuomintang.[80]

The eighty-member Philippines Chinese Youth Wartime Special Services Corps aided bombing victims in Manila but dissolved when the Japanese entered the city. The Chinese military council authorized Shi Yisheng, of the Kuomintang's standing committee in the Philippines, to convert the Chinese Volunteers of the Philippines (CVP) into a guerrilla force. They became the genesis of two groups, the USAFFE-supported US-CVP in the Baguio–La Union area under Li Bocai (Lee Pak-chay, aka Vincente Lopez), and the CVP under Shi Yisheng in the Calabugao Mountains in La Union.[81]

The leftist Philippine Chinese United Workers' Union formed the Anti-Japanese and Chinese-Protection Committee (AJCPC) and the Wartime Service Corps and petitioned Quezon and MacArthur for membership in USAFFE. Wang Xixiong of the AJCPC led four hundred Chinese women, children, and elderly out of Manila to Paete in Laguna. Xu Jingcheng and Chen Cunsheng took others to Bulacan. Meanwhile, Huang Jie and Cai Jianhua took the Wartime Service Corps to San Fernando, Pampanga, to train in irregular warfare. Away from Manila, the AJCPC re-formed as the Emergency Action Committee. Other leftists joined with the nationalists to form the Philippine Chinese Anti-Japanese Volunteer

Corps under Xu Zhimeng.[82] With up to three hundred members, the corps conducted nonmilitary operations, gathered food, and published the *Chinese Commercial Bulletin*. Meanwhile, the CVP grew to 761 men in Manila and its surrounding area, 89 more in Bicol, and 260 on Panay.

The guerrillas annoyed Homma. Unwilling to divert his combat units, he ordered his Luzon line of communication department, with support from the army air unit, to apprehend the "insidious elements" in Bontoc, Bayombong, and Zambales. Ambush and sabotage were the work of "bandits" and rightfully the responsibility of the local government. Homma thus instructed Filipino political leaders, including Manila mayor Jorge Vargas, to establish "a central administrative organ" and a "provisional consultative committee" to work with the Japanese administration.[83]

The Japanese were at a crossroads. In many personal encounters, Filipinos found them self-possessed. Isabel Yumol remembered her family seeing their first two Japanese soldiers. In a heavy accent, the older one identified himself as a colonel who taught at the University of Tokyo. His compatriot was a lieutenant who was once one of his students. They were lost and needed directions. The younger soldier used a translation dictionary to call Isabel "little sister" and shared a picture of a girl he called "my sister, same you, miss her."[84] The soldiers moved on, leaving behind a relieved Yumol family.

Marcos V. Augustin had a different experience. He had entered the USAFFE as a truck driver and was serving on a demolition platoon under Lieutenant Colonel Narcisco L. Manzano when engineers blew the Kalumpit bridges and trapped them behind enemy lines early on New Year's Day.[85] He destroyed equipment, dropped 130 rifles and cases of ammunition into the Pasig River, and headed south with a Lieutenant Vidan. In Pampanga they witnessed a Japanese patrol kill an old man who tried to stop them from beating his wife and raping his granddaughter.[86] The soldiers shot Vidan through the head and captured Augustin. Discovering his tattoo of an American eagle with the Stars and Stripes, they beat Augustin.[87] Though bound and tied, he managed to knock down a guard and jump from a truck into a river. Augustin then ran into the hills near Antipolo and under the nom de guerre "Marking" gathered a band of resistance fighters. Manzano went on to join the Free Philippines and to process information collected by their agents.[88]

Word of Japanese brutalities raced ahead of their columns. Soldiers shot and killed schoolteacher Buenaventura J. Bello in Vigan for refusing to lower a U.S. flag, and he became a martyr throughout the islands.[89] A man named Venancio—Pacita Pestano-Jacinto's family's "farm man"—told of what he had seen in Novaliches, eight miles from Manila. Soldiers detained all the women in the church overnight. "They were beasts, every one of them," Venancio said, "Worse than beasts, I tell you. We could not bear it, the cries and moaning of the women."[90] Men who defended the women were killed.

On a street in Angels City, two Japanese soldiers grabbed fourteen-year-old Maria Rosa Luna Henson as she gathered firewood. She screamed. A nearby officer berated the men and then grabbed Maria and raped her before passing her back to the others to share. In all, twenty-four soldiers raped her that day.[91] They took Maria with six other women to a rice mill near a headquarters. Ten to twenty Japanese soldiers would rape each woman every day for several months.[92] In August, they moved the captives to a larger facility.[93]

Filipinas suffered doubly from Japanese cultural attitudes toward women and subjugated people. In 1912 a British observer noted how a woman in Japan "is precluded from exercising a will of her own; and that the prince no less than the peasant is not slow to take advantage of a system that gives rein to the passions. . . . Thousands of women, and even little girls, are enslaved in a condition of moral degradation that has no parallel in lands where the teachings of Christianity are accepted."[94]

The Japanese military exploited conquered women systematically.[95] In July 1941 the army requested 20,000 "comfort women" for 700,000 troops in China and Southeast Asia—a ratio of 1 female for every 35 men.[96] In the Philippines, at first, soldiers forcibly abducted women from their homes or off streets for garrisons.[97] Records indicate that each company-sized Japanese unit detained about ten young women—many only girls—and soldiers raped each girl five to ten times a day.[98] The unpaid women also had to clean, wash clothes, and cook.[99]

The abuse of Filipinas cast the occupiers as monsters in native eyes. Villamor recalled, "The Japanese raped all Filipino women they got hold of, some of the men believed, and I was inclined to think this true, so many were the stories of horrors."[100] A guerrilla reported, "The degree to which they raped and otherwise brutalized legions of women led to the frequent remark that the Spaniards had built churches in the Philippines, the Americans had built schools, and the Japanese had built brothels."[101]

Quezon observed, "Many of the girls died from this brutal treatment and nothing could have been more certain to leave a permanent scar of deep hatred among the Filipinos against the conquerors than these awful crimes."[102] As Barrameda put it, "They not only raped women; they soiled Filipino womanhood by carting off their victims to army-run brothels to serve the libidinous drive of their soldiers."[103] General Francisco and General De Jesus found on Bataan an "increasingly grim determination on the part of our men to fight as they learned of the abuses and atrocities committed by the Japanese soldiers, especially the raping of Filipino women."[104]

CENTRAL LUZON, D25/R-1,024

On New Year's Day 1942 Homma's reconnaissance spotted large fires in Manila. At 2000 hours he ordered his 48th Division to prepare to rescue Japanese citizens and occupy the capital.[105] At that moment MacArthur was meeting with Quezon on Corregidor. MacArthur read a telegram from Washington that Quezon recalled saying that "I should be taken to Washington and function there as the head of the Commonwealth Government in exile and as the symbol of the redemption of the Philippines."[106] The asthmatic president was suffering terrible coughing fits in Corregidor's damp tunnels. He passed the cable to his cabinet, which determined he "should refuse to make the trip" under the assumption that "sufficient help would come from the American and Filipino forces to take the offensive and drive the enemy out of the land."[107] Quezon later confessed that he knew his "evacuation to America could be made in comparative safety" and he "was doubtful if help could come in time."[108] He remained on Corregidor.

In Nueva Ecija, Horan's officers were leaving him. Major Parker Calvert of the 43rd Infantry departed with Capt. Arthur Murphy and Pvt. Grafton "Budd" Spencer for Bataan. They made it to Montalban in Rizal before Japanese forces forced them back.[109] Meanwhile, Maj. Everett Warner and Capt. Manuel P. Enriquez reorganized remnants around Aritao, Nueva Vizcaya, into the 1st Provisional Guerrilla Regiment. Captain Guillermo Nakar joined them with what was left of the 71st Infantry Regiment.

On 2 January the society page of the *Manila Tribune* reported the wedding of USAFFE Captain Jose Laurel III, son of the prominent secretary of justice. A former student at a Japanese military academy, Captain Laurel had recently commanded troops at Mauban until his capture.[110] His timely release to get married signaled Japanese interest in placating prominent Filipino politicians.

At 1745 hours that evening, the 48th Division entered Manila with three infantry battalions. Fifteen minutes later another battalion with reconnaissance units from the 16th Division joined them. Japanese residents welcomed them enthusiastically.[111] Homma tapped two 48th Division infantry battalions to garrison the city, later joined by four from the 16th Division.[112] All schools across the Philippines closed, putting two million students on the streets.[113] Still, the lack of a decisive battle for Manila upset Homma's plans as he turned toward Bataan, an area he only knew from 1:200,000 scale maps.[114]

Quezon finally noticed Roosevelt had said Philippine independence would be *redeemed*. He asked MacArthur if that word indicated Roosevelt thought the islands irredeemably lost. "The General," wrote Quezon, "while not expressing a positive opinion, suggested the possibility that the transmission of the presidential message might have been garbled." Quezon had the word changed to "preserved" before relaying Roosevelt's message to units on Bataan.[115]

The next morning Chick Parsons awoke to discover Japanese sentries in front of his house in Manila with a sign on the gate declaring "Property of the Imperial Japanese Government."[116] Realizing his family faced internment, Parsons ran a Panamanian flag up his flagpole and informed the guards he had diplomatic immunity. Japanese officials verified his status with the Philippine government and reluctantly approved his neutrality. Parsons then spent days exploring the city and, with Katsy's help, filed reports he thought might be useful one day. Catholic priests supplied him names of people held by the Japanese. Disguised as a peasant, he met guerrillas in the jungles. Only once did police detain him, in Santo Tomás, but only for a few hours.[117]

On 3 January the Japanese announced martial law. In Naga they painted an outline of two feet in the front of the capitol. "All Filipinos passing by the building had to stand with their feet inside the outlines and bow to the Japanese sentries," a witness recalled. "A wrong bow brought a blow on the Filipino, so people practiced bowing."[118] Such measures doubled as a source for labor. Leon Parong of Tibgao executed a perfect bow but still faced instant arrest followed by a month of compulsory gang labor at the Pili airport.[119]

That afternoon three hundred Western men, women, and children reported to the University of Santo Tomás in Manila. Only hours before had Japanese officials selected the fifty-acre campus as an internment camp. Four hundred more internees arrived the next day, another five hundred on Tuesday, and hundreds more through the rest of the week. Luis de Alcuaz, secretary to the father rector, opened additional spaces, but conditions remained severely cramped. "Within 10 days, there were over 3,000 people in the camp, some 2,000 of whom were lodged in the main building, 700 in the gymnasium, and 400 in the annex," intern A. V. H. Hartendorp reported.[120] Americans comprised 70 percent of the interns, and 25 percent were British.

Filipino friends and neighbors arrived outside with food and other necessities. The routine crowds established exchange points with the internees through the gate, the fence, and the package line. "The Japanese were astounded and irked at the loyalty and affection shown by the Filipinos for their 'oppressors,'" Hartendorp recalled, "and at first attempted to drive the crowds off with blows, but they kept coming back."[121] After three weeks, the commandant banned internees from the front grounds and ordered all Filipinos not to approach the fence. Packages, many carrying hidden notes, still went in and out.

North of Manila, Horan reorganized what remained of the 43rd Infantry Regiment and withdrew to Kiangan, Ifugao. A week later, he secured an army radio in Bontoc and sent it to Warner, Enriquez, and Nakar in the 1st Provisional Guerrilla Regiment in Aritao.[122] Horan had Tech. Sgt. William Bowen and Pvt. Earl Brazelton of Camp John Hay's 228th Signal Company build him another radio from old sets and spare parts.[123] He contacted USAFFE and was told to fight as the 121st Regiment.

Horan tried to establish command of all guerrillas between Abra and La Union. Twenty miles to the east, Calvert commanded other remnants of the 43rd Infantry, mostly Ifugao tribesmen of the A and B companies from Bontoc and Philippine Scouts. Determined to protect their homes, they adopted the moniker "Calvert's Guerrillas." Horan moved them west to link up with Warner, but they never made a rendezvous.

American engineer Walter Cushing demolished his mine in Kalinga and ventured into Abra, where disorganized soldiers guarded armories for deployed constabulary units.[124] Cushing commandeered an armed training unit in Bangued and moved sixty miles to a mine in Batong that he knew held a radio that could reach USAFFE. He returned to Abra with the radio and two hundred men, including thirty Americans from an air warning unit under 1st Lt. Robert H. Arnold. Cushing's men were motivated but untrained and unorganized; Arnold provided military expertise and leadership.

Arnold led a New Year's Day ambush of a Japanese convoy on Highway 2 near Naravacan, but credit went to Cushing. Horan embraced the group, and Arnold became irritated "over the way Cushing was monopolizing the honor of founding and leading the guerrilla organization that was then attracting the attention of the people of Ilocos."[125]

Other guerrillas remained beyond Horan. In northwest Luzon, governor Roques Ablan led one hundred armed men in the Ilocos Norte, Ilocos Sur, and Abra Provinces. In Nueva Vizcaya, Philippine army sergeant Benedicto Erasmus reportedly promoted himself to lieutenant and led a guerrilla band. Rumors spread of another independent guerrilla group under a Major Gaular or Ganlan in Ilocos (still unidentified today).

On 5 January Carlos Romulo began daily radio broadcasts from Corregidor: "People of the Philippines! You are listening to the Voice of Freedom—from the battle front of Bataan!"[126] The Japanese countered with propaganda on radio KZRH, asking why Filipinos should fight and die for

America. Romulo responded on behalf of Quezon with a message "from a typical Filipino soldier in Bataan": "Be courageous and prudent. Do not offer futile resistance. Yield as far as your honor will allow, but no farther. Remember that if you cooperate with the Japanese you are fighting against me—against all of us."[127]

Eight days later Praeger led an attack for Cagayan governor Adduru that damaged the Japanese airfield at Tuguegarao.[128] Two days later he struck the Aparri airfield and bridges and culverts between the two fields. A Japanese counterattack drove him from Tuao into the mountains near Apayao, but the damage had already been done.

MANILA, D39/R-1,010

In the San Juan Catholic church just outside Manila on 15 January, underclass Philippine military academy cadets Miguel Ver and Eleuterio "Terry" Adevoso assembled sophomore and freshmen cadets to form a motivated but ill-equipped unit.[129] These "ROTC Guerrillas" pledged to collect intelligence for MacArthur, protect civilians and bolster morale, and fight behind enemy lines for USAFFE.[130] When a San Juan priest reported the youngsters to the Japanese, the group moved into the hills around Talbak. From a base in Banaba, they began harassing the enemy and eliminating collaborators.

Life on Luzon had become difficult. U.S. and Japanese troops confiscated all transportation. Strafing aircraft threatened main roads, and armed men roamed the jungles. With bridges destroyed and communications cut, nervous people seized on gossip. An editor at the *Herald* recalled, "The radio stations began broadcasting hectic warnings that paratroops were landing. There were rumors that the water supply had been poisoned; of uprisings among the large Japanese population at Davao."[131] In this chaos, guerrillas assumed a vital role as a conduit of trusted communication and news.

The invasion disrupted life in other unanticipated ways. Although Camarines Sur harvested a million sacks of rice above annual consumption, Commander Kuriyama, Lieutenant Colonel Tokiaki Nyhro, and Captain Hiroshi Ohtami prohibited export out of the province. The Japanese seized rice, abaca, and copra, paying little for 100,000 sacks, and sent it to warehouses in Iriga, Tigaon, and Libmanan under police guard.[132] Unpaid farmers could not buy items needed for the planting season. Shoppers left markets empty-handed.

The Japanese also closed the Chinese stores that made up 80 percent of retail. Commodity prices skyrocketed. In Naga, acting governor

Villafuerte ordered prices capped at 50 percent above prewar levels and asked the occupation authorities to get Japanese stores to cooperate. The Japanese association refused. "That early," Barrameda wrote, "the civilian population had begun to taste the bitter fruit of the Japanese invasion."[133]

At Homma's side when he entered Manila was Hideico Kihara, a longtime vice consul in Manila and consul general in Davao, to organize a new Philippine government.[134] Quezon had advised Vargas, Laurel, and others that "if they should be given an opportunity to co-operate in the administration of a civil government, they should accept it in order that the interests of the people and public order and respect for property should be safeguarded."[135] Laurel, Yulo, Benigno Aquino, Quintin Paredes, Camilo Osias, and Claro Recto formed a commission to meet Homma's chief of staff Lieutenant General Masami Maeda at Jose Yulo's house on 23 January.[136] Radicals Artemio Ricarte and Benigno Ramos were not invited.[137] They asked for a republic, not a commonwealth, and for head of government they proposed Vargas, "who only held an appointive position" rather than an elected one "in order that none of their acts might be interpreted as bearing popular sanction."[138] As historian Nicholas Tarling observed, Vargas was "politically 'neutral,'" reassured the elites, and served as an able "stand-in" for Quezon.[139]

On 17 January Vargas told reporters, "Let independence come in any form! We will co-operate!"[140] A week later the Japanese military administration issued Order Number 1 to establish the Philippine Executive Committee (PEC) with Vargas as chairman. Thirty-four prominent Filipinos formed an advisory council of state; any twelve could form a quorum. The PEC also created six government departments and some bureaus that "existed chiefly on paper."[141] Power resided with the Japanese. The next week, more than fifty commonwealth offices closed, and their officials and employees were "retired."

Vargas and the PEC prioritized issues thought to both please the Japanese *and* prepare the islands for independence. They endorsed a Japanese program to eliminate Western influence from Philippine schoolbooks and promote Japanese ideas of proper place and spirit.[142] The PEC also pushed a proposal to eliminate English and replace it with Tagalog, already established as the national language.

On 18 January Walter Cushing struck again and ambushed a column of sixty Japanese soldiers and ten trucks passing through Candon, Ilocos Sur. He then destroyed three cars—one carrying a Japanese general—and recovered American maps and plans for Bataan and Corregidor. Horan promoted Cushing to major. Although Lieutenant Colonel Moses and Lieutenant Colonel Noble had arrived at Horan's headquarters, they had yet to learn guerrilla methods.¹⁴³ Cushing seemed more ready for a leading role in the resistance.¹⁴⁴

CENTRAL LUZON, D43/R-1,006

With Wainwright in Bataan was Maj. Claude A. Thorp, the Fort Stotsenburg provost marshal and a veteran of Mexico and France. Thorp drafted a plan for organizing guerrillas behind Japanese lines and took it to Wainwright, who promptly rejected it.¹⁴⁵

Behind the scenes, MacArthur actually prepared for guerrilla war. He modified Sharp's mission in the southern islands: "When organized resistance was no longer practicable, he was to split his force into small groups and conduct guerilla [sic] warfare from hidden bases in the interior of each island."¹⁴⁶ On Luzon, he had G-2 (Intelligence) Col. Charles Willoughby quietly construct "an extensive network of prominent businessmen, plantation owners, miners, and newspaper people" to collect intelligence behind the lines.¹⁴⁷ Willoughby later described this as "a potential 'underground,' in case the Japanese were successful in over-running the Islands, a pessimistic possibility not publicly admitted."¹⁴⁸

Willoughby worked with Capt. Joseph McMicking "on a plan for certain communication workers to go underground and form nets should the Japanese attack."¹⁴⁹ The previous July, Willoughby and his deputy, Lt. Col. Joseph K. Evans, had organized the postal and telegraph service, the Philippine long distance and telephone company, the postmasters, and the Philippines civil service for just such a purpose.¹⁵⁰

Thorp went to MacArthur's adjutant, Col. Hugh Casey, who arranged for him to see the boss. Even though Thorp was shot in the left thigh while probing the front lines on 17 January, MacArthur approved his plan. Thorp departed Bataan with nineteen men and two women, including Lt. Charles Cushing (Walter's brother) and Capt. Ralph McGuire. With his wife stateside, Thorp brought along his secretary and mistress, Herminia "Minang" Dizon. Lieutenant Robert Lapham recalled, "This would have been a purely personal matter had not some of the men made jokes about it, thereby visibly reducing the respect some of them had for Thorp."¹⁵¹ The group started an arduous forty-day journey toward an arms cache at Camp Sanchez in the Zambales Mountains. With only a radio receiver, they were able to monitor broadcasts from USAFFE.¹⁵²

USAFFE G-2 also authorized Colonel Simeon de Jesus in Bataan to organize sixty agents from his 1st Philippine Constabulary into a clandestine military intelligence service "to collect, evaluate, and disseminate military information obtained in Bataan, Zambales, and Pampanga and other occupied areas, operating principally behind enemy lines."¹⁵³ Plagued by poor communications and slow procedures, however, the military intelligence service produced only limited results until the fall of Bataan.

Finally, MacArthur authorized Spanish-American War veteran Col. Hugh Straughn to organize a guerrilla force. He was already behind the lines around Antipolo in Rizal. The colonel began organizing the Fil-American Irregular Troops in central and southern Luzon.¹⁵⁴ Straughn asked Governor Escudero to join as a colonel and later enjoined Major Francisco Sandico to join his force.

TOKYO, D44/R-1,005

On 20 January Premier Tojo addressed the house of peers in the Diet to announce that Japan wanted each country and its people "to have its proper place and demonstrate its real character, thereby securing an order of co-existence and co-prosperity based on ethical principles with Japan serving as its nucleus."¹⁵⁵ The board of information further explained: "The people of Greater Asia are now confronted with the greatest opportunity in their history to build their common name according to the proud social conception of the world as a single family, each member thereof performing his functions according to his talent and ability for the good of the whole."¹⁵⁶

Tojo designated Hong Kong and Malaya as "absolutely essential" to Japan's defense. "As regards the Philippines," he said, "if the peoples of those islands will hereafter understand the real intentions of Japan and offer to cooperate with us as one of the partners for the establishment of the Greater East Asia Co-Prosperity Sphere, Japan will gladly enable them to enjoy the honor of independence."¹⁵⁷ If this offer did not win over guerrillas, it might at least convince the Filipino elites to police the countryside.¹⁵⁸

Japanese officials were frustrated with Homma, who had already exceeded the estimated thirty-four days needed to conquer Luzon.¹⁵⁹ He had vowed Mindanao and the Visayas would fall quickly after Manila.¹⁶⁰ The imperial general headquarters urged Homma to finish off USAFFE, but he pushed back and secured a promise for reinforcements. Before the Diet on 16 February, Tojo repeated his offer of Philippine independence in return for cooperation.¹⁶¹

The Japanese reassessed Filipinos as somehow "Asians but not Asians, Westerners but not Westerners.... They are self-indulgent, idle, fickle and frivolous." The Southern Army confirmed, "They adore the United States and make light of us."¹⁶² The Imperial Japanese Army issued Order Number 2 dictating six principles to guide Philippine teachers when schools reopened: promote relations between the Philippines and Japan in the new co-prosperity sphere; erase Western influences; elevate morals over materialism; promote the Japanese language and eliminate English; promote vocational education; and inspire in the people a love of labor.[163]

CENTRAL LUZON, D48/R-1,001

Applying lessons from Manchuria and China, the Japanese sent propaganda units to the Philippines. Most would remain in Manila to coordinate media and reassure Japan's citizens and soldiers. They had aircraft drop leaflets on Bataan: "Dear Filipino Soldiers! There are [sic] still one way left for you. That is to give up all your weapons at once and surrender to the Japanese force before it is too late, then we shall fully protect you."[164] Small detachments supported combat and constabulary troops. The Hitomi Propaganda Platoon, named after its twenty-five-year-old commander, Lieutenant Junsuke Hitomi, began "goodwill missions" to convince Filipinos hiding in the hinterlands to return to work.[165]

Ramsey noted, "In return for cooperation the Japanese promised fabulous prosperity within the pan-Pacific commonwealth of Asian peoples. This theme formed the centerpiece of their propaganda, and in the face of shortages and rationing the racial aspect was stressed."[166] As Kempeitai (military police) Colonel Akira Nagahama told Adalia Marquez, "We Japanese and you Filipinos are of the same color and it is only right and natural that our two people should be brothers. The American is of another color. He will never be your friend."[167] The appeals fell short: "Even if there was a noticeable lack of enthusiasm for the white man's reform, scarcely a hand was lifted in support of the Japanese. They clearly had failed to identify the interests of South-East Asians with their own."[168]

On 24 January Hitomi began thirteen days of operations in Batangas. Nearly out of maneuver room, MacArthur had cabled Washington: "I intend to fight it out to complete destruction."[169] Even so, Hitomi found that in peasant communities, "the people were completely opposed to us. . . . the objectives of propaganda activities based on respect and courtesy have not been achieved here."[170] Then he experienced an epiphany.

A ranking officer of the propaganda corps, Colonel Shigenobu Mochizuki, arrived to give a speech based on Kunmi Watanabe's imperialist and racist ideology. Julio Luz, a resident who had studied in Japan, translated. The quiet crowd slowly warmed to the speech and applauded loudly at the end. Isamu Wad, a local Japanese in attendance who spoke fluent Tagalog, explained to Hitomi what had happened. Mochizuki's speech was clearly confusing the peasants, so halfway through his interpreter began telling a story of how he once witnessed a Japanese man in a Nagoya shopping center go to great lengths to return a lost item to its proper owner. The Japanese, Luz concluded, were basically honest, so everyone should give them a chance. The crowd loved that story.

The lesson for Hitomi was obvious: Forget preaching the Greater East Asia Co-Prosperity Sphere and other things that did not matter to the people. Instead, use a simple, comprehensible and relatable argument: You Filipinos are caught in the middle of a war between Japan and the United States; the Japanese want to fight the Americans, not you; if you "sit it out" and do not support the guerrillas, the Japanese will leave you alone. Hitomi augmented his "sit-it-out" argument with "local Japanese residents, news reporters, photographers, and novelists in addition to Filipino entertainers, motion picture projectionists, public speakers, and physicians" to bring out crowds.[171] Through early March, the "Hitomi circus" produced results—helped, of course, by "special tactics" learned in Manchuria: "sneak attacks on guerrilla hideouts, using the prisoners rounded up for counterespionage, or taking the family members of the guerrillas hostage."[172]

Meanwhile in the mountains of Apayao, Governor Ablan and Lieutenant Feliciano Madamba spent weeks organizing guerrillas.[173] On 27 January they led a detachment to Solsona and recovered three hundred rifles, eighteen machine guns, and several crates of ammunition. The next day they ambushed and slaughtered a column of fifty Japanese soldiers entering Ilocos Norte. Excited local citizens rallied to Ablan. After a week a larger Japanese column under Major Kumatsu arrived, only to fall to a similar ambush. "This time," a guerrilla reported, "the Japs retaliated by bombing several of the inland villages and executing some twenty civilians at Banna, Ilocos Norte."[174] When Ablan continued his attacks, the Japanese answered with reprisals against the citizens of Nueva Era.

CENTRAL LUZON, D52/R-997

On 28 January Tokyo announced the new government in Manila. Commissioner Sayre pressed Quezon to publicly denounce the collaborators, but he refused, saying, "Any evidence of my faith in their loyalty would in itself serve to fortify their determination not to betray me; whereas, any indication that I considered them lost to the cause and practically traitors, would perhaps force them to go over to the Japanese."[175] By this time, Quezon needed morphine shots to calm his asthma attacks.

The Japanese bombed Port Moresby in New Guinea on 3 February and disquieted the fragile American-British-Dutch-Australian command. The next day U.S. Army chief of staff Gen. George C. Marshall cabled MacArthur for his plans to withdraw his wife, four-year-old son, and other officials from Corregidor to Mindanao or Australia.[176] MacArthur did not reply.

The submarine SS-202 *Trout* arrived at Corregidor to remove the Philippine treasury's gold, and intelligence officer Lt. Col. Warren J. Clear passed word to MacArthur of the recent Arcadia conference in Washington. British and American leaders agreed to prioritize operations against Germany. The war department concluded that it would take up to 7 aircraft carriers, 9 battleships, 50 destroyers, 60 submarines and auxiliaries, and 1,500 aircraft just to break through to the Philippines—"an entirely unjustifiable diversion of forces from the principal theater—the Atlantic."[177]

In Manila, the Japanese unleashed the Kempeitai on Philippine leftists. A raid on 24 January captured labor leader and Communist Party chairman Crisanto Evangelista, Socialist Party founder and Communist Party vice-chairman Pedro Abad Santos, and Angeles mayor Agapito del Rosario. The Japanese executed Evangelista and Rosario. Abad Santos spent two years in prison, became gravely ill, and died in 1945. Instead of seeking alliances with the revolutionaries, the Japanese beheaded their movement.

In early February, remaining communist leaders Luis Taruc, Mateo del Castillo, Casto Alejandrino, and other leftists gathered in Nueva Ecija to declare an end to the socialist AMT party. With Quezon out and the PEC under Japan's thumb, they considered declaring a new republic. Taruc recalled: "Our Politburo leaders emphasized in conversations with me that it was opportunism to put nationalism before Communism at that moment. They said we must merge the two in our minds."[178]

This was a pivotal moment for Filipino social revolutionaries. The war presented an opportunity to erase the old order, but the best chance to defeat the Japanese was to join with the Americans and Quezon. Taruc reasoned: "Ours was not a fight for America, except in the sense that we were allies, but a fight for Filipinos. I saw our resistance movement as being revolutionary, from which we would emerge free men in every sense of the word."[179] The group opted to continue a "united front" and ally with "moderate landlords" and "middle-class groups."

Leon Trotsky had said that when in the minority, the "party must assume the initiative in securing unity in these struggles" as long as it remained independent and led as the "vanguard of the proletariat."[180] They could tolerate "petty-bourgeois nationalism" as necessary to fight fascists. Taruc would later confess: "I know now from experience that the nationalism of the Communists is indeed opportunism, and that they use it for their own ends. Any nationalist who makes an ally of the Communists is going on a ride on a tiger."[181]

MANILA/CORREGIDOR, D59/R-990

MacArthur, cornered on Luzon, reorganized USAFFE into three independent commands on 4 February.[182] Wainwright still commanded in Bataan. A separate Harbor Defense Command held Corregidor. Sharp led the Philippine army's 61st, 81st, and 101st Divisions in the Visayan-Mindanao force.

Each night the Japanese-controlled radio station KZRH in Manila serenaded Corregidor with the tune *Waiting for Ships that Never Come*.[183] On 6 February the station interrupted its program to air a call from the venerable Emilio Aguinaldo asking MacArthur to surrender in the best interests of the people, just as he had done in 1901. The message from his old commander resonated with Quezon, who feared Tojo's promise of independence would win over "the less educated classes."[184] One night he protested to Romulo, "The fight between the United States and Japan is not our fight. I want to go back . . . and try to protect our people, Romulo, not America."[185] Quezon informed MacArthur he was considering "placing myself in the hands of the Japanese."[186] The general countered that the Japanese would isolate him and issue bogus statements in his name. Quezon considered asking Roosevelt and Japan to accept Philippine neutrality.[187] Over Vice President Osmeña's and Senator Roxas' objections, the cabinet let him send the request to Roosevelt.

Not everyone at KZRH stood with the Japanese. When their agents carted off broadcaster Johnny Harris to Fort Santiago prison for carrying a U.S. Army G-2 calling card, Jorge Vargas happened to be visiting. Encountering Yay Panlilio in the halls, he cautioned, "Watch your health, Yay. The weather is undependable."[188]

CENTRAL LUZON, D67/R-982

On 12 February Horan finally made radio contact with USAFFE headquarters and received authorization to reorganize his forces as the 14th Infantry Regiment.[189] The designation may have indicated an intention to create a conventional unit. USAFFE appointed Horan as commander of all forces in North Luzon, but then he lost communication with USAFFE until 19 March.

About twenty miles to the southeast in San Fernando in Mandili, Huang Jie and Cai Jianhua of the Wartime Service Corps supervised training of emergency action committee cadre. Veterans from Mao's army led classes: Luo Lishi and Guo Jian taught team organization, Xu Jingcheng gave lessons on United Front policy, and Guo Jian addressed the political work of the army.[190] Huang Jie then conducted guerrilla tactics on Mount Arayat. Their intention was to prepare Filipinos for a Maoist revolutionary war.

On 15 February Xu Jingcheng convened a leftist Chinese conference on strategy. They agreed on three priorities: help Filipino peasants and workers organize an anti-Japanese force; develop underground activities in Manila and central and southern Luzon, Iloilo, Cebu, Samar, and Cotabato; and return the four hundred Chinese refugees to Manila.

Xu Jingcheng established the Philippine Chinese Anti-Japanese and Anti-Puppets League, or Kang Fan, outside Manila and raised separate cadres for workers, store employees, youth, women, and Cantonese. The groups spread south to Bicol, the Visayas, and Mindanao. To "keep up the spirit of the Chinese through propaganda," they printed *The Chinese Guide* newspaper. Editors Zhang Siming and Huang Nanjun would increase circulation from an initial 350 issues in Manila to more than 3,000 across Luzon. The Kang Fan also supplied money, medicine, materials, and manpower to the Hua Zhi and later passed intelligence to the Manila unit, including targets for assassination to deter Chinese collaborators.[191]

The Chinese guerrillas used Edgar Snow's *Red Star Over China* as a text on P'eng Teh-huai's explanations of Mao's revolutionary theory and tactics.[192] In China, as in the Philippines, "imperialism, landlordism, and militaristic wars" had bankrupted peasant economies and created "a readiness among poor classes to fight for a change."[193] The war made social revolution possible. P'eng instructed to use hardships to motivate peasant revolution against elites; arm guerrillas in remote areas; ensure communist control of propaganda and organization; disarm the "exploiting class"; avoid battle against superior forces and keep moving; emphasize the political aims of revolution; and "use connection with the people to develop and use advantages in intelligence collection."[194]

Tactically, P'eng said guerrillas had to be fearless, swift, and intelligent, and, most importantly, they had to remain philosophically focused on class politics and eliminate all competitors to unify the masses. P'eng told Snow, "Only by implanting itself deeply in the hearts of the people, only by fulfilling the demands of the masses, only by consolidating a base in the peasant soviets, and only by sheltering in the shadow of the masses, can partisan warfare bring revolutionary victory."[195] P'eng concluded, "Tactics are important, but we could not exist if the majority of the people did not support us. We are nothing but the fist of the people beating their oppressors!"[196] Mao's veterans began by organizing a leftist cadre and imbuing them with these ideas.

CENTRAL LUZON, D79/R-970

Roosevelt broadcast a promise to soon send thousands of planes—to Europe. On Corregidor, Quezon exploded to Willoughby: "Where are the planes this *sinverguenza* [scoundrel] is boasting of? How American to writhe in anguish at the fate of a distant cousin while a daughter is being raped in the back room!"[197] MacArthur decided it was time for Quezon to leave Corregidor.

In the damp, unventilated Malinta tunnel, Quezon suffered a chronic cough and a temperature that spiked to 105 degrees.[198] Secretly, late on 18 February, MacArthur's staff put the president and his party aboard the submarine SS-193 *Swordfish*. The general also sent a box containing his papers, medals, and last will and testament.[199] At the war plans division in Washington, Brig. Gen. Dwight Eisenhower wrote in his diary: "Looks like MacArthur is losing his nerve. I'm hoping his yelps are just his way of spurring us on, but he is always an uncertain factor."[200]

Before departing, Quezon gave Roxas a letter instructing him "to act in my name in all matters not related to changes in policy."[201] After three days, *Swordfish* disembarked its passengers at San Jose de Buenavista on Panay. The party then traveled to Iloilo by car and to Bacolod, Negros, by steamer before PT boats under Cdr John D. Bulkeley took them to Del Monte, Mindanao.[202] As the Japanese entered the Visayas, the presidential party flew by B-17 bomber to Australia to set up a government in exile.

The day after Quezon left Corregidor, the Japanese bombed Darwin. Australian prime minister John Curtin pressed Churchill to return his country's three divisions from North Africa. Churchill demurred. On Saturday 21 February Curtin convened his cabinet and gained their assent to trade their divisions for a U.S. general to command the Australian theater. New Zealand concurred, and Churchill swiftly relayed the request to Roosevelt. At 1123 hours on 23 February, MacArthur received orders from the president to leave Corregidor for Mindanao and then Australia to take charge of a newly designated command.[203] MacArthur did not reply.

Many in the islands were losing hope. Ed Ramsey recalled, "We had been promised relief but none was coming, and all of us in Bataan shared a sense of betrayal."[204] Medical supplies ran out.[205] In their retreat the units had abandoned or destroyed medical stocks.[206] By the end of March, the chief surgeon of Luzon Force reported one thousand malaria cases per day, each requiring up to four days of intravenous treatment with quinine.[207] Sixty percent of medical personnel fell to the disease.[208] Conservative estimates state that 24,000 soldiers (25 percent of the total force) suffered malaria by April.[209]

Ramsey went to General Hospital Number 2: "I could hear and smell the place long before I saw it. There were rows of men on metal bedsteads hung with mosquito nets, suffering from every kind of sickness and wound. Their screams were terrible, and the stench hung thick upon the air, almost visible in the morning light."[210] "Many a man's hands were black, swollen and cracked from pellagra," Donald Willis recalled. "Others could hardly eat because of sore mouths from scurvy. I saw many men with their legs swollen to twice their normal size from beriberi."[211] Army doctors prescribed prolonged bedrest and special dietary and vitamin regimens made impossible by conditions. There was no medicine for dysentery.[212] A regimental surgeon reported: "I have seen men brought into the battalion aid stations and die of an overwhelming infection of dysentery or cerebral malaria before they could be tagged and classified for evacuation."[213] As Lapham concluded, "Bataan was more a medical disaster than a battlefield defeat."[214]

Meanwhile, Benigno Aquino campaigned across the islands for cooperation with the Japanese.[215] Social reform political leader Benigno Ramos and his peasant Sakdalista and Ganap followers aided the Japanese "by cutting communications behind Allied lines."[216] At the end of the month the PEC sent a telegram to Quezon arguing that "it is evident that further resistance in the Philippines will be futile" and calling for "the immediate cessation of hostilities in the Philippines."[217] They included a telegram addressed to Roosevelt: "We are co-operating with the Japanese forces in the re-establishment of civil government on the promise of the Japanese government to grant the Filipino people their independence with honor."[218]

On 28 February Quezon broadcast his response: "I urge every Filipino to be of good cheer, to have faith in the patriotism and valor of our soldiers in the field. But above all, to trust America and our great and beloved leader—President Roosevelt! The united nations will win this war."[219]

CENTRAL LUZON, D92/R-957

For Filipinos, the choice to collaborate or resist often came down to kinship networks. Private Gaudencio Vera of the Philippine Scouts returned home to Tayabas in early 1942 to lead one hundred of his kin into the mountains.[220] Poorly prepared, they turned to banditry to survive. Nearby, Vicente Umali, former mayor of Tiang, Tayabas, organized a group that would later claim ten thousand members in eleven regiments and become known as President Quezon's Own Guerrillas in Laguna and Tayabas.

In early March, collaborationist police from Candaba, Pampanga, captured eight members of a thirty-five-man communist guerrilla unit under Felipa Culala (alias Dayang-Dayang).[221] She was a peasant activist from nearby Mandili described as "a huge woman, manly, rough, and with a commanding personality that made her men tremble with fear."²²² She did not take the capture of her men lightly.

On 8 March Dayang-Dayang led a raid on the makeshift prison in the municipal building in Candaba and freed her men before retreating to Madili. Her success attracted ninety-five new volunteers to her unit. When Japanese patrols retaliated by brutalizing local civilians, Dayang-Dayang set an ambush that reportedly killed forty Japanese soldiers, eight police officers, and sixty collaborationist constabularies and captured thirty-eight weapons.²²³ It marked a turning point for the communists, "proving that the guerrilla movement could defeat a powerful enemy and pose a serious threat to the Japanese."²²⁴ Luis Taruc argued that Dayang-Dayang inspired numerous new guerrilla bands.

VISAYAS, D92/R-957

MacArthur again reorganized his forces, this time with an eye on guerrilla resistance. He gave Sharp command of the Mindanao force and handed the Visayan force's five central island garrisons to Brig. Gen. Bradford G. Chynoweth.²²⁵ USAFFE retained oversight of the Panay and Mindoro garrisons.²²⁶ MSgt. Paul Rodgers, the chief stenographer at USAFFE headquarters, explained, "MacArthur was hedging against the day when, in spite of Roosevelt's orders to him, and his orders to Wainwright, the command must collapse and surrender. With the four forces operating independently under his command, surrender of one would not tumble down the others."²²⁷ The separate commands could continue resistance. MacArthur biographer William Manchester observed that "Marshall, however, had decided to give Wainwright a third star and command of all the Philippine forces. That meant that Wainwright had the power to surrender all fighting in the islands and that the Japanese, aware of it, could threaten to execute everyone on Bataan and Corregidor unless he exercised it—which is exactly what happened."²²⁸

Chynoweth began planning a guerrilla campaign he called Operation *Baus Au* (Visayan for "Get it Back"). He oversaw "the large-scale movement of goods, supplies, and weapons into the interior for use later in guerrilla warfare."²²⁹ Much resulted from *cargadores* with the 63rd Infantry Regiment, which adopted a unit insignia of a carabao sled carrying a sack of rice with words *Baus Au*. The preparations, however, shook civilian confidence in the army's ability to defeat a Japanese invasion. On 10 March more Japanese troops landed on Mindanao.

CORREGIDOR, D95/R-954

Two hours after sunset on 11 March, Bulkeley steered his seventy-seven-foot PT-41 torpedo boat from the north dock of Corregidor Island.[230] In Manila Bay, the three other PT boats from Torpedo Boat Squadron Three fell into formation and headed to the open sea. Overhead, the last three P-40 fighter planes in the Philippines flew air cover. A network of coast watchers had reported a Japanese destroyer squadron heading toward Manila. Indeed, after becoming separated in squall-whipped seas, PT-41 narrowly dodged several Japanese warships. With his boat's worn-out 4,050-horsepower engines mustering only half their normal 50-mile-per-hour speed, Bulkeley needed 35 hours to cut through 560 miles of 15-foot waves and deliver Douglas MacArthur to the Del Monte pineapple plantation on Mindanao.

After MacArthur had ignored all orders to relocate to Australia, two urgent cables on 6 and 9 March finally compelled his move. Some thoughtful historians have concluded that by that time, MacArthur deserved to be relieved. Ronald Spector wrote, "His ill-conceived and grandiose plan to defend the entire archipelago had resulted in confusion and near disaster; it helped to produce the acute supply shortage which was sapping the strength of the Bataan forces."[231]

To the American people, however, MacArthur was an early hero of the war, leading America's boys in an intrepid fight against a dastardly enemy and desperately hanging on until promised reinforcements arrived. The general did his best to stoke this popular view. As Spector noted, "Of 142 communiqués released by his headquarters between December and March, 109 mentioned only one individual: MacArthur. When an action was described, it was 'MacArthur's right flanks on Bataan' or 'MacArthur's men.'"[232]

Politicians tripped over each other to praise MacArthur, and President Roosevelt gladly used him "to perk up civilian morale."[233] To lose this general could damage national confidence.[234] The president brought Churchill into a discussion with Secretary of War Henry Stimson about MacArthur's fate. The prime minister shared the telegram he had sent ordering General Lord Gort to relinquish his command at Dunkirk and return to England to avoid capture. The president read the telegram with great interest, and Stimson asked to borrow it. "It may be (for I do not know)," wrote Churchill, "that this influenced them in the right decision which they took in ordering General MacArthur to hand over his command to one of his subordinate generals, and thus saved for all his future glorious service the great Commander who would otherwise have perished or passed the war as a Japanese captive. I should like to think so."[235]

Roosevelt added a Congressional Medal of Honor and a public announcement of MacArthur's appointment to command the defense of Australia to both entice MacArthur and reaffirm his public high standing.

The public promise of aid must have played into the president's decision. MacArthur appeared ready to sacrifice himself—with his wife and young son—to demonstrate his faith in the promise that Roosevelt knew to be false. Unexpectedly questioned at a press conference on the yet-to-arrive aid, Roosevelt aberrantly stammered, "I wouldn't do any—well, I wouldn't—I am trying to take a leaf out of my notebook. I think it would be well for others to do it. I—not knowing enough about it—I try not to speculate myself."[236] America had neither prepared proper Philippine defenses nor built the kind of navy needed to break through during a war with Japan.[237] MacArthur's capture would therefore trigger questions Roosevelt would prefer not to answer.

On 14 March MacArthur and his party arrived at Del Monte's airfield in Bukidnon Province on Mindanao. Villamor observed, "He must have lost 25 pounds, living on the same diet as the soldiers on the Rock [Corregidor], and looked gaunt and ghastly."[238] The general seemed surprised there were no planes to carry him to Australia. Four planes had been sent, one crashed, one turned back, and two never made it. Finally, at 2000 hours on 16 March, two B-17 bombers piloted by Lt. Frank Bostrom and Capt. Bill Lewis arrived from Darwin to pick up MacArthur and fly him south.

MacArthur sent a letter to Quezon: "The United States is moving its forces into the southern Pacific area in what is destined to be a great offensive against Japan. The troops are being concentrated in Australia, which will be used as the base for the offensive drive to the Philippines. President Roosevelt has designated me to command this offensive and has directed me to proceed to Australia for that purpose."[239] He asked Quezon and his family to join him there. Three days later Bulkeley and his PT boats picked up Quezon and his entourage at Zamboanguita Beach on southern Negros.

MacArthur's move was not well received on Bataan. A U.S. Army history noted, "A large part of the faith in the timely arrival of reinforcements had been based on the presence of General MacArthur."[240] Ramsey said of the move: "Some hailed it as a prelude to a counter-invasion, clinging to the old stories about the hundred-mile-long convoy. But others, worn out from weeks of fighting, hunger, and sickness, saw it as abandonment. MacArthur had saved himself, they grumbled, and left them behind to die."[241] On Corregidor, as all troops went on quarter rations of about one thousand calories per day, Romulo reported: "On March 17th we learned MacArthur had entered Melbourne as a hero."[242]

Twenty-four hours later, riding a train to the continent's south coast, MacArthur accepted command in Australia. In another week, the combined chiefs of staff in Washington designated the Pacific theater an American responsibility. At the end of the month the U.S. joint chiefs of staff would divide the Pacific Ocean Area under Adm. Chester Nimitz and Southwest Pacific Area under MacArthur.

Switching trains in Adelaide Station on 20 March, MacArthur gave a short speech to the press: "The President of the United States ordered me to break through the Japanese lines and proceed from Corregidor to Australia for the purpose, as I understand it, of organizing the American offensive against Japan, a preliminary object of which is the relief of the Philippines."[243] In other words, he had not abandoned his troops; he had done his duty and obeyed direct orders from the commander in chief. He did not run away, he "broke through" enemy lines—in a way, he had advanced. Most importantly, he was going back. MacArthur concluded, "I came through and I shall return."[244]

MacArthur's memorable line was more than self-aggrandizement. It was a calculated attempt to influence several audiences simultaneously. First, of course, he wanted his soldiers not to think badly of him and to fight on in some desperate hope he could reverse their situation. Second, he wanted to openly defy the Japanese and show that at least they could not defeat *him* and in fact should fear his return. Third, and most importantly, he wanted to publicly commit the United States to return to the Philippines. Finally, he wanted to assure the people of the Philippines that their struggle was not over. In his memoirs, MacArthur said the phrase "I shall return" worked magic on the Filipinos: "It lit a flame that became a symbol which focused the nation's indomitable will and at whose shrine it finally attained victory and, once again, found freedom."[245]

In simple truth, as Ramsey noted, "America had failed to defend the Philippines, and the promised relief had never appeared. A trust had been violated, a confidence betrayed."[246] MacArthur's promise was a gamble that could regain or lose forever that trust. "On these three words will the hope of a whole country rest," Pacita Pestano-Jacinto wrote in her diary. "I wonder if MacArthur realizes how simply, how implicitly, this nation's trust has been placed in him."[247]

When MacArthur's train reached Kooringa in the far south of Australia, he learned there was no army waiting for him. Shocked and disappointed, he headed to his new headquarters in Melbourne to command 360 U.S. Army personnel.

3

The Death March
March–May 1942

TOKYO, D96/R-953

The day after MacArthur's departure—a move not made public for another week—Tojo announced a plan for Philippine independence for November 1943.[1] He then clarified the islands would first have to evidence "their cooperation with the empire," and even after independence, "military affairs, foreign affairs, economics, and other affairs shall be placed under the firm control of the empire."[2] Tojo had come to believe that the U.S. promise of independence had established Philippine expectations that prevented the country from embracing "the Japanese side."[3] On 13 March he set out on a two-week tour of occupied lands in Southeast Asia with stops planned for Manila and Davao.[4]

The war ministry tasked the Kempeitai to establish sections to process hundreds of thousands of Allied prisoners of war (POWs). Section one would run camps in Japan, China, Korea, Manchukuo, Formosa, and the Philippines.[5] The war ministry issued administrative regulations but left commanders free to run their camps. Inadequate resources and imperially sanctioned punitive attitudes led many to violate the standards set by the Geneva Convention.

CENTRAL LUZON, D97/R-952

In Manila, the Kempeitai established its headquarters in Fort Santiago. Elite officers worked as special agents in field cases, often in civilian clothes, with the Special Service Agency or military intelligence, while regular uniformed Kempeitai worked as guards or enforced military law.[6] They supported two types of trials: military court and civilian court. Later they began special courts martial without representation for defendants.

The capital had become a dangerous place. Pacita Pestano-Jacinto observed pro-Japanese spies: "Their field of operation is the street, the barbershop, the market stall, the street corners where men gather to air their views. The walls now have eyes and ears."[7] Yay Panlilio recalled: "Friends of other days now could be divided into three classes: those who had fallen away and could no longer be depended on; those who held aloof and would keep for the day when all could be explained; and those who fell in step, knowing the score, ready to pay the price—but not stupidly."[8] In March she walked out of the KZRH radio station and kept walking. After four days she made her way into the hills past Rizal, where she collapsed from malaria into a hut owned by a farmer named Igi.

SOUTHERN LUZON, D98/R-951

Homma could send only patrols against insurgents in Bicol. On 15 March one patrol with Ganaps searched a guerrilla area in San Nicolas in Camarines Sur. The wedding party of Venancio Borlagdan and Blandina Obstaculo was suddenly interrupted by a flare that preceded a barrage of gunfire.[9] The attack lasted for three hours before the soldiers ransacked and burnt the town. Sixteen-year-old Antonio P. Estrada witnessed "the exodus of barrio folks from San Nicolas to the town center of Canaman" in single file with personal belongings salvaged from burnt homes.

Nearby in Libmanan, long-time Japanese resident Miyahira Berto had gotten the Japanese to imprison electric company owner Patricio Genova.[10] Genova's son-in-law Elias Madrid, "a rich man in his own right," bought his freedom with a fine of P800, a sack of rice, and some gasoline.[11] Elias and his friend and reporter Leon S. A. Aureus then formed the Tangcong Vaca Guerrilla Unit (TVGU) under Madrid's nephew, Philippine army finance sergeant Juan Q. Miranda. San Aureus became executive officer and chief of propaganda. Elias became finance officer. In two days they had more than two dozen recruits. Mayor Roberto Requejo became an associate while simultaneously mediating with the Japanese.

On 13 March the TVGU demolished the Tucbasan bridge connecting Libmanan and Naga. Their attempts to blow nearby railroad bridges brought on the Japanese attack at the wedding in San Nicholas. A week later the TVGU ambushed two buses of Japanese soldiers and lost two guerrillas to grenades. The Japanese then increased patrols on the Naga-Pascacao road while local residents rallied to the TVGU.

Early on 28 March the TVGU ambushed a train on the Naga-Sipocot line, killing six Japanese soldiers and capturing an informer named Delfin Nepomuceno. Japanese reinforcements arrived and killed three civilians, including prominent citizen Jacinto Ursua, whose entire kinship network turned against the occupiers. The next month the TVGU liberated 30,000 sacks of rice from a warehouse in San Juan and distributed it to the people. They then sent patrols under Lieutenant Simeon Ayala and Sergeant Tomas Servidad to drive out Ganaps harassing citizens in remote barrios around Libmanan. Two days later a patrol led by Lieutenant Wilfredo San Sebastion killed eighteen Ganaps in Cabinitan, Ragay. That same day, the TVGU began issuing a mimeographed newspaper, *The Voice of Freedom*, edited by Aureus under his pen name, Rosau Eulanes.

One night the TVGU destroyed a large mill owned by Doña Flaviana Aspe de Ocampo and used by the Japanese association to provide rice to the army. Thirteen guerrillas ordered the guards to hand over their weapons and killed one who refused. The raiders then killed the Doña Babeng and her daughter Rebecca Ocampo because "their tongues were not too friendly."[12] "In an area where people were nearly universally pro-American," wrote Barrameda, "the killings, nevertheless, sent shock waves, primarily because of the prominence of some of the victims. The killings did tend to reinforce the upper-class notion about all guerrillas being power-mad and gun crazy."[13]

NORTHERN LUZON, D102/R-947

Ilocos Norte governor Ablan traveled to Apayao to use Praeger's radio to contact Quezon (whom he thought was still on Corregidor).[14] On 19 March Ablan reported to USAFFE that his guerrillas had killed six hundred Japanese soldiers and his free government still functioned in the hills and that he needed P100,000 for government workers who had not been paid since December.[15] Unable to fulfill the request, Quezon sent permission to "issue emergency notes as previously authorized by your provincial treasurer."[16]

Ablan passed word that the Japanese had brought Artemio Ricarte to Bitac, a town badly damaged for its resistance. He added: "Every day the hatred of our people against the Japs becomes more intense as they rob our homes, destroy property, kill civilians, and rape our women."[17] It seemed that almost everyone knew of a woman like twenty-four-year-old Manileño Gertrude Balisalisa.[18] When the Japanese forcibly drafted her husband, an engineer, to work on bridges, she was sent to the local commander's quarters to work as a housemaid. Japanese officers raped

Balisalisa and several other women in house several times every day. The officers forbade them from speaking and punished them with beatings. At least one girl was shot trying to escape.[19]

The Japanese military also exploited urban areas where "indigenous prostitution seems always to have flourished."[20] According to Theresa Kaminski, "Prostitution and gambling, both run from cabarets, continued with the cooperation of the police and other city officials."[21] Hartendorp added: "Cabarets and houses of prostitution sprang up all over Manila. The principal American residence districts, Ermita and Malate, were crowded with these establishments."[22] The army imported women from Japan, Korea, China, Spain, Russia, Indonesia, and Westerners caught in conquered territories.[23]

The *Manila Tribune* advertised for "good-looking and up-to-date girls," "mestiza waitresses with pleasing personality," and "complaisant hostesses" for work as waitresses, hostesses, masseuses, and dancers.[24] One observer noted, "The Japanese were always stressing in their propaganda that the Filipinos were Orientals and should consider themselves fellow-Orientals with the Japanese; but they did like *mestizas*."[25] George Hicks reported prices charged in Manila as ¥3.50 per night for Koreans, ¥5.50 for Japanese, ¥11 for Hispanics, and ¥13 for Americans.[26]

Many Filipinas with starving families answered the ads and became ensnared. Pacita Pestano-Jacinto observed, "The average Filipina is a sensitive woman but during these last years she has, no doubt, learned to be harder, less sensitive to pain. As the war drags on, necessity may yet teach her to be insensitive to shame."[27]

Auxiliary bishop monseigneur William Finnemann openly campaigned against the "comfort women" practices.[28] In October 1942 a Japanese commission retaliated by threatening to turn the convent of Holy Spirit Missionary Sisters in Mindoro into a brothel. According to Col. Wendell Fertig, the Japanese proposed "that he turn his girls college with all the girls over to them as a red-light house. He refused."[29] On 19 October the Japanese arrested Finnemann. Despite seven days of beatings and starvation, he refused to sign over the convent; the Japanese finally threw him into the sea off Verde Island near Batangas and reported the bishop had committed suicide.

Hoping to better understand the Filipinos, the Japanese propaganda corps organized a unit of writers, "the Pen Corps" (*pen butai*).[30] Kiyoshi Miki, a philosopher of Buddhist and German ideas trained in Kyoto and Europe, arrived in March to spend a year observing Philippine culture.[31] He found a resignation resembling Japanese subjective nothingness, but without depth, and a politeness lacking a philosophical context. He concluded that the Spaniards and Americans had given Filipinos an inferiority complex that they compensated for with habitual empty speeches and expensive clothes. Such observations reinforced racist notions of Filipinos as "an abundant source of human resources that could be harnessed for the benefit of the Greater East Asia Co-Prosperity Sphere."[32]

CENTRAL LUZON, D103/R-946

Luzon crawled with USAFFE stragglers, some trying to reach Bataan, others attempting to escape. Except for Philippine Scouts, they tended to fall in with any guerrilla outfit they encountered.[33] In Nueva Vizcaya, for example, Parker Calvert, Art Murphy, and "Budd" Spencer stumbled into the Lusod sawmill southwest of Baguio after failing to get through to Bataan and found Filipino soldiers wanting to join them. Unaware Thorp was nearby, Calvert led them north to Bontoc to find Horan. By now, Thorp, Straughn, and Horan had entered into a haphazard competition for support and prestige. Thorp's position improved tremendously on 20 March when a USAFFE team under Maj. Llewellyn Barbour completed a daring trip by PT boat and cross-country hike to deliver a two-way radio.[34] With it came operator Tech. Sgt. Bill Brooks, demolition specialist Sgt. Albert Short, and two Philippine Scouts.[35]

Meanwhile, miscalculation by the Japanese undermined their pacification efforts.[36] They had gained control over an area that produced 67 percent of the world's rice.[37] Yet a shortage in the Philippines threatened their legitimacy and control.[38] The Japanese Military Administration (JMA) responded with a program to introduce quick-growing Taiwanese *horai* rice with a promise to increase Philippine rice production by 300 percent.[39] Over the next eight months the media published glowing reports of tests proving how well the rice grew in the islands. In August, the *Manila Tribune* reported on a four-thousand-acre Ota Development Company model farm that met "military requirements in the Philippines: with expected yields of 100,000 bushels in 1942 and 750,000 bushels in 1944."[40] The JMA predicted *horai* would make the country self-sufficient in 1943. Until then, Japan would ship rice in from Vietnam.

The Ota Corporation oversaw rubber plantations in Cotabato and vegetable farms in Calamba for the Japanese navy. They confiscated lands for a slaughterhouse to provide the military with beef. They partnered with the Furukawa Plantation Company to run copra farms in Mindanao and with Daido Boeki to produce salt in Manila. Additionally, the JMA gave the 2,300-hectare International Harvester abaca plantation, lumber companies, and cotton plantations to the Furukawa Plantation.[41] Between

27 March and 7 April, the JMA announced the formation of "military-commissioned management of the Japanese developed mines."[42] It established the Philippine mining association to help reorganize, rebuild, and reopen local mines and oversaw legal changes that would allow the seizure of assets used by enemies or any public or semipublic property under military management.

The JMA also created the Philippine research commission to guide policies on economy, politics, ideology, education, religion, and race.[43] To bring Filipinos into their proper place, the commission endorsed replacing the ideas and practices of democracy and individualism with new concepts of morality, justice, and moral justice so as to harmonize duty and freedom.[44] The commission recommended building on Filipino values of kinship to create a form of Japanese polity casting the head of state as a father caring for his national family.

The Army's religious section brought Catholic bishop Taguchi from Tokyo to meet with Manila archbishop Michael J. O'Doherty, who "showed very little willingness to cooperate."[45] As an Irishman, O'Doherty said he had little influence over Filipino parish priests.[46] The Japanese turned to the bishop's two Filipino deputies, auxiliary bishop Guerrero and Father Rufino C. Santos. O'Doherty told Guerrero "to deal directly with the enemy and to do everything to protect the Church from harassment."[47]

Already, Romulo noted, "It was a common sight to see our priests praying over the ashes of the churches."[48] Japanese bombers seemed to deliberately target the Santo Rosa and Santa Catalina Catholic colleges and a number of churches. The Kempeitai swept nuns and priests into prisons. Using Santo Tomas campus as a detention camp also insulted Catholics. As one resident noted, "Every Catholic student in every Catholic school knows that the University of Santo Tomas is the largest and oldest university in Asia and in the Philippines."[49]

LUZON, D112/R-937

On 29 March prominent Philippine communists gathered in the forests between Nueva Ecija, Pampanga, and Tarlac with about two hundred armed followers and voted to create a new "People's Army to Fight the Japs" (*Hukbong ng Bayan Laban sa Hapon*), widely known by the acronym Hukbalaháp or Huks.[50] They elected Casto Alejandrino, Dayang-Dayang, Bernardo Poblete, and Luis Taruc to a military committee with Taruc as chairman and Alejandrino as deputy.[51] They agreed to accept short-term cooperation with opponents and even work with the Japanese, but their ultimate objectives were never to change, and Mateo del Castillo, later the political commissar, drafted guidance for using the war to create a new independent communist state.[52]

The Huks issued two controlling documents, *The Fundamental Spirit of the Hukbalaháp* and *The Iron Discipline*. The first called for equality and love between the Huks and the people. The second established unbreakable orders that made the Huks respected and feared.[53] According to neighboring guerrillas, however, many Huks—"including Taruc himself"—chafed under the regulations. Taruc explained, "I adjusted myself to Party discipline, irksome though it was, and tried to share the mind and outlook of my comrades of the Politburo and the High Command."[54]

The Huks created a wide base of peasant support.[55] Leonard Davis noted, "The method of indoctrination into the aims and purposes of the Huk was so thorough—ranging from lectures to writing textbooks and preparing historical pageants—that the people under the Huk sovereignty grasped the simple message, and could not help believing that a new vista had been opened up in which they, and not the landlords, were in control."[56] The organization grew rapidly.

Competing guerrillas reported that "most ordinary Filipinos who became Huks did so for reasons that had little to do with Marxist metaphysics."[57] Starving people came for food, the vulnerable for protection, victims for revenge, and criminals for the chance to loot. Food proved to be the strongest of inducements. In the Huk area, historian Lizzie Collingham noted, "Good weather ensured a rice bumper crop and many recall the period of 1942 to 1947 as the period in their lives when food was most plentiful."[58]

Taruc noted, "Whole squadrons came overnight from towns and barrios."[59] The Huks organized roughly one-hundred-man squadrons divided into platoons and squads.[60] Notable was a Chinese group called Squadron 48, also referred to as the *Wa Chi*, with ranks of merchants, teachers, and newsmen led by veteran communist guerrillas from Canton.[61] They took the number "48" from Mao's New Fourth Army and Eighth Route Army. The *Wa Chi* would provide military and political training for all Huks.

The Huks' reputation lingered as a sensitive subject long after the war. American communist William J. Pomeroy, who married a Huk, described them heroically. Lapham countered: "The vaunted idealism of the Huks existed mainly in the imaginations of those Western 'progressives' who see a reincarnated George Washington whenever some bloodstained bandit comes out of the jungle, rifle in hand, and starts talking about 'freedom' and 'social justice.'"[62]

The Huks' revolutionary fervor targeted many Filipinos. "Oftentimes," historian Teodoro Agoncillo explained, "it was necessary for them, in what they considered to be the interests of the movement, to liquidate those suspected, rightly or wrongly, of posing a danger to the organization."[63] Taruc later admitted that "errors were made and that innocent people died."[64] According to some estimates the Huks killed 5,000 Japanese—and 20,000 Filipinos.[65] To many, this was the price of social justice. "Others were like Carlos Nocum," wrote Lapham, "who joined in order to fight the Japanese but who disliked Marxist dogmatism and discipline so much that he and his men switched over to my LGAF [Luzon Guerrilla Armed Forces] forces in 1942."[66]

As one of its first acts, the Huks sent Alejandrino, Pampanga, mayor Fernancio Sampang, and peasant leader Benedicto Sayco to Bataan to meet with MacArthur, not knowing he had left the islands. Li Yongxiao claimed to have been with the delegation that met Thorp's executive officer, Captain Mackenzie, on Mount Arayat.[67] Lapham recalled seeing four or five particularly hard-looking Huks and believed one of them was Taruc.[68] They asked Thorp to be their military advisor. Blackburn recalled, "'Thorp said that he wouldn't be the military advisor, but that he'd run the whole damn show. This didn't sit well at all, and it resulted in quite a bit of friction between Thorp and the Huks."[69] Thorp moved his team to Camp Four on Mount Pinatubo in sight of Clark Field.[70]

On Bataan, the Japanese bombed clearly marked American Field Hospital Number 1, killing fifteen patients and administrators. This so enraged Filipinos that Japanese officials broadcast an unprecedented apology. Quezon then revealed in a broadcast from Melbourne that he had left the country to work with MacArthur and called upon "every Filipino to keep his courage and fortitude and have faith in the ultimate victory of our cause."[71]

On 1 April Homma's first reinforcements arrived in Luzon. He added service troops to Major General Kiyotake Kawaguchi's 35th Brigade of the 18th Division, augmented by the 124th Infantry Regiment from Borneo, to form the Kawaguchi detachment.[72] Four days later the 5th Division's 9th Infantry Brigade under Major General Saburo Kawamura, with the 41st Infantry Regiment, arrived from Malaya. Homma bolstered this group to form the Kawamura detachment. He planned to use these new detachments to conquer the southern Philippines.[73]

BATAAN, D118/R-931

On 3 April the forces defending Bataan endured six hours of heavy shelling. Ramsey recalled, "I was horrified and shaken by shellshock; it seemed that it would go on forever, this brutish killing and maiming, and that there was nothing I or anyone could do to stop it."⁷⁴ A determined Japanese assault breached the Philippine 41st Infantry Division. That evening, Homma sent representatives to deliver a message: "Follow the example of Singapore and Hong Kong and accept an honorable defeat."⁷⁵ Wainwright refused. Homma's troops continued their advance on Mount Samat. The defenders shared a poem penned by war correspondent Frank Hewlett: "We're the Battling Bastards of Bataan, No mama, no papa, no Uncle Sam, No aunts, no uncles, no cousins, no nieces, No pills, no planes, no artillery pieces, And nobody gives a damn."⁷⁶

Bataan's defenses began to crack. On 5 April the Japanese took Mount Samat from the Philippine 21st Division. MacArthur radioed Wainwright, "If food fails you will prepare and execute an attack upon the enemy."⁷⁷ He wanted I Corps to deliver a diversionary artillery barrage while II Corps assaulted to Olongapo Road and turned toward Subic Bay. If the attack failed, some men might still pass through the lines to the Zambales Mountains to fight on as guerrillas.⁷⁸ Unfortunately, USAFFE forces were too ravaged by starvation and disease to attempt a major attack.

Early on 7 April a Japanese bomber hit an ammunition truck parked by Field Hospital Number 1 at Bataan. Other aircraft returned to bomb and strafe the hospital, killing 89 soldiers and nurses and wounding another 101. This time there was no apology.

USAFFE made a temporary stand along the Alangan River until Japanese tanks forced them back. Realizing the end was near, the troops destroyed their ammunition and supplies. Wainwright doubled rations to deny food to the enemy. Sailors scuttled the submarine tender *Canopus*, the tug *Napa*, and the floating drydock *Dewey*. Some soldiers risked the shark-infested waters to swim to Corregidor. The sub SS-194 *Seadragon* removed the last twenty-one radio intelligence personnel.

Wainwright's men finally ran out of time. Early on 9 April USAFFE's II Corps commander, Gen. Edward P. King, sent a truce bearer to the Japanese lines. The Nagano detachment commander demanded that King appear personally. MacArthur radioed Wainwright that "under no conditions should Bataan be surrendered; any action is preferable to capitulation."⁷⁹ King defied both MacArthur and Wainwright and gave up 75,000 American and Filipino soldiers—the greatest number of men surrendered in U.S. history.⁸⁰ Wainwright stood alone with 10,000 men.

Many soldiers refused to surrender. In the 26th Cavalry Regiment, Capt. Joe Barker told Lt. Ed Ramsey, "Don't suppose I'd last long in prison camp."⁸¹ They worked down rivers and up the ridge of Mount Mariveles with a few rations and .45-caliber pistols. Ramsey recalled, "Everyone's lungs ached, everyone's stomach was empty."⁸² They picked up a lost U.S.

private, dodged Japanese patrols, and worked northward to the vicinity of Fort Stotsenburg.

Robert Lapham left the Philippine Scouts in Bataan with Albert Short and Esteban Lumyeb. Moving stealthily north through the Zambales foothills, they passed Camp O'Donnell and saw it was now a prison camp. In a nearby barrio, Filipino civilians mobbed the three men. "The experience forced us to face facts at last," said Lapham. "It was impossible to hide from Filipino civilians; we had to trust them."[83] In Lupao they met Sergeant Frederico Estipona and five 26th Cavalry soldiers. Exhausted, Short and Estipona remained in Lupao while Lapham and Lumyeb searched farther north for a base.

At 11th Division headquarters, Maj. Russell Volckmann and Capt. Donald Blackburn agreed to escape north.[84] They went with Martin Moses and Arthur Noble, both lieutenant colonels, to see Gen. William Brougher and ask permission to leave his division. The general did not give overt authorization but said, "If I was a younger man, I'd entertain the same thought."[85] Thinking smaller groups made smaller targets, Volckmann and Blackburn travelled apart from Moses and Noble.

Volckmann discovered his orderly had mistakenly emptied his musette bag of first aid supplies.[86] Blackburn added, "I really hadn't thought about quinine, or malaria, or dysentery, or beriberi, or any of those things. As a result, when we left our division, we were very ill prepared."[87] Hunger weakened the men.[88] "For anyone who has never gone hungry for a long time," recalled Volckmann, "I'm sure it is hard to understand this continual thinking about food."[89]

Corporal Alfred Bruce of the 31st Infantry and three lieutenants whom Volckmann remembered as Whiteman, Petit, and Anderson, along with a number of Filipino soldiers joined them. A Filipino scout they called Bruno, Jose Maddul from Ifugao, became an exceptionally valuable member of the team.[90] Whiteman and Bruce made it as far as Banban before they felt too sick to continue. They were never seen again.

Lieutenant Russell D. Barros of the 91st Infantry Division and some other American officers joined Marking's guerrillas near Rizal. Marking swore his followers to the U.S. Army's oath of enlistment.[91] He found Barros to be one "whose legs were raw from ankle to knee with tropical ulcers, and who had the best of intentions and forever said and did the wrong thing and somehow muddled through without getting killed." [92]

The refugee soldiers embraced the concealment of dense jungles. Yet they found incessant dampness eroded clothes and shoes and caused rashes. Stahl later complained, "The constant high humidity and moisture got into the bowels of our radio and shorted out critical parts."[93] Rattan thorns stuck in hands and feet and broke off under the skin. Willis remembered, "In the tropics most small cuts or scratches will turn into an ulcer if not constantly tended to."[94] The jungle held millions of small, biting creatures whose cacophony made some men go mad in the pitch-black nights. Others found comfort in the noise and dreaded any abrupt quiet. "I knew," said Ramsey, "that the sudden silence meant Japanese foot patrols."[95]

Leeches were relentless. "They were so numerous along the trail," Willis recalled, "that you could see them on the leaves of the trees and on the blades of the cogon grass, waving their thin bodies in the air, trying to find a passing victim to latch onto."[96] Maj. Steve Mellnik added, "Squeezing through small crevices—shoe and legging eyelets—they buried their heads in the flesh and began to suck blood. They apparently anesthetized the skin because we rarely felt their presence."[97] Removing them caused infectious sores.

"There is no way to keep the wounds dry; there is no sun to help the healing. The little wounds therefore grow larger, and rotten," Fertig complained.[98] Tropical ulcers often rotted to the bone. "It is easy to die in the world of the jungle," Fertig explained, "although death is apt to come slowly, beginning with the first fevers of any of a considerable number of diseases."[99] The jungle swallowed up many Bataan escapees.

After three days on the Dinalupihan-Olongapo road, Volckmann said, "I became so weak that I finally begged the rest of the party to go on without me, but they would not listen."[100] Blackburn recalled, "During the second week dysentery and malaria hit us, and this was just after we had gotten out of the Bataan Peninsula."[101] They found sojourn with the Guerrero family outside Dinalupihan who brought a doctor with liquid quinine urea to treat malaria, yellow jaundice, and beriberi.[102] Blackburn later reported, "I guess we got down to well under 100 pounds. We were like skeletons, and the food wasn't that appetizing."[103] The Guerreros were just one of countless Filipino families who provided the would-be guerrillas with indispensable sustenance.

Natives often offered traditional, interesting cures. People in Haliap said illness resulted from displeasing ancestors, and their shamans attempted to placate the deceased through offers of tapoy, betel nuts, and other foods spread on a blanket in *bacci* ceremonies. On a number of occasions Volckmann recalled, "Without asking me the pagan priest came in to play bacci for me. I recovered, so I never questioned their beliefs and customs."[104] Severe illnesses might require the forced feeding, ritual killing, roasting, and eating of a dog. Some dismissed such practices as primitive superstition, but Blackburn thought they had psychological merit "because the ritual distracted the sick man from his troubles and showed him 'that even strangers sincerely wanted him to get well.'"[105] He found too that respecting the native practices helped him connect with the people.

Not that many guerrillas were any more familiar with modern medicine. Faced with his first bout of malarial fever and chills, Ramsey took thirteen quinine pills. "The dose nearly killed me, and by morning I was delirious," he wrote.[106] Confused and stumbling in "horrible isolation and fever," he believed he was about to be captured. "I took my pistol from the holster," he remembered, "slipped off the safety catch, and pressed the muzzle to my temple. My finger was on the trigger, and I began to squeeze. But my mind would not let me."[107] At the last minute he turned his despair into anger against the Japanese and vowed to continue.

Travelling the jungle, Cpl. John Boone of the 31st Infantry Regiment came across Barker and Ramsey and told them that, under MacArthur's orders, Thorp had gone into the hills north of Fort Stotsenburg to "enlist any Filipinos and Americans who want to join into a guerrilla force that'll carry on the war behind Jap lines."[108] Noticing that Pvt. Gene Strickland was desperately ill, Boone advised Volckmann of a camp near Thorp where his men could receive medical care.

Brothers Bill and Martin Fassoth had converted their large sugar plantation deep in the Zambales Mountains near Clark Field into oasis for the escapees from Bataan.[109] Spanish-Filipino neighbor Vicente Bernia acquired supplies, money, and medicine through contacts in the Catholic church.[110] It was after Barker, Ramsey, and Strickland made it to the camp that they first heard accounts of the Bataan Death March.

On 9 April the Japanese marshalled prisoners from Bataan for movement to detention camps. They had expected 25,000 POWs but found 75,000 starving, sick, and exhausted captives. Instead of marching fourteen miles to small camps, they decided to march the men sixty-five miles to larger, hurriedly constructed camps and the rail station in Balanga.[111] Many haggard POWs faltered and were beaten or killed. "No words can describe the horror of it," one observer said, "the way the men clawed like dogs at the food that people in their pity threw at them."[112] "One elderly captain begged a guard to put him out of his misery with a single shot," survivors recalled. "A young American soldier was taken from the line and forced at gunpoint to beat the captain and bury him alive. The young soldier later committed suicide."[113] Up to 18,000 prisoners may have perished on the march. A number slipped away, often sheltered by Filipinos, to join the resistance.[114]

CEBU, D123/R-926

On the evening of 9 April coast watchers on Cebu spotted three Japanese cruisers and eleven transports off shore.[115] With Bataan in hand, Homma had launched the Kawaguchi detachment against Cebu and the Kawamura detachment at Panay. The two detachments would also join the Miura detachment in Davao to conquer Mindanao.[116]

The convoy split during the night, and at dawn the larger portion landed near Cebu City despite a challenge by several B-17s from Australia. Chynoweth's 6,500 soldiers were spread too thin to defend any one beach. "I had no idea of being able to stop the Japs," he explained, "but I thought we could spend two or three days in withdrawal."[117] He would then transition to his planned guerrilla warfare operations.

Lieutenant Colonel Howard J. Edmands commanded about 1,100 members of the Cebu military police regiment defending Cebu City's 150,000 residents. He held long enough to allow demolition teams to complete their work before falling back into the hills.[118] A pattern repeated: the Japanese advanced, the defenders withdrew. The Kawaguchi detachment reported defeating "several thousands of enemy" and "the subjugation of strategic positions on the island by the nineteenth."[119] Homma sent the 31st Independent Infantry Battalion to relieve the Kawaguchi detachment so it could prepare for Mindanao. Wainwright had conceded Cebu three days earlier and ordered Sharp to reestablish the Visayan-Mindanao force.[120] Still, Cebu's defenders remained intact with arms, ammunition, and supplies.

Thirty-three-year-old American Harry Fenton (born Aaron Feinstein) was a radio announcer on KZRC in Cebu City popular for his anti-Japanese broadcasts. When the war began, he claimed a commission from Chynoweth and went into the north Cebu hills to unite several guerrilla bands. It was said that he "trusted no one.... no one seemed to like him."[121] One guerrilla would add, "He's a madman. He's insane with hatred of the Japs. Anyone found with a single Jap yen in his pocket he immediately condemns to death. The same for anyone found living in occupied or controlled territory."[122] Fenton also refused to pay his men and had anyone who resisted him shot.

In southern Cebu, thirty-seven-year-old Mexican-American mestizo and mining engineer James Cushing—brother of Charlie and Walter—also claimed a commission as a captain from Chynoweth. He raised a guerrilla force around a core of USAFFE personnel and built a reputation for protecting civilians and fighting alongside his men. He was liked and respected.[123] In September, Cushing would lead one thousand guerrillas—the "Cebu Patriots"—with mortars against a Japanese garrison in Toledo.

On 11 April a Japanese patrol stopped a car carrying chief justice Jose Abad Santos, his son, and two soldiers. They took the judge and his son to a prison camp near Cebu City where he refused orders to collaborate. Before the end of the month, Major General Kiyotake Kawaguchi arrived to escort the two prisoners to Luzon.

The next day, Cebu guerrillas destroyed their last boat, PT-35. On Mindanao, the crew of PT-4 scuttled their boat while overhead, a U.S. 17th Pursuit Squadron P-40 flown by Lt. John Brownwell scored the last American victory over a Japanese aircraft in defense of the Philippines.

LUZON, D124/R-925

Homma's headquarters tracked "several hundred defeated enemy troops" hiding in the mountains of central Luzon east of the upper Cagayan River and three thousand more in the Zambales north of Bataan.[124] "Taking advantage of the weakness of our garrison force," a Japanese officer observed, "these units were engaged in disturbing public peace."[125] In Bicol, "several hundred defeated enemy troops and malcontents had changed into guerrilla units and were disturbing the peace" near Legaspi, Mount Isarog, and Daet.[126] More insurgents appeared around Luguna Bay southeast of Manila.

On 10 April Homma sent his 16th Division, the Nagano detachment, and the 4th Division to mop up these USAFFE remnants.[127] The 65th Brigade's Lieutenant General Akira Nara requested Lieutenant Hitomi's propaganda unit "for the purpose of getting the Philippine-American guerrilla forces in northern Luzon to surrender as well as persuading the local people to cooperate with the Japanese Army to restore law and order."[128] Governor Ablan countered with a news sheet produced by an intelligence network under former publicity and propaganda officer Pedro F. Alviat.

After clearing southern Bataan in seventy-two hours, the Japanese 4th Division with the army artillery unit joined the army air unit for an assault on Corregidor. On 13 April the 65th Brigade went to east-central Luzon, the Nagano detachment to west-central Luzon, and the 16th Division to the south of Manila.[129]

The next day in Washington Under Secretary of State Sumner Welles wrote to presidential political advisor Stanley Hornbeck: "The President has informed me that he thinks it highly desirable for President Quezon under present conditions to remain in Australia with his Government."[130] Three days later Hornbeck replied: "More than 1,000 miles from the Philippines, Australia has no system of communications with the Philippines, has no American press or Philippine press, and has more limited broadcasting facilities than this country."[131] Furthermore, winter in Australia would aggravate Quezon's tubercular condition. Roosevelt would have to reconsider.

Meanwhile, Lapham reached Umingan where retired Philippine Constabulary sergeant Juan Desear, farmers Juan Marcos and Emilio Casayuran, and grocer Filadelfo Macaranas recruited him to lead them in guerrilla warfare.[132] He accepted their offer. "Most Americans have merely assumed that guerrilla activity in the wartime Philippines must have been initiated by U.S. escapees like me," Lapham explained, "and that we then coaxed or bullied Filipinos into supporting us. This was not the case at all."[133] Most of the Americans hoped to either join U.S. groups or escape to Australia or China. Filipinos decided otherwise. "Overwhelmingly," Lapham wrote, "Filipinos came to us and begged us to lead them and help them fight their oppressors."[134]

Across the islands, Filipinos chose whether to invite Americans to lead their guerrilla groups. Many prudently saw in the Americans expertise in military tactics, organization, and leadership. Others calculated that having an American in charge would mean recognition and material support from MacArthur. Still others had more practical reasons: prewar politics, culture, and class divisions often made cooperation between Filipinos difficult, but all could agree to follow an American outsider.

For the Americans, the burden of leading Filipinos could be substantial. They had to cross cultures, join extended kinship networks, and become one with the people. Ramsey felt he remained "nothing but a symbol. A Paraclete reminding them of the promise of salvation. That promise had been made by the man whom they trusted more than any other and in whose distant shadow I stood: MacArthur."[135]

Lapham embraced his place. He made Umingan his base and reached out to local businessmen, plantation owners, and police. "Two concerns were of vital importance to them," he recalled, "first, we should not fight with the Japanese near Umingan, for they might take reprisals against civilians; second, something decisive had to be done about roving bands of former soldiers and outlaws who were terrorizing local civilians."[136] He also had to deal with the mayor of Umingan, who was pro-Japanese.

PANAY, D130/R-919

At dawn on 16 April the 4,160-man Kawamura detachment landed near Iloilo on southeast Panay. A smaller force landed north at Capiz. A final landing came forty-eight hours later near San Jose on the southwest coast. The landings went unopposed. Colonel Albert Christie's seven thousand defenders executed their preplanned withdrawals to the mountains where, in accordance with Operation *Baus Au*, they would wage guerrilla warfare.[137] The Japanese reported "very little enemy resistance" and occupied all strategic points in four days.[138] Two converging columns seized Capiz and the copper mines around San Jose but found USAFFE forces had reduced Iloilo City to ruins. Still, by 20 April Kawamura considered the campaign over.[139] A hastily assembled 1st Independent Infantry Battalion of the 33rd Independent Brigade relieved the Kawamura detachment for operations in Mindanao.

For Christie, the campaign was yet to begin. He had abundant arms, ammunition, and fresh water along with 500 head of cattle, 15,000 bags of rice, hundreds of cases of canned goods, and adequate fuel.[140] He began hit-and-run raids that brought a punitive Japanese expedition to San Jose. When a Filipino reported that Japanese troops were approaching, Christie organized a company ambush with bolos, spears, and bows and arrows that killed a large part of the enemy force and caused the rest to retreat to San Jose.[141] Even so, Homma reported Panay conquered and turned elsewhere.

WASHINGTON, D131/R-918

Roosevelt revisited the situation with Quezon and floated an idea of inviting the Philippine government in exile to sign the United Nations pact. State Department representatives cautioned that such a move would "be equivalent to formal recognition by us at this time of the independent status of the Philippines."[142] The United States could lose Quezon to a settlement with Japan. Welles suggested they wait until they could set a policy for all occupied countries. Five days later Roosevelt announced, "I am, of course, a firm believer in carrying through our promise of independence to the Philippines, but I do not think we should modify the present law by a step which might be considered to hold out a promise to them for immediate independence if, for example, the war were to terminate early in 1943. There might be a period of repair and adjustment for two or three years for which the United States should be responsible."[143]

AUSTRALIA, D132/R-917

On Saturday 18 April MacArthur formally accepted appointment as the commander in chief of the Southwest Pacific Area (SWPA). Even before leaving Corregidor, he had sent staff to Australia to coordinate with the Allied command. G-2 executive officer Col. Van Santvoord Merle-Smith worked with Royal Australian Navy captain R. B. M. Long to transform the highly effective allied naval coast watch service into an intelligence, propaganda, and special operations activity.[144] A well-connected Princeton grad, Oyster Bay New Yorker and former third secretary of state, Merle-Smith was an exceptional choice for the effort "severally handicapped by jealousies" between services, departments, and nations.[145] Furthermore, he had MacArthur's unequivocal support in bureaucratic turf fights. Merle-Smith set to work on an outline for an organization to be known as the Allied Intelligence Bureau and secured a promise from Australia for £45,000 as the Allies worked out command arrangements.[146]

MANILA, D132/R-917

On the afternoon of 18 April Japanese soldiers and Kempeitai in Manila suddenly rounded up all consular officials of neutral countries and hauled them off to prisons. Any white person on the streets received curses, slaps, and kicks.[147] News then spread of a remarkable event: that morning Brig. Gen. Jimmy Doolittle had led sixteen U.S. Army Air Force B-25 bombers in bombing Tokyo and other Japanese cities.

Among hundreds arrested, Chick Parsons was taken to the dungeons of Fort Santiago. He got word to American Helge Jansen, the "honorary consul" of Sweden whose wife was the actual Swedish consul. Jansen notified Panama, whose officials protested to Tokyo.[148] The Japanese transferred Parsons to the prison at Santo Tomás. By the end of May, a friendly doctor persuaded the authorities to let Parsons rest at home for one week.

The day after Doolittle's attack, Quezon and his party left Australia on the steamer SS *President Coolidge* bound for the United States.[149] Villamor met the wheelchair-bound president before his departure: "Jess, there is nothing I can do in Australia but vegetate," Quezon said. "You know I am not made for that. My place is in the United States. I must urge them to continue the struggle. They owe us a debt which must be paid."[150] Villamor asked what he could do to help. Quezon responded: "Go to the United States, and tell *los animals* [those animals] in Washington how badly help is needed in the Philippines."[151]

SOUTHERN LUZON, D133/R-916

On 19 April Faustino Flor's Camp Isarog guerrillas attacked Iriga and drove the town's mayor, Manuel Crescini, to seek refuge in Naga. With intelligence supplied by the Oligquino brothers and Adolfo Caro, Flor decided to push on against the garrison platoon in Naga.[152] Miranda agreed to assist. Coincidentally, Vinzons' Travelling Guerrillas attacked the forty-man Japanese garrison at Daet on 29 April with one hundred men, including six American miners deputized as lieutenants.[153] "The attack at Daet," Hartendorp noted, "was reportedly provoked by Japanese brutality in that area, where they shot down men, women, and children, just for being on the road or to see them jump, and by the abuses of Japanese-appointed Filipino officials."[154]

With the VTG distracting the Japanese, the next morning Flor assaulted Naga. Miranda and the TVGU arrived in the afternoon. On the second day, sixty-five men of Dianela's Camp Tinawagan guerrillas joined the fight. Lieutenant Jose Hernandez, son of a former Camarines Norte governor, arrived with a small band from Cabusao. The Buenaventura Plantado group came. Felix (Baro) Espiritu brought men from Camaligan, and Ricardo Gordenker arrived with more from Mount Isarog. Isabelo Payte led Isarog tribal bowmen firing flaming arrows across the Naga River into buildings occupied by the Japanese. Of the one thousand guerrillas in the attack, only about two hundred carried firearms.[155]

The guerrillas fought to the center of Naga and freed foreign nationals from the provincial prison. They also liberated the inmates' forty-two wives and children from Judge Manley's house near Puente Colgante. Japanese troops moved acting governor Villafuerte, his seven children, and his pregnant wife from their house to the capitol.

On the evening of 2 May Villafuerte's wife began hemorrhaging, and the worried husband sent a letter to the Japanese commander asking that they be released to the guerrillas.[156] Instead, their guards killed and cooked a stray dog to feed the family. The guerrillas then cut their water supply. Before dawn on 3 May a squad of Japanese soldiers broke out, taking the Villafuerte family with them. By sunrise the guerrillas held Naga.

Sweeping the city, the guerrillas arrested six Japanese-Filipino families and sent them to a camp in Curry, Pili.[157] Japanese resident Tancing Kitaguchi and her five daughters were not arrested but had to watch as guerrillas burned down their house with all their belongings. They then took Ancieta Pinon, Tancing's mother, to a TVGU camp to serve as a cook and washerwoman.

The escaping Japanese squad commandeered a fishing boat to take Villafuerte, his wife, and oldest son to Legaspi. At sea, Mrs. Villafuerte again began hemorrhaging, and her husband finally convinced the Japanese to go ashore at Vito, Siruma. He could not know that guerrilla Elias Madrid's wife and family were there. The party alit at 1900 hours on 4 May into the middle of a *santacruzan* ritual. The Japanese fired into the air, perhaps to disperse the crowd. Guerrillas fired back. The soldiers retreated to the jungle's edge and engaged in a nightlong firefight. Elias Madrid arrived by pumpboat near midnight with reinforcements and rushed to his wife, while the Japanese stole his boat and got away. The guerrillas found, executed, and beheaded Villafuerte, his wife, his son, and their companions.[158]

CENTRAL LUZON, D135/R-914

Barker and Ramsey tired of the Fassoth camp and its air of defeatism and insubordination. They found Negrito guides who agreed to take them to Thorp's camp near Mount Pinatubo. Though seriously ill, Private Strickland made them promise to take him along. When the party arrived at their destination on 21 April, the shivering Strickland said, "I told you I'd make it."[159] On their second day in camp, twenty-one-year-old Gene Strickland died, simply worn out by malnutrition, illness, and fatigue.

The fall of Bataan had visibly shaken Thorp. Lapham wrote, "It has been alleged that at this juncture Colonel Thorp simply gave up. That is not what happened. We had general discussion about various possible actions, and at length Thorp brought it to an end by announcing that we could all do as we liked: surrender to the Japanese, stay with him, or strike out on our own."[160] Thorp would fight on, for now.

Farther south, Volckmann and Blackburn, again overcome by illness, returned to the Guerrero family home to recover. "They knew that if they hid us and shared their scanty means with us," Volckmann acknowledged, "the Japs would surely torture and kill them if they found out."[161] On 23 April Guerrero contacted his prewar employer, a Mr. Demson, who moved the refugee soldiers deeper into the mountains to a camp that he ran away from all main trails.

"Bandits" raided a nearby camp, killed Demson's wife, wounded his son, and stole their belongings. The raid attracted Japanese patrols that forced Volckmann and Blackburn to spend several days hiding in a creek bed. Guerrero watched the Japanese and reported: "They moved down those trails that they could find, and each time they passed a house or an evacuation camp they sprayed it with bullets and kept on going."[162] Soon the Guerrero family departed, leaving Volckmann—now also suffering beriberi—and Blackburn. A week later, Demson ceased sending supplies and vanished.[163]

Meanwhile, the Japanese spent five days shelling Corregidor with a huge 240-mm Type 96 howitzer they had brought to Bataan. On 25 April as bombers hit Darwin, they added nightly artillery bombardments of Corregidor. Fifteen of Wainwright's men died when two shells from the howitzer destroyed the entrance to a command tunnel. In the early evening of 2 May, 1,600 bags of gunpowder, each 62 pounds, in the Geary gun battery magazine exploded, killing fifty-six soldiers and wounding hundreds more. The next day the submarine SS-190 *Spearfish* removed twenty-seven soldiers, nurses, and civilians as two thousand Japanese soldiers prepared to board fifteen barges just across the bay in Bataan.

MINDANAO, D142/R-907

Homma planned a multipronged attack to secure Mindanao: the Miura detachment moving in from Davao and Digo, the Kawaguchi detachment east and north from Cotabato and Parang, and the Kawamura detachment west from Macajalar Bay.[164] Ultimately, the detachments would link up along the Digos-Cotabato stretch of Route 1.

Lieutenant Colonel Reed Graves of the Philippine 101st Division awaited a Miura detachment attack in the Cotabato-Davao sector.[165] One American, however, would later confess, "Most of the men who fought on Mindanao never fired a live round before they went into battle."[166] Yet when Miura attacked on 28 April, Graves' men held. Early the next day, the 4,852-man Kawaguchi detachment landed near Cotabato and Parang ninety miles west of Davao. The 101st Division's surprisingly robust defense ended when Japanese aircraft forced them to fall back.[167] Kawaguchi marched east and so threatened Graves that Brig. Gen. Joseph P. Vachon ordered his withdrawal on the evening of 2 May.[168] The next morning the Kawamura detachment landed on Macajalar Bay, 125 miles northwest of Davao.[169] For six days the Japanese advantages in artillery and aircraft undermined all Filipino-American defensive efforts.

MANILA, D149/R-900

On 5 May Tojo arrived in Manila, where collaborationists orchestrated a warm reception covered by a fawning press. Nearly 400,000 people, many waving Japanese flags, greeted the prime minister. Bands played along his route. Tojo told the crowd: "I am glad to state that upon my arrival in this country, I see everywhere tangible evidence of your growing desire to cooperate more closely with the Imperial Japanese Government."[170] Commissioner of justice Jose Laurel led responding cheers of "banzai!"

During a meeting with Tojo, PEC presiding officer Jorge Vargas expressed how happy he was that Filipinos and Japanese were working together to create a new Philippines. He explained, "We have been an orphan in Asia, a spoiled child among the Asian peoples. Living in an alien culture, we have forgotten our innate culture, but Japan has pulled us up to the level of a member of the Greater East Asia Co-Prosperity Sphere."[171] After three days Tojo returned to Japan without visiting Davao, while newspapers advertised the second shipment of rice from Saigon to Manila.

Tojo likely received a briefing on an effort to convert the Araullo high school in Intramuros into a new constabulary training academy where select cadets would take a three-month course under Japanese supervision. "From the Filipino point of view," Agoncillo wrote, "the creation of the Academy was a preparation for retaliatory measures to be taken by the Academy graduates, upon the insistence of the Japanese, against the guerrillas or, as the Japanese called them, bandits."[172] To oversee the constabulary, JMA director-general General Yoshihide Hayashi created a department of peace and order.

The Philippine research commission studied American achievements in the islands pertaining to individual rights, local government, and secular education and found faults with each.[173] Education, for example, was centered on liberal ideals such as law and literature, which led Filipinos astray from the manual labor the Japanese felt best suited them. Filipinos also lacked any sense of self-sacrifice and duty to the state. The JMA sought to eradicate these Western influences and re-educate Filipinos.

The JMA created a government training institute to inculcate Filipino administrators in "moral, intellectual, and physical'" ideals that would "make them better fit to perform their duties under the New Order."[174] Graduates were to exorcise all non-Japanese ideas from textbooks and teach a new Japanese-influenced language called "Nippongo."[175] Commissioner of education Claro Recto received orders to reopen schools under a Japanese-Filipino committee and set 1 June for the new school year, but a lack of teachers and an unwillingness of parents to send their children stymied his efforts.[176]

CORREGIDOR, D149/R-900

Following a bombardment of 16,000 shells, just before midnight on 5 May Homma hit the east side of Corregidor with 2,000 infantrymen. Intense fires killed or wounded 1,200 men of the assaulting force. Yet by 0930 the next morning, they achieved a solid toehold on the island fortress. Counterattacks by U.S. Marines failed to dislodge the invaders, who were now reinforced with tanks.

At 1230 hours a representative of Wainwright crossed the Japanese lines near Cavalry Point under a flag of truce to arrange a meeting to discuss surrender. An hour later Wainwright arrived at the left flank of the Japanese 4th Division. He sent a coded message to General Sharp granting him command of all USAFFE forces outside Corregidor. The Japanese escorted Wainwright to Cabcaben, but because he only offered to surrender Corregidor, they sent him back and continued their attack.[177] Later that day General Short radioed MacArthur from Mindanao: "North front in full retreat. Enemy comes through right flank. Nothing further can be done. May sign off any time now."[178]

Wainwright told Homma that he commanded only Corregidor and had no authority to instruct other forces to surrender. That was by MacArthur's design. However, Homma knew Army chief of staff General Marshall had promoted Wainwright to command all forces in the Philippines and had even seen an order issued by Wainwright announcing his assumption of USAFFE command.[179] The Japanese general demanded Wainwright surrender all forces. The American protested that he had no way to communicate such an order, having already destroyed all radio equipment on Corregidor. Homma offered him two alternatives: surrender all forces, or face continued attack. Wainwright agreed to coordinate the unconditional surrender of all USAFFE forces.

At 2345 hours on 6 May 1942 a white flag flew over the headquarters on Corregidor. Five minutes later, over the Philippines broadcasting network from Manila, Wainwright instructed all U.S. commanders in the islands to lay down their arms.

MANILA, D151/R-898

Between 14 and 25 May, Japanese planes flew Wainwright's staff to Cebu, Panay, Leyte, Negros, and Samar to coordinate their surrender (see map 3.1).[180] Imperial army garrison units followed.

The day after Wainwright's surrender, the Japanese unloaded six thousand American and Filipino prisoners off barges at the yacht club on Dewey Avenue for a march through crowds in Manila, just as they had paraded Australian, British, and Dutch prisoners through throngs of jeering natives in Singapore and Batavia. A Filipino historian reported, "The Manileños did jeer at those ragged troops, but their very raggedness seemed to symbolize something more profound, the fraying of American confidence, of Manila's confidence in America. Many Manileños ran behind Japanese guards and offered the prisoners cigarettes and food—it was like a sentimental gesture to an old friend leaving, perhaps never to return."[181]

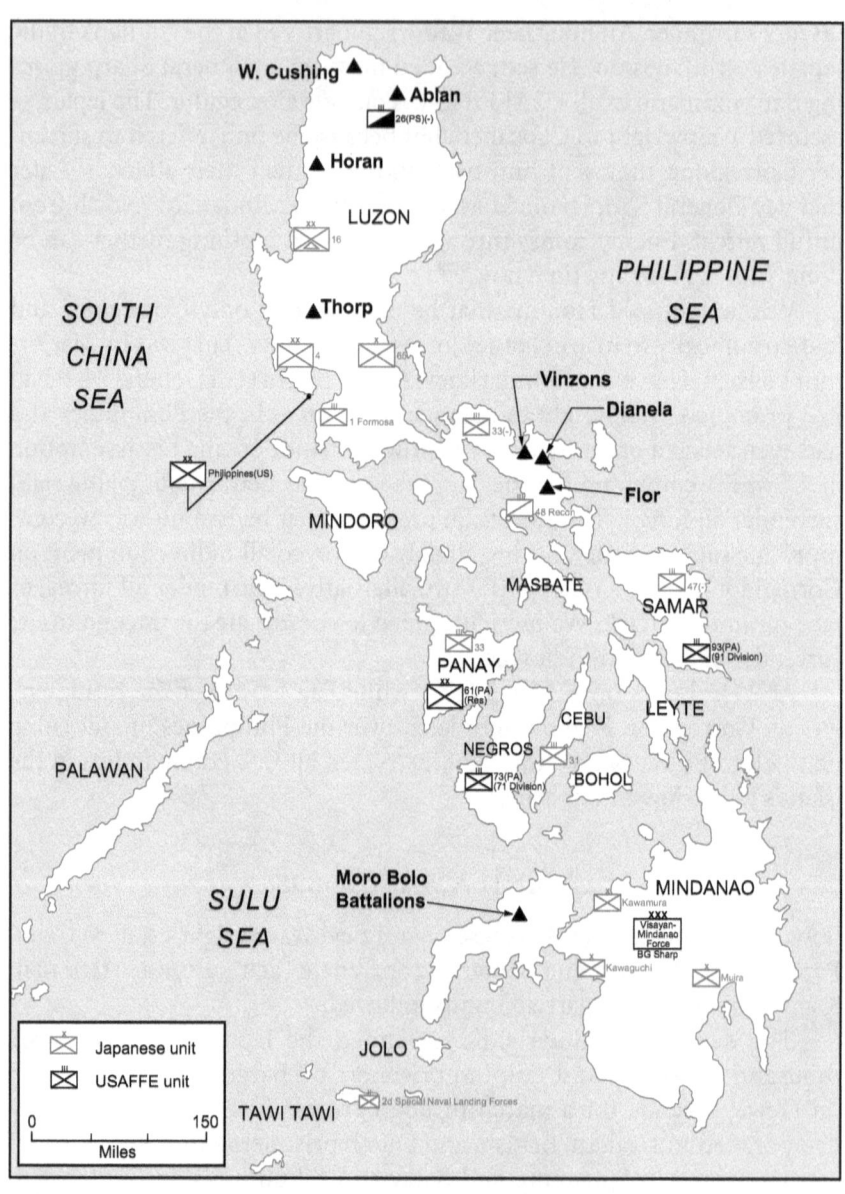

MAP 3.1. Situation, 8 May 1942

PANAY, D152/R-897

Brigadier General Christie obeyed Wainwright's orders to surrender the Americans of his 61st Division (Philippine Army), but he granted his Filipino soldiers permission to leave. G-3 (Operations) Captain Macario Peralta, division engineer Captain Leopoldo Relunia, and 3rd Battalion, 63rd Regiment commander Captain Julian Chaves promised not to organize any guerrilla resistance for two months so as not to provoke retribution upon prisoners. Peralta took some soldiers north, Relunia east, and Chaves to the island's center. Other groups assembled under Braulic Villasis in Capiz and Cerilo Garcia in the northwest.

Across the islands, armed men used the war to settle old grudges. In Iloilo, Juanito Ceballos led fifty soldiers into rural Zarraga in search of judge Vincente Mapa, who had once sentenced him to prison for theft. They found and executed the judge. The band then killed an abusive farm owner, Sabas Gustilo. The murders drove local elites into the arms of the Japanese for protection.[182] When Ceballos began hunting the politically powerful Lopez brothers across Iloilo, he was captured in an ambush and later executed.

Peralta proved a natural guerrilla leader. "People who have known him report that he is a strong character, a good organizer, aggressive, sure of himself to the point of being cocky, and a strong nationalist," SWPA noted, before adding, "He tends to be impetuous, lacks experience, is on occasion arbitrary and sometimes lacks follow-up on his ideas. He wants the Panay guerrilla organization to be a purely Filipino accomplishment."[183] Peralta tolerated Americans on his island but excluded them from his organization. This made SWPA wary. Over the next four months, Peralta would gradually bring many units into a guerrilla version of the 61st Division under his command while containing the small Japanese garrisons in San Jose (Antique), Capiz, and Iloilo City.

Iloilo provincial governor Tomas Confesor escaped detention in Manila to return to Panay. The provincial governors of Antique and Capiz surrendered, but Confesor held government in the hills. "He is impetuous," U.S. Army intelligence reported, "and was known as the 'stormy petrel' of Philippine politics because of this trait alone."[184] Confesor established a police force known as the provincial guards, a robust messenger organization, and a radio station. People gravitated to Confesor. Peralta and the other 61st Division officers, on the other hand, were outsiders, Tagalogs from central Luzon. As a result, Peralta entered into a contest for power against Confesor.

A Kang Fan delegation with Cai Zhensheng, Guo Jian, and Ji Rongfang had also arrived on Panay "to organize the underground activities."[185]

Iloilo was home to more than 3,500 Chinese, their second largest community in the Philippines. In 1936 Commercial Secondary School teachers Chen Qushui and Zheng Shimei had founded the Chinese Salvation Association, which now directed Chinese youth on Panay to guerrilla warfare. In 1938 Wu Zhaisheng, Gong Taoyi, and Wu Jinshui turned a reading club in brothers Zhang Jisheng's and Zhang Guamian's bookstore into the National Salvation Society to mobilize students and shopkeepers against the Japanese.[186] Although the invaders scattered the society's fifty members, the Kang Fan established a Southern Island branch on 7 July and began publishing an underground *Southern Island Guide* newspaper.

MINDANAO, D153/R-896

Major General Sharp felt well positioned on Mindanao to wage irregular warfare and hesitated to surrender.[187] His 81st Division Commander, Brig. Gen. Guy O. Fort, was organizing thousands of motivated young Moros in Bolo battalions under Muslim leaders along highways in Lanao. When the Japanese landed at Davao, however, the untrained units dissolved.

Still, Japanese actions incited resistance. After witnessing Filipinas customarily kissing the hands of two American priests in Pikit, for example, Japanese sentinels bayonetted the priests, put their bodies in sacks, tossed them in a river, and continued plundering, raping, and killing.[188] Similar outrages in Midsayap and Kabacan in Cotabato Province—"the Judgment of Knives"—spurred the reconstitution of Bolo battalions.

Before Corregidor fell, Moro lawyer and USAFFE First Lieutenant Salipada Pendatun and his brother-in-law Datu Matalam Udtog organized a Bolo battalion near Catabato. Pendatun, a former classmate of Peralta's at the University of the Philippines, blocked the Digos-Kabacan road with several others until the Japanese ran them off.[189]

As his executive officer and chief of staff, Pendatun selected constabulary Major Edwin D. Andrews, a thirty-seven-year-old American mestizo graduate of the Philippine Constabulary academy who had attended the Federal Bureau of Investigation school in the United States.[190] Andrews was thought to have "never got over a racial insult suffered during his training days at flying fields in the southern United States."[191] Leaving his command of the Zablan airfield, he took two hundred rifles provided by assemblyman Manuel Fortich and helped Pendatun defeat Japanese garrisons at Kibawe, Maramag, Valencia, Mailag, and Malaybalay.[192] By the end of 1942 they would have 2,400 men in Bukidnon Province and more in the surrounding areas. Andrews boasted: "We had the necessary services such as quartermaster, medical, transportation, ordinance, and finance. We had a regular hospital running with six doctors and twenty nurses, in short a regular force functioning under the leadership of this young Muslim lawyer."[193] It was an impressive force.

On 11 May Sharp received word from MacArthur: "Orders emanating from General WAINWRIGHT have no validity. If possible separate your forces into small elements and initiate guerrilla operations."[194] The coastal cities had few roads to the interior, and Short held strong positions. Then Wainwright reported that Homma threatened the prisoners on Luzon if all U.S. forces in the Philippines did not surrender. Sharp radioed MacArthur that he would follow Wainwright's instructions. His decision to surrender, Keats wrote, "was so complete and sudden that civilians and army remnants were stunned and demoralized."[195] SWPA noted, "One by one the thin, uncertain lines of communication between General MacArthur's reconstituted headquarters in Melbourne and the tortured Philippines three thousand miles to the north were fading into silence."[196] Allied organized resistance in the Philippines had ended.

4

Alone
May–August 1942

MINDANAO, D155/R-890

Many men refused to follow Sharp in surrender. Mining stock millionaire and recalled Navy lieutenant Samuel J. Wilson, owner of Wilson Building in Manila, was in Lanao when he learned the Japanese had interned his wife and children in Santo Tomas. He joined the resistance. Jordan Hamner, Charles M. Smith, and Athol Y. "Chick" Smith were mining engineers on Masbate. They obtained a sailboat and escaped to Panay. When Cebu fell, they moved to Mindanao to build roads for Sharp. When he surrendered, they made their way to an American plantation camp owned by a Mr. Deisher near Momungan.[1]

Many who did surrender had second thoughts. Pvt. Robert Ball and Sgt. William A. Knortz capitulated at Malaybay but escaped to join the resistance. The Japanese released German citizen Waldo Neveling from Davao prison to encourage Westerners to surrender, but he headed into the jungle and joined the guerrillas.

Lieutenant Colonel Wendell W. Fertig, an American mining engineer and Army reservist, was working on an airfield in Lanao when he heard Sharp had surrendered. He set out with Navy CPO Elwood Offret and Army captain Charlie Hedges for Mirayon Province to link up with the 81st Division.[2] At the house of Salvador Lluch, a trader between Christians and Moros, they learned General Fort had also surrendered. Lluch redirected the men toward Deisher's camp.

CENTRAL LUZON, D160/R-889

As Japanese units finished mopping up west-central Luzon, Homma sent two battalions of the 10th Independent Garrison Unit and the Miura detachment to Mindanao to relieve the Kawaguchi and Kawamura detachments for other theaters. The Nagano detachment moved to Negros, Bohol, Leyte, and Samar. The 2nd Independent Infantry Battalion garrisoned at Cebu and Panay. At midmonth the Olongapo detachment (aided by Sharp's staff officers) worked to pacify the Visayas and Mindanao.[3]

Corregidor's holdout had "put some of the weakness of the [Japanese] High Command on show—most conspicuously the clashes of personality, differing priorities, and individual ambitions."[4] Homma expected guerrillas to follow Wainwright's orders and surrender, once informed of those orders. To be sure, after receiving a letter from Wainwright, Horan surrendered and helped convince others to follow suit.[5] In Isabela and Nueva Vizcaya, Maj. Everett Warner surrendered the bulk of his 14th Infantry Regiment, leaving Nakar to command the remainder. Pursued by Japanese patrols, he dispersed his men to avoid destruction and obtain food and shelter.[6]

Walter Cushing took command of 121st Regiment troops. Monitoring a radio from the Batong mine for news, he began distributing a newsletter called *The Echo of the Free North*.[7] Calvert and Murphy gathered remnants of the 43rd Infantry Regiment in Benguet and moved north to Bontoc to join Horan, only to find that he had surrendered and left orders for them to do the same. After much debate, they opted to ignore the orders and seek out Moses and Noble.

VISAYAS, D161/R-888

The Japanese met with spontaneous resistance across the Visayas. The government of Dumaran Island off northeast Palawan collapsed when the Japanese seized the capital of Puerto Princesa, leaving brigands to freely roam the countryside. In Danlig, American mestizo brothers and cattle ranchers Alfred and Paul Cobb organized a home guard to restore law and order. While protecting civilians and supporting the extralegal government, they ambushed Japanese patrols attempting to seize the rice harvest.

About 190 miles to the northeast, twenty-six-year-old senior inspector of the Romblon-Mindoro district constabulary, Major Jose M. Ruffy, was commanding sixty constabulary troops near Pinamalayan when the Japanese landed on Mindoro. Volunteers increased his unit to about 250 men, about half of whom were armed. Ruffy organized a Bolo battalion headquartered near Naujan and prepared to battle the invaders.

Three hundred miles to the southeast, Japanese troops marched into Bohol's capital Tagbilaran and seized the manganese mines on Panglao and Guindulman islands. Captain Victoriano Blancas surrendered his USAFFE garrison, leaving Bohol governor Agapito Hontanosas to the Japanese. Blancas' executive officer, First Lieutenant José M. Maneja, refused to surrender and led followers to a mountain base he called "Camp Liberty." The volunteer guard, formed prior to the war by Quezon's order, joined them as a Bolo battalion. Armed only with their curved knives, they acted mostly as couriers, *cargadores*, and sentries.

The *cargadores* who transported supplies across the jungles were the unsung heroes of the resistance. "Wearing brief loincloths and amulets, they ate with their fingers and indicated the time of day by pointing to the sun," Steve Mellnik remembered. "They possessed remarkable strength. A four-foot, ninety-pound Ata would carry a seventy-five-pound load all day without complaint."[8] They seemed always present and ready to assist. At least one guerrilla would admit, however, that often parties of armed guerrillas would recruit them "sometimes, I fear, with a bit of 'persuasion.'"[9]

The guerrillas also relied on these volunteers as runners to carry messages. "We are only for small jobs," one runner said. "We carry word from the mountains down to those who are working secretly in the towns and cities."[10] The couriers had to be physically tough, familiar with the territory and the people, able to avoid the Japanese, and trustworthy. Short trips on maps often translated into long travels when complicated by steep hills, dense jungles, and treacherous rivers. Incredibly, sufficient numbers of capable volunteers applied. Most had wanted to fight but lacked proper arms. "The runners' main importance was quite different anyway," Lapham reasoned, "since I always had more volunteers than I knew what to do with, making runners of a considerable number gave them a chance to do, and feel they were doing something useful."[11]

Communication networks could be complicated. Volckmann would develop the "Land Communication Company" that included three east-west and three north-south message routes with relay stations.[12] Blackburn explained, "We had way stations, or message centers, set up every four to six hiking hours, depending on terrain. And, we kept nine men and a noncom in each of these message centers."[13] The centers copied each message so that Volckmann could adjust to any that fell into enemy hands. Messages marked "rush" went out anytime. Using miners' helmets with carbide lamps, they moved at night. A message from Ilocos could reach Kalinga, about 225 miles distant, in two days. A message traveling over seventy miles from Kiangan to La Union—seven days' hard march over mountains—took two days.

Messengers pulled extra duty as scavengers, sentries, and spies. "Our couriers are real heroes!" wrote Mellnik. "They enter Davao City, call on friendly officials, borrow money, and buy clothing, medicines, and salt. Then comes the dangerous part—smuggling the stuff out of the city!"[14] Like the *cargadores*, the messengers were all native Filipinos.

CENTRAL LUZON, D168/R-881

Thorp's Luzon Guerrilla Force (LGF) patrolled around their base on Mount Pinatubo north of Bataan. On 24 May Thorp returned with an entourage to Timbo to find Joe Barker and Ed Ramsey waiting. Moses and Noble arrived a little later.

Ramsey was struck by the natives in camp. "While we waited, the people of Timbo were wonderfully kind to us," he recalled.[15] They fed the Americans, provided medical aid, and offered companionship and entertainment. Sympathy and kindness drew the Americans into their common cause. "Up until this time I had thought of the Philippines only as a post; now I began to see it as a place, and a people," Ramsey wrote. "We had failed in our defense of them, leaving them in the hands of their enemies. They ought to have owed us nothing; instead they were sharing what little they had with us and risking their lives to help us."[16]

Barker and Ramsey had already begun recruiting guerrillas from veterans, police, and government officials. Refugees in Timbo constructed a base for them a mile and a half upriver from Thorp's camp. They appointed eager young Processo Cadizo as a sergeant. News reporter Alejandro Santos and policeman Fausto Alberto joined them from Manila. Philippine scout Claro Camacho became a key aide and ran the headquarters at their new base.

When Thorp arrived, Ramsey told him of their nearly completed camp. The colonel, however, no longer resembled the leader Ramsey knew from Fort Stotsenburg. "Now he was thin and rather frail, worn out from months in the jungle," Ramsey noted. "His hair had gone completely white, and his manner was merely gruff."[17] A runner reported Japanese troops approaching, and the natives scattered. Thorp sent the Americans to hide among local families.

A local Negrito named Pandora with a wife and two children housed Ramsey in their riverside hut. They were small people who wore only loincloths and spoke very little Tagalog. As the family went about their daily lives making arrows and tending to the children, Ramsey felt an intense isolation and drifted into dark thoughts. "Fighting behind Japanese lines, no weapons, no organization, no army—it was madness," he mused. "I would be captured and shot, or worse, and I had no one to blame but myself."[18]

Northeast of Manila, the young ROTC guerrillas also confronted disillusionment. Many went home. Eleuterio Adevoso and Miguel Ver moved their headquarters into the Sumulong Rest House and renamed their group "the Hunters." Adevoso organized a raid on a building in the Union College of Manila used by the Japanese as an armory. Disguising themselves as Japanese soldiers, the Hunters duped a janitor, slipped past the guards, and removed all 136 rifles to a new camp at Malabanca.

Months later the Hunters would try to repeat their success at the Mapua Institute of Technology, but alert Japanese guards captured two of their members, who broke under torture. A Hunters' sergeant spotted them leading a Japanese patrol to their base camp in Antipolo, but Ver disregarded his warning. On the morning of 4 July the Japanese attacked. Although the Hunters killed twenty-five enemy soldiers, the Japanese killed Ver.[19]

LEYTE, D168/R-881

Japanese troops landed unopposed on Leyte on 24 May and rolled over the island in twenty-four hours. Colonel Thomas Cornell, the Leyte-Samar commander, surrendered his Provisional Regiment of the 91st Division. A Sergeant Terraz escaped to lead guerrillas until he was killed. Sergeant Antonio Juan took over the group but was also killed. The unit then split between Ciriaco Centino and Filemon Pabilona. Second Lieutenant Alejandro Balderian promoted himself to lieutenant colonel to organize guerrillas in Northern Leyte with supplies from a camp at Jaro. Isabelo Centino, who fought under Balderian, joined his father Ciriaco. They promoted themselves to major and led their Centino guerrillas in Jaro, Pastrana, and Palo as part of Balderian's group. First Sergeant Pabilona promoted himself to lieutenant colonel and expanded his group around San Miguel, Babatngon, Alangalang, and unoccupied Tacloban.

Before Cornell surrendered, he appointed Lapus as commander in Bicol, pending the return of the more senior Sandico.[20] By the time Sandico appeared in late May, Lapus' guerrillas had become a robust and aggressive outfit of several hundred men based in Carachayon. They moved to Dolos, assigned seventeen men to protect Governor Escudero, and temporarily disbanded. This incited Lapus' deputy, Sayoc, to secretly cooperate with Escudero to overthrow Lapus. When he found out, Lapus fired Sayoc.

Other guerrilla units rose up on Leyte. Lieutenant Blas Miranda (alias Colonel Briguez) commanded in the area from Palompon to Baybay.

Technical Sergeant Felix Pamanian assumed the rank of lieutenant colonel and established a separate band in the Mount Capoocan area of Northern Leyte, joined soon after by a group under USAFFE Captain C. Corpin from Biliran. On Panaon Island off southern Leyte, U.S. Navy Yeoman Lieutenant Gordon A. Lang, Major Porfirio E. Jain, and Lieutenant Jose Nazareno formed their own guerrillas.

MANILA, D168/R-881

On 20 May assemblyman Benigno Aquino wrote Vargas to call Japanese attention to the dangers of "bad elements, otherwise known as 'the USAFFE' in Central Luzon."[21] Most Filipinos were more concerned with routine Japanese abuses. Ten-year-old Lita Yumol walked to school with her little brother, careful to avoid smiling while passing a Japanese sentry, to bow deeply, and to make certain her brother did the same. "There have been cases when people, even children, who fail to do this are stopped or called back and slapped on both cheeks; then told to bow low," Lita noted. "And father has warned us of this."[22]

Slaps were a particular point of cultural contention. "Slapping has become the order of the day," Pacita Pestano-Jacinto wrote in her diary. "It is the Japanese way of proclaiming that they are the masters."[23] Historian John Dower explains, "In their penchant for slapping non-Japanese Asians about, Japanese soldiers, especially enlisted men, were treating others in the same way their superiors treated them."[24] Even so, the insulting slaps gave weight to rumors of worse atrocities.

Witnesses claimed that the Japanese "arrested, maimed, and murdered Filipinos by the tens of thousands and did so in myriad horrible ways: whipping them, starving them, setting fire to the hair in their armpits, pulling out their fingernails, giving them showers of boiling water, abusing and killing their children in front of them, and chaining them to slabs of iron in the burning midday sun so that they slowly fried to death."[25] Jesus Villamor detailed specific incidents: a young Filipina who slapped back at a Japanese soldier on Rizal Avenue in Manila was stripped and tied to a pole in the city square; a boy in Negros was tied up in a house that was set on fire so he was burned alive; a guerrilla caught on Panay was skinned.[26] Suspected guerrillas had lips or ears cut off, hands soaked in gasoline and set on fire, or the soles of their feet cut open before being forced to walk in sand. "There was the 'cutting' torture," Panlilio reported. "The Jap would rush the victim with bayonet or saber, as if to dispatch him permanently, then would deflect or pull the thrust to inflict a lesser wound or slice off only a nick of flesh. A slip meant death, but what of it?"[27]

In other ways the Japanese displayed disdain as indifference. During the invasion they destroyed the Misamis water and power stations and never bothered to repair them. "With all their promises to the Filipino people about the 'Co-Prosperity Sphere,' they made no attempt to help rebuild any of the damaged property," Don Willis recalled. "As a matter of fact, they usually pulled out any plumbing, wiring, pipes, or machinery and shipped it off to Japan. I noticed that was true all over the Philippines."[28]

NEGROS, D170/R-879

On 26 May the Japanese landed at Dumaguete, capital of Negros Oriental, the last unoccupied province. When Davao fell, Col. Roger Hilsman Sr., commander of the 101st Division on Mindanao, had gone to Negros to plan a "little Bataan" defense of Mount Kanlaon with a provisional force, but he fell ill in March and left for Cebu. Staff officers such as G-3 Major Salvadore Abcede thought a "little Bataan" a bad idea. When Col. Robert MacLenan arrived to fill in for Hilsman, they convinced him to divide Negros into five sectors for guerrilla warfare. Expecting orders to surrender, MacLenan relieved all his American commanders and replaced them with Filipino officers who could carry on the fight.

Abcede divided the 74th Infantry among majors Ernesto Mata, Pullong Arpa, Francisco Gomez, and Fortunato Roque. When the Japanese landed in April, Hilsman made a surprise return to Negros. Eight days after Corregidor fell, he surrendered and ordered his men to do the same. Arpa, Gomez, and Roque obeyed. Mata and Abcede refused and led men into the mountains.[29]

The Japanese reached Bacolod on the north coast of Negros by 20 May. The remaining 1,000 Filipinos of the original 4,500-man Negros force burned Banago wharf, the Diza electric oil deposit, the Socony gasoline tank at Santo Niño, and the alcohol tank near the Bacolod-Murcia Central rail yard. Pushed by a superior force, however, Abcede disbanded his troops with orders to regroup when called. Meanwhile "wild units" used resistance as a "pretext for plunder."[30] Abcede regrouped his troops and "liquidated" the bandits to restore public safety.

The students and faculty of Negros' Silliman University in Dumaguete had a reputation as champions of free government and dreaded the Japanese. American Henry Roy Bell, a popular twenty-year physics professor and former athletic director, transferred university equipment and personnel to Malabo and Lake Balinsasayao. Villamor later described Bell as "robust and vigorous, looking more like a professor of physical education than of physics."[31]

Bell set up a camp at Malabo, assisted with the creation of a free provisional government, and helped organize Silliman students and alumni into several Bolo battalions. Former student and ROTC instructor, Major B. N. Viloria, led one battalion, and a USAFFE lieutenant who escaped from Mindanao led another. High school teacher Felix Estrada and Leon Flores commanded battalions closer to Dumaguete. Victor Jornales and Sergeant David Cirilo assumed command of two more. All followed Bell's guidance.

The Japanese occupied the outer plain of Negros and drove guerrillas, hampered by poor logistics and communications, into the rough central interior and southern coastal mountains. Bell had buried parts for a radio in the mountains near Dumaguete. With the help of USAFFE radioman Lieutenant Louis Vail, an American mestizo from northern Negros who escaped from prison in Fabrica, he recovered the parts, assembled a radio, and began trying to contact the outside world.[32]

MINDANAO, D175/R-874

A Japanese infantry battalion established a garrison at the former U.S. Camp Keithley on the northern shore of Lake Lanao. Four miles to the southeast a Kempeitai squad, a JMA liaison office from Davao, and a telecommunications unit settled in Dansalan. Lieutenant Yusuke Goto commanded the liaison office to oversee administration and business matters while JMA civilian Seiji Kogo ran special operations and liaisons with influential Moro leaders. Goto arranged a garrison battalion for Parang on the eastern edge of the island.[33] Kogo recalled from his studies at the University of the Philippines Madiki Alonto, the son of prominent Lanao Muslim Domocao Alonto, along with leading Cotabato politician Ugalingan Piang. Seeing his son in Japanese hands, Alonto became a passive collaborator while Piang worked to convince Moros near Goto's headquarters to lay down their arms.

Cotabato was also home to 1,500 Chinese, largely Kuomintang loyalists. Wu Wenguo, Lin Zhengren, and Huang Ruihua of the leftist Cotabato Chinese Mutual Aid Society led its seventy members and their families inland to Pilayan.[34]

NORTH CENTRAL LUZON, D178/R-871

Walter Cushing searched northern Luzon for other guerrillas. In Tarlac, he secured help from a Spanish manager of a sugar processing plant that produced alcohol for the Japanese. In Manila, he found several Philippine officials still loyal to the exiled government. They provided Cushing with false documents identifying him as a priest, a Spanish mestizo, and an Italian mestizo. With these and bluff and luck, he narrowly avoided capture and contacted guerrillas in La Union and Ilocos Sur before making his way back to Abra.

Russell Volckmann had been desperately ill for weeks. On the last day of May he wrote in his diary: "To my disgust, many of the nights I have almost hoped not to wake up in the morning."[35] He vowed to leave the malarial lowlands for the mountains. In early June, after more than a month in the Guerreros' jungle shack, he and Blackburn followed their host to his family home where a doctor injected them with shots. After three days, word reached them that the Japanese were on their way. Volunteers carried the two Americans back to the Guerrero camp.

By mid-June Volckmann was just beginning to walk again when Petit and Anderson visited and informed him of the Fassoths' camp.[36] By now Bill and Martin Fassoth, along with Bill's wife Catalina, had saved 104 of the roughly 400 Americans known to have escaped the Bataan Death March.[37] They had even secured a doctor and medical supplies. Volckmann thought, "It sounded too good to be true."[38] On 22 June, ignoring pleas from the Guerrero family, the two Americans headed out. Despite malaria, jaundice, and beriberi, they completed a long day's march and stumbled into the Fassoth camp. Blackburn recalled, "The illness hit Volckmann real bad. What do you call it, dysentery and hole [sic] nine yards, so we lost weight. I guess we got down to well under 100 pounds. We were like skeletons, and the food wasn't that appetizing."[39]

Between fifty and eighty Americans lounged about the camp on bamboo cots listening to KGEI radio out of San Francisco. Neighbor Bernia continued to risk his life to purchase supplies, often on credit from patriotic local merchants.[40] Blackburn thought the soldiers treated the Fassoth brothers badly and were "very derogatory of Bernia."[41] The refugee soldiers enjoyed rice and salt twice a day, but the diet aggravated Volckmann's beriberi. He recalled, "My ankles and my feet became so swollen that I could hardly walk, and I couldn't even get my shoes on."[42] On the first morning in camp, big red-headed sergeant Red Floyd told Volckmann and Blackburn, "Now, look, let's get the name of the game straight, if you guys want to stay here I want you to recognize that there is no such thing as rank. The war is over."[43] The two officers decided not to argue.

Meanwhile, Homma had established the Manila defense force to garrison the capital with a few permanently assigned units.[44] Regular army units were needed elsewhere, and guerrillas were a matter for the

Philippine police. At the end of May, the 47th Infantry Battalion (minus one company) left the Manila defense force for Davao to join the 17th Army.[45] In the months ahead, three other companies of the 40th Infantry Battalion would leave for Sumatra.

The Japanese army occupied strategic cities in the islands and began exploiting resources. Their garrisons were too formidable for the guerrillas, but their lines of supply looked vulnerable. They therefore tasked the 63rd Lines of Communication Sector to reorganize units around Manila to repair infrastructure sabotaged by the retreating Americans and increase production and storage of war materials. Short on manpower, the 63rd imported two thousand Aborigines from Formosa's so-called Takasago volunteer corps in early 1942 and organized them as the Formosan labor service corps for work in supply depots.[46] The ad hoc Army Road Unit (the 38th and 39th Field Railway Units) supported supply by repairing roads and railways, while the Army Railway Battalion (3rd Battalion of the 6th Railway Regiment) reopened the Damoritis and Tarlac line. In return, supply units provided personnel, hospitals, and "local coolies" to combat units.[47]

To foster better public relations, on 5 June the Japanese granted amnesty to tens of thousands of Filipino POWs as an advertisement of their good intentions and to bolster the workforce. The release also signaled to guerrillas that they too could lay down their arms and go home. Chick Parsons was among those paroled from Santo Tomás. He never spoke about his month in prison, but he had emerged without several fingernails on his right hand.[48] The authorities ordered Parsons to gather his family with one trunk and one suitcase and prepare for shipment "home" to Panama as part of an exchange with neutral Latin American countries.[49] Parsons realized his family faced a customs inspection but, unbeknown to him, his wife packed his improvised intelligence file in their suitcase. Adding to his worries, Katsy's mother Blanche refused to leave the islands while her son Tommy Jurika was held as a POW on Cebu.

Without Blanche, the Parsons sailed to Formosa with eight other civilians under armed guard aboard a Japanese military hospital ship. There they underwent the customs inspection. Only by placing their smallest child innocently on their suitcase did they keep their papers hidden from distracted Japanese soldiers and avoid being shot. The Parsons flew on a captured U.S. aircraft to Shanghai where they embarked on *Conte Verde* bound for Singapore and Lourenço Marques in Portuguese East Africa. Officials there completed the citizen exchange, and the Parsons finally boarded a U.S. chartered repatriation ship, the Swedish MS *Gripsholm*, bound for Rio.

VISAYAS, D182/R-867

On Negros, fifty-year-old Lieutenant Colonel Gabriel Gador had been the 7th District Commander (Negros and Siquijor) when war began. Because he could not get along with his junior officers, Sharp transferred him with his staff to Mindanao. In June, Gador returned to Negros saying Sharp had sent him back to organize guerrillas, but he then went into the hills and became inactive. Meanwhile, thirty-year-old Major Hermenegildo Mercado, one of Peralta's classmates at the infantry school, organized guerrillas around Guilhulngan. In September, Gador reemerged and convinced Mercado to join his command. Gador's habit of promoting relatives to senior positions prompted an argument with Mercado, who withdrew his men from Gador.

On nearby Bohol, Gador's former subordinate Philippine army Third Lieutenant Ismael P. Ingeniero organized what would become that island's largest resistance group, the "Behind the Clouds" guerrillas. U.S. Army intelligence reported: "Ingeniero is described as a weak character, and inclined to take orders from Gador, whom he alone recognized as commander of Negros Oriental."[50] Reports suspiciously indicated Ingeniero had been visiting his wife in Panay during the Japanese invasion and added: "It is said that Ingeniero obtained command by a quasi-political deal and through the support of Senator Carlos Garcia."[51]

Despite the rumors, Ingeniero "was somehow getting things done."[52] He communicated with Cebu and, aided by Governor Conrado Marapo and Senator Carlos Polistico Garcia, rallied the people on Bohol. Villamor later reported that under Ingeniero, "All able-bodied men aged 16 to 60 drilled daily and stood guard, without arms but with sharp bolos hanging from scabbards tied around their waists, at guard houses one to two kilometers apart. Some women as well, those up to 30 years of age, also drilled, and, to feed the soldiers each Boholano family was giving each month: one *ganta* of rice, one chicken, two eggs, and ten centavos."[53] By May 1943 Ingeniero would have 4,000 guerrillas with 194 officers bottling up enemy troops at Tagbilaran and in the Guindulman manganese mines.

CENTRAL LUZON, D186/R-863

Marking learned that the Japanese were abusing 115 Americans, mostly pilots and engineers, at a makeshift prison in the Cine Lumban movie theater in Laguna.[54] He decided to liberate those POWs. Lumbang's mayor agreed to turn off the town's lights and prevent all local dogs from barking on the night of the attack. (As one guerrilla said, "If there was one constant in the Philippines, it was that [at] any given time and place one to a dozen dogs would be barking."[55])

On the moonless night of 11 June Marking led forty-five guerrillas across Laguna de Bay, tied up the mayor for appearances, and took up positions around the prison. "Marking shot a sentry, the signal for a tensely aimed volley," Agoncillo reported, "and guerrillas sprang into the clearing to shoot and bludgeon the remaining guards and grab their guns."[56] Marking called the POWs to join him, but only one, George Lightman, answered. A U.S. Army captain among the prisoners ordered the rest to remain. The guerrillas left with Lightman and some captured weapons. In the following days, the Japanese executed ten of the POWs as punishment for the one who escaped.

Meanwhile, aware of chief justice Abad Santos' execution in May, Manuel Roxas surrendered in Davao. As Quezon's former secretary of finance and speaker of the house of representatives, there were few more prominent men in the Philippines. A Colonel Jimpo rushed Roxas to Manila. Knowing Roxas had been a liaison between Quezon and MacArthur, Kempeitai chief Colonel Akira Nagahama ordered him executed for suspicion of leading guerrillas. Old friend José Laurel demanded Roxas' release, saying he was too valuable to execute. Laurel pushed a decision into August as Fourteenth Army chief of staff Colonel Takaji Wachi ordered an English-speaking priest, Gen Kawahara, to investigate. Father Kawahara reported: "Roxas' influence turned out to be far greater than we had originally imagined" and concluded that he should be spared and won over "to our side."[57]

Outside Manila, Barker added two more organizations, Squadron 111 in Umingan and Squadron 300 in Lupao, to the LGF. Thorp issued General Order Number 1 making Capt. Wilber Lage his adjutant and Sgt. Bill Brooks his radioman and organizing four LGF sectors: north under Praeger, west under Capt. Ralph McGuire, south under Capt. Jack Spies, and the East Central Luzon guerrilla area under Barker with Ed Ramsey as adjutant and Bernard Anderson as chief of staff.[58] Lapham, commanding companies to the north, became Thorp's inspector general. The senior U.S. Army commander tried to recreate an Army unit with American officers and felt ready to bring all other groups on Luzon under his umbrella. Praeger scavenged guns and ammunition from the fields around Bataan. "He also liquidated spies and collaborators energetically and undertook some sabotage," recalled Lapham.[59] On 4 July Praeger commissioned Apayao governor Marcelo Adduru as a U.S. Army major and made him executive officer in their combined Cagayan-Apayao guerrilla force.

Closer to Manila, the Huks allowed the Hua Zhi freedom of action in return for food, intelligence, guides, and a promise to help them train in guerrilla tactics.[60] Veteran Chinese communists assisted the Huks in establishing a political and military training school on Mount Arayat using Chu-teh's *Fundamental Spirit of Guerrilla Tactics* along with Snow's *Red Star Over China* as manuals.[61] After gathering weapons from Bataan, the Hua Zhi regrouped on Mount Pasbul for tactical training and political indoctrination per Mao's *The Guerrilla War* and *The Strategic Problem in Anti-Japanese Guerrilla War*. In early September they would return to Mount Arayat with 78 armed men, but their combat record would remain surprisingly sparse: an ambush and capture of 32 Japanese in San Isidro on 8 December; killing 37 Japanese at Kanunpa in January 1943 at the cost of 5 killed and 3 wounded; and ten more engagements in February, March, and April, killing 286 Japanese and capturing 24 while suffering 19 killed, 18 wounded, and 6 missing.[62] More surprising, Bernard Anderson reported to SWPA that the Hua Zhi was "100 percent pro-American, pro-Filipino and pro-Chinese Chungking [Nationalist] regime."[63]

Thorp sent Barker, Anderson, and Lieutenant Colbert Pettit to liaise with the Huks. On 7 July Barker presented letters from Thorp offering USAFFE recognition and support to the Huks if they joined his command. The West Pointer apparently tried to impress the Huks with his presence and promises of future remunerations. Taruc thought Barker an irritating elitist who was trying to coerce the Huks into subordination. The Huks claimed ten thousand members in Bulacan and Pampanga, far outnumbering Thorp's small headquarters. "We told them that we would follow them militarily, but that we must be free to have our own political program which had as its objective democracy and independence," Taruc remembered. "We told them we would not put Filipino patriotism on sale for back-pay promises."[64]

The Huks were fighting a different war. The Americans wanted to defeat the Japanese and restore the prewar Philippine government; the Huks sought to erase colonialism and overturn the prewar government. They drew support for their agenda from the recent Atlantic Charter authored by Roosevelt and Churchill that promised the right of self-determination to all people. "Given these fundamental disagreements," Lapham wrote, "the best the conferees could manage was a paper promise to 'cooperate' and share equipment and supplies, while allowing the Huks 'independent action' on 'organizational and political matters.'"[65]

After the meeting, letters allegedly signed by Thorp, Barker, and Ramsey circulated across northern Luzon announcing Huk-USAFFE cooperation and demanding all local citizens surrender their weapons to the Huks. "Barker and I were reluctant to believe the reports of this deception," Ramsey confessed, "until we saw the letters ourselves bearing bad forgeries of our signatures."[66] Tensions rose. One of Lapham's units met with a Huk group and shared a dinner. "When my men awoke the next morning," he wrote, "the Huks were gone, and so were our guns and supplies."[67] He added: "Early in the war we spent as much time fighting the Huks and various pro-Japanese individuals and groups as we did combatting the Japanese themselves."[68]

North of Camp Sanchez near Umingan, Lapham endured severe bouts of malaria and dysentery while overseeing the establishment of a base he called Camp Manchuria for its remoteness. It operated in parallel with his first camp in Lupao. Lapham had left Thorp two months earlier with one hundred Filipinos and now commanded nearly twice that number with companies in the separate camps. He promoted himself to major (Ramsey followed suit). Federico Doliente came to Manchuria with ten men. "If Johnny Marcos was our best recruiter and trainer in 1942, Doliente proved to be the best fighter," Lapham remembered. "Soon he became my most trusted companion on patrols."[69] Jeremias C. Serafica arrived with fifty armed guerrillas, and Lapham made him commander of Squadron 207 in the Cuyapo-Guimba-Munoz area of central Luzon.

Lieutenant Juan Pajota of the Philippine army 91st Infantry Division escaped from Bataan to return home to Nueva Ecija. He was small but steady, tough, and unassuming. He was also not ready to stop fighting the Japanese. Pajota sought out Lapham. According to author Hampton Sides, the American saw in him "a very unflamboyant guy with a natural bent for leadership. He was resourceful, organized, and extremely imaginative. . . . He knew all the mayors of all the barrios. He was familiar with the realities on the ground, every quirk of the water buffalo paths, every river bend. Whatever men or arms might need to be mustered, Pajota had the political wherewithal to make it happen."[70] Lapham commissioned Pajota to raise several squadrons in Nueva Ecija. Soon, he had eyes and hands in every village. Behind every successful American guerrilla commander was at least one Filipino like Pajota.

Lapham heard that Umingan's collaborationist mayor was threatening citizens for information on the guerrillas. Doliente volunteered to handle the matter and set out one night with a patrol. At sunrise a few days later, he returned to Camp Manchuria with a gunnysack for Lapham. In it was the mayor's severed head. "I am not especially squeamish," Lapham confided, "but that experience was a shock."[71]

Thorp faced an unexpected challenge from Col. Gyles Merrill of the 26th Cavalry Regiment. One of the highest-ranking men to escape the Bataan Death March, Merrill believed himself to be the senior U.S. Army officer in the Philippines. He had tried to persuade the Fassoth brothers to convert their camp into a guerrilla base for him, but Bill and Martin refused. Later that summer he established a base north of Manila Bay from which he hoped to command all guerrillas in the islands. With him were Col. Peter Calyer, Capt. George Crane, Captain Richard Kadel, and Pvt. Leon Beck. They would recruit into the ranks of their Zambales guerrillas a local college-educated farm boy, Ramon Magsaysay, who would one day become president of the Philippines.[72]

SOUTHERN LUZON, D213/R-836

At the end of June Camarines Sur guerrilla leader Lieutenant José Hernandez delivered to Vinzons a request from Wainwright's personal secretary, Lt. Robert Silhavy, for a meeting. Vinzons agreed to meet him in Barcelonita on 8 July; he granted his troops a fifteen-day furlough and headed to the meeting accompanied by his father and provincial governor Basilio Bautista. Along the way, the Japanese—aided by a former guerrilla named Villaluz—captured them. They paraded Vinzons before a crowd in Labo before imprisoning him in Daet.[73] A week later the Japanese arrested his wife, Liwayway, and his children, Alex and Aurora.

Vinzons refused to collaborate and smuggled out a single written message: "Tell Rafael Quiñones, fight and continue."[74] Quiñones was Vinzons' first prewar protégé in the Young Philippine party. Following a week of torture, garrison commander Major Noburo Tsuneoka confronted Vinzons on the night of 15 July with a paper signed by fifty natives identifying him as *dorobo* (bandit) and threatened him with death. Vinzons replied, "Nothing can make me happier than to die for my country, Major. You will too—" before being interrupted by the thrusts of Noburo's bayonet. Vinzons died that night. His family was never seen again.[75]

AUSTRALIA, D207/R-842

In Melbourne, MacArthur craved information from the Philippines. For months he heard nothing. Then in early June Allied coast watchers relayed reports of transmissions from someone named Bell on Negros.[76] On 8 June Merle-Smith submitted his plan for an Allied Intelligence Bureau (AIB) to the commander in chief of Australian military forces, General Thomas Blamey, with MacArthur's enthusiastic endorsement. At Blamey's suggestion, MacArthur appointed Colonel G. C. Roberts, the director of Australian army intelligence, to lead the AIB but MacArthur ensured his control by placing U.S. Army officer Maj. Allison Ind as Roberts' deputy.

Later that month the Federal Communications Commission station KFS near San Francisco, California, received a radio message addressed to MacArthur from a station calling itself VCJC.⁷⁷ Suspicious of a Japanese trick, the station ignored the signal before finally forwarding the repeated calls to the Army signals intelligence service, which passed it to the war department in Washington for a lengthy authentication process. By coincidence, Lt. Col. Joseph K. Evans served as the chief of Southeast Asia section at the war department after previously serving as deputy G-2 in Manila where he had helped Willoughby establish the secret intelligence network with a crude cipher code.⁷⁸ Evans was able to verify the source: VCJC was Peralta on Panay.⁷⁹ Unfortunately, Peralta's radio could only communicate when atmospheric conditions were just right, meaning it sometimes took weeks to exchange messages.

On 2 July Merle-Smith tasked Ind to draft a directive organizing the AIB, and four days later Roberts endorsed it. Ind spelled out their mission: "Obtain and report information on the enemy in the Southwest Pacific Area, and in addition, where practicable . . . weaken the enemy by sabotage and destruction of morale, and . . . render aid and assistance to local efforts in the same and in enemy-occupied territories."⁸⁰ First, the AIB would have to gain an accurate awareness of the state of the resistance. Ind organized four AIB sections. Section C under Captain Commander Eric Feldt of the Royal Australian Navy volunteer reserve handled field intelligence. Ind further divided Section C into three regional subsections: northeast area, the Philippines (Philippine regional section [PRS]), and the Netherland East Indies.

On Luzon, Warner had passed his radio set to the 14th Infantry Regiment's Major Nakar, who had since repeatedly tried to contact SWPA. On 10 July a coast watcher in Java finally picked up a faint Morse code signal and passed it up the chain of command. Ten days later, SWPA G-2 read the message.⁸¹ Nakar called to MacArthur, "Detachment of Fil-American forces—we have not surrendered and are actively raiding northeast towns of Pangasinan, including Dagupan."⁸² A senior SWPA officer later described, "His message was the first clear proof that loyal Filipinos, led by MacArthur's soldiers who had escaped capture, still fought on. It dramatically confirmed MacArthur's faith that they would and he determined to do all in his power not only to support it but in time to exploit it as a powerful adjunct to Allied arms."⁸³

This was a critical moment. "I had acquired a force behind the Japanese lines that would have a far-reaching effect on the war in the days to come," MacArthur wrote. "Let no man misunderstand the meaning of that message from the Philippines. Here was a people in one of the most tragic hours of human history, bereft of all reason for hope and without material support, endeavoring, despite the stern realities confronting them, to hold aloft the flaming torch of liberty."[84] Nakar received his long-awaited response: "The courageous and splendid resistance maintained by you and your command fills with pride and satisfaction. It will be my privilege to see that you and your officers and men are properly rewarded at the appropriate time. MacArthur."[85] The SWPA commander promoted Nakar to lieutenant colonel.

On 20 July SWPA moved from Melbourne to Brisbane, and the AIB moved into the Heindorf House office building. Guards on the ground floor limited access to the AIB; guards on the PRS floor kept out the rest of the AIB. The PRS communications team worked in shifts of one officer and two or three enlisted men. According to radioman T/Sgt. 4 Bob Stahl, a teletype connected the desks in the code room to "some mysterious location where a radio station transmitted and received our messages."[86] Communications from the Philippines were sparse, sporadic, and unverified. Stahl remembered, "This made my job very boring, with nothing to do but read books, work crossword puzzles, or sleep."[87] Ind took charge of the PRS and began sorting out radio contacts.[88]

At MacArthur's urging. Willoughby pressed the AIB to strengthen communications with the resistance.[89] On 7 August Ind received a worrisome report from Nakar: "Intelligence report reveals that enemy has detected the existence of our radio station, possibly by geometric process, and detailed a large force to look for us."[90] After a message on 22 August Nakar went silent.[91] Ind recalled, "G2 left little doubt in our minds: the obvious precariousness of the equipment in the Islands, the lack of secure ciphers and, above all, the contradictory nature of the information that was beginning to come out underscored the need for an observer placed there and controlled by GHQ."[92] The first question was who to send.

NORTHERN LUZON, D215/R-834

JMA plans for the Philippine economy were clearly failing.[93] The invasion had cut off the 84 percent of prewar exports sold to the United States. The new administration also forfeited the 80 percent of the country's prewar revenues paid in taxes by the Westerners now imprisoned.[94] That 1 percent of the population also comprised the people who provided key business and government services. On top of all this, Japan burdened the islands with economic exploitation and an army attempting to live off the land.

Hardships piled up. Filipinos had too few jobs and too little wages. Income fell below subsistence levels. "The jobs still open to them had been scaled down, salary-wise, to the point of ludicrousness," Villamor reported. "A telephone operator in Manila receiving 120 pesos before the war was now getting 15 pesos for the same work. Public officials used to monthly salaries of 300 pesos were lucky to now get 40 to 50 pesos."[95]

People warily eyed food prices. In June, the Japanese-run National Rice and Corn Corporation began rationing rice at about two and a half pounds per person per day; by October that ration would fall to a little more than half a pound per person per day.[96] The Japanese government had "succeeded, in an astonishingly short space of time, in running down the entire region, pushing back the progress which had been made towards modernity and re-establishing its pre-colonial isolation, undoing the process of urbanization and driving the hungry population back into the countryside to undertake subsistence farming."[97] The JMA assigned rice retailers to the corporation to improve production and distribution with a new federation of rice growers cooperative supporting their efforts. A new food control association did the same for other foods. Other cooperatives controlled livestock and fish.

Non-food commodities fell under the control of the Philippine Prime Commodities Distribution Control Association, but the Japanese continued to monopolize commerce and paid front men in worthless occupation scrip.[98] As a Philippine historian wrote, "Most of the associations were headed by Japanese, with Filipinos as token members of the various boards."[99] None of the organizations permitted free markets. The JMA granted a new Federation of Filipino Retailer Associations authority to control retail prices, but that also failed to correct supply.

On 19 July cotton specialists arrived in Manila from Japan.[100] The next day the JMA announced several new policies, and the Philippine Executive Committee rubber-stamped five-year targets for producing 100,700 U.S. tons of cotton per year by cultivating 1,124,330 acres of farmland.[101] This was not to satisfy Filipinos but to support the Japanese war effort.[102] They planned to reclaim idle land and convert forests, rice paddies, and sugar cane fields. The JMA also assigned cultivation districts to nine cotton companies. As Yoshiko Nagano noted, their goals were impossible to reach.

NORTHERN LUZON, D220/R-829

The Hitomi propaganda platoon travelled the Mountain and Ilocos Provinces in Luzon with U.S. officers calling for the guerrillas to surrender.[103] By mid-summer the unit embraced a mix of punitive tactics—raids, arrests, hostages, and firepower—while still spreading its "sit-it-out" propaganda.[104] The "hostile propaganda" strategy persuaded 117 guerrillas to surrender and led to the capture of 2 machine guns, 116 rifles, 39 pistols, and 21 hunting rifles.[105]

In July, Hitomi moved his unit into Ilocos Norte and was shocked to witness guerrillas there shoot and kill an American officer he brought in to convince them to surrender. Governor Ablan commanded the area's guerrillas with lieutenants Madamba and Isabelo Monje. Local assemblyman Edwin T. Medina, defeated in elections twice by Ablan, supported the Japanese as governor with followers in the constabulary.

Hitomi used all his weapons: the circus techniques, hardline activities, visits by General Ricarte, and medical support to locals provided by freed Philippine army doctors. In August Monje surrendered, and 125 guerrillas followed, with 23 pledging to cooperate with the Japanese.[106] Hitomi arrested 14 more and reported capturing 86 pistols, 51 rifles, and 2 pieces of heavy artillery. Local constabulary forces joined the Furuki battalion in sweeping up guerrillas. The Japanese would declare Ilocos Norte cleared on 12 August.

MINDANAO, D225/R-824

During July the Japanese Fourteenth Army detected a rise in lawlessness on Mindanao.[107] Long fraught relations between hill-dwelling Muslim Moros and coastal Christians were unraveling.[108] The mountain Muslims considered lowlander Christians soft and fearful; lowlanders thought of mountain people as ignorant barbarians. For centuries they had exchanged raids for food, goods, and women, but for the last four decades the Philippine Constabulary kept the peace. According to Fertig, "During the period of American rule in the Islands, the number of lowland women carried off to Lanao's mountains was more or less minimal, but the sudden intrusion of the Japanese resulted in a kind of legal vacuum which was immediately filled by ancient custom, and the paying-off of old scores."[109] The Japanese suspected Americans were behind the unrest.[110] Many troublesome natives were in fact pro-Americans, among them chief Datu Tambuyong in the Taglibi area and Captain Arolas Tulawie in the Luuk-Talipas sector.

The imperial army promised to "wipe out the malignant Moro elements" and "win the hearts of powerful chiefs."[111] The JMA brought Teofista Guingona, the former commissioner of Mindanao and Sulu, and his assistant Ciriaco Raval to Davao and illogically appointed Raval—a Christian—provincial governor. Prejudiced views of Moros were not unique to the Japanese, however. American guerrilla Charlie Hedges wrote: "These hills Moros live according to the Koran as interpreted by some illiterate, flea-bitten imam who heard from some crooked hadji what was supposed to be in the Holy Book. What they get out of it boils down to polygamy, slavery, and brutality."[112]

The Japanese battalion in Dansalan launched a subjugation campaign, attacking Wato on Lake Lanao, killing twenty-four villagers and burning eight homes. This and similar efforts to terrorize the population in Cotabato turned the people and created many guerrilla Bolo battalions. Datu Aliman gathered six hundred men between Kidapawan, Cotabato, and Mount Apo in Davao Province. Datu Mantil Dilangalan, with his two brothers, raised one thousand men (half of them armed) in the Midsayap-Dulawan-Pikit area. From Midsayap to Lebak, twelve-year U.S. Navy veteran Major Froilan Mascardo Matas led five hundred Christians in the "Matas Militia" force. He became known as "the God of Midsayap" and "was reported to be brave determined but reckless and defiant."[113]

In August, Pendatun attacked the Japanese at Pikit, Cotabato. Success brought him new recruits. With a larger force he attacked Kabacan and secured the Digos-Kabacan road by September. Gradually Aliman, Dilangalan, and others united under Pendatun at Bukidnon. Others opposed to him described him to SWPA as an anti-American lawyer and self-promoted brigadier general "deeply involved in Moro politics and protected by a princely family."[114]

Elsewhere on Mindanao, Fertig, Offret, and Hedges reached a Moro village ruled by Datu Soong. Young men came out to kill the Americans, but the datu showed letters of commendation he had once received from Lt. John J. Pershing and Gen. Arthur MacArthur. He provided Fertig with guides to Deisher's camp, where they found about thirty American soldiers and sailors who had given up on the war and intended to spend the duration hiding in an unhealthy, muddy mess. Fertig remembered, "They resented officers, would not take orders, and would do nothing but sit there, rotting in the jungle, living off the store of Army rations which Deisher, a three-hundred-pound old prospector and boar hunter, had somehow acquired."[115] Fertig and his group, now including Jordan Hamner and Charles Smith, moved on to the home of Mrs. MacMichael, an old Moro widow of an American Spanish-American War vet. Her open, sunny home seemed to work wonders on Hedges' malaria.

On the Fourth of July Fertig sat on a high hill near Dansalan looking down on the National Road. Below him, the Japanese paraded a long line of ragtag and malaria-ridden POWs before the citizens of Mindanao. In an open truck at the head of the column, they displayed Brigadier General Short. The POWs shambled forward, tied together foot and hand with telephone wire. Whenever they lagged, Japanese guards beat them or jabbed them with bayonets. When they fell, they were stabbed.[116] Watching from above, Fertig decided he would never surrender. He would fight.

When Wainwright surrendered, Governor Pelaez pleaded with U.S. Army Lt. Col. Ernest McClish to stay with his regiment and keep law and order in Misamis Oriental. McClish recalled, "I couldn't surrender and let the province fall apart!"[117] He organized guerrillas in Imbatug, Bukidnon. Escaped POWs Robert Ball, Anton Haratik, and William Knortz joined him. They ambushed a patrol near Medina. McClish and Col. Clyde Childress fought the Japanese in Butuan until both sides ran low on ammunition and then returned some captured soldiers to the Japanese with a proposal: "Keep your men out of my territory and I'll keep mine out of yours!"[118] They negotiated a truce and divided the town, even agreeing to share the single store.[119] The free government ran schools, courts, tax collections, trade, and printing of money. McClish searched for other guerrillas and would eventually find Fertig.

NEGROS, D229/R-820

Through the summer Abcede based his men in Kabankalan with much of their prewar supplies and at least six hundred rifles, making them one of the best-armed guerrilla units in the Philippines. With locally raised officers, they enjoyed access to nearby supplies and a partnership with former Bacolod mayor Alfredo Montelibano who acted as governor of Free Negros. "Under his management the civil government of resistance had grown into a stability that was amazing in time of war," said Abcede. "Free Negros not only had treasurers and auditors, it had officials in the municipal level, including policemen and clerks, fiscals, and judges."[120] Local citizens sent about 20 percent of all food gathered in the area to support the guerrillas.

One witness described the twenty-nine-year-old Abcede as having "a rather shy self-effacing look. Yet he had about him the air of quiet confidence. He looked like a leader."[121] A U.S. Army estimate said: "He is aggressive and often given to snappy judgments but is never afraid to admit mistakes. He is hearty and frank and well liked throughout Negros."[122]

Enrique Torres, now a major, formed a unit under Abcede near Sinalbagan. Major Hermenegildo Mercado, a thirty-year-old classmate of Peralta at the infantry school, organized another group from Guilhulngan north to Negros Oriental. A man known as Puring, thought to be Philippine army Private First Class Casiong Gemillan, led a lawless band with about fifty USAFFE weapons in the hills between Vallehermoso and San Carlos in Negros Occidental. His brother, illiterate ex-convict Margarito Gemillan, served as his deputy. They attacked the Japanese, guerrillas, and civilians alike.[123] Reportedly, Abcede's guerrillas killed Puring, and his brother took over the organization. The Puring guerrillas would melt away during the fall of 1944.

Killing Puring was just one example of guerrillas maintaining law and order. "This was no easy task," wrote Lapham. "No code of law anywhere governs the activities of guerrillas, and where we were, there were no effective courts or judges either."[124] Constabulary Lieutenant Colonel Claro Lauretta commanded the battalion in Davao and saw how vital security was to winning popular support. "Do you know what happens when no one will enforce law and order?" he observed. "The strong take from the weak: food, belongings, wife, and even life!"[125] People gravitated to whomever kept them safe.

Without prisons, supplies, or any desire to act as jailers, guerrilla chiefs rarely detained anyone long. Lapham wrote, "Consequently, punishments for misdeeds had to assume forms other than confinement. For some minor offenses, a man might be punished by being put on KP or assigned to look after the horses, but for something serious there was usually little real choice between setting an accused free (with perhaps a stern lecture) and executing him." Lapham identified three capital offenses: "looting, rape, and giving aid and comfort to the enemy." He later admitted, "I never kept records of the uglier cases we had to deal with."[126]

The TVGU dispensed death for treachery, treason, rape, and murder. A TVGU commander said, "In the Third Battalion under Captain Leon Aureus if one is found wanting, he was immediately separated from the group by firing squad."[127] Such measures would make incorporation into MacArthur's command impossible. Meted out justly, however, they could win over the people. Blackburn recalled a captain in the Cagayan Valley accused of raping a girl. "I had the evidence, the torn underwear, and an abundance of testimony. He used the excuse that the parents were collaborators, which they weren't, and that that gave him the right. So, we formed a company in the town and executed the captain in front of all the people. By God, if you're not letting your people get away with these things, then this gets around."[128]

CENTRAL LUZON, D237/R-812

Colonel Hugh Straughn added local volunteers and soldiers escaping Bataan to his Fil-American Irregular Troops (FAIT) around Antipolo. Expanding south and east of Manila, he brought other guerrillas into the FAIT, including the President Quezon's Own Guerrillas and, for a while, the Hunter's and Marking's guerrillas.

Yay Panlilio met Marking when she arrived at his camp in July. She recalled, "Tall, well-muscled, but lean, Major Marcos V. Augustin, alias Marking, stood with his fists on his hips, his feet planted wide, and his head high and a little back."[129] The twenty-nine-year-old Irish-American Filipina caught his eye. She continued, "Hotly we looked at each other. I saw a fighting man. He saw a defiant woman. We burst into laughter, having found each other."[130] Quickly, they became lovers. Marking named them both colonels and appointed her co-commander of his guerrillas.

Panlilio and Marking made a volatile pair. Agoncillo explained, "Where Marking was raw, Yay was polished. Marking, brusque and uncouth, was a man of action who seldom, if ever, thought of consequences. Yay, a civilized woman, was calculating and sophisticated."[131] A U.S. Army report observed: "The leader of the group is Marcos Villa Agustin [Marking], but the backbone of the organization is a woman known as Yay Panlilio."[132] Under her influence Marking agreed to join Straughn as the FAIT 1st Brigade, which grew into a large outfit of "full-time fighters in the hills; part-time saboteurs, working for the enemy and undoing all they had done; propagandists writing, printing, passing their down-in-black-and-white defiance; men and women training themselves as intelligence agents, learning to observe and retain and evaluate what they saw and to convey the information accurately and quickly."[133] They dreamt of bigger things.

Meanwhile, Terry Adevoso reassembled the Hunters after Miguel Ver's death to avenge their fallen leader. In August he led an ambush against two hundred Japanese soldiers on the Rizal-Laguna road. When the firing was over, they reported 127 dead enemy soldiers.[134] The victory gained the Hunters popular support and new arms, supplies, and recruits. In the following months Adevoso sent subordinates out to new areas to raise new groups with names such as Birds of Prey, Cobras, Eagles, Hawks, Hornets, Sharks, Vipers, Wild Cats, Wild Buffalo, and *Lapu-Lapu* (after the Visayan who killed Magellan). The Hunters spread from Rizal to Laguna, Cavite, Batangas, and Tayabas.

MANILA, D237/R-812

An irritated imperial headquarters removed Homma from command of the Fourteenth Army for the failure to take the Philippines on schedule. On 1 August Lieutenant General Shizuichi Tanaka arrived in Manila to take charge. A former Kempeitai chief in China, he had been a Shakespearean scholar at Oxford for three years, served as a military attaché in the United States and Mexico, and had led the Japanese delegation in the victory parade in London after World War I. He had even once met MacArthur.

The Philippine capital appeared tranquil. One of its residents recounted, "It is an uneasy kind of peace; tension and fear are still ever present because the Japanese go on midnight or early morning raids of neighborhoods looking for guerrillas that they had been informed reside or are hiding in that neighborhood."[135] The Japanese routinely used anonymous Filipinos disguised with sacks over their heads to point out suspected guerrillas from lineups of local men. Those pointed out were quickly carried off to prison. "It is the custom of the Japanese police," Pacita Pestano-Jacinto noted, "never to tell one why."[136] "If the young man resists and fights, he is tackled and bayonetted," Isabel Yumol remembered, "and if his family comes to his aid, they, too, are bayonetted."[137]

In another effort to combat resistance, in September the PEC issued Executive Order Number 77 establishing JMA-controlled "neighborhood associations" in Manila.[138] Over the next nine months, the JMA would create 13,192 neighborhood associations containing 900,000 citizens in and around the capital.[139] A guerrilla testified, "If a person wanted to go from one town to another, before he could leave the barrio, he had to have a pass stamped by the barrio lieutenant, then take it to the municipality and the Japs would pass on it; then he could go to the next town where the Japs would again stamp it."[140] It was harder for people to risk support for the guerrillas.

NORTHERN LUZON, D246/R-803

Guerrillas who had not fought in Bataan, such as Walter Cushing, Ralph Praeger, and Guillermo Nakar, conducted a flurry of attacks following Wainwright's surrender. The Bataan escapees, on the other hand, remained largely inactive. Lapham explained: "For me, the first eight or nine months of the war were by far the hardest because I was sick so much of the time. Like many others, I was already beset with malaria and dysentery when I came out of Bataan in February."[141] Just the sight of capable men ravaged by illness could discourage action. In August, American miner Patrick O'Day reported to Volckmann for duty.[142] Before the war he had been an imposing man of over six feet and two hundred pounds, but dysentery and malnutrition took their toll. Volckmann recalled, "I'm sure that when we met him he didn't weigh over a hundred and forty pounds, and he looked so weak and thin that it didn't seem he could stand up against a stiff breeze."[143] These men needed time to recuperate before entering the fight.

Che Guevara once observed: "The doctor's role in guerrilla warfare is a highly important one. Not only does he save lives, but he strengthens the morale of the sick and wounded."[144] Forty years earlier, the U.S. Army saw how tropical diseases could drop 10 percent of troops within three days of arriving in the Philippines and 33 percent within a week. It was not unusual to see 50 to 75 percent of unit personnel on sick reports.[145] Even in peacetime doctors noted that American soldiers succumbed to a tropical malaise they termed melancholy or nostalgia. The Army surgeon general concluded: "Residence in the tropic regions at or near the sea level is unfavorable to the health of Northern races.... nobody—no white man—lives in the tropics over a long period who does not deteriorate in practically every way."[146] Concern was so great that in 1934 Congress restricted soldiers' tours in the islands to not more than two years.

Filipinos were also not immune to mosquito-borne illnesses. After the Japanese began forcing captured Filipino soldiers into three constabulary companies in Langnan, Bontoc, and Lubuagan, the ladies' club in Baguio complained to provincial governor Hillary P. Clapp, "Our soldiers from the mountains are not used to the lowlands, and the mosquitoes. They are dying. Won't you do something to get them out of the lowlands?"[147]

Malaria was the most dangerous malady in the islands. Several species of mosquitoes caused the illness by introducing four different microscopic parasites into the blood. These mosquitoes bred in water, lived in and near forests, and attacked their victims between 2000 and 0100 hours—conditions associated with guerrilla operations.[148] The malarial mosquitoes lived below two-thousand-foot elevations, where population centers are normally found.[149]

While the quickness, severity, and duration of symptoms varied, malaria was almost always harshly debilitating. Typically, victims suffered a period of chills that, left untreated, turned into "paralyzing shivering," followed by a burning fever with headaches and great thirst, and finally "drenching sweats" as the fever broke.[150] Even after a victim recovered, "full-blown attacks" could recur every one to three years.[151]

Another mosquito common to the Philippines carried both yellow fever and dengue fever. After three to six days, yellow fever produced roughly four days of moderate to severe fever, headaches, muscle pains, nausea, vomiting, and possible hepatitis and hemorrhagic fever.[152] Symptoms included soreness behind the eyes, inability to concentrate, insomnia, extreme fatigue, and loss of appetite. Army physicians noted, "The malaise and depression are generally so great that the patient keeps his bed voluntarily."[153]

Dysentery caused "mucus in bloody discharges from the intestine" and amplified the symptoms of the other tropical diseases.[154] Protozoal dysentery, first pathologically described in the Philippines in 1900, resulted in chronic diarrhea, "colicky pain, a distended and painful abdomen, with furred tongue and loss of appetite."[155] *Leishmanian* dysentery produced "persistent fever, anemia, and cachexial [a wasting loss of weight] condition with the ultimate enlargement of the spleen and liver."[156] Signs of infection usually appeared about three days after contamination and lasted for ten days. The victim suffered severe dehydration resulting from diarrhea, vomiting, and sweats. Poor diets aggravated the symptoms. Beriberi was common and was caused by inadequate amounts of vitamin B or thiamine, which was abundant in beans and peas.[157] It affected nerves, caused weakness, and could result in paralysis and congestive heart failure.

The guerrillas had little medical training, yet even skilled medical personnel would have found it challenging to identify and treat their ailments. Malarial parasites affected many organs and produced symptoms that mimicked a host of other diseases.[158] The guerrillas were often infected by different strains of malaria coincident with many other tropical illnesses. A successful treatment of one causative parasite led to its replacement by a second or third.

Beyond the physical effects of these infirmities lurked a more treacherous disorder. By the time Ramsey arrived at the Fassoth camp, it had improved sanitation, plenty of food, and a doctor and a nurse, but these were not always enough. He watched camp personnel try to nurse one lieutenant back to health. "Instead," Ramsey noted, "he was obsessed with the idea that his government had deserted him and left him helpless before his enemies. And so, while everyone around him was regaining weight and health, he continued to decline until finally, for no reason the doctor could identify, he died."[159] Blackburn identified the lieutenant as Bell, an engineer from the University of Colorado.[160] Ramsey noted, "It drove home to me once again the truth of which I was already aware, that mind and attitude together shape will, and when the will is lost, defeat follows."[161]

VISAYAS, D244/R-805

Between 8 and 26 August a string of uprisings started in Negros and spread across the Philippines. The Japanese responded with a plan for an autumn campaign to pacify the islands.[162] It included a sudden roundup and reimprisonment of the Filipino POWs previously granted amnesty. On Panay, they used those reincarcerated POWs as forced labor, which greatly angered the natives, but Tokyo was facing a rising worker deficit at home and simply had no manpower to spare for the Philippines.

Haseba Sueto of the Mitsubishi Nagasaki shipbuilding works recalled, "By 1943 the shortage of labor had become the most pressing problem at war plants."[163] Before the end of the war the authorities would bring more than 30,000 Allied POWs to Japan as forced laborers, and 3,526 of them would die there.[164]

The guerrillas intensified the worker shortage in the islands. For nearly a year they delayed the opening of copper mines in Chobutan, Pilar-Cadiz, and Sipalay that the JMA had granted to Mitsubishi Kogyo and Ishihara Sangyo. Carlos Amores, a security guard at the Nihon Kogyo manganese mines in Busuanga, secretly organized hundreds of guerrillas armed with pistols, knives, and clubs before suddenly killing all twenty or so of the Japanese employees at the mine and most of the Japanese residents in the town.[165] The guerrillas then sealed the mine with dynamite and destroyed stocks of ore before heading into the hills.

Despite such problems, on 22 August Ishihara Sangyo delivered its first shipment of iron ore from the Larap Mine (Kalambayangan). For six months a man named Pastrana, who had managed the mines before the war for the Lepantao company, helped get Larap operating by stripping equipment from mines at Paracale, including two diesel train engines with track, eight barges, power generators, and other items.[166] Under army protection, Mitsui Kozan began extracting copper ore from the Mankayan copper mine in northern Luzon. To get these mines working, the JMA and Fourteenth Army stripped ten idle gold mines around Baguio of materials previously imported from the United States. They also hired a Japanese resident of Manila who worked as a machinist at the Balatoc mine to oversee the transfer of power generators from Suyoc and Balatoc.

When the Japanese sufficiently guarded the mines, however, guerrillas attacked the transport along the Naguilian Road through Baguio toward Poro. "As a result," one historian wrote, "not only was the transport of materials, equipment, and extracted ore, slowed down, but the availability of truck drivers and general workers was also seriously affected."[167]

These attacks were just part of the guerrilla efforts to disrupt Japanese exploitation of resources across the islands. They interrupted workforces and diverted the Japanese from preparations to defend the islands. In Bohol, guerrillas abducted and killed Japanese employees at the Nihon Kogyo manganese mine. Remaining workers fled, and production halted. The Japanese army had to increase security and coerce workers to restart production. Guerrillas on Panay intimidated Filipinos from answering the Ishihara Sangyo company's call for two thousand workers to reopen the vital copper mine in Antique.[168] Between 23 and 27 September the guerrillas attacked the mine and killed twelve to sixteen Japanese employees. Only the air attacks broke their siege. By the end of the year the Japanese army had to garrison the mines and guard 385 POWs brought from Manila to get the mines operating again. When representatives of the Taiwan Takushoku, Kurha Boseki, Toyo Menka, and Toyo Boseki companies arrived in Negros to develop cotton fields, guerrillas forced them to retreat to Luzon.[169]

On Cebu, the Tai Kogyo company won the contract for the Toledo copper mine, but guerrillas delayed them for eight months.[170] Cushing and Fenton had combined forces and established dual command, with Fenton as administrative commander headquartered in Maslog and Cushing seven miles away leading the combat units from a base at Mangalon Heights. They organized battalions with staff sections along U.S. Army lines. "The Cebu area long enjoyed the reputation for having killed more Japanese than any other area," SWPA later noted with the caution: "In their efforts to stamp out Japanese and Japanese sympathizers, the men, reportedly under Fenton, went to extremes and many wanton killings of innocent citizens were reported."[171] Suspecting local politics might have colored such reports, MacArthur's staff added: "Although there was a certain amount of killing and destruction, it appears possible that this feature was exaggerated by Kangleon, Fertig, Parsons, and Ingeniero, who had ambitions regarding Cebu."[172]

Meanwhile, on 20 August the Negros guerrillas elected Professor Bell to organize their forces. He recruited Chinese merchant Manuel Sy Cip to obtain supplies. Seeking an experienced officer to take charge, Bell asked Gador, but he declined.[173] Bell turned to constabulary Major Placido Ausejo, a fifty-one-year-old Silliman University graduate. "He is disciplined, mature in judgment and a good organizer," wrote U.S. Army intelligence, "all excellent assets in establishing a guerrilla movement about to go wild."[174] In October Ausejo renamed his one-thousand-man guerrilla force as the 75th Regiment. Headquartered in Malabo, it won popular support.

Gador decided to raise his own guerrilla group and challenge for command of Negros and nearby Negros Siquitor, where retired Philippine scout Major Benito Cunanan had organized two battalions of guerrillas and drove off several attempted Japanese landings. Cunanan's men even assassinated the Japanese-appointed governor. In October he would ignore Gador and join his guerrillas to Ausejo's 75th Regiment as the 4th Provisional Battalion.

On Panay, Peralta entered into a contretemps with Confesor over personnel, supplies, money, citizens' rights, and control of the provincial guards.[175] By now Peralta had eight thousand men in the Free Panay guerrilla forces, with Confesor's long-time political foe, assemblyman José Zulueta, leading a rival free government. Confesor, however, still retained the people's loyalty and guarded them against guerrilla transgressions. The contest devolved into an uneasy balance: Peralta would not interfere with either Confesor's government or his provincial guards as long as Confesor provided 75 percent of taxes to Peralta. With this, nearly 15,000 united guerrillas joined to hold at bay the more than 5,000 Japanese troops on Panay.

In northeast Palawan, Alfred and Paul Cobb continued to expand their home guard from Danlig by adding a unit on Dumaran Island. Alfred made contact with American airmen from the 48th Material Command hiding on Cuyo Island. Some of these men agreed to join his force on Palawan, while others would connect with Carlos Amores on Busuanga. They collected food, arms, boats, and other supplies and drafted plans for attacking Puerto Princesa.

When Amores organized the attack on the Busuanga mines, he went to Danlig to ask the Cobb brothers for help. Eventually Japanese counterattacks and a lack of food forced Amores to withdraw with about one hundred men to Sibaltan in northern Palawan. There he officially joined the Cobbs as C Company in the Palawan special battalion. This brought the Cobb group to about 150 armed men, but the guerrillas attacked no more in Busuanga, they only gathered intelligence.

CENTRAL LUZON, D254/R-795

Outside Manila, Harry McKenzie, an American miner married to a Filipina named Mary with a six-year-old son, arrived to join Lapham. "Harry was a proverbial diamond in the rough: he had little formal education but was faithful and dependable," Lapham recalled. "I soon made him district commander of Nueva Ecija as well as my executive officer—in effect, my right-hand man."[176] Mary's cousin, Manuel Bahia, became Harry's adjutant.

Volckmann and Blackburn had now spent two months in the Fassoth camp and wanted out. The camp wallowed in despair. "I mean, most of the talk that you would hear was, 'They're not ever coming back. How are we going to survive?'" Blackburn recalled.[177] The refugee American soldiers rejected military rank, order, and discipline and were outright belligerent.[178] Sanitation literally went out the window. Through leadership by example, the two officers gradually reasserted rank and structure and instituted a program of slit-trench latrines.

Bernia warned the two American officers that an increasing number of armed bandit gangs calling themselves guerrillas were abusing people in the local area. "He felt the need to get something organized to control all of this," Blackburn recalled.[179] Bernia asked Volckmann and Blackburn to go with him to see Colonel Merrill and decide on how to combat the bandits. Eagerly, they started north on 18 August. As always, Filipinos along the route fed and sheltered the Americans and at times provided carabao carts for their travel.

They met Merrill near Natividad, wrote Volckmann, "but it was obvious to us that the colonel was still in bad shape."[180] They saw prewar acquaintances Lt. Pete Calyer and Capt. George Crane, who were staying with other Americans as guests of a Chinese mestizo family named Jinco.[181] The officers stayed for three days, and Merrill gave them a message to deliver to Thorp. When it was time to move, the men were reluctant. Blackburn explained, "The Jinco daughters prided themselves on their cooking, and I'm telling you, those Chinese gals could really put it on. They were beautiful girls."[182] Good food, fresh linen, and comfortable beds tempted them to stay, but Volckmann and Blackburn again headed north.

On 20 August the party came across Wainwright's former cook, who swore he had recently seen the general on a train headed for Manila where he was to be shipped to Formosa. That evening Volckmann and Blackburn arrived at Thorp's camp near Timbu, west of Fort Stotsenburg. The colonel struck his visitors as being willfully uninterested in the war and irritated by anyone determined to fight.[183] Volckmann and Blackburn delivered Merrill's message. Volckmann recalled, "Thorp burst into a rage because the letter seemed to assume that Merrill was the supreme commander of guerrillas on Luzon."[184] "He believed that he was the only legitimate one authorized to do this," observed Blackburn. "He assumed a very arrogant attitude about it."[185] Whether Merrill realized it or not, Thorp had received authority directly from MacArthur. After an exchange of messages, Merrill accepted recognition from Thorp as a subordinate commander in Zambalese, but the two men would never work together.

At Thorp's camp Volckmann took note of the men around him. "Many became extremely pessimistic, firmly convinced that we had no chance to survive—to them it was only a question of time and events." He spotted a second group who seemed more "determined and optimistic" per day, defying desperation. Finally, he identified a third group: "They sank to the level of beasts, and became so self-centered in their fight for existence that they would stoop to anything, regardless of the effect on others. Stealing, cheating, lying, or even murder came easy to them if to their distorted minds it seemed to be to their advantage."[186]

After two days in camp, Volckmann and Blackburn concluded: "Thorp had no brains."[187] Upon learning that Moses and Noble had passed through on their way north, they asked for a guide to search for the two colonels. Thorp agreed to have them escorted as far as Hukbalahap territory. On 24 August Volckmann and Blackburn departed with a Filipino guide, nicknamed Kid Muscles. They skirted the internment center at Camp O'Donnell before reaching the base of sixty-year-old Huk leader Esuebio Aquino, who displayed ill will toward Thorp.[188] After Volckmann declined Aquino's offer to become his military advisor, the Huk offered quarters and food for the night and a guide to take them farther north in the morning.

WASHINGTON, D265/R-784

Chick Parsons arrived with his family in New York City on 29 August and learned the Navy had listed him as officially missing in action. He settled his wife and children with family in North Carolina and then reported for duty in Washington, D.C., where he delivered his intelligence file from Manila to Colonel Evans in Army G-2.[189] Parsons also contacted old friends like Peter Grim, his former boss in the Luzon Stevedoring Company. Grim, now a U.S. Army Transportation Corps colonel in Brisbane, brought Parsons' story to the attention of the AIB.[190] With few Army units in the Pacific and the Army staff focused on the pending invasion of North Africa, the burden of collecting and analyzing signal radio intelligence fell to MacArthur's Central Bureau Brisbane.[191] They needed help. Before long, SWPA sent a message to Washington: "SEND PARSONS IMMEDIATELY—MACARTHUR."[192]

5

Islands at War
August 1942–January 1943

NORTHERN LUZON, D268/R-781

Thorp's Central Luzon Guerrilla Force was well organized and staffed when he scheduled a conference of his district commanders for 29 August at his headquarters at Camp Chavez on Mount Pinatubo.[1] A Tagalog runner named Rodriguez betrayed the meeting to the Japanese, but he got the date wrong, and the Japanese raided twenty-four hours too early. Thorp escaped with his staff to Santa Juliana in Tarlac Province, where his mistress's uncle, former mayor Marcos Laxamana, greeted them.

To the north near La Paz, Volckmann and Blackburn arrived at Lapham's headquarters on 1 September and found him confined to bed with a high fever and being tended to by African-American Spanish-American War veteran Mr. Brunch, who "carried a lot of influence in the area."[2] Three days later, with guides provided by Lapham, they headed farther north to find Moses and Noble. A native's timely warning enabled them to dodge a Japanese ambush and reach Charlie Cushing's camp near San Nicolas.[3] A number of guerrillas there were incapacitated by malaria, including the 11th Infantry Regiment's Lieutenant Rufino Baldwin, who would later raise a guerrilla force in the Itogon mining area.

Volckmann and Blackburn met American gold miners John French and Herb Swick, who agreed to take them to Noble and Moses in Benguet. Along the way, they felt noticeably invigorated by the crisp, clean mountain air. They encountered the emaciated Patrick O'Day, who was sharing a house with a Belgian priest.[4] A native arrived with a message from Moses and Noble asking to meet at Barrio Benning.[5]

On 9 September the four officers finally met. The colonels briefed their visitors on the situation across northern Luzon: Walter Cushing led the 121st Regiment, Nakar commanded the 14th Regiment, Calvert had the 43rd Regiment, and Praeger led guerrillas in Cagayan Province. They believed Ablan still had a force in Ilocos Norte. Philippine army captain Ali al Raschid led guerrillas in Kalinga Province, and Baldwin was starting to build a command in Benguet. To the north, more guerrillas followed Bado Dangwa, the former transportation executive. It all sounded impressive but disorganized. Volckmann asked Moses, the senior officer, if he had command of all these guerrillas. "No," he answered, "to date we have been surveying the situation and have been resting to get our health back."[6] He thought Volckmann and Blackburn needed rest too. The next day Swick took the two to a doctor near Uding while Moses and Noble headed back north.

Four families resided near the abandoned mines around Uding. The elderly Pearsons were Americans from Itogon. With them were their son, his wife, and the Moule family. Filipino Dr. Biason, who had studied in Minnesota, and his wife, a nurse from Wisconsin, also came from Itogon. "After a few hours with them I felt that I had been lifted into a new world," Volckmann wrote, "and that I was farther away from the war than at any time since it began."[7] Their crude houses had running water from a nearby stream and a water-powered automobile generator. Each night a different family fed the visitors. Volckmann began to regain his health, but Blackburn's illnesses seemed to linger.

Swick led Volckmann to the abandoned Bodok mines, where a caretaker kept a house and mill. Volckmann cut some machine belts to repair his worn-out shoes. At the nearby mining camp at Equip, he encountered O'Day, the Belgian priest, a Private Gattie, and a miner named Harris. The six-thousand-foot-high camp had good air and abundant mountain rice, camotes, cabbage, pork, chicken, and beef. Blackburn was soon well enough to join them and brought a message from Noble and Moses calling for a meeting on 1 October. After two weeks at Camp Equip, Volckmann and Blackburn set out to see Thorp at Caraw.

Meanwhile, Walter Cushing left his 121st Infantry Regiment around Abra for Kabugao to see Praeger and use his Buhay mine radio to report to SWPA. He would provide the first details they received of the Bataan Death March. Ignoring Praeger's warnings, Cushing set off to find guerrillas reportedly harming civilians in Isabela Province. Near Jones, he and three of his men accepted a farmer's invitation to dinner. Afterward, a waiting Japanese patrol shot and killed Cushing and his men. As told to Volckmann: "Cushing fell wounded, and though riddled with bullets, he managed to empty all but one round from his .45 revolver into the Japs. The remaining round he put through his head."⁸

Still, the resistance continued. Japanese patrols in Abra captured most of Cushing's officers, including his successor, Capt. William Arthur. Major George Barnett managed to evade the enemy and rally remnants of Cushing's guerrillas northwest of San Fernando, La Union.

Dennis Molintas, a farm school principal and army reserve major who had not been activated, reported to Moses, who authorized him to raise a guerrilla company. Later Moses would combine Dangwa's force with Molintas' to form the 12th Infantry Regiment. Volckmann commented: "Dangwa was undoubtedly the most influential and respected native in the Mountain Province.... He possessed an unusual understanding of his people; he was just, and his word was as good as gold. To the majority of the natives, his word was law."⁹ Moses formed the 66th Infantry Regiment around Baguio by adding the 43rd and 11th Infantry to the 12th Infantry Regiment. Unfortunately, Japanese patrols killed Captain Jack Spies on his way to command this new unit.

MANILA, D287/R-762

Colonel Naokata Utsunomiya arrived in Manila to assume duties as both the Fourteenth Army deputy chief of staff and the JMA director of the general affairs department. He intended to deal with the Filipino elite "as gentleman [sic] in order not to insult their character."¹⁰ He began on 20 September with an army department of information–sponsored Catholic mass at San Marcelino for religious section members about to return to Japan.¹¹ They dedicated the mass to feudal lords Ukon Takayama and Joan Naito, Japanese Christians who escaped persecution and settled in Manila in 1613.

At the same time, Bishop Taguchi completed four months drafting four documents he hoped would gain Catholic Filipino support.¹² He was under pressure from the Japanese to remove all foreign priests, but they comprised more than half of the priesthood in the Philippines and 10 percent of church administrators. Yet Taguchi knew the Vatican had promised in 1926 to place Philippine priests in the parish hierarchy and schools. Removing the foreigners could satisfy the military, please Filipino Catholics, and separate the church from the guerrillas. Taguchi decided to risk irritating the Vatican and follow JMA orders.

There were other possible church reforms with potential popular support. Many Filipinos had long resented special tax exemptions enjoyed by church estates and the legal mandate requiring Catholic education in public schools. Bishop Taguchi proposed to allow taxes on all church property not used for religious activity and to make Catholic education optional in public schools. Contrary to JMA wishes, however, he insisted that the church be allowed to operate Catholic schools. Taguchi also asserted that changes to church policies had to be done with Vatican approval. He would join Toyoaki Ono of the religious section, Belgian priest Father Bromman of Manila, and Tokyo-appointed former chancellor to France Ken Harada in a special emissary mission to the Vatican.

Outside Manila, Ramsey became so ill that Barker carried him back to the Fassoth camp. An escaped POW doctor, Captain Warshal, tended to him while Barker assessed the camp. Its more than one hundred American refugee soldiers seemed none too anxious to leave. Ramsey recalled trying to recruit them but was told: "We're not guerrillas. If we're captured we will be treated as prisoners of war. But if they take us with you, we might all be killed."[13] He found no volunteers, and some told him to leave and never come back.

Barker and Ramsey paused to reconsider guerrilla warfare. Barker admitted, "I guess I was absent the day they taught that at the Point."[14] In fact, the U.S. Army did not teach guerrilla warfare. Thorp passed them a copy of Mao's book on guerrilla warfare he had obtained from the Hukbalahaps. It taught that guerrillas should "stay on the defensive but assume the initiative, take advantage of the terrain," "stay flexible but organized and avoid pitched battles," and most importantly, build "credibility and get the people on our side."[15] Barker, however, balked at the politics in Mao's guidance. "Our job isn't to start a revolution," he noted, "it's to prepare for MacArthur's invasion. We're military men, not politicians."[16]

Travelling south, Ramsey suffered another malarial fit just as he entered a barrio where terrified locals warned him of a Huk war party in town. Assisted by his aide Cardizon, he climbed into a hut to meet the Huk leader, and a dozen armed men grabbed him as he passed out. Ramsey awoke in darkness to hear voices arguing in the Pampanga dialect. Cardizon explained that a Huk lieutenant was telling his men that Taruc had denounced Ramsey as a German spy and ordered his execution.[17] Cardizon then dragged Ramsey under the hut's rear wall and across cane fields into the jungle a few steps ahead of the pursuing Huks.

Before Ramsey made it to his new base at Porac, the Japanese raided nearby Timbo, burned the village to the ground, and scattered its inhabitants. The attack spurred five local leaders to join Barker and Ramsey, and Barker cast his eyes upon Manila as a source of supplies, money, and intelligence. Alejandro Santos and Fausto Alberto volunteered to return to their homes in the city and establish guerrilla cadres. "Garish, gigantic billboards now plastered the city, the guerrillas said, proclaiming 'Asia for the Asiatics' and 'Drive out western imperialism,' and setting forth, painfully, the rules and regulations under which the Filipinos were expected to live."[18]

Santos and Alberto made contact with resistance groups already in Manila. By the end of the month they were funneling information to Barker, who sent it by messenger to the southern islands for relay to SWPA. Local volunteers—men and women—acted as couriers. "They went understanding full well that if they were caught they would be tortured for information and then executed," Ramsey observed. "Many we never saw again."[19] Kempeitai Colonel Nagahama had a list of targets for bounty hunters, headed by Thorp, Moses, Noble, Praeger, McGuire, Barker, and Ramsey.[20] Undeterred, Joe Barker would sneak into Manila at the end of October.

In Pampanga, Major Emilio Hernandez brought four guerrilla bands to Lapham with future squadron commanders Gemeniano de Leon and Albert Short. Soon after, Japanese patrols hit the area hard and pushed the guerrillas back twenty-five miles into Pantabangan. "Short was shot in the arm during a skirmish with a rival band of Filipino guerrillas," Lapham recalled, "and while he was still weak from his wound the Japanese renewed their pursuit. In attempting to escape from them, he was shot and killed."[21]

Truckloads of Japanese unloaded near Umingan and spread out into the jungle. Natives warned that patrols would raid Camp Manchuria in revenge for the beheading of the Umingan mayor. Lapham's men slung their ailing commander into a hammock and carried him away. Several times he ordered them to "put me down beside the trail and let me die in peace."[22] Esteban Lumyeb responded: "Not now, sir. We can make it. You will see, sir."[23] One night in a house just outside Umingan, the Japanese came in the front door as Lapham and his bodyguard Lalugan escaped out the back.

On 20 September collaborator Benigno Aquino sent a seven-page plan to the Japanese for the issue of a five-million-peso bond to buy arms and ammunition for the constabulary. Aquino wanted a native force able "to diminish the activities of the lawless elements."[24] The Japanese did not act on his plan.

The new pacification campaign in northern Luzon caught a number of guerrillas. According to Agoncillo, "One of them, Lieutenant Leandro Rosario, actively collaborated with the enemy and pointed to Nakar's hideout."[25] On 29 September a Japanese patrol conducted a raid near Jones, Isabela, and captured Nakar and his radio. It was more than a simple betrayal. Contact with MacArthur had increased Nakar's desire to maintain communication. Without codes, however, he had to provide "long and detailed instructions for codes and deceptive timing to mislead the Japanese."[26] The long and frequent transmissions enabled Japanese direction-finding equipment to plot Nakar's location. Despite months of torture, he refused to cooperate. Finally in October 1943 the Japanese beheaded Nakar in Manila's North Cemetery.[27]

Without their leader, most of the 14th Infantry's five thousand men surrendered.[28] What was left passed to 2nd Battalion commander Lieutenant Colonel Manuel Enriquez. He concentrated on coordinating with neighboring regiments and daringly located his headquarters inside a nacoco store (a trading post authorized by the Japanese) in Baguio. It was a brilliant choice, as agents could easily come and go posing as salesmen.[29]

One evening in Pantabangan, ill with malaria, Lapham sat on the edge of hill and gazed at the distant barrios. "Never in my life have I felt so alone, so misplaced, so utterly estranged from normal human existence."[30] He felt his forces were hopelessly disorganized and scattered. He observed, "When the physical resources of troops have been sapped by chronic disease and protracted semi-starvation, their will to fight declines along with their ability to do so."[31] Idle moments magnified fears and tested guerrilla leaders. The remedy was to stay active.

In Bicol, Vinzons' deputy Major Francisco "Turko" Boayes, rallied the scattered VTG and by the end of September joined the TVGU under Juan Q. Miranda.[32] Turko moved from Camarines Norte to Camarines Sur with hopes of leaving behind a bad reputation. Under the TVGU's strict policies, his men notably "never once molested any civilian."[33] Turko justified the VTG's past repute as just a part of guerrilla warfare. "But rape can never be an inevitable extreme measure or put more bluntly, a war policy," Barrameda wrote. "Neither is the public humiliation and killing of non-combatants, collaborators as they may have reportedly been."[34] After several uneasy months, Turko would withdraw from the TVGU and again become independent.

MINDANAO, D279/R-770

After a Muslim force under Manalo Mindalano attacked a Japanese garrison at Ganassi, Lieutenant Sunao Yoshioka retaliated on 12 September with an advance on guerrillas he thought were near Tamparan on Lake Lanao. His company ran into an ambush by bolo-wielding Moros and suffered nearly complete destruction.[35] After that, the Japanese at Ganassi decided it best to remain in their garrison and avoid antagonizing the Moros.

The Japanese had assumed Moro bands such as the one under "Brigadier General" Busran Kalaw were anti-American, but they turned out to be against anyone who was not Moro.[36] New groups rose up across Mindanao: Macario Diaz in Masgad, Major Garcia in central Surigao, and Captain Tomanning at Lianga. According to SWPA: "These small groups were loosely controlled and behaved as bandits in their areas. They inflicted damage against property, refused to submit to each other and gave the guerrillas a bad name generally."[37] Some weaker bands, such as those under Manuel Fortich and Vincente Leuterio in southern Bukidnon, joined Pendatun as he campaigned with 2,400 men to drive the Japanese out of Kibawe, Maramag, Valencia, and Mailag.

On 6 October Japanese troops on the inter-island steamer *Tular* tried to dock at Misamis City harbor but were surprised and driven off by guerrillas firing from the old Spanish fort under an American flag.[38] Former USAFFE soldiers, Philippine Constabulary, Philippine Scouts, U.S. Navy personnel, and civilians formed bands east of the town, north of Agusan, and around Surigao. "They were led by natural leaders," SWPA later reported, "who assumed their responsibilities for various reasons—personal aggrandizement, banditry, desire to fight the Japs or establishment of law and order."[39] Private First Class Clyde Abbott of the 14th Bomb Squadron and Lieutenant Pedro Collado of the Philippine Constabulary led guerrillas that drove off a Japanese patrol trying to establish a puppet government in Balingasag.[40] Groups such as those led by U.S. Army Air Corps veterans MSgt. James McIntyre at Claveria and MSgt. Alfredo Fernandez at Malitbog, however, forfeited many opportunities by refusing to cooperate with each other.

In response to the ambush at Misamis City harbor, the Japanese sent the 10th Independent Garrison's five battalions to the Mindanao district and the 11th Independent Garrison's four battalions to the Visayan district. The 16th Division remained in garrisons in Southern Luzon, and the 2nd Regiment and 4th Battalion of the 65th Brigade occupied Northern Luzon.[41]

When the Japanese invaded Mindanao, American mestizo Luis Morgan was a Philippine Constabulary lieutenant in Kolambugan.[42] One guerrilla described him as "outgoing but demanding, almost arrogant. He had a swashbuckling air about him, with a tommy gun strapped across his chest."[43] Just before Sharp's surrender, Morgan received orders to take his troops to Lake Lanao. Instead, he burned down a sawmill in Kolambugan and headed for distant Baroy, picking up about four hundred Filipino soldiers along the way. The Christian town of Baroy was suffering from Muslim raids. Morgan reportedly gathered the town's roughly thirty Moro men, women, and children into a warehouse and slaughtered them with machine gun fire.[44] He then set himself up as a warlord, demanding money and food for his men and a new woman for his bed each night. Constabulary Lieutenant Bill Tate, son of an African-American buffalo soldier and a Moro woman, deserted the bureau of constabulary to offer Morgan information on Mindanao's guerrillas.

In August Morgan had learned Fertig was in his area and sent Tait to deliver a proposition. Self-promoted to captain, Morgan suspected Filipino officers of higher rank would try to take over his growing force. To block them, he proposed to spread a rumor that MacArthur had sent a brigadier general to command the Mindanao resistance. He asked Fertig to show up at Baroy and claim to be that general. He would let Fertig play the boss while Morgan ran the show as chief of staff. Tait invited Fertig to visit Morgan and discuss the plan.

Fertig had his own ideas. He had assumed that, eventually, some guerrillas would seek his leadership. Only then, from a position of strength, would he join any group. Morgan was welcome to come see him, Fertig told Tait, while he considered his offer. Two weeks passed. Local citizens grew more resentful of Morgan, and erstwhile rivals espied his command. On 10 September Morgan at last went to Fertig. Maintaining a posture suited to his superior rank, the American officer grilled Morgan on why he had not followed orders and gone to Lake Lanao. He asked for plans and staff studies, tables of organization and equipment, and rosters.[45] When a humbled Morgan returned three days later with all requested information, Fertig was wearing the silver stars of a brigadier general fashioned from coins by a local Moro silversmith.

Fertig decided to accept command of Morgan's guerrillas, but not as a figurehead. He renamed the force the 106th Regiment and set out to unite all Mindanao's guerrillas under his command. Coincidentally, Captain Joaquin Dismal in nearby of Misamis Occidental asked for help to attack a Japanese garrison. Fertig sent Morgan and Tate, and they successfully cleared Misamis Occidental and the north coast of Zamboanga. Meanwhile, fifty-one-year-old Lieutenant Colonel Ciriaco Mortera arrived from Misamis Occidental with a remnant constabulary force to join Fertig.

On 18 September Fertig issued an ambitious proclamation addressed to "the United States Army Forces in the Philippines [USAFIP]." He announced that he had raised the American and Filipino flags in Misamis Occidental and Northern Zamboanga and reestablished the Philippine commonwealth government in liberated areas under military authorities. Where civil laws conflicted with military laws, he proclaimed that military law prevailed. Fertig signed his declaration as "W. W. Fertig, Brigadier General, USA, Commanding Mindanao and Sulu Force."[46]

Fertig suspected that Morgan resented his authority and, given time, would work to replace him. He decided to send Morgan around Mindanao to find and recruit guerrillas for his organization. If Morgan succeeded, it would prove his loyalty. If he failed, Morgan would look weak and incompetent. If something unfortunate happened during the trip, it would be a problem solved for Fertig. In the meantime, Fertig would improve his units, gain their loyalty, and organize a civil government.

On a whirlwind inspection of Misamis Occidental, Fertig found Charlie Hedges' old motor pool still in good order. His men got the province's telephone system working. Offret, who knew a thing or two about engines, supervised the reopening of the coconut oil factory in Jimenez that had employed many local citizens.[47] Fertig absorbed many local guerrillas, but the American Air Corps enlisted men who led north coast bands between Talakag and Sumilao departed to find their way to Australia.[48] U.S. Army Lt. Col. Robert V. Bowler recruited their men into the 111th and 112th Regiments of Fertig's 109th Division. Major Manuel Jaldon organized guerrillas around Alubijid, Misamis Oriental, into the 109th Regiment. Eventually Fertig would add the 117th Regiment in this area.

Bowler thought his area's terrain, supportive people, and scarcity of enemy troops were ideal for guerrillas. He determined to hide as much as possible and fight when he had no other choice. "My principal assets are anonymity, lack of roads, and friendly neighbors," he told Fertig. "The Japs know we operate in the hills, but they estimate our potential at five percent of what it is!"[49] This was remarkable, for Colonel Yoshinari Tanaka, the commander in western Mindanao, believed "General Fertig" held Misamis with seven thousand guerrilla troops.[50] "Communities provide us with shelter, information, and food, and we never involve them in operations," Bowler said. "When the Japs sweep through friendly barrios, my men fade into the hills; if necessary, they bury their arms and become farmers!"[51] Steve Mellnik later observed, "Though Bowler's personal qualities did much to stimulate guerrilla cohesion, it was local leadership—Americans who settled in Mindanao after the Spanish-American War—that enabled Bowler to expand the organization."[52]

Fertig instituted a training program dedicated to tactics and soldier skills and administrative procedures for his staff, "careful to record service information so that someday his men could collect back pay."[53] Civilian volunteers used crude molds to shape curtain rods into .30-caliber bullets. In a shed in Dipolog, Lieutenant Sol Samonte mixed quicksilver from thermometers with other chemicals to make fulminate of mercury for percussion caps. An ordnance factory in Jimenez turned old springs into new ejectors for Enfield rifles. In a rice mill near Oroquieta, a handpicked crew carved hardwood plates for printing Government of the Free Philippines notes that (without authority) promised redemption at face value after the war. Outside Bonifacio, Geraldo Almendres filled the floors of a hut with parts scavenged from radios and a movie sound projector in an effort to create a long-range transmitter and receiver. Finally, Fertig had his men manufacture soap, an item in great demand, to trade on Negros for sugar to produce fuel.

Nothing came easy. When Morgan confiscated boats, fishermen objected, and local economies and diets suffered. Fertig decided he needed a civilian government for such problems and recruited highly respected judge Florentino Saguin as chief of state. Others stepped forward to fill administrative positions. Fertig sought an alliance with the local Catholic church, but Irish Jesuit Father Calanan could offer only his sympathy while insisting on outward neutrality. Unofficially, however, many priests and nuns became vital agents for the guerrillas.[54] To encourage cooperation, Fertig ordered his headquarters personnel to attend weekly mass. He also actively courted the support of the Doña Carmen Ozámiz and her family, whose highborn Spanish mestizo kinship network long held sway in the province.

Sam Wilson took over the printing of money and kept meticulous books for the treasury. Robert Ball was put to work with the radio development section and later became district communication officer. Kenneth Baylay, sick with malaria, escaped a field hospital with thirteen patients and spent months wandering Moro country. After his best friend John Grant was speared to death by Magahats, Baylay joined Pendatun. Sensing hostility from Ed Andrews, however, he left with American Leonard Merchant to find Fertig. He notified Fertig of a very capable West Pointer and World War I veteran named Colonel Frank McGee working on Pendatun's staff.

Roy Bell arrived unexpectedly from Negros in search of food and money. Fertig agreed to send food, military supplies, and Mindanao emergency currency to Negros. In return, Ausejo's 75th Regiment pledged itself to Fertig. Bell helped Almendres and Ball complete a radio. Ball then used a code cylinder Fertig carried to tap out a message to the world: "WE HAVE THE HOT DOPE ON THE HOT YANKS IN THE HOT PHILIPPINES."[55] They failed to realize that without a crystal, their transmitter slid across a broad band of frequencies. Even so, Fertig's message was heard—at the radio station KFS in San Francisco, whose operators dismissed the slang-filled message in obsolete code on multi-frequencies as some kind of Japanese effort to jam Allied radio traffic. Any response could encourage further jamming.[56]

CENTRAL LUZON, D304/R-745

During the first week of October, Japanese interrogators broke a runner from the Fassoth camp, and he gave away its location. Fortunately, word reached Bill and Martin in time to disband their camp. A local Negrito with three young wives took Ramsey, Doctor Warshal, and Martin Fassoth to a hut in higher hills. When the men returned, they found the throat-slit bodies of guards among the smoking remains of the camp. They met up with Bill Fassoth and learned that after the Japanese raid, many men had returned to the camp when the Japanese surprised them by returning to finish the job. They killed thirty Americans and captured five.[57] Bill decided to surrender for fear of what the enemy might do to his family.[58] The Japanese had learned to strike kinship networks. "A means more penetrating and effective could not possibly have been conceived," Volckmann observed, "for while the average Filipino has very little national or state feeling, his family ties are strong and sacred to him."[59]

Ramsey said his goodbyes and headed for his friend John Boone's camp north of Manila near Cabanatuan. He had recruited Boone from the East Coast Luzon Guerrilla Force (ECLGF) and promoted him to captain. The good-natured Boone fell in love with a woman he had held prisoner after executing her husband for collaboration.[60] Ramsey performed their wedding ceremony.

On 23 October Thorp learned that Minang's uncle, ex-mayor Laxamana who had welcomed them to Umindang, had been captured. Six days later as they prepared to move, the Japanese attacked and seized Thorp and his staff. Rumors circulated that Laxamana had betrayed him for money. "The guide he had chosen for Thorp, Andres de la Cruz, was released at once by his captors and given back his gun, though the others remained 'hog tied,'" Lapham noted. "Laxamana received a handsome reward for his treachery. Afterward, he was protected by the Japanese and helped to invest in real estate from which he made a great deal more money, though he may have eventually ended his inglorious career buried alive by guerrillas."[61] Minang also avoided prison but eventually became guerrilla Ray Hunt's lover. Lapham said, "Understandably, he esteemed her highly."[62] Lapham, Anderson, and Ramsey took over Thorp's organization.

Thorp's capture erased his arrangement with the Huks, who fought some Americans and maintained decent relations with others. They escorted Bernard Anderson south to organize guerrillas, and Merrill dealt with them "because he admired their pugnacity."[63] Blair Robinett, Joe Barker, and William J. Gardiner also worked with the Huks. Blackburn, Volckmann, Crane, Anderson, Ramsey, and James Boyd remained wary.

Clay Conner served in Anderson's new Squadron 155 in command of several hundred Negritos. He openly admired the Huks' organization, arms, and leaders but noticed that the Japanese almost always raided his positions a day or two after contact with the communist guerrillas. "Then he saw Huks go into small barrios and take guns away from USAFFE guerrillas there," Lapham wrote. "Finally, when he was saved from a Huk ambush only by the loyalty and quick wits of some of his Negrito followers, the last of his illusions about these smart, brave, 'progressive,' anti-Fascist warriors evaporated."[64]

It is interesting to note how the Negritos, who averaged slightly under five feet tall, were routinely described as short. The average Philippine guerrilla only stood between five feet and five feet six inches tall, weighed about 110 to 120 pounds, and was between seventeen and twenty-three years old.[65] They often wore uniforms taken from their fallen enemy and from a distance were almost indistinguishable from the Japanese. Parsons learned one quick method of identification—Japanese never went barefoot, and Filipinos seldom wore shoes. In theory, they earned the same pay as American soldiers, but they received maybe ten to fifty pesos of scrip each month, which they called *tinghoy*—worthless—because there was nothing to buy.[66]

Carlos Romulo studied the Japanese soldiers early in the war and made some generalizations: "His weight is from 95 to 125 pounds; his height is five foot three inches; his age is twenty-three; his length of military service is one and a half years. He comes, as a rule, from the farm."[67] Villamor noted differences between early Japanese regular army troops and later green replacements: "They were in much better physical appearance than the transient casuals coming from Japan and proceeding to the front, who were younger, weaker, and smaller. One agent reported seeing a whole battalion of these soldiers, and not one of them was over five feet in height."[68]

The Japanese field units, however, enjoyed advantages over the guerrillas in firepower, training, experience, and unit cohesion. In addition to naval gunfire, aircraft, and sometimes tanks, the Japanese were routinely armed with .30-caliber water-cooled machine guns, so-called knee mortars, automatic rifles, and grenades.[69] According to U.S. military intelligence, the Japanese arms "were of first-rate design and construction," with firearms as effective as Allied weapons but simpler to use.[70] "And the Japanese soldier had the advantage over the American and Filipino," observed Romulo, "because he is used to living on almost nothing. We were willing to strip comfort to the minimum. But to him that minimum was a luxury."[71]

Japanese regular troops could be fierce in battle. B. David Mann fought them in Bataan in 1945 and later wrote, "Japan's leaders blundered many times during the war, but no one can dispute that the individual Japanese infantryman was among the best the world has ever seen. For tenacity, determination, bravery, and devotion to cause, he has few if any peers."[72] As Yuki Tanaka explained, "The new military ideology—which placed so much weight on the concepts of no surrender, loyalty through blind obedience, and honor in dying for the emperor—spread throughout the Japanese armed forces with little apparent resistance."[73] One soldier, Yutaka Yokota, added, "There's an old expression, 'Bushido is the search for a place to die.' Well, that was our fervent desire, our long-cherished dream. A place to die for my country."[74]

Blind courage contained a paradoxical weakness, however. As historians Meirion and Susie Harries observed, "The utter disregard for danger was rooted not in hope but in resignation to the inevitability of defeat."[75] Veteran Suzuki Murio later admitted, "Soldiers like me had no idea why we were fighting this war. We were treated as nothing more than consumable goods."[76]

Tactically, the Japanese operated on exact and predictable timetables. Officers told Quezon, "Everything with them is like a railroad time schedule."[77] A witness described a typical raid on Claver, Mindanao, on 30 November 1943: "A Japanese cruiser and several small craft shelled the town and the surrounding hills. They sent landing craft with assault troops ashore and moved inland to a distance of about three miles."[78] The soldiers appeared reluctant to venture beyond the range of their naval gunfire support or stay too long in guerrilla territory.

As the imperial headquarters stripped away top-line units for other fronts, green conscripts and reservists took their place.[79] In 1940 professionals outnumbered reservists in the Japanese army by a ratio of 2.4 to 1; by 1943 the army contained 1.5 reservists for each regular soldier.[80] Lapham watched the new arrivals closely and concluded, "Their maneuvers were broad, general sweeps, often appearing to be field exercises for green troops fresh from Japan."[81] Another guerrilla recalled, "The Japanese occupation army was made up of conscripts, not regular army troops, and they were not the bravest of soldiers."[82]

The green replacements were hesitant warriors. Lapham reported, "The Japanese disliked going into the jungle at night so nocturnal ambushes were rare."[83] Others described their patrols as "chronically noisy. . . . We could often hear their conversations and their clanging equipment long before we encountered them."[84] Some guerrillas assumed their enemy was trying to avoid contact.[85] An enlisted soldier of the 32nd Regiment from Osaka gave credence to this impression: "Why die when you've already lost? I guess if you've been long on the battlefield, you know instantly whether the enemy's going to shoot or not. Anyway, that was my philosophy: As long as I don't fight, I'll make it home. I believed in that."[86]

Many of the new soldiers were almost children. In a poignant interview, Miki Hanada, a six-year Red Cross nurse, recalled the "student soldiers" sailing on her hospital ship for the Philippines (in violation of the Geneva accords because the U.S. Navy sank so many troop ships). Instructed that "books are unnecessary," they left many favorites behind. "Giving up works by Ishikawa Takuboku and Hermann Hesse must have felt as if they were bidding farewell to their youth," she recalled. "The books were heavily underlined. Images of their faces as they gallantly saluted upon disembarking are burned into my memory."[87]

To compensate for the weak replacements, the Fourteenth Army relied on numbers. A guerrilla later remembered, "A few bursts of rifle and submachine gunfire from a concealed position would disperse them quickly. On one occasion, however, they came after us in force and routed us completely."[88] In September 1943 the Japanese sent 1,500 soldiers on a three-pronged attack in Iloilo Province in Panay.[89] Troops surrounded their targeted area, "then the patrols cut through, over and over again, like cutting pie."[90] Guerrillas could not stand against large numbers, especially when backed by airpower. The Japanese also targeted unprotected villages. "Fifty Japs could surround a town," Yay Panlilio wrote, "one town after another or several towns at the same time—surprise it, pouncing by truckloads, dumping men there at dawn, or creeping into sentry position before day broke. Anybody could come in. Nobody could go out."[91]

To maintain numbers, the Japanese often forced Filipinos into volunteer guard organizations. Guerrilla reports of high Japanese casualties often included numbers of these constabulary, *ronda*, or "yuin" Filipino auxiliaries.[92] In fact, the Japanese would remove or destroy their own dead to prevent them from falling into guerrilla hands. One guerrilla reported that the Japanese habitually threw their dead into native huts and set them on fire.[93]

Unable to physically destroy the resistance, the Japanese tried psychological domination. When they rebuilt the Forbes bridge in Iloilo City on Panay, the Japanese forced anyone passing "to bow from the waist down before the sentinels representing the Emperor of Japan."[94] "The new masters were brutal and arrogant," wrote Villamor. "They slapped people around at the slightest provocation. They bathed in the nude in the public plazas, shocking the Filipinos. They plundered, commandeering stocks of palay and corn, destroyed and dismantled private homes for firewood."[95] Rape, torture, and execution were ultimate expressions of domination.

Yuki Tanaka of Hiroshima University has argued: "In literal terms, Japanese soldiers were obviously the physical perpetrators of such atrocities. In psychological and ideological terms, they were also the victims of an emperor system that legitimized such atrocities in the name of the emperor."[96] Within Japan, the enlisted soldiers were considered a low social class, but in the colonies, they represented the emperor, the highest possible position in society.[97] Tanaka explained, "This led in many cases to unbalanced psychological states: extremes of self-abnegation in relation to the Japanese domestic hierarchy alternating with excessive self-regard in relation to colonial non-Japanese. The repressed resentment of the former was often expressed in violence toward the latter."[98] The violence served to reinforce a martial self-image in green troops. Before joining the guerrillas, Panlilio once talked with a Japanese officer who was angry at seeing one of his sentries sharing photos with Filipinos on the street. "Look what your country is doing to our army," he said. "You mean you have to keep them away from the people?" she asked. He nodded and said, "Otherwise they go soft."[99]

AUSTRALIA, D308/R-741

On 11 October Capt. William L. Osborne and Capt. Damon J. "Rocky" Gause completed a 159-day journey of more than 3,200 miles from the Philippines to northern Australia via Palawan, North Borneo, Tawi, and Makassar Strait.[100] Dodging violent storms and the Japanese navy, the two travelled from Corregidor on a twenty-foot sailboat rather than surrender. Delivered to Brisbane eleven days later, the barefoot and tattered escapees reported to MacArthur, who exclaimed, "Well, I'll be damned."[101] The two men provided the "first direct personal information from the Philippines" delivered to SPWA.

Major Ind and Maj. Joseph McMicking Jr. had been working on a plan since July to insert agents into Mindanao. On 21 October the AIB created a special Philippine subsection under Ind to supply, fund, and communicate with the guerrillas.[102] The section reworked the plans for: "a) re-establishment of radio communications with the Islands; b) intelligence collection by means of clandestine agents or parties; c) establishment of escape routes for [allied prisoners]; and d) establishment of lists of emergency supplies to be run into the Islands by air or submarine."[103]

At Amberly Field near Brisbane, McMicking introduced Ind to Captain Jesus Villamor, famous for shooting down two Zero fighters in an antiquated P-26. Villamor made it known that he wanted to go back to the Philippines, and Ind arranged for his transfer to the 81st Air Depot Group. The AIB then promoted Villamor to major.[104] Days later he was at his new desk when AIB controller Colonel Roberts handed him a directive initialed "O.K. MacA." It listed several specified tasks for Operation Planet: establish a military intelligence network with communications throughout the islands; develop a covert "subversive activities and propaganda" organization; establish contact with individuals known to be loyal; conduct an "intelligence survey" of Japanese political, civil, and military intentions; and report on "Japanese military, naval, air strengths; dispositions, equipment, quality, morale, training etc."[105] Villamor instantly accepted the mission.

SWPA denied a request from Villamor to recruit friends in the United States, including Massachusetts Institute of Technology graduate Luis Lim and Annapolis-trained Roberto Lim, the sons of General Vincente Lim. Instead, he spent six days traveling Australia and evaluating hundreds of Filipino volunteers before selecting eight finalists for special training: Rodolfo Ignacio, Delfin YuHico, Patricio Jorge, Dominador Malic, Emilio Quinto, Susano Amodia, Virgilio Felix, and Pedro Cariago.[106] At Victoria Barracks in Brisbane, Australian army captain Allan Davidson led the men in mornings of physical training and courses on infiltration techniques, navigation, and sabotage, followed by afternoons and evenings learning Morse code, cypher systems, and radio communications.[107]

The AIB recognized that long-distance radios would be critical to Villamor's mission.[108] Available radios used shortwave frequencies (1.6 to 30 megahertz) that travelled by either low-power ground waves limited to five to ten miles range or higher power skywaves that at certain times could bounce off the ionosphere for thousands of miles. To employ skywave, however, operators had to calculate frequencies, signal path, interference from solar radiation, and antennae length. The better trained the operator, the better the chance of success.

The AIB equipped the Planet team with civilian radios used by Allied coast watchers: the Australian 3BZ and ATR4.[109] The roughly two-hundred-pound Amalgamated Wireless 3BZ used batteries or a pedal generator and fit into three sixteen-by-ten-by-ten-inch steel boxes that passed nicely through a submarine hatch.[110] Most importantly, the 3BZ was mildew-, rot-, and fungus-resistant. The Radio Corporation of Melbourne's "tropic-proofed" ATR4 (Australian Transmitter/Receiver Model 4 portable radio) weighed twenty-three pounds and fit into a backpack.[111] For both radios, power limited range. The fifteen-watt 3BZs normally had a range of about four hundred miles.[112] The 1.5-watt ATR4s had shorter range, although some agents reported "surprising results of over several hundred miles."[113] To span the 3,600 miles to Australia, Planet carried an 80-watt transmitter specially built by the U.S. Army Signal Corps.[114] Emilio Quinto, former communication officer on *Don Isidro* and a wireless station on *Arcturus*, would operate it.[115] Later teams would carry the commercially available long-range HT-9 transmitters built by Hallicrafters of Chicago, Dutch-built 30-watt NEI-II/IIIs, or specially built radios for use as relay base stations.[116]

Submarines were harder for the AIB to get. MacArthur's staff had to barter with the Navy for the Southwest Pacific Force's twenty submarines in Australia—twelve in Brisbane.[117] "In return for submarine assistance, it was agreed to obtain for the Navy specific naval information," they noted, "and to establish coast-watch stations at points specified by Navy to provide information on shipping lanes and traffic densities, and later to provide targets for submarines."[118] Wary of "the somewhat uncertain military capacity of Philippine guerrillas at this time," the AIB worked with the Army Signal Corps to prepare distinct radio networks for their insertion teams, the coast watchers, and the guerrillas.[119] From the start, SWPA wanted an intelligence network free from guerrilla involvement.

It is notable that Washington forfeited potentially valuable assistance for AIB operations because of racial policies. Director of the office of war information Elmer Davis asked Roosevelt to allow Japanese-Americans to enlist in the military to counter Japanese propaganda that framed the war as a racial conflict in "the Philippines, Burma, and elsewhere."[120] Powerful opposition within the administration nevertheless restricted Japanese-Americans to support and intelligence roles.[121]

CENTRAL LUZON, D308/R-741

On 1 October Moses proclaimed himself commander of all guerrillas in north Luzon in a new organization he called the United States Army Forces in the Philippines, North Luzon (USAFIP-NL).[122] This now included Ablan and Praeger in Apayao; Enriquez's 14th Infantry in Nueva Vizcaya; George Barnett in La Union; Lapham and Charles Cushing in Pangasinan and Nueva Ecija; Dennis Molintas in Benguet; and Volckmann, with Blackburn as his executive officer, around Benguet.[123] Moses ordered all units to attack the Japanese on 15 October.[124]

Volckmann arrived at Tocod on 11 October to coordinate with Baldwin. One hour after midnight on 15 October, Baldwin attacked and destroyed the Japanese garrisons at Sanhiglo and Balatoc that guarded the Itogon mines.[125] Volckmann wrote: "I had now only to wait for reports from the other areas and hope that our plans had been carried out there with equal success."[126]

Volckmann sent Blackburn to select a new base and arrange another meeting with Moses and Noble before heading off to use Praeger's radio to inform Australia of his attacks.[127] Praeger reported that his

Cagayan-Apayao force held off the Japanese and protected local free government. He added: "I can organize 5,000 able-bodied trainees, R.O.T.C.s and intelligence men provided we would be furnished arms and ammunition."[128] He also informed MacArthur that Moses and Noble had escaped capture on Bataan and had organized six thousand guerrillas north of Manila.[129] The AIB moved to work out a code with Praeger to send him priority intelligence requirements. Two days later, Moses and Noble visited Volckmann on their way to Praeger's radio.[130]

Blackburn feared the 15 October attacks had only "alerted the Japs to presence of the guerrillas."[131] Volckmann went to meet him at Uding and became the guest of honor at a surprise birthday party held by the American refugees. Afterward, he reflected on his situation and became troubled: "To my mind it was just a question of time and how much the Japs would take before they came boiling out into the mountains to try to wipe out the guerrilla menace."[132]

Traveling to Bodok, Volckmann noticed many deserted huts—a sign the Japanese were about. He found the Lusod sawmill badly damaged and looted but decided to make it his new base. Over the next week Blackburn put the camp in order and restored phone lines. With bodyguards Bruno and Emilio, they welcomed a mine mechanic named Deleon, an elderly native woman who served as their cook, and a young man who volunteered as a guide. Volckmann offered scrip to local leaders for men and supplies, promising reimbursement from the U.S. government.[133]

Then the Japanese counterattacked. In the first week of November they forced Baldwin's guerrillas out of the gold mining area south of Baguio. Patrols moved south through Bodok and appeared on the west bank of the Agno River. They moved in force against Volckmann in Lusod. Shells hit the camp. "This convinced me," he noted, "that they had definite information about our presence and the location of our headquarters."[134] From 10 to 15 November Volckmann retreated farther up the mountains and watched the enemy question natives about him and Blackburn by name. "Well, they were constant," recalled Blackburn. "And, boy, they were everywhere."[135] A patrol of fifty troops passed within a stone's throw of the Americans' hiding spot. On the sixth day, the Japanese—Volckmann counted 350 soldiers—departed.

Volckmann moved his group to Uding, which they found ransacked and burnt. They then headed north. "The Japanese were still in the area," he reported, "and as we went along we could see numerous native villages going up in smoke."[136] He pushed on to Equip to link up with Moses and Noble and found the village empty and smoldering. Volckmann retreated south toward Ifugao while spreading the word that he was continuing north. "Through bitter experience we had learned never to disclose our true route to the natives," he wrote. "Though the majority of them were quite loyal, Japanese torture had a way of making them talk."[137]

PANAY, D329/R-720

The Japanese Fourteenth Army transferred the Hitomi Propaganda Platoon to Panay to support the 170th Independent Infantry Battalion at Iloilo, Capiz, and San Jose. Their task was formidable: separate the people from increasingly strong guerrilla units. Unlike Luzon, where diverse native ethnic groups had long adapted to living among a strong foreign administration, the people on Panay were more homogenous and independent. Convinced that his higher headquarters would not appreciate his "sit out the war" arguments, Hitomi camouflaged his pitch. When the imperial headquarters sent two female reporters, Kikuko Kawakami and Tsuyako Abe, to report on field propaganda efforts, Hitomi arranged a charade. He gave locals an impassioned speech in Japanese about the Greater East Asia Co-Prosperity Sphere while his interpreter delivered his "wait and see" speech in the natives' language.[138] The reporters left unaware of the deception. Hitomi received credit for the surrender of thirty American officers and one thousand guerrillas.[139]

Japanese occupation practices continually undermined Hitomi's efforts. As Blackburn reported, "When the Japs came they mistreated the hell out of the people in those barrios where Americans had been, and the natives who had fed them, or in any way had indicated that they were sympathetic to the guerrillas."[140] In Iloilo, Japanese soldiers grabbed sleeping thirteen-year-old Tomasa Solingnog when her father jumped to her defense. "My father was struck with a sword by Captain Hiruka," she recalled. "I ran to where he lay and embraced him only to find out that his head was already severed from his body. I cried hysterically, but the Japanese mercilessly dragged me out of our house."[141] They took her to a two-story home with a bathroom in every room that housed many women. At least four men raped her each day and forced her to do laundry. "I cannot remember for how long I was inside the mess house," she later testified, "because I felt that I was already losing my mind. I'd always remember my father and then I'd cry."[142] She eventually escaped, only to be caught by a Japanese officer who made her his mistress and servant. Stories such as hers radiated across extended Filipino kinship networks.

In need of SWPA support, Peralta had the head of the bureau of posts radio station in Iloilo, Mariano Tolentino, move a transmitter to his headquarters in Sara, but it could not reach Australia.[143] Tolentino then secured a more powerful transmitter from an abandoned British freighter. On 30 October he broadcasted uncoded messages for MacArthur and Quezon that were picked up by KFS in San Francisco, which relayed them to Royal Australian Air Force station KAZ in Darwin the next night.[144]

Peralta claimed to command eight thousand guerrillas and announced: "[We] control all Panay interior and west coast. Civilians and officials ninety-nine percent loyal. Supplies could be dropped [by aircraft] away from towns, and subs could make coast anywhere more than twenty miles distant from [larger towns]."[145] To SPWA, this seemed too good to be true. In Brisbane, Merle-Smith told MacArthur the message was "probably bona fide, but mixed with exaggeration."[146] In Washington, Colonel Evans asked Chick Parsons if the message might be a Japanese trick. Parsons thought it probably authentic but said the only way to know for certain was to send someone into the Philippines. Evans asked if he was volunteering, and Parsons answered that he probably was.[147] By 17 December Parsons was on his way to Brisbane.[148]

Still suspicious of a Japanese ruse, KAZ did not respond to Peralta until 5 November, when it informed him that his message had been received and passed to MacArthur. Knowing Peralta was without a cipher, SWPA hesitated to communicate further. Peralta signaled: "All codes destroyed before surrender but we have cipher device M-94. We have sweated blood to contact you and tell you our needs. Are you going to let us down now [?]"[149] Peralta suggested SWPA contact his old division staff school classmate Lieutenant Colonel Jaime Velasquez, who was traveling with President Quezon to obtain a "key phrase for cipher device M-94."[150]

The war department notified SWPA of their efforts in "developing possibility of cryptographic system with both Peralta and Praeger."[151] After a few more weeks KFS forwarded to Peralta a message from the war department: "Break the coded message using as key word in combination cipher device M-94 followed by double transposition in the name of place where President Quezon and Governor Confesor last dined together?"[152] It was several weeks before the Panay guerrilla solved the riddle and constructed a code for secure communications.

Peralta sought SWPA's approval to unite all Philippine guerrillas into a Fourth Philippine Corps under his command.[153] He had already reached out to Abcede and Ausejo on Negros, Miranda on Leyte, and Merritt on Samar, placed the 61st Division under Relunia, and—he thought—cut an agreement with Fertig. His claim of eight thousand men certainly impressed MacArthur.[154] The Japanese only had eight hundred troops on Panay. On the other hand, Peralta reported that he had declared martial law and had captured and sentenced to death Panay's puppet governor,

"Hernandez of Capiz." This posed legal problems. SWPA responded: "As regards your military forces your authority is defined by military laws and regulations with which you are acquainted. As regards civilian communities and populations you have no authority except that which permits you to take action to preserve the safety of your forces."[155]

Peralta's communications indicated something else: he had no Americans in his organization. This was deliberate, because he wanted to better position Filipinos for independence after the war. The combination of Peralta's apparent braggadocio, extralegal acts, and hyper-nationalism concerned SWPA and led Ind to urge that any parties inserted into the Philippines avoid "contacts and possible entanglements with the undoubtedly energetic and ambitious Peralta."[156]

SWPA would later report: "In the exchange of messages with GHQ during November, December, and January, Peralta apparently assumed that GHQ had no radio contact with or knowledge of Fertig."[157] His efforts to command all the islands raised the possibility that he could someday take the Philippines out of the war by accommodation with the collaborationist government or the Japanese, or even pose postwar problems for U.S. policies. Such fears made for an uneasy relationship between SWPA and Peralta.

VISAYAS, D335/R-714

Mindoro tempted Peralta. The Japanese had easily chased its small constabulary into the hills, where they coalesced into a guerrilla band. "Many reports on guerrilla activities in Mindoro are unclear or ambiguous, but it is clear the conflicting ambitions of guerrilla leaders have led to increasing friction between groups and have prevented effective unification of command," U.S. Army intelligence observed.[158]

One of the largest Mindoro groups was under constabulary commander Major Ramon Ruffy who was an outsider Batangueño from Luzon. A rival group formed under Captain Esteban Beloncio, an army reservist and school principal in Oriental. Ruffy had the loyalty of the constabulary; Beloncio had the people. In September, American army radio technician Sergeant Charles H. Hickok arrived and organized about thirty other Filipinos, but the larger organizations undermined him. In November, Hickock reached out to Peralta, who authorized him to take charge on Mindoro under the Fourth Philippine Corps. Peralta then replaced Hickok with a Filipino.

On Negros, Abcede continued to build a force near Tanjay, while Torres battled the Japanese near Buenavista. By November Abcede claimed seven thousand followers, although many were family members, and he received an offer from his old classmate Peralta for a promotion to lieutenant colonel in his corps. At Peralta's urging, Abcede tried to recruit Ausejo to his south and Mata to his north.[159]

On Romblon, Philippine merchant marine Captain Constantine C. Raval had been allied with Peralta since March. By November he had organized a small, fragile band of guerrillas who had little to do. Still, Peralta valued Romblon as a strategic stepping-stone toward Luzon and gladly absorbed Raval into his Fourth Philippine Corps.

Only Marinduque, north of Panay and east of Mindoro, eluded Peralta. Japanese troops had landed there on 7 July and forced the small constabulary garrison under Lieutenant Sofronio T. Untalan to surrender. Peralta would insert agents in early 1943 to gain of control Marinduque as another stepping-stone to Luzon and would have Lieutenant Colonel Enrique Jurado bring back Hickok from Tablas Island to organize stopovers for agents.

During the summer, lawyer and congressional representative Cecilio A. Maneja returned from Leyte to his home on Bohol and gathered men into an East Bohol battalion. Seeing how divided and mutually suspicious the island's other guerrilla groups were, he arranged a meeting of all leaders at Batuan in November. The conferees agreed to unite all guerrillas under Philippine army major Ismael Ingeniero from Luzon and form a free government on the island.

LUZON, D329/R-720

The Japanese continued to campaign across northern Luzon. "They were often led by Filipinos who knew the trails throughout the area where we were operating," Blackburn recalled. "And from November 1942 to August 1943, the Japs were constantly mopping up the mountains and coastal areas."[160]

A Filipino claiming to be a Captain Edades walked into Lapham's headquarters. Several native guerrillas recognized him as a Philippine army officer who had attended West Point. He looked and talked the part. Lapham gave Edades a command north of Umingan, where he began eliminating collaborationist Ganaps. Pleased, Lapham sent Federico Doliente with guerrillas to assist Edades against the Japanese. Edades instead ordered Doliente to attack a fellow guerrilla, the young Telesforo Palaruan. "Fortunately," Lapham recalled, "Doliente knew his own countrymen better than I did."[161] Doliente hesitated and talked to Lapham. Together they confronted Edades. "It was soon evident that he was not the real Captain Edades at all but a mere con man," Lapham recalled.[162] The imposter fled a short distance and continued to rob local citizens. "This time we brought his career to a sudden end, which so outraged his wife that she threatened to take the whole story to the Japanese," Lapham reported before adding ominously, "Whether she would have done so, nobody knows, for she abruptly disappeared and was never seen again."[163]

About this time Ramsey received an invitation to meet a colonel from Wainwright's staff who was in hiding. Though emaciated by malaria and dysentery and down to 120 pounds, Ramsey rode a carabao sled to the nice home of a wealthy Filipino planter where the colonel resided with half a dozen other American officers. The soldiers, wearing repaired and pressed khaki uniforms, were in far better shape than their visitor. Ramsey explained the organization Thorp had built and offered to transport them back with him. After a pause the colonel said, "I knew Thorp before the war. Good man. Do give him my regards when you see him."[164] Feeling worse for his effort, Ramey made the long ride back to camp alone, resentful of the men who chose comfort over duty.

MINDANAO, D334/R-715

Reestablishing MacArthur's prewar designation, Fertig renamed his command the 10th Military Independent District. His situation was good. Schools had not yet reopened, but that helped recruitment. Food was plentiful: there were pineapples from Del Monte plantations near Cagayan de Misamis, potatoes and vegetables from the Bukidnon hills near Talakag and Claveris, and coffee and rice from the Panguil Bay area and east coast of Surigao. He started clearing carabao trails from Misamis Oriental and Balingasag into Bukidnon to transport salt and the chinchona bark needed to combat malaria. Trails from Talakag would be used to transport food.

Fertig went with Morgan to Vatali to recruit a guerrilla group. Morgan then went on to Zamboanga and sent Lieutenant Abdulrahim Imao, a Moro from Jolo, to organize guerillas on Sulu. Imao took with him Sergeant Ursula Simpek and, in December, moved to Siasi to organize a few armed guerrillas and attack a weak Japanese garrison. On Christmas they captured thirty rifles and some ammunition and then held together against aggressive Japanese counterattacks.

SOUTHERN LUZON, D336/R-713

In Bicol, Dinasco Dianela led guerrillas on the east coast near Caramoan. He claimed to have been a U.S. Army captain and had commanded sixty-five men at Naga in May. When the Japanese counterattacked in June,

Dianela reached a truce with them that held until November, when the Japanese again began arresting and harassing civilians. Now, from his base in Camp Tinawagan, Dianela prepared to go back on the warpath.

To the west, on 8 November Miranda led sixty-seven TVGU men in a two-and-a-half hour ambush of a Japanese convoy in Taguild in which they killed the Japanese commander in Naga, Colonel Susumo Takechi, 2 captains, 2 lieutenants, and between 168 and 200 enlisted men.[165] Five days later, the commander in Libmanan, Colonel Inuye, sent a letter to "Capt. MIRANDA BANDIT CAPTAIN": "You forget that you are Filipino, an Oriental. You want to serve the white people who had escaped already from the Orient. Bear in mind that we are determined to have peace and order in the place at all costs, even to the extent of sacrificing worthless lives."[166]

Japanese units in Camarines Sur ordered residents of Libmanan, Pamplona, Sipocot, Lupi, Ragay, Del Gallego, Gainza, Camaligan, Cabuso, San Fernando, Milaor, Minalabac, and Bula to concentrate in their town centers within seventy-two hours. After three days, paid informers led soldiers, Ganaps, and collaborationist constabulary troops in a two-week sweep of the mountains in search of guerrillas. "They killed unknowing men, women, and children of all ages whom they chanced upon," Barremeda reported, "torched even the lowliest hut and shack; slaughtered farm animals; and destroyed crops and other food sources."[167]

CENTRAL LUZON, D358/R-691

In Manila on 30 November, the JMA department of general affairs head Colonel Utsunomiya met with his branch chiefs to examine how the USAFFE guerrillas coordinated their activities. He announced that the JMA had to refocus on economic exploitation. Utsunomiya prioritized the extraction of copper but added: "The conditions under which such developed mineral resources are being transported to Japan cannot be termed favorable, and I see no room for optimism in the future."[168] They had to overcome the resistance.

Force favored the Japanese. Conditions favored the guerrillas. The Japanese sought to tip this balance with networks of informers. Volckmann described their methodology. First, they gained the support of a prominent citizen, usually with money or favors. The prominent citizen would then recruit others thought to be vulnerable to persuasion. They in turn monitored others' behavior. "This system became so effective in some areas," Volckmann noted, "that civilians could not cooperate with the guerrillas without being reported to the Japs."[169]

By this time the collaborationist Ganap and Sakdal farmers' movement, once praised by American governor-general Frank Murphy, had established a new identity.[170] Panlilio explained, "There had been a reason for their discontent. Under the cacique system—an absentee landlord system—they had labored in an economic slavery that had kept them in debt years ahead of their hours."[171] The peasants had been exploited with little food, money, or respect. When Benigno Ramos turned Ganap and Sakdal rosters over to the Japanese, "Few could escape collaboration even if they would, the majority believed that their day had come."[172] They became a Japanese-trained "Philippine Fifth Column" given free range to loot their countrymen.[173]

On the war's first anniversary, the Japanese mandated participation of all government employees in a big parade in Manila. Vargas gave a speech: "It is our great fortune that the Imperial Japanese Forces have shown a deep sympathy and complete understanding of our erroneous conduct."[174] Authorities ordered free streetcar rides and free showings of a documentary on the bombing of Pearl Harbor at the Lyric movie theater. However, an attendee recalled, "When President Roosevelt's picture was shown, the audience clapped and cheered but when Hirohito's picture was flashed, no applause. The Japanese officers pounded the floor with their sabers until the lights came on and the audience driven out of the show."[175]

The veneer of celebration failed to cover deepening antagonisms. According to Villamor, "One year after the Japanese entry into the city, murder, rape, and attacks on small children were still commonplace."[176] Furthermore, a historian noted, "With the press completely in their hands, the Japanese began to exercise thought control."[177] "All books must pass through their hands," Pacita Pestano-Jacinto wrote. "It is not salable unless it has the violet 'passed' stamp."[178] The military censored the press and put all newspapers under the direction of the Manila Simbun-sya run by the *Osaka Mainichi* and the *Tokyo Nichi*. "The new company," the Japanese announced, "has been established for the purpose of further clarifying the invulnerable position of the Nippon Empire, now in the midst of the creation of the New Order in Greater East Asia, of making more thoroughly understood the purpose of the Military Administration in the Philippines, and of propelling with greater force the materialization of the New Philippines."[179]

Nearly simultaneously, the administration outlawed existing Philippine political parties and issued PEC executive order number 109 that created a new party called "the Association for Service to the New Philippines" (*Kapisanan ng Paglilingkod sa Bagong Pilipinas*), better known by the acronym KALIBAPI. Secretary of agriculture and commerce Benigno Aquino became director-general of the KALIBAPI.[180] He quickly declared,

"The KALIBAPI seeks to eradicate the physically debilitating effects of Occidental vices by encouraging manly sports and games, outdoor activities and closer kindship to the son and soil of the land."[181] Two days later the PEC announced the party would "assist the Filipino in fully comprehending the significance of, and in strengthening his adherence to, the Co-Prosperity Sphere of Greater East Asia by subordinating himself and his interests to those of the Philippines."[182]

NORTHERN LUZON, D366/R-683

On 8 December Volckmann and Blackburn, although suffering a malaria attack, took up residence in a thatch hut in a new camp near Kiangan. Nearby were three American women, United Evangelical Church missionaries Myrtle Metzger and Lottie Spessard, and Mrs. Anna Kluge, wife of a missing American lumberman and guerrilla captain.[183] Spessard, a nurse, looked after Blackburn. Indispensable aide Bruno travelled in and out Ifugao where his father had once been a chief and secured supplies on credit through a local man, Mr. Herrin, who also brought sugar, beans, cooking grease, coffee, tobacco, and soap.[184] Bruno also acquired native wine known as *tapoy* boiled from rice, drained under banana leaves, and fermented for several days. Through trial and error, Volckmann happily discovered that a powder resulting from that process was good for making ersatz hotcakes.

The nearly ninety-year-old Chief Timicpao of Kiangan was a relative of Bruno. "He wore a G-string, had all kinds of gold nuggets draped around his neck, as was extremely alert and astute," recalled Blackburn.[185] Timicpao offered his full support to the Americans and helped build their camp. He also warned of a fiercely belligerent chief named Kimayong in neighboring Haliap. Volckmann and Blackburn decided to visit this chief and found him to be about thirty years old, short, and mild tempered. He told them, "You're not secure where you are. I want you to come and live at my place. You don't want to live in this camp."[186] The Americans negotiated a truce between the rival chiefs and enjoyed support from both.

Bruno brought news that the Japanese were conducting a strong propaganda campaign advertising a parade of military victories and cajoling Filipinos to join in the greater co-prosperity sphere. Their theme: "The Americans will never be able to return to the Philippines—they have been defeated at the hands of the Japanese Imperial Forces."[187] They also renewed offers of amnesty to Filipinos who surrendered, turned in arms, or handed over Americans.

Spessard, Metzger, and Kluge introduced Volckmann and Blackburn to a trusted merchant named Formuka. He led them to a man named

Lanag who ran the city dispensary and could get medicine.[188] The two contacts relayed information about everyone in town. "There were a lot of Philippine Scouts and Philippine Constabulary in the area who had their weapons," Blackburn noted. "They were apprehensive as to what the Japanese were going to do."[189] About thirty of the well-trained former troopers joined Volckmann's ranks.

The Japanese had put three new bureau of constabulary companies—filled by recently released Filipino POWs—in Blackburn's district at Bontoc, Lubuagan, and Kiangnan. "They were the sons, uncles, grandfathers, fathers, or whatever, of the people that we had, and they knew this interior better than we did," observed Blackburn. "So, I said, 'I've got a problem. I've got to get control of that Constabulary.'"[190] He learned that the commander in Kiangnan, Captain Emiliano Dunuan, and his sergeant, Pedro Dunuan, were fellow veterans of the 11th Infantry Regiment. Blackburn invited them to patrol his area so that they could meet. He told them, "This is kind of silly, you're looking for us. Why don't we help each other and when the time comes, I'll induct you into the Army and you'll be one of my battalions or companies?"[191] They agreed.

VASAYAS, D370/R-679

On Leyte, Blas Miranda called a conference of the resistance groups around Ormoc to both expand his organization and dissuade banditry. The attendees, including Major Marcos Soliman and Captain Aristoteles Olaybar, agreed to work together in a new Western Leyte Guerrilla Warfare Force.[192] Under General Miranda, the force's six regiments recruited justices of the peace from each of their towns to serve as judge advocates.[193] Miranda also secured the cooperation of the former collaborationist mayor of Ormoc, Catalino Hermosilla. In return, some claimed, Miranda's guerrillas killed Hermosilla's "enemies."[194]

Meanwhile on Negros, Bell and Abcede again asked Gador to command the island's guerrillas. Gador again declined, claiming he first needed SWPA's invitation because he did not want to be held responsible for preexisting conflicts between guerrillas. Mata and Abcede then went to Peralta and joined his Fourth Philippine Corps. Peralta named Abcede commander of the 72nd Division (Negros) with Mata as both his chief of staff and regimental commander. Left out in the cold, on 11 December Gador issued a belated memorandum claiming command over all forces on Negros based on what he said was an appointment from General Sharp.

The next day KAZ in Darwin exchanged coded messages with Panay.[195] SWPA told Peralta, "As our intelligence unit covering the maximum territory you can perform great service."¹⁹⁶ He took this as authority to spread his network into Luzon. Bicol in the south and Batangas on the northwest coast seemed to be the most promising areas. The first required securing Masbate Island, then roiled by disputes among guerrillas. The second required control of Tablas Island and Mindoro or Marinduque.

Lapus received Peralta's emissary, Relunia, a fellow Bicolano who explained that, in accordance with MacArthur's wishes, Peralta needed an intelligence net on Luzon. He wanted Lapus to reassemble his men as the 3rd Battalion, 67th Infantry Regiment, 61st Division, Fourth Philippine Corps.¹⁹⁷ Lapus accepted both the assignment and a promotion to major and began forwarding all his reports to Panay.

Salvador Escudero had been serving Lapus as governor and providing him with P20,000 from provincial funds. Suddenly, Escudero accused Lapus of "embezzlement and banditry" and broke with the guerrilla leader. He then accepted an offer delivered by Crisoldo de la Paz from Colonel Straughn to serve as a colonel in the Fil-American Irregular Troops. Taking with him the 17-man bodyguard provided by Lapus, Escudero began building what would become the most powerful guerrilla force in Sorsogon, peaking at 1,500 men, and soon began fighting pitched battles against Lapus.

MacArthur, then at Port Moresby, mulled over Peralta's effort to take "command of the fighters in the Visayas."¹⁹⁸ On 17 December the SWPA commander radioed Peralta: "You will continue to exercise command. Primary mission is to maintain your organization and secure maximum amount of information. [Combat] activities should be postponed until ordered from here. Premature action of this kind will only bring heavy retaliation upon innocent people."¹⁹⁹ This contradicted guerrilla orthodoxy. As Mao had argued, attacks were crucial to maintain the people's support, and the loss of popular support led to "the danger of defeat and destruction."²⁰⁰

"We could give peasants a reason to be grateful to us," Lapham explained, "we could stimulate their loyalty to their own government and to the United States, and we could cause them to fear us more than our foes."²⁰¹ They needed to demonstrate their ability to attack the enemy. As Fertig put it: "The [Filipino] population wants to see dead Japs. Without public support, no guerrillas."²⁰² Lapham added, "In crises, notoriously, people everywhere look not for more discussion but for leaders who will reassure them and then act."²⁰³ Radios, however, had placed the guerrillas firmly within MacArthur's chain of command, subjecting them to higher priorities than their own.

MacArthur further restricted Peralta: "You cannot—repeat cannot—operate under provisions of martial law in the Philippines occupied as they are by the enemy. It is not—repeat not—practicable to issue money."²⁰⁴

SWPA instructed Peralta to pay his guerrillas with certificates to be honored by the United States and promised to review the matter in later messages. These instructions unwittingly favored Governor Confesor in his power struggle with Peralta. Three days later, SWPA received a response: "Field Marshal MacArthur from Lieutenant Colonel Peralta. Missions assigned us will be accomplished. Humblest soldier had blind faith in you and America."[205] "Field Marshal" was, of course, the rank MacArthur had worn before the war when he worked only for Quezon.

SWPA passed another message to Peralta: "Authority to Combat Team Leaders to execute spies by 'drum-head Court Martial' is not authorized by our Rules of Land Warfare."[206] Villamor later learned that Willoughby privately described the guerrilla executions as "probably ample to make some of our departed Judge Advocates General stir restlessly in the graves."[207] Lapham, among others, had accepted as immutable fact that guerrilla war was "a mean, dirty, brutal struggle to the death, devoid of any principle or sentiment save to survive and win."[208]

Guerrillas had neither the food nor the manpower to keep prisoners. Ramsey remarked: "Each unit was dealing with the issue on its own, which meant that some prisoners were being executed while others were being released. In the latter case the result was almost always raids, which meant the capture, torture, and killing of our own people."[209] He issued instructions: "It is the policy of the guerrilla forces to execute prisoners who threaten us. There is nothing else we can do."[210] Ramsey later explained, "Consequently, whenever one of our units captured a Japanese or a Filipino collaborator or spy, he was interrogated briefly and then killed."[211]

The guerrillas also dealt harshly with spies, collaborators, and turncoats. Ramon Magsaysay recalled orders from Captain Ralph Maguire to liquidate any captured collaborators.[212] Volckmann recalled, "Those who were spying for the Japs were apprehended and eliminated; every effort was made to find the kingpins in every spy net that was uncovered."[213] Killing a Filipino, however, could bring retribution from his whole kinship network. Magsaysay warned McGuire: "Liquidate one member of a family, and his entire tribe will turn against us and our cause."[214]

SWPA, of course, could never authorize such extreme actions, and the guerrillas risked severe punishment under the Uniform Code of Military Justice. "I knew the Japanese would almost certainly execute me if they ever caught me," wrote Lapham, "but that my own country might punish me after the war for fighting the enemy I simply could not imagine."[215] By keeping the guerrillas separate from his army—not providing pay and allowances—MacArthur actually protected them from legal penalties for their actions.

The blood sport of guerrilla warfare had its own way of reckoning. Ramsey witnessed an execution in Colonel Manahan's Mountain Corps Regiment. Standing over the kneeling prisoner, the executioner thrust a bayonet down behind the left collarbone into the heart. "The man died almost instantly," Ramsey observed.[216] Silently, the executioner wiped the blood off his bayonet with a palm leaf and went back to his daily duties. Ramsey later saw that the executioner was an undersized fifteen-year-old boy whom the men feared. He haunted Ramsey. "He was the executioner," he wrote, "but it was I who had created the policy. He was merely the instrument of my own decision, one that involved a violence more intimate and personal than anything else I had experienced in the course of the war."[217]

LUZON, D378/R-671

TVGU leader Miranda sent Lieutenant Vicente Villa from Bicol north to San Narciso, Tayabas, to seek out Captain Epifano Vera in hopes of securing weapons. Villa discovered the captain had been captured and executed by the Japanese. Gaudencio V. Vera, a former cook with the Philippine Scouts who escaped from Bataan to his home, Lucena, now ran the Tayabas guerrillas under an assumed rank of general. When Villa addressed the new leader without reference to this rank, Vera had him arrested and executed. "How Sergeant Vera managed to assume Captain Vera's position taxes the imagination," commented Barrameda.[218]

Miranda accepted an invitation from Captain Lorenzo Padua of the Camp Isarog guerrillas to meet at Camp Isarog II and arrange a merger of their groups. Leaving Leon Aureus in temporary command, Miranda departed on 20 December with an armed escort and arrived at Padua's camp midday on Christmas. The next day the two leaders agreed to bring Padua's Isarog guerrillas into the TVGU, with Miranda in overall command and Padua as his deputy. In Barrameda's words: "The protocol was prepared on sheets of ruled pad paper by a strikingly beautiful intelligence officer in Padua's camp, Lieutenant Constancia Estrada from the town of Baao, Camarines Sur."[219] The teenage Estrada, already a veteran of several guerrilla bands, had been twice captured and had even witnessed her brother killed while helping her on an escape. She was in Japanese hands on 8 December when Padua freed her while capturing Japanese interpreter Denzo Kuriyama. Padua executed Kuriyama. Miranda fell in love with Estrada at first sight and decided to remain a while longer at Padua's camp.

AUSTRALIA, D378/R-671

The day Miranda departed for Camp Isarog II, Lieutenant Franklyn H. Young Jr. with his wife and child, Albert Klestadt, three Moro crewmen, and another woman arrived at the coast of Australia after a five-month voyage aboard a forty-five-foot boat. Young was an American mestizo in the Philippine army who had spent time with Thorp. He had left Bicol in July and travelled through Samar, Leyte, Cebu, Negros, and Panay, where he linked up with German-born Klestadt, an experienced yachtsman wanted by the Japanese for his work for the British ministry of information in Manila.[220] They sailed to Zamboanga and Australia. Young brought with him a report from Thorp for MacArthur telling of "large guerrilla groups existing in central Luzon" and "important and lucid information of enemy and guerrilla activity in the areas through which they passed."[221] Taken to Melbourne, the two escapees briefed the G-2. From Young and Klestadt, Villamor "learned that the guerrillas they had seen were disorganized, ragged and hungry, moving about in small arguing groups, and desperate for some sign of recognition."[222]

By now Villamor had whittled his team to five: Delfin YuHico, Patricio Jorge, Dominador Malic, Emilio Quinto, and Rodolfo Ignacio.[223] In Brisbane on 27 December they disguised themselves as cargo handlers and boarded the submarine SS-211 *Gudgeon*.[224] Before departing, Villamor met with MacArthur, who told him, "I shall see you when you come back. Better yet, I shall see you upon my return to the Philippines."[225] That night they departed for the islands.

LUZON, D389/R-660

From Manila, Barker sent word to Ramsey that all was well and that he was swearing in guerrillas recruited by Santos and Alberto. Barker then relayed news of Thorp's capture and his own assumption of command of the Luzon Guerrilla Force. Ramsey was now head of the ECLGF. "I ought to congratulate you," Barker wrote, "since, according to our agents in Manila, you are now number two, behind me, on the Kempeitai's death list."[226] Ramsey learned too that west-central Luzon guerrilla leader Captain Ralph McGuire was dead. He somberly noted, "One of his own men had cut his head off and taken it to the Japanese. . . .We were not, as Mao had suggested, fish in the sea. . . . we were minnows in an ocean infested with sharks."[227]

Ramsey wanted to follow Barker to Manila but deemed it too dangerous. Under new counterintelligence chief Lieutenant General Kamekau

Baba, Kempeitai chief Nagahama had stepped up his program of spies, raids, rewards, and torture.[228] Baba ordered Nagahama to use Sakdalistas to create a network of informants known as the Makapili—"out-and-out individual collaborators with the Japanese" reporting directly to Baba.[229] Laurel protested this "volunteer militia of opportunists and Japanophiles" that Nicholas Tarling described as "the kind of people the elite had feared."[230] They were effective. Within two months Baba had a composite sketch of Ramsey on his desk and a P250,000 bounty on his head.

After organizing the ECLGF in Bataan, Ramsey headed north to find Lapham and Charles Putnam, a hard-drinking American mining engineer who did double duty in the Army reserve. Putnam had spent most of his forty-odd years in the Philippines, accepted a commission as an artillery captain on Bataan, and organized guerrillas in the Lingayen Gulf. "He had lived among the Filipinos, obviously liked them, and understood them well," Lapham noted, "He behaved toward them like an amiable despot and was extremely popular with his 'subjects.'"[231]

MINDANAO, D389/R-660

On Mindanao, Jordan Hamner and Charles Smith reunited with Chick Smith, who they found working for Morgan. For two months, the three men pestered Fertig with a plan to sail to Australia when the monsoons began. Though he thought their scheme foolhardy, Fertig eventually gave his okay. Their first attempt failed after two days at sea, and they returned to make better preparations.[232] Hamner and the Smiths reinforced a twenty-one-foot sailboat that Morgan had acquired in Naga, and locals supplied an eight-horsepower kerosene engine for use when the winds slackened. Two Filipinos joined the crew: a Moro named Lakibul Nastail, and a Christian named Eugenio S. Catalina. On 4 December they set sail from Labangan in the boat they renamed *Or Else*. Before they cast off, Fertig whispered to Charlie Smith a radio call sign only the two of them would know. If Smith made it to Australia, he was to radio back using the call sign "MSF" which stood for "Mindanao-Smith-Fertig."[233]

Against all odds, *Or Else* arrived off Australia on 31 December.[234] The crew had sailed through the Celebes Seas and the Morotai Straits, stopped for food and water in New Guinea and the island of Kai, and then ran straight south to Australia's Cobourg Peninsula. Along the way they managed to stay one step ahead of Japanese ships, dehydration, starvation, and hostile natives. After going ashore for water, they headed west, came to the Cape Don lighthouse, and at 0300 hours on New Year's Day made contact with coast watchers. An Australian patrol boat delivered them to Darwin three days later.[235] On 12 January Hamner and Smith reported to SWPA the existence of Fertig's Mindanao guerrillas. MacArthur's G-2 reported: "This development was an important link in the future plans of intelligence coverage."[236]

After Morgan completed his recruitment tour of Mindanao and returned to Misamis, Fertig sent him out again on 12 January with eighty men of the General Headquarters Expeditionary Force to recruit on Leyte and Negros. He tasked Morgan to spread the word that only guerrilla leaders with Fertig's USAFIP would be designated "authorized" commanders.

Fertig promoted 61st Division veteran Clyde C. Childress to lieutenant colonel and chief of staff of the 110th Division in Zamboanga. Childress had developed much of Fertig's supply operations: fuel and rice from Surigao carried up the Cadabaran road or sailed on bancas. Fertig also created a USAFIP navy with the large twin-mast motor banca *Athena* under Captain Vincente Zapanta as its flagship, armed with a homemade smoothbore cannon that was replaced later with a 20-mm cannon and .50-caliber machine guns.[237] (After several successful encounters with the Japanese, the crew would burn *Athena* in mid-1944 to prevent her capture.) Fertig's navy grew to include the inter-island passenger launch *Treasure Island* with its high superstructure and seventy-five-horsepower diesel engine, the light tug *Rosalia* with a fifty-horsepower engine, the motor banca *So What, Nara, CAPT Knortz,* and *Narwhal.*

Major Frank McCarthy Jr. organized guerrillas for Fertig in the Malangas area of southern Mindanao and quickly extended his command to the Kabasalan area, which was rich in rubber plantations. McCarthy's men actively collected latex to use in trade. By 1944 Fertig would incorporate the group as the 115th Regiment under Major Angel Medina.

In Cotabato Province, Pendatun remained outside Fertig's command. He had expanded his original Bolo battalion of Moros into a diverse Muslim-Christian guerrilla movement known as the Bukidnon-Cotabato force that controlled the Cotabato Valley and southern Bukidnon. In mid-January Pendatun attacked a Japanese garrison in Malaybalay from the south, but Bowler's promised support from the north never came, and the attacked failed.

In his diary on 6 January 1943 Fertig summarized reports from across the Philippines: U.S. submarines had forced Japanese ships to sail in the shallows; seventeen transports sat idle in Manila Bay awaiting repairs; the Japanese scrounged all the scrap metal they could find for shipment to Japan; a large, unexplained explosion occurred at Fort McKinley that reportedly killed "seven truck-loads of Japs"; Filipinos paid a 35 percent luxury tax on everything; the boulevards in Manila were empty.[238] He also noted a discussion between a Japanese engineer and a Filipino doctor: "Japan is now preparing for a long war, perhaps ten years. Manila is the paradise. In Japan everyone wears short pants with plenty of patches and no socks. Government ask more money but people cannot give for they do not have. Japan lacks raw material. No cotton, no iron. Dr. questions 'But Japan is winning war?' Oh, yes, but Americans very stubborn, will not hands up as Japan thought."[239]

6

The Aid

January–May 1943

LUZON, D393/R-656

On 4 January Japanese patrols captured the 121st Infantry Regiment's new commander, Captain William G. Peryam, in Abra Province. He joined Thorp, Nakar, and others in prison. Walter Cushing and Spies were dead. Negrito tribesmen had beheaded McGuire. The Fassoth camp lay in ashes, its proprietors in custody. Barker was on the run in Manila. Merrill hid in the Zambales, while Moses and Noble moved about in fits and starts. Volckmann and Blackburn stood ready to lead, but Ramsey and Lapham were not keen to follow.[1] Japanese units in Bicol harassed Dianela's Camp Tinawagan guerrillas south of Tabgan. On 7 January they raided Padua's camp in Balayan and shot Miranda in the left leg. His new love Estrada got him to Camp Isarog, where they would spend the next year together while Aureus ran the TVGU.

Ramsey and Captain John Boone made it to the coast of Bataan to recruit guerrillas. Boone was preoccupied with combating the Huks and dispersed his five regiments to their homes. Villagers celebrated Ramsey's arrival, and many joined his ECLGF. Returning to Dinalupihan, however, he received devastating news. On 8 January the Japanese had captured Barker's bodyguard who, after three days of torture, led patrols to Barker. "Thousands of people were being arrested," Ramsey noted, "including hundreds of our operatives and senior officers. The Manila network had been dealt a heavy blow."[2] Ramsey issued General Order Number 1 announcing his command of the ECLGF and appointed Fausto Alberto as head of the Manila section.[3]

Farther north, Moses reorganized his staff: Thomas Jones as G-1 (personnel and administration), Praeger as G-2 (intelligence), Noble as G-3 (plans and operations), and Adduru as G-4 (logistics).[4] They used Praeger's radio to optimistically inform MacArthur that they had "unified command, and control six thousand guerrilla troops in provinces north of Manila."[5]

PANAY, D396/R-653

Order on Panay deteriorated with the reincarceration of paroled Filipino POWs in June 1942. Resentment increased when the Ishihara industries began using "low level Japanese" to forcibly recruit miners. At the end of the year the Japanese replaced Lieutenant Colonel Seno as commander of the garrison in Antique with China veteran Lieutenant Colonel Ryoichi Tozuka.[6] He continued mopping-up and punitive expeditions while preparing an early January surprise attack on Mount Dila Dila and Mount Baloy to capture 61st Division commander Relunia and his chief of staff Chaves. Captain Toshimi Kumai, the garrison adjutant, reported: "Even though the main forces had tanks deployed in the area, the results were not great. The troops only captured a guerrilla [noncommissioned officer] and the mother of Lieutenant Colonel Chavez."[7]

Kumai described one of his patrols' typically frustrating experiences. Scouting along the Suage River with twelve men, they came to an open area surrounded by a banana grove. Lance Corporal Taniyama was on point seventy yards out front, followed by several soldiers from the radio section. Suddenly they saw a young woman waving happily, but she disappeared as they approached. "Instantly, there was a volley of shots from the surrounding trees. Lead shots hit Taniyama directly and killed him on the spot," recalled Kumai.[8] After a lengthy exchange of fire with some sixty guerrillas on the edge of the jungle, Japanese reinforcements arrived, and the guerrillas vanished. Soldiers groping in the darkness found their point man's beheaded body. Kumai continued, "As we stood around the remains of Lance Corporal Taniyama, we were seething with strong feelings for retaliation."[9] A campaign of looting, burning, and killing ensued.

NEGROS, D403/R-646

On 14 January the submarine *Gudgeon* crept along the southern tip of Negros.[10] At Catmon Point, Lieutenant Commander William Shirley Stovall Jr. landed Villamor's Operation Planet team with their equipment. Losing one raft during insertion, the team chose to leave behind medical supplies and propaganda material and carry forward high-priority radio equipment.[11] They brought enough spare parts to operate for at least twelve months.[12] Stovall then departed to reconnoiter local islands.

After a march to Tolong, Villamor established a base in a nipa hut near Sipalay looking southwest on the Sulu Sea. The ubiquitous Professor Bell appeared and helped Emilio Quinto set up radio station 4E7 with his eighty-watt transmitter. Late on 26 January Quinto began tapping out calls to "KAZ" (RAAF Darwin) more than 1,600 miles away.[13] After numerous attempts, KAZ responded and passed word to SWPA.[14] Elated, Ind reported to MacArthur's chief of staff, who replied, "The first to go in, but not the last. We're on our way!"[15]

Almost immediately, the "jungle telegraph" spread the word, "Villamor is here!"[16] Negros guerrilla Higinio de Uriarte recalled, "The general rejoicing and enthusiasm caused by Villamor's arrival were indescribable and impossible to control."[17] Operation Planet represented "the Aid," the beginning of the end of the war, yet Villamor was under orders to stay out of local affairs. The AIB later explained: "He arrived at the time the organizations of Abcede, Ausejo and Gador were full blown and Peralta and Fertig were attempting to gain control of Negros guerrilla affairs."[18] Abcede was the first to visit Villamor and told him, "I control about seven thousand men, and every one of them has been waiting for an eternity to hear just one word—Recognition!"[19] Abcede had groups of thirty men with ten Enfield rifles and other arms conducting hit-and-run tactics and reconnaissance. He even tasked his men to kill at least one Japanese each day.[20]

Abcede shared his understanding of the guerrilla situation: Praeger in Cagayan Valley, Walter Cushing in North Luzon, Fenton and James Cushing in Cebu, and Wendell Fertig in Mindanao (see map 6.1).[21] Among the Filipino guerrillas he knew of were Governor Ablan, Peralta, Manuel Enriquez, Nakar, Mata, Ausejo, Kangleon, Magsaysay, and Gador. However, Abcede complained, "Corporals are promoting themselves to sergeants, sergeants are becoming lieutenants, lieutenants are fancying themselves as captains. Overnight, some officers are turning into generals."[22]

Villamor passed these reports to SWPA with "recommendations on the solution of local problems, particularly on the command situations."[23] SWPA feared he was venturing into local politics and denied Villamor authority to settle the guerrilla disputes. Gador sensed opportunity. He and Ausejo had remained outside Abcede's control on Negros. Hearing Fertig wore brigadier's stars, Gador proclaimed himself a major general.[24]

Abcede believed Gador was a troublemaker who wanted to "command all Negros . . . the entire Philippines," while Ausejo was mature and diplomatic and had the loyalty of both his men and local civilians.[25] Ausejo,

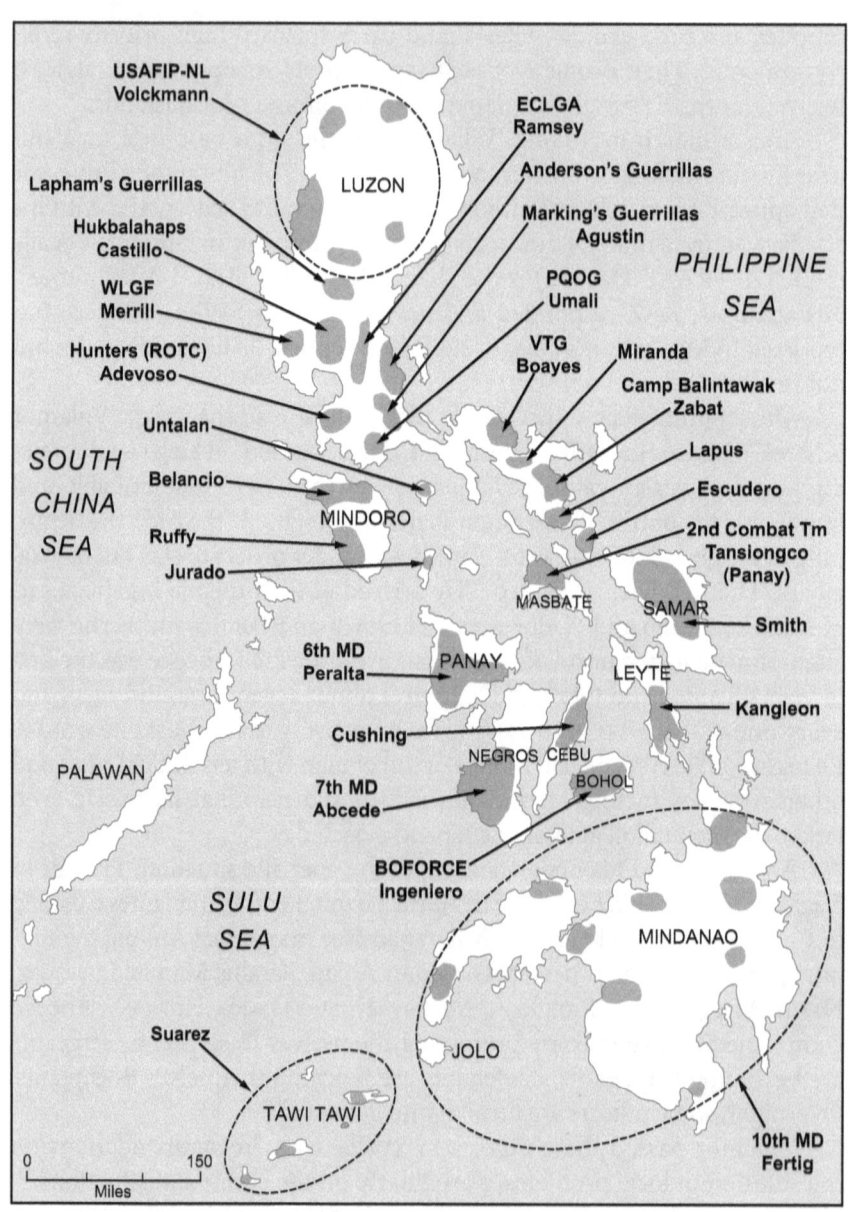

MAP 6.1. Major guerrilla units tracked by SWPA G-2, 1943–1944

however, had pledged to Fertig—it took him twenty days to get a message to Abcede but only four to reach Fertig. Villamor noted, "When he thought of Fertig, Abcede became furious."[26] Abcede ranted: "Does he think that the Filipinos cannot fight or stay together unless they have an American leading them?"[27] Through Peralta, he had gotten SWPA to promise: "Will investigate identity and activities of Brigadier General Fertig and will advise you as soon as possible."[28] Abcede sent Fertig a message saying that MacArthur had been informed of his obstinacy and added: "Your laying claims to control Oriental Negros without controlling the whole island has [resulted in] unpleasant incidents. I can hardly blame Major Ausejo for hesitating to come under the control of this Headquarters."[29] Fertig ignored the message. In the meantime, MacArthur informed Abcede: "You will continue to exercise the command, relay this [to] Gador, Ausejo, Fertig, and Cebu."[30]

Peralta presented another kind of challenge for Villamor. The Panay commander had already brought Bernard Anderson, the Free Philippines, the Hunters, and some other Luzon guerrillas into his net.[31] SWPA instructed Villamor to send a "highly trained, thoroughly astute individual" to meet Peralta without letting him take control of the mission.[32] Villamor chose Delfin YuHico, who carried a miniaturized cipher system sewn into his shoes.[33] Villamor asked Bell and Bill Lowry to make a detour to see Fertig on their way to deliver codes to Cebu, where Fenton and Cushing were attempting to repair an old RCA radio station transmitter.[34] Villamor then planned to go with Patricio Jorge to Mindoro before heading to Manila. Quinto, Malic, and Ignacio would remain with the Negros station.[35] First, however, Villamor felt he had to resolve things between Abcede and Fertig.

MINDANAO, D403/R-646

Fertig sent Charles Hedges to deal with growing numbers of armed Moros. Forty-eight-year-old Hedges had worked for years in the Kolambugan lumber mills and had demonstrated an ability "to maintain the favor and support of the Moros" before he returned to active duty to command the Motor Transport Company in Dansalan.[36] American educator Edward M. Kuder volunteered to assist Hedges in turning a Bolo battalion under Manalao Mindalano and the Marano Militia Force into the eight-thousand-man 108th Division.[37] Yet many Moros hesitated to join Hedges. Busran Kalaw of Momungan, Datu Laguindab of Ganassi, Joseph Sanguilla of Mumay and Madakus, and Datu Buntalis of Masiu valued their independence. An Army assessment noted: "The efforts of Busran, Kalaw,

Mindalano, the Sultan of Ganassi and many others to bring the Moros into line is a monumental tribute to their respect for the American people."[38]

Back in Australia, Hamner and the two Smiths convinced SWPA and Army intelligence to let KFS answer the incessant "hot Yanks" radio calls emanating from the Philippines. One morning Fertig's radio operators informed him of a message received during the night: "KFS calling MSF." Fertig knew instantly it was Charlie Smith.[39] He called back and KFS responded: "Use as key first name of second next of kin and city of residence second next of kin."[40] Using his oldest daughter Patricia's name and their hometown of Golden, Fertig broke the code and could talk to SWPA, just like Peralta.

Fertig rushed to inform MacArthur, "Have strong force in being with complete civilian support.... Large number of enemy motor vehicles and bridges have been destroyed. Many telephone poles have been cut down, food dumps burned, and considerable enemy arms and ammunition captured. Thousands young Filipinos eager to join when arms available. Ready and eager to engage the enemy on your orders."[41] KFS instructed Fertig to sit tight.

The Japanese coincidentally broadcast news that their planes had destroyed the guerrilla headquarters on Mindanao, killing Fertig and driving his forces into the hinterland.[42] Intelligence officials in Washington again doubted their radio contact from Mindanao. They sent federal investigators to visit Fertig's wife and daughters in Colorado to gather information they could use to confirm their contact's identity. Until then, Fertig would hear nothing from SWPA.

MANILA, D403/R-646

Concerned about U.S. submarines in the Philippines, the Japanese high command compelled the imperial navy to "close or put under strict control, the straits wherever the conditions require."[43] Lagging Filipino interest in the Greater East Asia Co-Prosperity Sphere was not as easily addressed. Fourteenth Army chief of staff and director of the JMA, Lieutenant General Wachi, announced: "To quicken national independence . . . citizens of the Philippines should liquidate their past focus on the reorganization of the economy and return as quickly as possible to their true East Asian indemnity both spiritually and intellectually."[44]

Counterintelligence corps' General Baba unleashed Makapili informants against the resistance. "Although very small in number," Ramsey recalled, "the Makapili were insidious, for they were extremely secretive, wore no uniforms, and were indistinguishable from their countrymen in towns and villages."[45] Baba also stepped up patrols and raids, increased the use of torture, and offered rewards for the heads of guerrilla leaders. Romulo recalled: "The Japanese had two overwhelming arguments for collaboration: bloodhounds and food."[46] The baying hounds could sniff out any hiding place. Romulo added: "The power of rice was even more sinister. Rice had become more valuable than gold."[47]

In Tokyo on 14 January an imperial headquarters–government liaison conference debated withholding independence until they saw adequate Philippine cooperation.[48] They decided Japan should grant independence "upon areas as qualify for it in the light of their past political development, if this is deemed advantageous to the prosecution of the Greater East Asia war and the establishment of Greater East Asia."[49] They expected Philippine independence would decrease strains on the military, assuming that Filipinos willingly policed themselves and supported Japan.[50]

Unemployed Filipinos did not support Japan. To placate them, the PEC established a bureau of employment, which ordered that no one could more than work fifteen days in a row so as to allow others opportunities at employment.[51] Ironically, the only people looking for employees seemed to be the Japanese, but nobody wanted to work for them. Major Mikio Matsunobu, an intelligence officer in the Fourteenth Army, received orders to organize Ganap party members at Fort McKinley into a labor battalion that became known as the Yoin or Yuin, from the initials for the "United Nippon." Some Yuin would even receive arms and uniforms.

On 25 January Manila lawyer Marcial P. Lichauco wrote in his diary, "A sensational wholesale arrest by Military Police began five days ago."[52] The Japanese raided the Manila law offices of Senator Quirino, arresting everyone there for suspicion of guerrilla activities, and taking into custody anyone who entered the office over the following three days. "A total of nearly 300 persons were thus taken in custody," Lichauco noted, "all of whom are now languishing in Fort Santiago."[53]

The pressure was wearing on the guerrillas. South of Manila, Marking developed malaria, while five abscessed molars incapacitated Panlilio. She refused to allow Marking to risk himself in combat but demanded that he control his men. "I found early that it was hard for him to bear the shackles of leadership," she wrote, "as it would have been for anyone. And I made him hate me because I insisted on it."[54] Panlilio observed, "Not every man knows the difference between commandeering and banditry. . . . A rifle *should* be a trust; *actually, it is a power over the life and death.*"[55] She had become Marking's conscience as well as his love.[56]

NEGROS, D416/R-633

After three days of failed attempts, Quinto finally got through to SWPA on 27 January and sent Villamor's first message: "So far so good though have had several hair-raising experiences."[57] Villamor reported that increased Japanese patrolling had made travel risky, mistakenly said that Peralta had given his Fourth Corps to Fertig, and asked SWPA to reissue its orders for guerrillas to lay low and avoid reprisals. SWPA answered the next day with orders for Villamor to remain in Negros and determine the "trustworthiness [of] main guerrilla leaders in Visayas and Mindanao."[58] They wanted a recommendation on either Peralta or Fertig for overall command—or should they remain separate? Subsequent messages informed Villamor of Nakar's and Thorp's captures, Praeger's radio contact, the possible loyalty of Luzon constabulary chief Augustino Gabriel, Fertig's control of Mindanao (without a radio), and broken radio communication with Peralta. The messages also authorized the printing of scrip but prohibited guerrillas from imposing martial law.

At Cartagena, Villamor asked Abcede for men and received fourteen volunteers. He decided to form three-man communications teams: "I wanted two men for the radio station I planned to establish, and the odd man as the 'pacifier.'"[59] He established a program to pass along the skills his agents had learned at Victoria Barracks. Lieutenants Modesto Castañeda, Enrique Abila, Roberto Luzuriaga, William Zayco, Arthur Zaycom, and Raymundo Teruel were the first graduates. They deployed to the capital and reported that "Manila was infested with spies and puppet police. Throughout all of Luzon morale was low, and elsewhere it was not a great deal better."[60]

By now Villamor had noted differences between guerrillas and regular soldiers. Because they did not defend ground, guerrillas relied less on discipline and embraced malleable attitudes to keep men in camp.[61] Leaders routinely disbanded units and sent men home to evade the enemy, lower logistical burdens, and keep up morale. When U.S. Army Lt. Russell Barros advised Marking and Panlilio to "keep the orders going" so that their subordinates did not "break up or slow down," the guerrilla leaders refused. "If they want to fight on," Marking explained, "they find us first, tell us what they want to do; then we advise them on how it should be done, and finally we give them orders to go ahead and do it."[62] That was the guerrilla way. Most notably, regular soldiers focused on the enemy, while guerrillas fixated on the people.

MANILA, D418/R-631

On 29 January Manila newspapers carried a speech by Tojo to the Tokyo Diet exhorting Philippine cooperation and announcing, "Under these circumstances and on condition that further tangible evidences of cooperation are actively demonstrated, it is contemplated to put into effect the statement made previously in the question of Philippine independence in the shortest possible time."[63] In celebration, the KALIBAPI declared 8 February a public holiday and scheduled pro-Japanese demonstrations. Benigno Ramos led Ganap rallies that "harangued the people with purple prose describing the nobility of the Japanese aims and their magnanimity in promising independence to the Philippines."[64] A story on the front page of the *Manila Tribune* even claimed all resistance had ceased.[65] Fertig noted shortly afterward, "Both Tokyo and Manila have spent considerable time in their radio news broadcast telling about peaceful conditions in the Philippines; how the Filipinos are helping in the co-prosperity field while actually the Filipinos call it Prosperity-Ce-Tagalog, slang meaning 'Your Prosperity.'"[66]

The JMA was more concerned with farm fields than battlefields. Friction over cotton led to the creation of the Philippines Cotton Growers Association with ambassador Shozo Murata as chairman.[67] The JMA reported 23,150 acres of cotton planted—an increase of almost 1,400 percent since October, but still less than 3 percent of their announced goal. Moreover, as traveling reporter Koichi Kayahara discovered, the Japanese routinely failed to advance enough money to contracted farmers to cover the costs of equipment, irrigation, planting, fertilizer, and insecticide—although they did pay a wage for irrigating and spraying.[68] As a result, ginned cotton harvests would reach only 20 percent of the JMA's 2,470-ton goal.

On 20 February the JMA approved an "Agenda for Implementing Cotton Cultivation Projects in the Philippines for the Year 1943" and the "Agenda for the Determination of Cotton Cultivation Areas in the Philippines." These plans built upon sugar industry policies adopted the previous July and August and converted to cotton production 46 percent of 643,000 acres previously dedicated to sugar cane.[69] Already, however, conversion of farmland had contributed to the severe and growing rice shortage. In Manila, the price of a sack of rice rocketed from 30 to 200 pesos. Only the Japanese, able to print money at will, could afford bulk purchases of rice. Hunger forced more people to Manila, nearly doubling the city's prewar population.

MINDANAO, D425/R-624

On 5 February KFS relayed war department requests for Fertig to confirm his identity. His frustration mounted when Bell informed him that Peralta had radioed MacArthur's headquarters "that certain officers, including one Wendell Fertig, were trying to usurp his command."[70] Then on 14 February Peralta nearly captured the Japanese Fourteenth Army commander in an ambush near Iloilo. He even sent staff officers to Fertig, which the American somehow interpreted as an offer for him to take command of Peralta's corps. From Negros, Villamor perceived: "They were behaving like kids in a dispute for the leadership of a neighborhood gang. And all through the officer ranks there spread the fever of competition."[71]

MacArthur was fed up. He sent new orders instructing "All Guerrilla Leaders" to limit hostile contact with the enemy, to concentrate on developing intelligence nets, and to report "promptly names of superior officers, and other items of military intelligence."[72] He sent Peralta and Fertig three directives: one banning the printing of money, the second keeping guerrillas under their current commanders, and the third designating Peralta as "military guerrilla chief of temporarily occupied enemy territory."[73] Confused and irate, Fertig fired off a message to KFS with instructions to relay to the war department: "As senior American officer in the Philippine Islands I have assumed command of Mindanao and Visayas with rank of brigadier general xxx As the leader of the guerrillas forces we have reactivated the US[A]FIP and established civil government in the hands of duly elected commonwealth officials xxx Money is being printed by them and loaned to US[A]FIP xxx Fertig."[74] It was not wise to challenge MacArthur. On 11 February KFS informed Fertig his call sign was no longer MSF but WYZB and assigned him to KAZ, MacArthur's headquarters in Brisbane. Fertig resent his long message to KAZ. SWPA responded, "KEEP YOUR SHIRT ON YOU ARE NOT FORGOTTEN."[75]

Something definitive had to be done about the guerrilla chain of command. "The problem of finding [a] commander suitable for the overall situation was a difficult one and would take time and trouble," SWPA noted. "Recognition of individual local commanders appeared to be the most satisfactory solution and G-2 unhesitatingly recommended the establishment of island commands on the basis of pre-war Military Districts."[76] One thing was certain: MacArthur would have no one other than himself in command of all forces in the Philippines.

On 13 February SWPA reactivated the prewar USAFFE military districts (see map 6.2).[77] MacArthur approved Fertig as commander of the 10th Military District (MD), which included Mindanao and, for the time being, Sulu. He ordered Fertig to develop an intelligence net in the 9th MD area

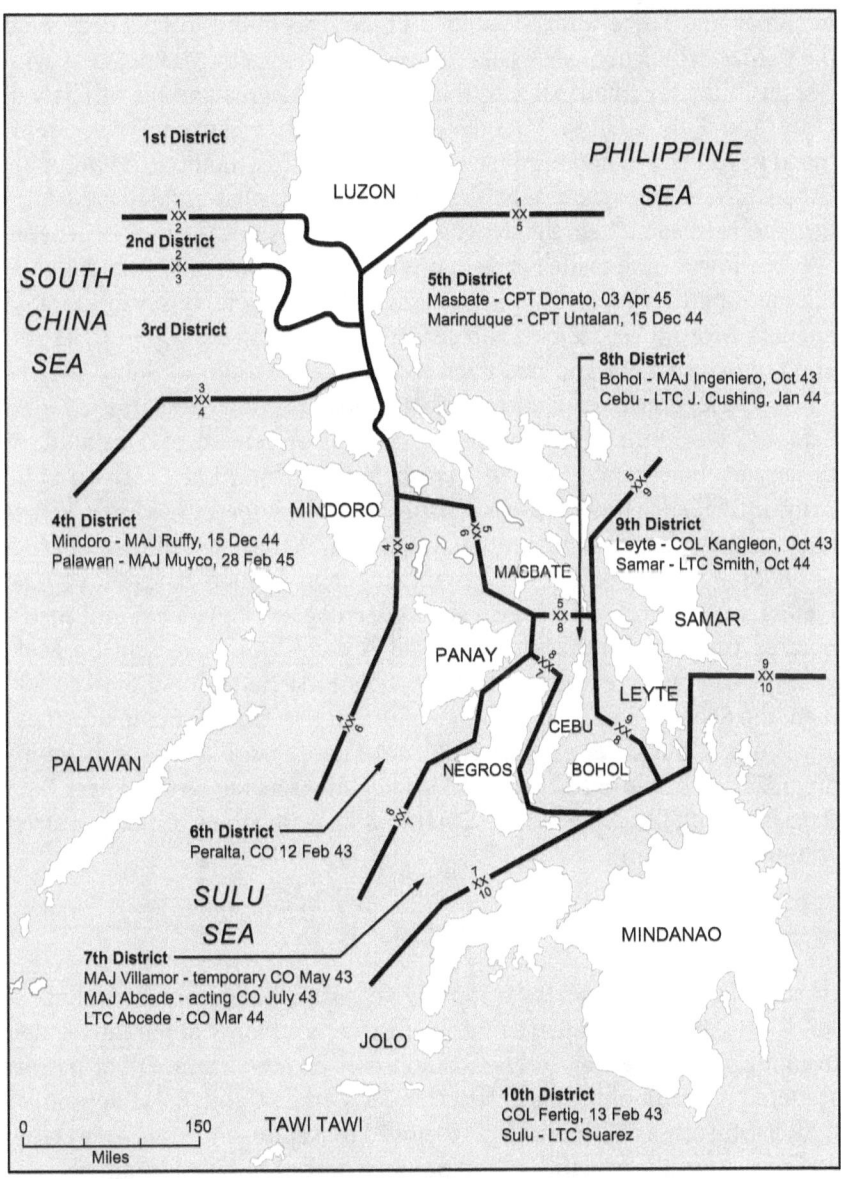

MAP 6.2. Military districts and SWPA-appointed commanders, 13 February 1943

of Samar and Leyte until a qualified officer was found to take command there. MacArthur named Peralta commander of the 6th MD of Panay with responsibility for intelligence in the 7th MD of Negros and the 8th MD of Cebu and Bohol. These boundaries effectively recognized Fertig's command in Mindanao and terminated Peralta's multi-island Fourth Philippine Corps. SWPA also specifically identified both guerrillas as lieutenant colonels and reminded them that no guerrilla was to assume the rank of general.

The lower rank made Fertig apprehensive of senior officers in his area. First among them was Colonel Alejandro Suarez, a forty-seven-year-old Spanish-Moro mestizo who had served in the constabulary in Cotabato and Sulu since 1914 and had risen to become governor of Sulu. After he followed General Fort in surrender, the Japanese moved Suarez to Cotabato and gave him command of that province's bureau of constabulary. In January he escaped to Tawi Tawi before reaching Bato Bato on Sulu. Army intelligence noted: "He is reliable, capable, knows the Moros well, is respected and has many friends among them."[78] He also outranked Fertig.

Suarez integrated thirty constabulary men at Bato Bato under First Lieutenant Alejandro Trespeces with guerrillas on Tawi Tawi and incorporated twenty men under Lieutenant Abdulrahim Imao sent by Morgan.[79] Subsequent recruitment brought his First Battalion at Siasi to 200 men, the Second Battalion at Jolo to 250, and the Third Battalion on Tawi Tawi to 350 men. Fertig reached out to Suarez who agreed to have his organization become 10th MD's 125th Regiment headquartered near Bato Bato.[80] Eventually, SWPA would name Sulu a separate military district with Suarez as commander.

LUZON, D426/R-623

In early February Japanese troops again swept across northern Luzon. Raids on Ablan's headquarters deep in the mountains apparently failed to capture the governor, but he would never be seen again. Other patrols scattered Thorp's old First District under Parker Calvert. He appointed Arthur Murphy as his adjutant and moved to Kapangan, Benguet, to reorganize around the remaining Philippine Scouts of the 43rd Infantry.

On 6 February the *Manila Tribune* front page featured the banner headline "GUERRILLAS SURRENDER!" The story said 1,367 misguided Filipinos and USAFFE soldiers had surrendered and pledged their loyalty to Japanese forces. "Co. Susuki" had told them: "I, acting on behalf of the Commander-in-Chief of the Japanese Imperial Army, hereby accept your surrender because I am very grateful. And I also forgive your previous offenses entirely, letting bygones be bygones."[81]

That same day Moses and Noble arrived at Praeger's headquarters to spend two weeks using his radio to talk with SWPA.[82] They confirmed that they had ordered all U.S. forces in the Philippines to "limit hostilities" in favor of collecting intelligence in accordance with MacArthur's instructions.[83] Yet they contradicted themselves, often in one message, in regard to popular morale, guerrilla status, and their intentions, and they appeared to be in less than complete control.[84] Meanwhile, more than one thousand Japanese troops were converging on Praeger's radio.

Not every guerrilla was willing to lay low. Leon Z. Cabalhin of Marking's guerrillas set a seventy-man ambush on the Koyambay-Tanay trail with an air-cooled .30-caliber machine gun recovered from an airplane.[85] They encountered a patrol of 150 Japanese and claimed to kill 93, who were later discovered to be engineers headed for the Angelo mine. The Huks also ignored Moses but invited coordination with USAFFE guerrillas. Their numbers had increased to a point where they divided central Luzon into five districts.[86] They bought—or stole—enough arms and ammunition to make a formidable force. Lapham's executive officer, Harry McKenzie, received one of the first Huk invitations. Lapham recalled, "En route to the appointed meeting place he was ambushed and shot in the chest."[87] Harry's men fled, but his wife Mary and his adjutant, Manuel Bahia, stayed with him as the Huks took them prisoner. When the Japanese happened to raid the Huk camp, Mary and Manuel pulled Harry into the jungle and back to the Luzon Guerrilla Armed Forces (LGAF).

MINDANAO, D438/R-611

Based on Villamor's and Hamner's reports, SWPA decided to send their next submarine to Fertig.[88] Chick Parsons arrived in Brisbane on 18 January with a plan for a mission to the Philippines. With MacArthur's approval, Parsons drew up priorities for supplies: signal equipment, medical provisions, arms and ammunition, food, clothing, and "morale builders" such as cigarettes, chocolate, gum, magazines, and a fifty-pound can of wheat flour "for Communion wafers."[89] Medical supplies were most critical, "especially a quantity of atabrine for use against malaria."[90] Parsons would also bring cathartic pills to combat dysentery and sulfathiazole to treat pneumonia and staphylococcal infections.[91]

SWPA G-2 reported: "Prior to this time, the C-in-C [MacArthur] had ruled that no American personnel would be permitted on penetration missions, but Parsons secured special permission at the last moment and was allowed to go on the first supply run to Mindanao and to remain on Mindanao as an observer of the guerrilla organization there."[92] Parsons recruited newly promoted Major Charles Smith, fresh from his trek on *Or Else*, along with two Moros for their knowledge of Mindanao and its people.⁹³

At midnight on 5 March the submarine SS-198 *Tambor* under Lt. Cdr. S. H. Armbruster placed Parson's Operation Fifty team ashore at Laganan near Tukuran in Zamboanga, Mindanao.⁹⁴ Parsons went ashore with neither a disguise nor a weapon and encountered a group of natives that, by rare chance, included his former washerwoman. A local guerrilla leader gave him a sixty-foot diesel-powered lighter captured from the Japanese. Boldly flying an American flag, Parsons shuttled supplies ashore. By the time Japanese patrols arrived in response to exaggerated rumors of six submarines landing hundreds of men, the guerrillas had carried the team and their cargo into the jungle north of Oroquieta. Parsons sent a message to Fertig: "Urgent have four tons supplies for you from down under signed Lt. Comdr. Parsons and Smith."⁹⁵

Fertig was overwhelmed by the thought of four tons of supplies.⁹⁶ He calculated that the haul came to 1.3 pounds per guerrilla, but he found it did not break down that easily and required 160 men or 25 carabao carts for transport. Parsons told him that only MacArthur's personal interest had produced these provisions. In other words, Fertig owed MacArthur loyalty. Parson also relayed SWPA instructions that Fertig should develop a radio net, establish coast watchers, and construct secret airfields. Fertig was now a link in the SWPA chain of command.

Fertig shared his fears that his organization could dissolve at any moment. In fact, Major Angeles Limena's 109th Regiment had just attacked the headquarters of neighbor Major Manuel Jaldon. "Finally," Fertig recounted, "mutiny has broken out and threatens this whole crazy structure."⁹⁷ Limena's attack would last for four months.

Parsons reminded Fertig that MacArthur wanted intelligence, not combat. "Those radios we brought you are for information," he said. "You are to establish a flash line [immediate priority communication] of watcher stations along the coasts, and pass the word to us of Jap ship movements."⁹⁸ Fertig disagreed. His priority was fighting. He told Parsons: "Now as far as the Japanese are concerned, the over-all strategic objective is very simple. It is, *Kill the bastards*."⁹⁹ No go, replied Parsons. If he wanted more SWPA support, Fertig would have to toe the line.

Morgan was just ending an unsuccessful ten-day attack supported by McClish's 110th Division against the Japanese at Butuan. The result was a loss of face for Morgan—which was fine with Fertig. McClish had moved to the Clacveria-Malitbog area, where he convinced independent guerrillas to join the USAFIP under James E. McIntyre and U.S. Army Air Corps Lt. Alfredo Fernandez. He recruited other guerrillas under Rosaurio Dongallo in the vicinity of Gingoog Bay, and they became the 110th Regiment of McClish's division. MacArthur's recognition—manifested by the delivery of supplies—had demonstrably made Fertig's recruiting much easier.[100]

On 23 February Fertig learned of his assignment as 10th MD commander.[101] He revealed to Parsons his strategy to coerce local support. Except in one area on the east coast, the Japanese had driven most of Mindanao to the guerrillas. Fertig worked to get his enemy to drive that last part of the people to him. He explained: "We practice sabotage and assassinate Japanese in that area, to provoke the Japanese into making the kind of reprisals that *will* put the people on our side."[102] It was a cruel but effective policy, adopted by a great number of guerrillas.

Parsons and Smith were surprised when Fertig told them that Manuel Roxas was a key source of his intelligence.[103] The AIB had wondered about Roxas' loyalties after he had refused Quezon's invitation to accompany him to Australia. As MacArthur biographer William Manchester noted, "Whether or not he stayed on MacArthur's instructions is unclear. The General later said so, but contemporary documents are confusing."[104] The Japanese had released Roxas from prison under pressure from Laurel but kept him under close watch. MacArthur joyfully received the news about his former liaison. "Briefly reports from Manila indicate that the politicians are trying to play the game," Fertig continued. "Except for Aguino [Aquino] the others are still with us. Even Laurel is at heart OK. The common people are definitely pro-Americans with the cocheros [horse-drawn carromata cab drivers] extremely so. Morale is high and they are just waiting."[105]

The diary of Marcial Lichauco supports Fertig's assertion. Early in the occupation he asked an elderly cochero if he was happy that the sudden lack of automobiles had increased his business. "Mister, I drove a carromata during the last few years that the Spaniards were here and I have kept up my profession during the forty-two years the Americans have been in our country and not once had a Spaniard or American so much as insulted or abused me," he answered. "But the Japanese have been here only three months and, so far, I have been slapped twice and kicked three times."[106]

Fertig told Parsons he needed money. To raise funds, he had his men gather up all the hair curlers in Misamis Occidental and establish a monopoly on styling women's hair.[107] Parsons worked to get Quezon to alleviate Fertig's problems by approving a guerrilla-staffed Mindanao currency board and authorizing it to print emergency currency.

Fertig illustrated guerrilla operations with another story. He had learned of Japanese soldiers who confiscated what they thought were *camotes* (a type of sweet potato) from Negritos, but the tubers were actually *camoteng cahoy*. Though similar in appearance, if not peeled, diced, and soaked for three days in a fast-running stream, *camoteng cahoy* contained cyanide when ripe. The feasting confiscators quickly turned blue and died. Fertig then made it a rule for his guerrillas to mix all the *camoteng cahoy* they could find into the baskets of *camotes* the Japanese purchased in local markets. Surviving Japanese soldiers became notably wary of local merchants.[108]

Fertig seemed a promising choice to command in the Philippines. Options elsewhere were less appealing. Noble and Moses lacked control.[109] No one was listening to Merrill. The several leaders in Bicol fought a tug-of-war. In the Visayas, Villamor seemed beset by local guerrilla politics, and Peralta posed other problems. But then again, MacArthur had pulled the reins on Fertig.

PANAY, D440/R-609

As for Villamor, Peralta was the best choice for overall command of the guerrillas. On 20 February SWPA reminded him: "As you know Peralta named commander of Panay district only."[110] The next day SWPA informed Peralta: "Commander of districts will operate under control [of] this headquarters and assignments will be subject to review on basis of performance."[111] MacArthur reaffirmed Fertig as 10th MD commander and Peralta as 6th MD commander.

To divide Peralta and Governor Confesor, the Japanese tasked Iloilo provincial governor Fermin Caram to write to Confesor and ask him to surrender to local commander Colonel Furukawa to bring "peace and tranquility to the suffering people of Panay."[112] Confesor, a thoughtful man with degrees from the University of California and the University of Chicago, recognized Caram's plea as a cipher for larger questions. Why risk death in fighting the Japanese? What could be worth the sacrifice? What were they fighting for? Confesor's reply of 20 February would become one of history's rare inspirations to a people.

Confesor declined to surrender because, he reasoned, peace and tranquility were beyond Filipinos as long as Japan and the United States were at war. "This is a total war in which the issues between the warring parties are less concerned with the territorial questions but more with forms of government, ways of life, and those that affect even the very thoughts, feeling, and sentiments of every man," he wrote. "In other words, the questions at stake with respect to the Philippines is not whether Japan or the United States should possess it; but more fundamentally it is: what system of government should stand here and what ways of life, systems of social organizations and code of morals should govern our existence."[113]

He believed that through resistance, the Philippines could become one nation formed according to their will.

If Japan truly had the Filipinos' best interests at heart, Confesor argued, they would withdraw and proclaim the islands neutral. If not, then the terms set for independence were false and unachievable. "I agree with you when you say that our people are 'experiencing unspeakable hardships and sufferings because of these hostilities,' but you should realize that our people are bearing these burdens cheerfully because they know that they are doing it for a good and noble cause," he answered Caram.[114] Japan had forced an unacceptable way of life and system of government upon Filipinos. Fighting them proved Filipinos worthy of choosing a better way of life and system of government. Confesor explained,

> In other words, this war placed us in the crucible to assay the metal in our being. For as a people, we have been living during the last forty years under a regime of justice and liberty regulated only by universally accepted principles of constitutional government. We have come to enjoy personal privileges and civil liberties without much struggle, without undergoing any pain to attain them. They were practically a gift from a generous and magnanimous people—the people of the United States of America. Now, that Japan is attempting to destroy these liberties, should we not exert any effort to defend them? Should we not be willing to suffer for their defense? If our people are undergoing hardship now, and are doing it gladly, it is because we are willing to pay the price for these constitutional liberties and privileges.[115]

Confesor believed the United States championed democracy and would honor its promise to grant independence. The Japanese, on the other hand, routinely condemned democracy and liberty. Filipinos had to choose between the two, a choice that would decide their "national principles." To surrender for "peace and tranquility" was to forfeit worthwhile principles as a basis for a new, independent nation. As an exemplar, he cited Abraham Lincoln, who accepted civil war as the price for higher ideals. Confesor closed with a quote: "Suffering affords for the practice of many virtues—virtues which develop greatness and nobility of soul."[116] The letter was popularly embraced, as Pacita Pestano-Jacinto wrote, as "the answer of not one Filipino, but of all who are being coerced, duped, and corralled into an independence trap."[117] Filipinos posted the letter everywhere.

On 2 March propaganda platoon leader Hitomi reported from Panay: "The enemy has gained the upper hand in applying pressure on the citizenry. . . . propaganda speeches without a show of force are of no value at all."¹¹⁸ He asked for troops. Lieutenant Colonel Ryoichi Tozuka, the commander of the 107th Independent Infantry Battalion (also known as the Panay Defense Force), answered with a "collective barrio operation" to forcibly relocate rural islanders to urban areas so as to separate them from the guerrillas. He tasked Hitomi to persuade the peasants to move. After reporting this to the propaganda corps headquarters in May, a plane from Manila arrived to take Hitomi to Fourteenth Army vice chief of staff Utsunomiya.

"Collective barrios have already failed on the China mainland," Utsunomiya scolded Hitomi, "The only effect that they have is evoking the wrath of the people."¹¹⁹ He added, "I can't believe that there is some fool now trying to implement the same plan out on Panay."¹²⁰ Utsunomiya relieved Hitomi of his platoon and reassigned him to a desk in the department of information (*Hodobu*) in Manila.¹²¹ Thus ended Hitomi's tailored propaganda program.

The Japanese renewed efforts to leverage the Catholic church. On 6 March the PEC, through Laurel's interior department, ordered the church to "inculcate in the minds of their faithful or flock, loyalty to the constituted authorities and the absolute necessity on the part of all Filipinos to cooperate whole heartedly with the present administration in the establishment of peace and order in every nook and corner of the Philippines."¹²² Laurel issued a circular that stated: "Far from being political, the collaboration of all Churches is, in the ultimate analysis, a religious enterprise demanded by conscience."¹²³

SOUTHERN LUZON, D450/R-599

In Bohol, Turko built a new VTG camp in Caramoan in late February. "Soon reports of rapes and other crimes against civilians in Caramoan surfaced," Barrameda wrote. "Pitched battles ensued between the VTG and Camp Tinawagan men, some of whose relatives were said to have been violated and maltreated by Turko's men."¹²⁴ Dianela's kin were among the VTG victims; when he protested, Turko chased Dianela to Padua's camp in Goa.¹²⁵ Turko forced Dianela's capitulation and absorbed his Camp Tinawagan guerrillas into the VTG. He then ordered the combined force to find and kill Miranda.

Turko's VTG and Padua's Camp Isarog guerrillas became unequal partners: Padua's men logged forty-six actions between 27 January 1943 and 26 December 1944, while the VTG fought only four.¹²⁶ Yet Turko maintained disproportionate influence. He also married Emilia Teoxon, bringing her powerful Caramoan family into his kinship network.

With a twelve-man escort, TVGU commander Miranda limped along on crutches from Tangcong to Bahi, where on 8 March, after six days in town, he married Estrada. Townspeople came to him to complain about extortion and rape by VTG men under returned resident José Benvenuto (Benut). When Miranda ordered the VTG to stop, they ignored him. Resident Ramon Piano then went to Turko, who sent Sergeant Floresta to investigate. "Apparently the sergeant saw Miranda's young wife and liked what he saw," noted Barrameda.[127] After Floresta left to report to Turko, VTG men plotted to poison both Miranda and Elias Madrid at a dance on 14 March, but their targets failed to show. Floresta returned to Bahi a few days later with Turko and Dianela and a large force. He claimed Miranda's wife as *balato*—something of a gratuity due for service—with the ostensive intention of giving her to Turko. Cooler heads, assisted by the arrival of Judge Bajandi, calmed the situation, and Turko left town.

Turko and Dianela then ordered Miranda to report to Camp Tinawagan where—Madrid discovered—they planned to arrest him on charges of banditry and usurpation. After a shootout with some VTG men, Miranda and his wife left Bahi with eleven men on 21 March and headed for the remote town of Viga, far from Turko's influence. There Miranda would spend the next three months recuperating from his injuries.

Events grew more complicated in March when Escudero fell ill and went to Samar to recuperate. Lapus exploited his absence by convincing Merritt to chase Escudero off Samar. Lapus, who backed Miranda as the commander of the TVGU, was now in a strong position, but Zabat continued to recognize Aureus as head of the TVGU in hopes of recruiting the unit. In May, Peralta received delegates from both Lapus and Escudero looking for support. The next month Lapus traveled to Masbate to meet Zabat and attempt to iron out their differences.

NEGROS, D464/R-585

Incredibly, Villamor had to learn through the jungle telegraph that a SWPA team under a "Commander X" (Parsons) with Captain Charles Smith and three others had landed on Mindanao. "This mysterious commander was working to bring the independent groups on the huge island into line under Fertig," he believed.[128] Mellnik clarified, "Though outwardly frank, Chick was most mysterious about his origin and mission."[129] There was also a mysterious dynamic within the Fifty team. On 16 March Fertig observed that Smith "encoded a telegram for the South. He would not let Parsons read it so he left in huff."[130]

With YuHico off to Panay, Jorge to Bohol, and Lieutenant Bartolomeo C. Cabangbang on Mindanao, Villamor chose Bell to go to Cebu in late March. Bell had convinced him that it would be better to send an American to see the erratic Fenton. Then on 28 March Japanese troops landed in southern Negros. Quinto reported to SWPA, "Japanese land, sea and air activities started very suddenly. Locations menaced."[131] Four days of fighting dispersed the Planet team.

From Panay, YuHico sent a positive impression of Peralta: "He has ten thousand men, half of them armed, with sub-machine guns and assorted firearms. He rules with an iron hand, under martial law, threatening to execute spies by drum head courts martial. His agents are everywhere. He fills the airwaves with messages to MacArthur."[132] YuHico informed Villamor, "He doesn't have much faith in you. He says your identity and mission are all over Negros and other islands."[133] Peralta clearly wanted it known that Villamor was not a suitable choice to lead the Philippine guerrilla movement.

Peralta also urged Quezon to publicly denounce Vargas. Villamor countered that Quezon should refrain from denouncing Vargas or any other apparent collaborators. Any denouncement, he argued, "will undoubtedly encourage the shoot on sight policy of our soldiers which has already caused so many unjustified killings and which has actually boomeranged against us in that it has forced loyal people to seek Japanese protection."[134] That Villamor's family was part of the Filipino elite made him perhaps a bit more understanding of their place in the occupation.

In fact, collaboration came in shades of gray. Lapham, like most guerrilla leaders, sensed that "probably 90 percent of ordinary Filipinos, both farmers and local officials, in their hearts preferred Americans and American ideas to their Japanese counterparts."[135] As time passed without any sign of MacArthur's return, many Filipinos acclimated to Japanese suzerainty. As Marquez wrote: "By this time, after more than eighteen months of occupation, some of the men and women residents of Manila had begun to 'play ball' with the enemy."[136] Asunción Pérez added, "It is human nature. It could happen in America. It was happening in Europe before the war came here. It will happen wherever there is tyranny, oppression, and a price for betrayal."[137]

Some collaborationists simply desired respect. When Isabel Yumol received second prize in school for Japanese recitation and won applause from several occupation generals, a neighbor commented, "You know, our little personal triumphs, like this, permitted and appreciated, make us feel less oppressed and subjugated."[138] Most collaboration, however, was clearly coerced. Villamor explained, "To some extent the whole country was a prison camp."[139] Volckmann added, "No civilian, even though loyal and sympathetic to the cause, could be expected to render support if he were sure to be reported to the Japs and shortly thereafter to lose his head to a Samurai sword."[140]

The reality of collaboration was often ugly. One day, a Mr. Gongong from Kiangan, who had been raised by American missionaries and graduated from Silliman University, applied to Volckmann to become a spy. After a week to reconsider, he took the oath of service and performed well on his first two assignments. On his third mission, however, the Japanese found his USAFIP-Northern Luzon (NL) pass. They sent Gongong, who had a family, to a reeducation school in Manila. After a few months he emerged as an officer in the Japanese-controlled constabulary. "Our agents next reported that he was making public speeches denouncing the United States and asking the people to cooperate with the Japanese," Volckmann wrote.[141] Gongong took command of a constabulary company in Kalinga, where the guerrillas found and killed him.

Many collaborators were simply duped. Magdalona Leones walked into the 1st Battalion, 121st Infantry Regiment, USAFIP-NL, in La Union and reported that a Filipino agent from SWPA had arrived in Manila and sent her to fetch the rosters of all guerrilla units in the area. The agent had shown her official-looking orders and U.S. Treasury checks to prove his identity. Guerrillas escorted Miss Leones to Volckmann. A background check verified that she had been raised by American missionaries and was a friend of Volckmann's associates Miss Metzger and Miss Spessard. Volckmann decided to hold Miss Leones until he could check out the agent in Manila. After two weeks he received a report: the agent was a spy for the Japanese named Reyes.

The USAFIP-NL inquiry triggered a Japanese roundup of American missionaries in Manila. Informed of this, Leones accepted Volckmann's invitation to join his guerrillas. She moved fearlessly about Manila collecting information through her church contacts. Despite being detained three times with incriminating evidence, she always managed to get back to the guerrillas to carry on her work. "Maggie was eventually formally enlisted into the Philippine Army and inducted in to USAFIP, NL," Volckmann recalled. "After the war she was awarded the Silver Star, the only woman in USAFIP, NL to receive such a high award."[142]

MINDANAO TO LEYTE, D463/R-586

Fertig provided Parsons with another boat, the sixty-foot diesel Mitsui launch *Nara Maru*, to establish a radio station on the heavily trafficked

Surigao Strait between Mindanao and Leyte.[143] Parsons went ashore at Medina in McClish's area and was surprised to find a guerrilla "service company" ready to fuel his boat with fuel distilled from coconuts.[144] McClish also provided personnel for a coast-watching station and a .50-caliber machine gun for the boat. When Parsons got to the tip of Surigao City, the most desirable site for coast watchers, he found the Japanese already searching for him. He turned north across the strait for the finger-like Panaon Island pointing toward Leyte.

The next morning, a team of "yellow" guerrillas greeted *Nara Maru*. They had desperately opened a wayward sea mine to get picric acid to treat their jungle sores and got coated with the yellow dust. Parsons left Lt. Truman Hemingway and McClish's men with a radio to report on ship traffic and continued north to Leyte.

Meanwhile, guerrilla coast watchers reported seeing a ship sunk off Davao. Most Navy attacks had gone unconfirmed, but this report proved coast watchers could give them credit for sunk ships.[145] Elated, the Navy offered the AIB submarines, coast watchers, and net control stations to forward reports to naval intelligence in Perth.[146] Getting guerrilla leaders to be as enthusiastic for coast watchers was another matter. Parsons had to explain to Fertig: "One torpedo in half a second can blow up more ammunition than the Japs can shoot at you in a year. Another can kill more Japs on a troop transport than all the guerrillas in the Islands could ever kill."[147]

Before passing through the one-hundred-foot-wide Panaon Strait, Parsons sent runners ahead to coordinate with Lieutenant José Nazareno's men defending the channel. Still, *Nara Maru* took friendly fire that damaged external fuel tanks. The guerrillas had only received a warning: "Look out for a launch arriving this afternoon."[148] Parsons entered into his journal, "I have been fired upon by friends many more times than by the enemy."[149]

Before the end of March, Parsons reached Maasin in southwest Leyte, where he learned that rival guerrilla groups had just killed forty-five of each other's men. "Captain" Gordon Lang, former Sixteenth Naval District yeoman, led one band.[150] American mining engineer Chester "Major X" Peters and his wife Julia Manapasi, also known as "Joan of Arc," led the other. Parsons visited both and found them incompatible and unreliable. He then went to old friends Miguel and Mariano Jesus Cuenco, who advised him that the only person with the status to unite all the Leyte guerrillas was Colonel Ruperto Kangleon of San Roque at the southern tip of the island.

The former constabulary commander on Cebu and Bohol was the senior Philippine officer on Leyte and had commanded the 81st Infantry Division before being captured near Davao.[151] Kangleon, fifty-one years old, told Parsons he was too old and too tired to play another role in the war. Parsons' promise of recognition and support from MacArthur, plus the faith of the Cuenco brothers, convinced him to finally say, "You have made my duty clear, Commander Parsons. I have no choice. You may tell General MacArthur that I am at his disposition."[152] Satisfied, Parsons headed to Malitbog in southern Leyte on his way back to Mindanao.

Parsons had overlooked other guerrillas on Leyte such as Blas Miranda, Alejandro Balderian, Ciriaco and Isabelo Centino, Antonio Cinco, Filemon Pabilona, and Felix Pamanian, among others, across the island's center and north. Willoughby would later admit, "Miranda may have had possibilities not evident at the time but was frozen out by Kangleon-Fertig-Parsons."[153] Historian Elmer Lear, however, suggested a possible explanation for Parson's selection of Kangleon: he was the most palatable choice to the Philippine elites.

Some accused Blas Miranda and his Western Leyte guerrilla warfare force of "radical tendencies hostile to property interests."[154] Hacienderos of western Leyte such as the Mejia and Tan families had long feared tenant revolt and saw ill intent behind Miranda's diversion of harvests from markets, protection of delinquent tenants, and confiscation of lands for communal farming. "To be sure," Lear argued, "one might argue that from such beginnings collective farms in the Marxist sense might emerge. Hypothetically, this eventuality cannot be dismissed."[155] Whatever their motivation, Miranda, and men like him, threatened to alter social power dynamics. Miguel and Mariano Jesus Cuenco would likely have recognized this threat.

NORTHERN LUZON, D456/R-593

To avoid capture by the Japanese, Praeger disassembled his heavy homemade radio at Kabugao on 8 March and ordered it moved one mile to Bulu.[156] Pursuing patrols employed threats and bribes to find his new headquarters.[157] The guerrillas finally reassembled the radio at Camp X several miles outside of Dampalan, where Captain John Simmons battled through malarial fits to maintain communication with the outside world.[158]

Praeger's decision to move his radio merits examination. The U.S. Army had learned long ago that Filipinos would tire of "impotent" guerrilla efforts and "withdraw their material and moral support."[159] As Fertig said, "Any guerrilla has to keep the pressure on, everywhere and all the time, killing Japs. Otherwise, no public support."[160] If Praeger retreated without a fight, the people might perceive his force as impotent.[161] Yet forty porters were required to move his radio, with its batteries, generators, fuel, spare parts, and so forth. It demanded an early decision as whether to fight or flee. If he stayed too long, he risked losing the radio. If he left in time, he might look weak. Philosophical debates about "winning the people" came down in practice to decisions like when to move a radio. Praeger chose to move quickly.

Moving meant Praeger went off the air. On 20 March Moses and Noble, who now claimed six thousand guerrillas, sent out runners with a frantic message to "All Guerrilla Leaders":

> Send your men out to all barrios in your territory and search for a "ham" or amateur radio operator who is capable of constructing a transmitter that will carry 300 + 400 miles. Try to get him all the spare parts you can to construct the transmitter as well as the power unit and generator. Induct him into the U.S. Army. Place set on highest mountain in your vicinity. You are authorized to sign vouchers for all materials necessary to build this set. Also procure on regular commercial battery radio set in order to receive short wave messages. Make every effort to get this in operation by May 1st.[162]

Coincidentally, the AIB instructed Villamor to smuggle a radio into Manila. He had José Casteñada memorize the construction of a radio, disassemble it, and pack the parts in a consignment of fruit. With two Planet members, Casteñada sailed to Luzon and brazenly walked past Japanese checkpoints all the way to Manila, telling curious enemy soldiers the fruit was reserved for an officers' mess.[163] He arrived at the house of AIB agent Frank Jones, reassembled the radio, and brought Manila into the Planet net. Villamor then sent Rodolfo Ignacio to smuggle a relay radio to Major Ricardo L. Benedicto on Mindoro.[164]

Guerrilla leaders without radios had to travel to communicate. In March Ramsey took a long, dangerous journey north through the area occupied by ten thousand Japanese troops near Fort Stotsenburg. At Tarlac he met with Captain Manuel Reyes, who guided him through Nueva Ecija and Pangasinan provinces. Ramsey organized guerrillas in Bayambong, Claro Camacho's home. Bernard Anderson, who now ran guerrillas in Bulacan and Tayabas, went with Ramsey to organize east central Luzon. Meanwhile, a "pro-Japanese Filipino agent" obtained Anderson's organizational roster and sparked a purge that badly hurt the ECLGF.[165]

Travel became more difficult on 17 March when the PEC issued Executive Order 137 expanding neighborhood associations beyond Manila "as a tool to keep them informed on the presence of guerrillas."[166] Males eleven and older acted as sentries with bamboo drums to warn of strangers entering towns.[167] The requirements for identification cards, checkpoints, and surveillance in exchange for allotments of food and medicine bred resentment.¹⁶⁸

The dwindling supply of food also raised native anger. The commander of the occupation forces on Leyte, 36th Independent Infantry Garrison Battalion Colonel Yoshitsugu Omori, issued a proclamation: "With respect to the food problem, I say that all of us have to make some personal sacrifices. This is the consequence of war. . . . Nobody knows when this war will end. Let us plant our own rice. This constitutes one of our moral disciplines. Sky-high price [sic] of commodities is an American philosophy. Price [sic] should be controlled by the government. But the government cannot do this work alone. All of us have to work together. As long as the war lasts, there will be problem of food."¹⁶⁹

News suddenly rocked the guerrillas: Charles Cushing had surrendered. "Charles was a nervous man and, unlike his brothers Walter and James, had never seemed to me to be cut out for guerrilla life," Lapham rationalized.¹⁷⁰ The Japanese had captured and imprisoned Cushing's wife in Santo Tomas and released her under the promise that she would convince her husband to surrender. Under Telesforo Palaruan and Feliciano Nobres, Cushing's remaining guerrillas joined Lapham's LGAF.

In a broader campaign, Panlilio recalled, "The Japs patrolled oftener and oftener, in groups ranging from 30 to 150. We moved back. We moved forward. We side-stepped. We sat tight."¹⁷¹ From August through April, Marking dodged patrols in and around Kalinawan, Rawang, Makantog, Sulok, Mayton, and Kanumay. "Those who failed to move got run over," said Panlilio.¹⁷²

Farther north, Japanese patrols captured governor Marcelo Adduru on 1 April.¹⁷³ Shortly thereafter, the one hundred men of Ablan's Cagayan-Apayao guerrilla force went inactive in the hills near Carazi, Ilocos Norte. Then on 13 April Captain Manuel Enriquez surrendered and entered Fort Santiago prison. Volckmann reported, "The Japs had taken Enriquez's wife and children into custody as hostages, and at his wife's pleading Enriquez surrendered."¹⁷⁴ The remaining one thousand armed men of 14th Infantry passed to Major Romulo Manriquez.¹⁷⁵

NEGROS, D486/R-563

On 7 April MacArthur sent a message to Villamor: "Information that serious friction exists between allied military groups in Negros is profoundly disturbing particularly in present dangerous circumstances. I am directing all leaders faithfully to cooperate against the common enemy."¹⁷⁶ Villamor called for unity, but Gador refused and pulled rank. Peralta continued to support Mata on Negros, Fertig endorsed Ausejo, and Villamor concluded that Abcede was best suited to command.

The next day Villamor complained to SWPA that Peralta had ordered the arrest of any Filipinos released by the Japanese and had even planned to furnish other guerrillas with "transmitters purposely constructed to be incapable of transmitting to you."[177] Villamor believed Peralta was a good soldier, but the incident left him fuming with exasperation.[178] In despair, Villamor requested guidance from MacArthur or Quezon on "taxes, courts and their jurisdictions, money, status of men taken into the services since the fall, etc." and said, "I feel that unless policies are established soon there is a danger that the Army will eventually lose the full backing of the civilians without which the Army will not long exist."[179] SWPA understood and noted: "The commanders have always been somewhat distrustful of one another."[180] Villamor argued that the Philippines needed one commander, and that commander should be a Filipino.

LUZON, D488/R-561

Lapham received information and much-needed money from prominent Manileños of the Escoda group, young female socialites organized in part by New York *Herald Tribune* reporter Tony Escoda and his wife Josefa. (Many members of the group, including the Escodas, would be caught, imprisoned, and beheaded.)[181] One of them, Ramona "Mona" Snyder, happened to be visiting family in the countryside when a cousin serving as a Lapham lieutenant mentioned that his leader was nearby and severely ill. "Though she had never seen me before," recalled Lapham, "she showed up one day well supplied with money, medicine, and provisions and began to try to nurse me back to health."[182] Later introduced to Ramsey, Mona fell in love. According to Lapham, "In rapid succession she became his girlfriend, then an intermediary between him and Manuel Roxas."[183]

The occupation was especially dangerous for women like Mona Snyder, who lived under constant threat of assault, rape, and prolonged sexual servitude. Yet a legion of women joined the resistance. Many entered women's auxiliary service units to sew clothes, act as nurses, or provide entertainment. Women also served as vital intelligence assets and couriers.[184] The Escoda group raised money and supplies.[185] In Bicol, the Daughters of Tandang Sora and the Daughters of Liberty provided intelligence and first aid and acted as camp orderlies.[186] They also organized food sales cooperatives to raise much-needed funds and personally delivered the monies by bravely passing through both Japanese checkpoints and guerrilla skirmish lines.

Many women made their marks as individuals. As a cabaret hostess for Japanese officers, Claire Phillips gathered intelligence and earned the nickname "High Pockets" for smuggling messages in her bra.[187] American Dorothy de la Fuente posed as a Filipina and ran the *Tsubahi* bar reserved by the Japanese military. She collected intelligence and cash for the guerrillas until she was arrested and disappeared into Fort Santiago prison.[188] Five-foot-tall nurse Lieutenant Estella Remito amazed Don Willis with her ability to lead marches through jungles and over mountains at a pace of twenty miles per day.[189] Trinidad Díaz, a cashier in the Binangonan cement factory, served as one of Marking's lieutenants, "policing the district with her own men, liquidating a spy, laying an intelligence network to catch more."[190] Captured during an ambush, she survived thirty-two days of torture before she died.

Then, of course, there was Yay Panlilio. A newspaper reporter and radio broadcaster before the war, she left her children and became Marking's lover and co-commander. She explained, "War was our marriage, the guerrillas our sons."[191] Many men around Marking resented her, and she eventually had to confront his bodyguard, Cabalhin. "He said something, I said something," Panlilio remembered, "he placed his hand on his sidearm, I challenged him to pull it and reached for my own."[192] Marking also drew his gun on his bodyguard, who left in tears. It remained a tough world for Panlilio. Marking would throw her about, slap her, fire weapons near her, and even hold her underwater. Panlilio remembered him warning: "'Don't forget you belong to me. I catch you making eyes, I'll black them both.' And my unspoken retort, 'If I weighed 135 and you weighed 90, it'd be the other way around, buddy boy.'"[193]

Some guerrilla leaders tried to ban romantic entanglements. Ramsey and Barker thought it best to remain celibate. "We had heard reports of guerrilla officers compromised by their relations with local women," Ramsey explained, "either directly through treachery or because of a jealous boyfriend or husband."[194] Lapham concurred, "Romantic attachments sometimes caused trouble: leaders and whole units were betrayed to rival units or to the Japanese by 'other women,' outraged wives, vengeful husbands, or disgruntled boyfriends."[195] Many units established codes of conduct to prevent liaisons between male and female guerrillas that often led to jealousies and undermined discipline. "Code violators were summarily dismissed to prevent bad blood and demoralization in the organization," wrote Barrameda.[196] Human nature frequently won out. Not only did Ramsey become involved with Ramona Snyder, but the Huks also reportedly placed a warrant on him "for making improper advances to Filipino women."[197]

Guerrilla memoirs attest to their inexorable attraction to Filipinas.[198] They pursued local customs of courtship ranging from politicking with parents, exchanging betel nut bags and rolled cigarettes, and meeting under the trees outside dance halls, to ritual abductions of young women from their homes.[199] Willis once turned down a concubine sent to him as a gift from a wealthy benefactor but noted, "The practice wasn't that unusual in the Philippines, as many businessmen had girlfriends living in apartments or houses conveniently located close to their places of business."[200] On Samar "almost all of the Americans had their own huts, equipped with native housekeepers of the female variety."[201] Fertig's men were happy to be stationed in Lanao, where, as writer John Keats explained: "It was not that the Moro girls were immodest; they were merely helpful. They sincerely believed that men sicken if they do not enjoy regular sexual intercourse, and it seemed that none of them wished the Americans to become ill."[202]

Many romances came with pre-set limits. Herminia Dizon would never be more than Thorp's mistress. Villamor married Maria, who nursed him through desperate illness in June 1943, but divorced her when the war ended.[203] Henry Clay O'Connor married the Negrito daughter of a chief, had children with her, and left her when MacArthur returned.[204] Bob Stahl wistfully recalled a platonic relationship with a beautiful daughter of mayor Jesus Medenilla of San Narciso. He accepted a silver ring from her, not knowing that by local custom she meant for him to slip it on her finger at their wedding. After he returned to the United States, he received a letter from one of the disheartened girl's cousins asking for the ring back.[205]

For the Japanese, relations with Philippine women were more problematic. In Korea, miscegenation was encouraged as a method of colonial incorporation but found the practice had a double edge. The policy encouraged unity, but it also justified harsh measures against any Koreans who failed to meet Japanese expectations: "In other words, it was precisely the assumption that Koreans and Japanese had the opportunity to be equals that legitimated abuse against those deemed (in)different."[206]

The Japanese sought to reform Filipinas. The JMA's Philippine research commission recommended Philippine women confine themselves to the affairs of the home and accept that they "are not in themselves ... needed in passing judgment upon questions of public policy."[207] They wanted Filipinas to accept traditional Japanese female values and "work quietly and unobtrusively in the family and for the neighborhood associations, enabling their husbands to work outside, completely freed from the cares of their families, thus drawing to themselves the unbound gratitude and respect of their men."²⁰⁸ To instill such values, the commission recommended reeducation in separate schools for girls.

CENTRAL LUZON, D487/R-562

Marking's guerrillas began assassinating Japanese military police in Manila.²⁰⁹ On 8 April the chief of the Central Luzon military police, Captain Ikeda, responded with a letter offering Marking a chance to surrender within ten days or face attack. "I hope you will understand this present situation, and be a historic man for the establishment of the New Philippines," Ikeda wrote.²¹⁰ At Panlilio's urging, Marking reluctantly dispersed his men and ordered them to lay low. Ikeda then began a three-week campaign and detained, tortured, and executed many civilians.

During a full moon on 18 April Japanese patrols arrived at Marking's base on Mount Kanumay. For a full day, they killed or drove off guerrillas and burned the local crops and then left. Suddenly they returned. For four days Marking and forty-nine of his followers managed to stay one step ahead of their pursuers before finally slipping through the enemy lines to safety.²¹¹

NORTHERN LUZON, D495/R-554

By mid-March Blackburn was finally well enough to leave Volckmann's camp in Ifugao and begin searching for guerrillas in Benguet. He explained, "My objective was to find out who was still around after the intense Jap patrol activity, and what the attitude of the native population was after such an ordeal."²¹² After two weeks, he returned with an American, Mr. Fish, who recounted enemy activities in the area since Moses' October attacks. "I learned that large quantities of weapons had been captured when the Japs moved out," Blackburn reported, "and that a lot of guerrillas had been captured. People had been scattered to the four winds."²¹³ The Japanese had also captured Herb Swick in Uding and shot Dr. Biason's wife Daisy.

Fish agreed to go back to Benguet and find guerrillas. After he left, Blackburn and Volckmann learned the Japanese knew they were in Antipolo and were heading their way. The two escaped by night to Haliap, where Volckmann continued to try to organize his force and extend his intelligence network. "To supplement our fixed agents, we employed special agents who traveled widely under various guises as merchants or peddlers," he recalled.²¹⁴ Not until 16 April, however, would Volckmann's search parties find a radio receiver for his headquarters. "This was the start of the beginning," remembered Blackburn.²¹⁵

VISAYAS, D497/R-552

On 18 April Vargas visited Negros and Panay with chief justice José Yulo. The Japanese apparently felt satisfied enough to transfer the 2nd Infantry Division to the southeastern area, yet the JMA department of industries complained that the Antique copper mine had not reached the ore extraction phase.[216] In April the Fourteenth Army fired the mine's manager, Mineo Mori, and would replace him with Hideo Yamazaki in July. Not until twelve months later would Antique reach its extraction target of 19,000 tons of copper ore, but guerrillas and a lack of transportation would close the mine in November 1944.

Vargas blamed Peralta for turmoil on Panay. He reported to the JMA, "Capiz is totally hopeless. Not a single official was in office. Provincial and municipal officials have been taken by guerrillas."[217] Asked about Confesor, Vargas answered, "He is hopeless. Nobody can make him give up. We will go get him!"[218] He suggested that the Fourteenth Army should arm the Iloilo constabulary so they could get Confesor and "clean up" the province.

The Southern General Army authorized the formation of a military auxiliary of "locally recruited non-Japanese soldiers attached to the Japanese military in order to supplement military action."[219] The auxiliary units in the Philippines would eventually include "the Navy Free Unit" in Zamboanga, the Pro-Japanese Unit in Nueva Ecija, the Standing Army in Negros Occidental, and the National Unity of the Children of Rizal in Laguna and Rizal provinces.

Meanwhile, Bell returned to Villamor on Negros. He reported that when he landed in Cebu seven weeks earlier, Fenton's men "escorted" him to their headquarters in Balanbar, where he found two previous delegations imprisoned. In a fit of rage, Fenton told Bell, "Tell Villamor we don't want him or anyone else to butt into our affairs."[220] Bell noted, however, that Fenton and Cushing had a well-organized, armed force that had killed a great many Japanese—and local politicians—and besieged the garrisons in Toledo, Carcar, and Cebu City.

Bell offered recognition and aid from SWPA, but Fenton replied, "To hell with that stuff. We don't want 'recognition' or anything like that from MacArthur or anybody else until the American flag is flying over here again."[221] Fenton had Bell and his men ushered from the island with a warning: "Tell Villamor next time not to expect the return of anyone he decides to send—if he is crazy enough to do so."[222] James Cushing walked Bell to his boat, saying he hoped his report would not be all bad before quietly adding, "But I cannot go on like this much longer."[223]

As Blackburn later realized, the guerrillas' power "represented a beautiful way for the people to get even with their enemies."[224] Certainly this dynamic marked the more than sixty executions Fenton ordered between July and December 1942.²²⁵ Before the war, his aide Ramon Durano, the "Caesar of Cebu," had lost a race for the first district congressional seat to Osmeña ally Celestino Rodriguez.²²⁶ "Under Fenton's authority," Michael Cullinane explained, "Durano is said to have used his position in the guerrillas to arrest, try, and summarily execute prewar political figures in the First District suspected of collaborating with the Japanese. After the war, it was alleged that many of these executions were part of a systematic elimination of the political allies of Celestino Rodriguez."²²⁷ To prevent similar malfeasance, Blackburn and Volckmann said, "We felt that we should make the judgment [on executions], even though it sounds dictatorial, because we didn't have any axe to grind other than the accomplishment of our mission, whereas, many of these people had a hell of a lot of axes to grind."²²⁸

Fenton's isolation secured his absolute authority, but it was not all by design. He somehow managed to use a radio station identified as WJE. MacArthur's G-2 described this as "one of the more unfortunate incidents in the history of radio contacts in the Philippines."²²⁹ On 14 February 1943 the war department notified SWPA that WJE broadcasted "in the clear, information of value to the enemy and would not cease despite War Department orders."²³⁰ SWPA asked Villamor and Peralta to get Fenton to stop his broadcasts. After about thirty days the station went silent and then fell into Japanese hands. The Cebu guerrillas would remain without a radio until Villamor provided one in late 1943.

MINDANAO, D504/R-545

Fertig's agents made contact with a band of three hundred Chinese guerrillas under Albert I. N. Kwok east of Jesselton in North Borneo where 10th MD Lieutenant José Valera raised money and arms.²³¹ After Moro traders informed Kwok of Suarez's guerrillas in Tawi Tawi, he persuaded them to take him there in May. He made a second trip to Tawi Tawi in June with money and medical supplies. As a reward, Fertig commissioned Kwok as third lieutenant.

Fertig decided to send the disgruntled Morgan on another round of travels, first to Leyte to unite the 9th MD (Leyte and Samar) under Kangleon.²³² Unsuccessful there, Morgan moved on to Siquijor and recruited guerrilla Major Benito Cunanan to command Cebu. Cunanan relied on Morgan's authority as a SWPA agent, but Cebu's guerrillas were not persuaded. When Cunanan's effort fell apart, hard feelings developed between him and the 10th MD.

Morgan went to Negros to recruit Gador to lead the 7th MD. He also provided arms and other supplies to Villamor—and regaled him with how he had made Fertig a general by "taking a lesson from *Mein Kampf* that a lie will be believed if it is big enough."[233] Morgan said he had turned beaten men into the guerrilla organization across Mindanao. Villamor thought Morgan a "proud and brave man," a "restless man, frustrated by orders that came later to only 'annoy' the enemy."[234] He added, "I wondered if Morgan was aware that Fertig not only had pushed him up [promoted him] but had in effect thrown him out of the command. I had intelligence reports to this effect. Fertig wanted Morgan out of the way."[235]

Villamor believed Morgan was oblivious to Fertig's designs and wrote: "He had been spreading Fertig's name everywhere, throughout the Islands, without really realizing that the Filipinos felt this was their cause, and they weren't about to step in line behind some unknown American."[236] Villamor warned Morgan that Fertig would always favor Americans with the best accommodations, equipment, and assignments. Morgan was a victim of remnant colonial exploitation, and Villamor advised him to end his tour.

Meanwhile, on 30 April, SS-211 *Gudgeon* under Lt. Cdr. W. S. Post Jr. spent five days attacking enemy ships before delivering six men of the Pleven team under Second Lieutenant Toribio Crespo with three tons of equipment to Pucio Point, Panay (see map 6.3).[237] *Gudgeon* then brought four more tons of supplies to Tawi Tawi and Mindanao before spending another eight days sinking Japanese light vessels with its deck guns and heading for Pearl Harbor.

Parsons arrived in Bukidnon, Mindanao, to settle the dispute between Fertig and Pendatun. He met "General" Pendatun in the Del Monte section in the southern Cagayan Valley, where he commanded a large Moro force assisted by a robust staff including Americans.[238] The organization was self-sufficient, with livestock and farms and their own powerful radio station. Pendatun saw no reason to work under Fertig. Not until he staged a demonstration against enemy troops barricaded in a school building in Malaybay did Parsons see a way to convince him otherwise.[239]

After failing to dislodge the enemy with machine guns and homemade bombs, Pendatun sent in a buffalo strapped with aerial bombs modified with dynamite fuses to finish the job. Parsons casually mentioned that with the mortars and bazookas he provided to Fertig, Pendatun's force would be far more lethal. Mention of "the Aid" did the trick.[240] Pendatun contacted Fertig by radio and accepted his standing offer to serve as a major in the 10th MD and redesignate his men as the 117th Regiment.[241] On 3 May, however, Bowler informed Fertig anew that Pendatun's executive officer,

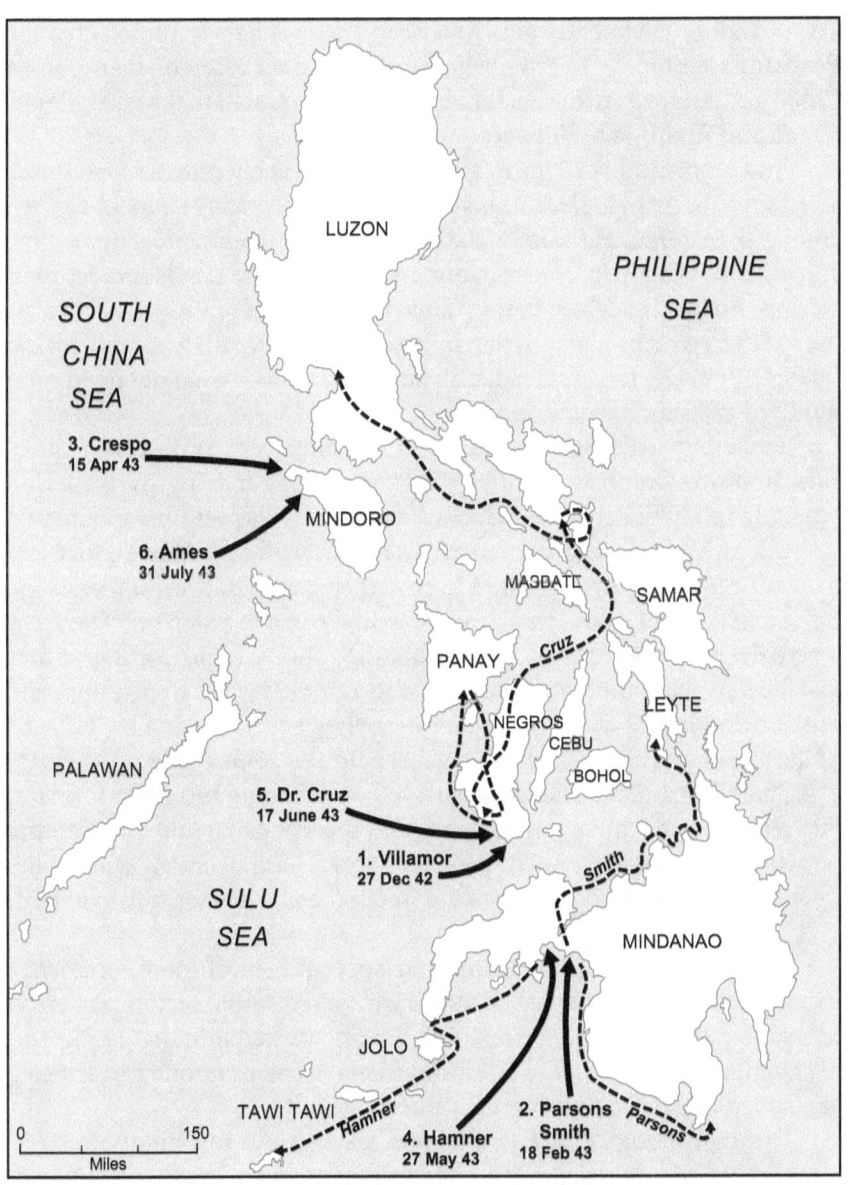

MAP 6.3. AIB missions to the Philippines, December 1942–July 1943

Ed Andrews, "is violently anti-American [and] is largely responsible for Pendatun's attitude."[242] Fertig called former Lanao assemblyman Tomas Cabili and Andrews to his headquarters and sent Cabili to the guerrillas in Lanao and Andrews to Villamor on Negros.

To command his 109th Regiment, Fertig recruited James Grinstead, a retired U.S. Army officer in his early fifties with many years of service among the Moros. He was "a stable and careful commander in a difficult area."[243] With help from Parsons and Kuder, more bands sprang up in Nasipit, Buenavista, Cabadbaran, and the lower Agusan River to become the 113th Regiment under Syrian mining engineer Khalil Khodr, "a highly intelligent, brave, forceful leader."[244] Somehow Khodr even obtained nine hundred arms for his new outfit.

Returning to Fertig's headquarters, Parsons went to observe a guerrilla ambush. Outposts reported Japanese troops moving on a routine schedule in big boiler-plated trucks.[245] The guerrillas set up an L-shaped ambush on a narrow stretch of road in a mountain forest. At one end, a few men with tommy guns were told to shoot windshields, tires, and engines. A lieutenant told Parsons the Japanese would come to a stop fifty feet from where the guerrillas opened fire because they always came to a stop at that distance. At that point guerrillas dug and camouflaged a trench opposite of the firing line to catch the Japanese as they exited the trucks, because under fire they always exited the trucks and ran to that side of the road. The guerrillas waited. The trucks arrived on schedule and came to a stop fifty feet from the initial engagement, and the troops ran out and into the pit where they were executed. Parsons wrote, "I am definitely a guerrilla. I see no sense in risking annihilation in open combat when you can fight, kill, run—and, later, fight again."[246]

Fertig's embrace of the Moros and appointment of more Americans irritated Morgan. Adding to Villamor's whispered suspicions about Fertig, Morgan's constant female companion Sinang warned him that Fertig and his countrymen were out to get him.[247] Pendatun's promotion over Morgan added one more straw on the camel's back.[248]

Through Fertig's contacts, Parsons reached out to Philippine senator José Ozámiz to discuss "the establishment of an Intelligence Net in Manila."[249] The senator, from the prominent Mindanao Spanish copra planters, had earned a law degree at Columbia University in 1929 and had remained in the government to gather intelligence for the guerrillas.[250] On 25 May Ozámiz arrived by boat with Jose Maria and Pelong Campos to meet Parsons and Fertig.[251]

The senator was one of many prominent agents in contact with Parsons. Juan Elizade was a wealthy polo-playing son of a Manila family invested in sugar, shipping, and insurance companies. With his brother Manuel, he organized the underground "28 Men of Fort Santiago," who circulated in social circles and business communities to collect information from Japanese commercial and political contacts.[252] Parsons also communicated with industrialist and statesman Salvador Araneta, Women's Society of Christian Service Manila District president Mrs. Asuncion Perez, Mabini Academy founder Dr. Jose Katigbak, and Menzi Company founder and chief executive officer Hans Menzi. President of the Sanitary Division in Lanao and Philippine army reserve captain Dr. Antonio Montalva also visited Parsons. Among other contacts were A. F. Gonzales, Antonio Pertierra, Enrique Priovano, Prasedes Verona, and Mary B. Stagg.[253]

Ozámiz reported that some people in Luzon supported the Japanese and were well rewarded for it.[254] Most of the people, however, simply endured. To get food and other rationed necessities, they joined the neighborhood associations that required spying on friends and neighbors. Ozámiz explained, "It is difficult to persuade those, who otherwise would be helpful, that they have a higher duty to their country than to the families."[255] Parsons commissioned Ozámiz as a Philippine army lieutenant colonel.[256]

On 5 May, KZRH radio broadcasted news of Tojo's return to the Philippines in front of cheering crowds orchestrated by Vargas under orders from Consul Kihara.[257] Twenty-four hours later at a "day of gratitude" ceremony in Manila's Luneta Park, Tojo announced: "You Filipinos today are going to wipe away your mistaken Americanism . . . and return to your true character as a nation of great East Asian origin. . . . we urge you all to cooperate in winning the Greater East Asian War more actively . . . and be invested with the crown of national independence as quickly as possible."[258] On 9 May the first anniversary of Corregidor's surrender, Vargas publicly called on "misguided remnants of USAFFE" to surrender.[259] Fertig reported, "KGEI commented 'Tozyo [Tojo] visit to the Islands will be restricted by the activities of the Filipino-American troops.' This is one of the first official admissions of our activities." [260]

7

Divisions
May–October 1943

NEGROS, D523/R-526

On 14 May Villamor suggested to SWPA that he be made permanent commander of the 7th MD. They told him to concentrate on getting the Negros guerrillas to cooperate and report malcontents to MacArthur "for appropriate disciplinary action when circumstances permit."[1] SWPA reminded Villamor to designate a permanent district commander when he thought the time was right. Villamor decided on Abcede with Gador as chief of staff. He would commission Bell as a major to serve as both Negros civil administrator and chairman of a 7th MD research board. Villamor also established a free government under Negros Occidental's popular prewar governor Alfredo Montelibano, a thirty-six-year-old wealthy planter described as "aggressive, a tireless worker and exacting in his demands for work done" and "a program socialist fighting for the welfare of the poorer class."[2]

On 28 May Villamor announced the new staff assignments at a meeting with Abcede, Ausejo, Montelibano, Bell, and Romero Intengan. Gador came late. The attendees asked for medicine, money, radios, arms, and recognition. Villamor demanded cooperation and threatened, "I will shoot any son of bitch who doesn't get the message. . . . My command is temporary, and when I see fit, when one of you shows me that you can command respect and cooperation from all others, I'll make him the permanent district commander."[3] That seemed to work. Villamor ordered the guerrillas to wear their prewar rank, which brought violent objections from Gador. The Planet commander informed SWPA that Gador was "a better politician than soldier" and "does not believe in uniting Negros."[4]

Villamor called another conference for the third week of June to announce command arrangements. Mata, Abcede, and Ausejo offered their support, but Villamor received little backing to remain as 7th MD commander. Gador arrived with a large armed escort and agreed to be Abcede's executive officer. A Japanese patrol unexpectedly landed nearby and burned Bell's camp. "Gador and most of his men fled without assisting in the local defenses though he had a position assigned," Villamor reported.[5]

LUZON, D532/R-517

The Japanese campaign in northern Luzon abated with the arrival of the rainy season. Merrill organized the western Luzon guerrilla force in the Zambales Mountains northeast of San Marcelino. Another one thousand men rallied under Antonio Francisco around Castillejos. Newly promoted majors Ramsey and Lapham went to see Charlie Putnam in the Lingayen Gulf. Everywhere they went, Filipinos asked one question: When would MacArthur return? "His name was like an invocation to them, a holy word that had special power and meaning," Ramsey remembered. "None of them doubted his promise to return, but they were anxious to learn when the invasion would come."[6]

Putnam agreed to organize Pangasinan Province for Ramsey as part of Lapham's force. Waving an arm, he shared his command philosophy: "We control these people. We hold their lives in our hands. Being a guerrilla leader is like being a king, Ramsey, you have absolute power over people."[7] He described his Igorots and Ilongots as headhunters and, sometimes, cannibals who invited Japanese raids as an opportunity for spoil. "That's guerrilla warfare, and as far as they're concerned I'm no captain, I'm the king."[8]

Volckmann established lines of communication out of Ifugao while Moses and Noble watched increased Japanese activity in Apayao. They expected Praeger's radio to go off the air again. A week later a large force captured 2nd Battalion's captain Rufino Baldwin, who had been, in Volckmann's words, "terrorizing the Japanese in the area south of Baguio for many months."[9] Baldwin's fiancé had called him to her house. When he arrived, Japanese troops took him prisoner. Calvert promoted Grafton Spencer to command the 2nd Battalion.

The Japanese neared Haliap, causing Volckmann to ask for Kamayong's help in moving his headquarters. The chief sent four shamans to hold a *bacci* ceremony. They spread out tobacco, rice, and other items on a blanket, chanted, and slaughtered four small chickens. The entrails indicated that the Americans would be safe where they were after the shamans concealed chicken legs on the approaches. Volckmann protested to no avail. "The Jap patrol did come to the very foot of the hill upon which our camp was located," he recalled, "but upon arriving at the spot where the chicken legs were buried they changed their direction and went on down the river valley!"[10]

MANILA, D537/R-512

On 28 May fifty-five-year-old Lieutenant General Shigenori Kuroda arrived to replace General Tanaka in command of the Fourteenth Army. Kuroda's thirty-three years with the army included tours socializing as a military attaché in England and India.[11] Barrameda observed, "In Manila, Kuroda spent much of his time on golf, geishas, and goofing off—and because discipline became lax, he was soon on bad terms with many of his senior officers."[12] Kuroda would make few preparations to defend the islands because he considered them "obviously indefensible."[13]

A week earlier the year-old Greater East Asia Establishment Council issued a report calling for cultural programs to draw occupied lands closer to Japan.[14] One promising effort was the special overseas students from the southern regions program that sent native future leaders to Japan for education and acculturalization. By the fall, 116 students from the territories were in Japan—among 27 from the Philippines were the sons of Vargas and Laurel.[15] Another twenty-four young Filipinos went the following year, meaning Filipinos comprised one-quarter of all students in the program. Only the Filipinos, however, complained about instructions to reject "lazy" Western humanist attitudes in favor of rigorous, disciplined Japanese outlooks.[16]

The day after Kuroda's arrival, 63 Japanese transports arrived in Manila with 150,000 troops, of which 50,000—many of them "Indo-Chinese and Burmese recruits"—took up stations in and around the city.[17] The army scheduled construction to begin in October of munition storage sites in Manila, Corregidor, Lamao, Kalaklan, Tabaco, Cebu, Iloilo, Davao, and Cagayan.[18] Villamor's agents provided daily details of the Japanese moves in the Visayas and Luzon.[19] He then fell sick. When Maria nursed him back to health, he proposed, and she accepted.

BRISBANE, D541/R-508

At SWPA, the first thing MacArthur did each morning was look for the reports from the Philippines.[20] The AIB now had agents on Mindanao, Negros, Tawi Tawi, Cebu, Panay, and in Manila. The general became more determined "to weld the scattered groups into unified and responsible forces through the designation and support of responsible local commanders."[21] SWPA G-2 noted this as "the approximate end of the preliminary or pathfinding phase of intelligence development."[22] It was time for a more robust staff to prepare for MacArthur's return.

SWPA drafted a plan to transform the AIB Philippine subsection into a larger Philippine regional section under the G-2 (see map 7.1). Given more supplies, submarines, and personnel, the PRS was to establish bases in Mindoro and Samar, conduct intelligence penetration of Luzon, and close gaps in the existing intelligence nets south from Luzon. MacArthur approved the PRS and recalled from Washington old Philippine hand Col. Courtney Whitney Jr. to lead it. "He was ideal for such an assignment," wrote MacArthur. "A prominent Manila lawyer, his thirteen years there had made him thoroughly familiar with Philippine conditions and personnel."[23]

Notified of his new assignment, Whitney arranged to have the Signal Corps organize the 978th Signal Service Company to support infiltration missions.[24] Ignoring AIB plans to secure one hundred volunteers from the stateside 1st and 2nd Filipino Regiments over a two-year period, Whitney inspected the regiments and quickly hand-picked four hundred men for PRS missions.[25] The PRS then organized the "volunteers" into the 3217th Reconnaissance Battalion.

On 23 May Whitney arrived at SWPA. Six days later he attended a conference in Sutherland's office to clarify "the relationship of G-2 to the AIB and, more particularly, the Philippine Regional Section, AIB, as well as the responsibilities for both."[26] MacArthur explained Whitney's new mission:

> His objectives were the formation of a battle detachment in every important Filipino area, alerted to strike against the enemy's rear as our battle-lines advanced; to secure fields adjacent to military objectives into which our airmen might drop with assurances of immediate rescue and protection; to arouse the militant loyalty of a whole people by forming resolute armed centers of resistance around which they could rally; to establish a vast network of agents numbering into the thousands to provide precise, accurate, and detailed information on major enemy moves and installations; to create a vast network of radio positions extending into every center of enemy activity and concentration through the islands; to build on every major island of the Philippines a completely equipped and staffed weather observatory to flash to my headquarters full weather data morning, afternoon, and night of every day; to implement an air-warning system affording visual

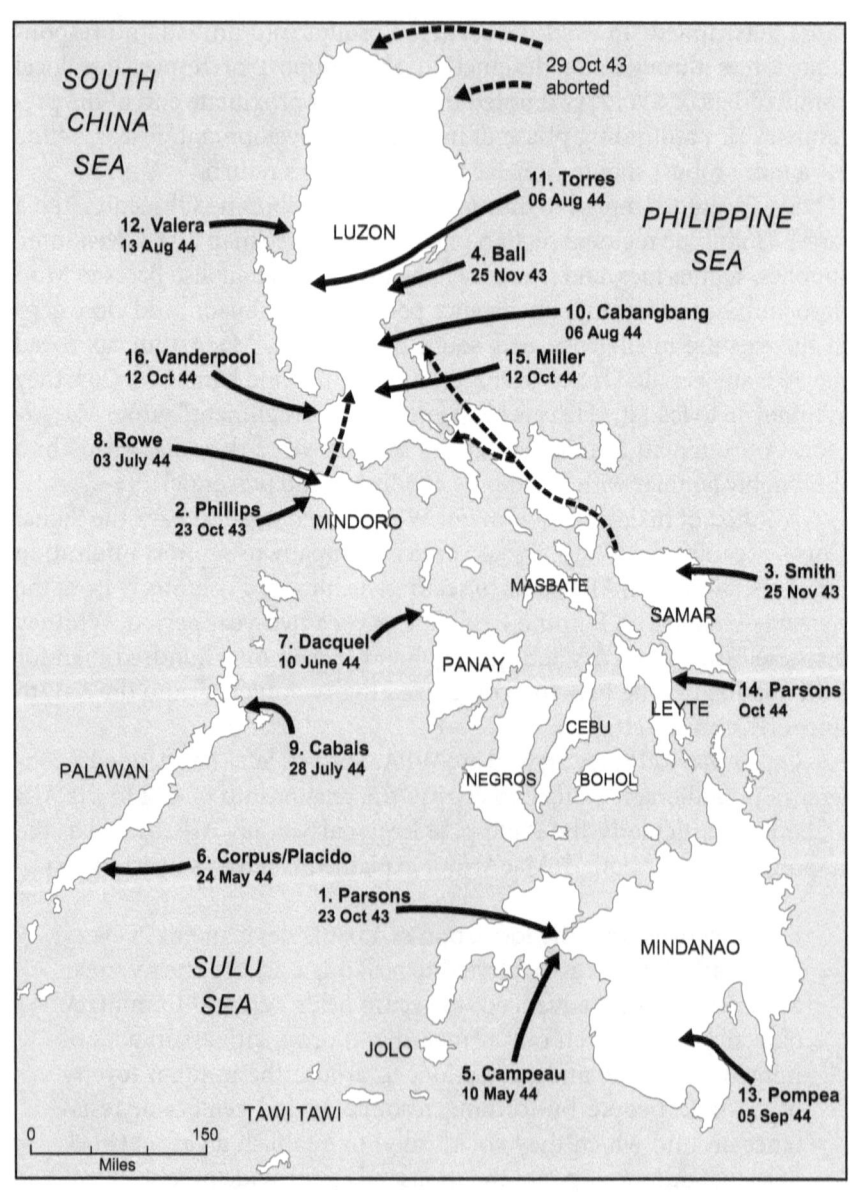

MAP 7.1. Philippine regional section missions, October 1943–October 1944

observation of the air over every square foot of Philippine soil to give immediate warning of enemy aircraft or naval movement to our submarines on patrol in Philippine waters; to apply close interior vigilance so as to secure for our military use enemy documents of value; and to exploit any other aids to our military operations that might arise.[27]

Despite the carryover of AIB personnel such as Major Ind, transition to the PRS opened a gap between ongoing guerrilla intelligence collection and new SWPA missions. Five years later MacArthur's G-2 acknowledged that "several previously established channels were ignored or not fully exploited, especially the Villamor net," while the "new channels developed were all under American leadership and were based mainly on personnel from Australian bases."[28] Focused on MacArthur's return, the PRS sidestepped the predominantly Filipino irregulars to place U.S. Army missions under regular Army officers. That those officers were white pricked Filipino sensitivities to historic imperial and racial prejudices.

The PRS used AIB facilities at Camp Tabragalbra and Frazer Island near Brisbane to prepare agents for its missions. Army Signal Corps Lt. Louis Brown trained American and Hawaiian-born Filipino volunteers to be guerrillas, coast watchers, aircraft spotters, and weather observers.[29] By August the camp held 125 officers and men, with plans to increase to about 800.[30] At any one time five groups of twenty-five volunteers entered phase one drills without being told "the reason for this training or their possible destinations."[31] The groups rotated through "Ranger type training and School of the Soldier."[32] The AIB then selected students for fifty-six days of advanced training on guerrilla operations, Japanese and local cultures, and cryptography.

Parsons coordinated supplies for the PRS and for submarines with the 7th Fleet staff while Whitney oversaw all liaison with guerrillas. In June the submarine SS-202 *Trout* delivered the five-man Tenwest team under Capt. Jordan Hamner to Labangan, Mindanao, with two tons of supplies, including six thousand rounds of .30-caliber and two thousand rounds of .45-caliber ammunition.[33] Though impressive, the amounts fell well short of the 50 million .30-caliber rounds and 20 million .45-caliber rounds Fertig had requested in March.[34] Hamner brought Lt. Franklyn Young Jr., returning after his escape with Albert Klestadt, to establish a radio station near Zamboanga City. Then "after a short review with Col. Fertig," they were off to Tawi Tawi to provide radios to Suarez.[35]

After attacking transports and destroyers off Celebes, SS-200 *Thresher* under Lt. Cdr. Harry Hull transported Hamner and his agents to Sulu to set up a radio station on the Sibitu Passage.[36] On 9 July Hull delivered

Hamner and the remaining five members of his team to Catmon Point, Negros, with 500 pounds of supplies and 40,000 rounds of ammunition before heading to Pearl Harbor for an overhaul.[37]

Hamner's mission would not end well. In November the AIB would send supplies through British agents based on Borneo. SWPA instructed the two teams to establish radio contact but noted: "Neither party had much interest in inter-communications and their failure to take any such action in this connection was received with a certain amount of prejudice against Hamner."[38] Suddenly SWPA noticed Hamner had problems with malaria, his teeth, and an ear growth. The PRS later recommended that SWPA not reward Hamner for his service in the islands.[39]

Despite increased support, the guerrillas continued to struggle. As Blackburn stated, "About the time you'd think you got over with an illness, bam! You were hit with something else."[40] Just moving in jungles caused casualties. Noble lost an eye to a tree branch.[41] Lapham fell into a hole one night and broke his shoulder, and an ill-trained medic made him a poorly constructed cast. "His [the medic's] replacement," recalled Lapham, "seeing at once that the cast was unsuitable, cut it off and discovered that what had originally been a simple break had been made a good deal worse by the misplaced efforts of his predecessor."[42] Lapham underwent surgery and received a larger cast.

Psychological challenges aggravated physical hardships. Volckmann believed relentless tension awoke dormant character defects in many men. He wrote, "Each day they became more depressed and listless, and with few exceptions these men readily gave up when forced into a tight spot. If overtaken by fever or some other tropical illness, they often displayed no determination to fight back and as a result usually died within a few days."[43] He found remedy in sound organization, coherent operational direction, and firm military discipline.

By June famine and shortages were wearing on guerrillas and civilians alike. "Locusts had stripped the coconut palms of their leaves, making branches stick out like the ribs of umbrellas. A bar of soap was like a precious jewel," Villamor recalled. "People moved about in clothing they had worn for months, men and women walked barefoot or in shoes with soles made from bits of old automobile tires."[44] Malnourishment increased susceptibility to disease—often spread by released POWs and furloughed guerrillas.[45] "And everywhere," Villamor added, "there was the nagging, persistent question: When *would* aid come?"[46]

The bonds connecting guerrillas and the people were strained. "We guerrillas considered that we had a right to civilian support," Lapham wrote, "since we were risking our lives against common enemies and of course could not operate without food and equipment. Yet civilians only had so much to give anyone; if pressed too hard they might starve."[47] The resistance groups innovated methods for obtaining support. Some "taxed" locals through a free local government or by direct requisition. Most tried to limit demands on those closest to them for fear of losing both popular support and the loyalty of guerrillas with local family.[48]

Few villages paid taxes with money; most donated food or other goods. Guerrillas also purchased goods with scrip they printed or left IOUs and tried to keep records of payments. The USAFIP-NL guerrillas signed receipts. Yet balance sheets failed to reflect the tense debates over scarce financial resources that could rip apart organizations. "How many quarrels we had had over finances!" recalled Panlilio of her dealings with Marking.[49] Guerrillas lucky enough to receive cash from SWPA encountered strict accounting rules.[50] Lapham actually declined $50,000 in genuine Philippine pesos because of SWPA's rules. "I did not keep formal records of such 'sales,' or of contributions either," he explained, "because I thought it dangerous to write of benefactors in record books that might be seized by the enemy."[51] Bernard Anderson took the money but later could not account for $20,000 he gave to Alejandro Santos.[52]

Cash was key for obtaining medicines, often through the black market. Guerrillas could get weapons from raids, black markets, or old battlefields; the LGAF collected nearly three thousand rifles from Bataan.[53] They could distill fuel from coconuts.[54] As for other items, Willis noted, "I was beginning to realize that if you ever want anything and can't find it, all you have to do is go to a Chinese merchant in town, and he probably will have it or can locate it."[55]

Food remained a most elusive commodity.[56] Blackburn remembered, "We got control of the towns, and the mayors were directed to appoint food administrators who would work with my food administrator. We would tax the mayor for so much rice and other food stuffs, and his food administrator would gather it up."[57] Even the most loyal Filipinos, however, had limits. It was said of Ernesto Felix, a volunteer home guard battalion commander in central Luzon: "He fed his children with one finger; and devoted the other nine to the fighters."[58] The Japanese captured Felix and tortured him to death.

Starvation became the price of resistance. American guerrillas lost on average about 40 percent of their body weight. They survived on such concoctions as *ginamoose*, which Stahl described as "a slurry of boiled baby shrimp, small enough to qualify as maggots. I've never eaten maggots, but they couldn't have tasted worse than *ginamoose*."[59] They ate carabao blood: "We would set the cup by the fire and let the blood congeal. Then we dumped out the lump of blood, sliced it, and put it on our rice or fried it and ate it with our rice."⁶⁰ They made the most of staples like the tree fruit *tuba*. Gatherers scaled palm trees daily, sliced *tuba* buds, and hung bamboo buckets to collect the dripping juice. A day later, they gathered the juice into a larger bucket and repeated the process. After one day, the juice tasted like beer. After five days, it served as the base for a kind of pepper vinegar. After ten days, it could be triple-distilled and used as gasoline. This caused a problem: "It was not unusual for [drivers] to siphon the fuel from the tank along the way to mix a few highballs."⁶¹

Coconuts were a vital, versatile item. The palms furnished thatched roofs, baskets, and hats. The husks made for firewood and ash to make lye. A guerrilla recalled, "The un-matured meat inside is a jelly-like consistency but very pleasant to eat."⁶² The half-inch-thick meat of a ripe coconut was 68 percent oil. Mixed with water, it made milk to pour on toasted rice and sugar for cereal. Native women shaved coconut meat and boiled the slivers in a fifty-five-gallon drum until the oil settled on top. "Then they had a nice clear oil for cooking, for lamps, or for anything else which oil could be used for," Willis remembered.⁶³ Guerrillas learned to strip the husk off a mature coconut, punch holes where the shell connected to the tree, pour in a tablespoonful of sugar, plug the holes, and bury the coconut six inches below warm sand. "Wait at least a week before removing it from its 'oven.' Voila!" Stahl recalled. "You have a cupful of sweet-tasting alcohol not unlike Southern Comfort (if you have enough imagination)."⁶⁴

The general shortages made the Japanese pacification campaign of early 1943 particularly effective. Blackburn recalled, "Things were tough all over. The people were afraid to support guerrilla units.... And, there was no protection from all the spies and informers who were beginning to spring up."⁶⁵ While meeting with Huks, Ramsey collapsed with what he later believed was a "mild stroke" with "fits of paralysis and unconsciousness."⁶⁶ Blackburn would soon abandon operations "to go to Uding to receive another series of shots for his fever."⁶⁷ Volckmann retreated into the Zambalese mountains and reported: "The clean pine odor and the cool refreshing air of this beautiful country made me feel like a different person. Already I felt that by the grace of God I would again get strong and well."⁶⁸ Like many others, he traded opportunity to attack the enemy for healthier living conditions.

LUZON, D543/R-506

Late on 3 June at Number 9 Third Street in Manila, Antonio Bautista of the Free Philippines sent his children and household staff to the movies.

He and his wife Adalia Marquez held a dinner with U.S. Army Col. Narcisco Manzano, law professor Jose B. L. Reyes, journalist Rafael R. "Liling" Roces Jr., and popular resistance leader Lorenzo Tanada. Each was hostage to the loyalty of the others. Arrest of one could lead to the execution of the others. "That was the beginning of the end of peaceful period I may have hoped for," recalled Adalia.[69]

Two days later at 0600 hours, Roces played a round of golf with PEC president Jose Laurel and several doctors at the Wack Wack golf and country club in Mandaluyong.[70] On the seventh tee, a man with a .45-caliber handgun shot Laurel twice in the back. The doctors hurried him to the Philippine general hospital, where medical personnel joined by JMA chief surgeon Colonel Ishii saved his life. The Kempeitai launched a massive search for the gunman, rumored at first to be one of Marking's men known as "Little Joe." Laurel urged compassion for his attacker and wrote, "I condemn cowardice and treachery but I must respect the political ideology of people plunged into desperation in a situation in which I played an important role."[71] According to Agoncillo, the Kempeitai apprehended and executed Captain Palma Martin, a member of Colonel Enrique Arce's Hunters guerrillas unit, but Laurel later identified his attacker as former boxer Feliciano Lizardo.[72] Whoever the attacker, the act was a warning to collaborators. "People speak in whispers of a blacklist, which contains the names of several very prominent collaborators, supposedly marked men," noted Pacita Pestano-Jacinto. "The inference is that guerrilla bands have become bolder, more active, that the policy is to do away with political men who have no compunction about making their pro-Japanese sentiments public."[73]

On 9 June Volckmann learned boldness had its price. Kalinga, Moses, and Noble left a cave near Lubuagan to go for supplies. "According to the story that we heard," recalled Blackburn, "they had native boys they'd send out in front of them, supposedly to scout the trail, but the scouts carelessly let it be known that 'the colonels are coming, the colonels are coming.'"[74] The Japanese tortured the runner to locate the American officers. "The captured colonels were rushed to Bontoc, the capital of the Mountain Province," Volckmann wrote, "where the Japanese commander forged an order by the colonels directing all guerrillas to surrender."[75] Blackburn added: "The morale of personnel and the units hit a new low, if you could call them 'units.' The men suffered from the lack of food and medical supplies. We just didn't have anything."[76]

Volckmann assumed leadership of the two thousand USAFIP-NL guerrillas dispersed in small groups with few arms and little ammunition. With Praeger's radio offline, he had no means to communicate with

SWPA. "Anti-resistance feeling mounted so high in some areas that it was impossible to send even a native runner through those areas without having him apprehended, tied on a pole like a pig, and carried to the Japs," he noted.[77] On 20 June Japanese troops struck near Volckmann's camp in Haliap. That night he wrote: "Hid our surplus things and went to our hide out."[78] Over the next few weeks, residents reported Japanese soldiers asking about Volckmann and Blackburn by name. The two guerrillas left Ifugao.

MINDANAO, D552/R-497

Fertig was bedridden in Liangan with intestinal illness when Hamner landed near Labangan on 12 June. He lamented, "The casa is the one place in the whole world in which it is almost a pleasure to be sick. The war seems so far away and yet it is just across the bay.... Unless the offensive starts very soon, we are lost, for we can't meet the full force of the enemy."[79] Japanese troops alit in nearby Misamis, and Morgan left them unopposed, later claiming to have followed orders to lay low. When he finally sent guerrillas into Misamis, contrary to Fertig's orders, it was only to seize arms from those who had fled.[80] On top of this, Fertig heard that "Andrews is continuing his anti-American conversations."[81] In a severe rebuke to Morgan, the 10th MD commander named Robert Bowler as his chief of staff and added more Americans and Moros to his organization.[82]

Fertig then uncovered a Moro spy ring centered on an agent named Quizon, whom he found "reporting my movements and indicating the possibility of an early attack."[83] Increasingly paranoid, Fertig sent Captain William Knortz to Surigao, Major Garcia into central Surigao, and Captain Tomanning to Lianga with orders to eliminate any restless guerrillas. In September Knortz, a fearless U.S. Air Corps corporal and a "firm dealer in organizing recalcitrant guerrilla groups," would drown when his boat to Agusan capsized.[84] This was a doubly tough blow for Fertig, as it followed the suicide of Bill Lowry.[85]

Meanwhile, Parsons was with the Ozámiz family in Jimenez on Iligan Bay when guards on the beach sounded an alarm. While others hastily departed for the jungle, Parsons inexplicably decided he had time for a nap. Awakened suddenly by Japanese soldiers breaking down his front door, he barely escaped out the back with his papers.[86] He traveled for a while with a group under Father Calanan before they headed back to Jimenez to recover a can of wheat flour for communion wafers. Parsons broke away to begin a long trek to rejoin Fertig.

MANILA, D556/R-493

On 16 June Tojo announced that within a year, Japan would grant the "honor of national independence" to the Philippines. The PEC quickly formed a preparatory committee for Philippine independence (PCPI). Three days later, a KALIBAPI convention selected the committee's members: Aguinaldo, Aquino, Osias, Paredes, Recto, Vargas, Yulo, and Roxas (who declined due to illness and recommended first Aquino and then Laurel). The next day Kuroda approved the committee with Laurel as chairman, and the delegation headed to Tokyo.[87] Although Roxas declined, authorities sent him to Tojo, who convinced him to join the constitutional assembly.[88] Utsunomiya oversaw the drafting of a new Philippine constitution, which ironically undermined the JMA: there was less incentive for either Filipinos to work with the Japanese or for the Japanese to pursue long-range plans.[89]

Laurel's selection as PCPI chair indicated a change of fortune for PEC chairman Vargas. Fourteenth Army chief of staff Wachi observed: "No one had been so much taken advantage of and so abruptly rejected by Japan as Jorge B. Vargas. . . . he had been treated as a puppet not only by the Japanese, but also by the prominent Filipinos."[90] The Japanese had hoped Vargas would entice Quezon to join the occupation government. With Quezon ensconced in Washington, Vargas was no longer needed. On 15 July the JMA ordered Alejandro Roces' TVT newspapers to "play down Vargas" and "play up Laurel."[91] The papers began by quoting Laurel: "Vargas cannot handle the situation: If I were given the chance to head the government, I would place all who opposed me under the machine gun."[92]

Roxas kept guerrillas informed about the PCPI. By now Villamor had a robust radio network spanning Negros, Panay, Cebu, Samar, Mindoro, and Leyte.[93] His couriers on Luzon connected Bicol, Laguna, the Cagayan Valley, and Manila.[94] Captain Buenaventura Villanueva (Benny Newcastle) ran spies for him in Manila, including former speaker Jose Yulo, newsman Arsenio Lacson, and University of Santo Tomas professor Manuel Colayco. Catholic priest Father Francisco Avendaño operated a radio transmitter from his church in Manila and sent information through Laguna to Negros and Australia.[95] One of Vargas' press relations officers in Malacañang Palace, Vincente Alvarez, even put coded information in his broadcasts on KZRH that Villamor passed to SWPA.[96]

SOUTHERN LUZON, D557/R-492

Turko continued to send his VTG guerrillas across Bicol after TVGU leader Miranda. In the second week of June a few VTG men under

Lieutenant Rafael Quiñones and Lieutenant Jesus del Valle arrived in Viga, where they converted the Our Lady of the Assumption convent into their headquarters and looted the church. Turko arrived on 17 June and met Miranda in the nearby barrio Rizal. In a heated exchange, Miranda called the VTG deserters. "At this point Quiñones went for his gun, not knowing that Miranda was a fast draw and a dead shot," Barrameda wrote. "Quiñones was dead, a .45-caliber bullet in his forehead, before he even hit the ground."[97] Another VTG man went to shoot, but Miranda gunned him down too. Miranda's party relieved Turko and his men of their bullets and then split up and fled.

Turko returned to his base to Caramoan to gather a larger posse before chasing after Miranda. In Bato, his men caught and killed TVGU Sergeant Manuel San Juan. They would spend July searching in Catanduanes. On 2 July Miranda left Virac in Catanduanes with a small group north to Batan Island, Albay, where he rendezvoused with Faustino Flor. The two decided to join Lapus in Bicol. Miranda continued to Masbate before reaching Panay in mid-August. Over the next month he would confer at least twice with Peralta's chief of staff Relunia in search of recognition and support. There he learned of his promotion to major, on Lapus' recommendation. In mid-September Miranda would leave Panay for Iloilo.

During July Aureus and Padua came to a new understanding. They divided Camarines Sur into five districts, two for Padua and three for Aureus.[98] This ended Padua's agreement to serve under Miranda. Zabat again saw opportunity. In August he settled his differences with Aureus and Padua and brought them into his organization as his 53rd Regiment with Padua in command. He then convinced Turko to join his growing organization as the 54th Regiment.

VISAYAS, D562/R-487

SWPA informed Villamor that they would soon withdraw him from the Philippines, perhaps based on Fertig's assessment: "Unification of Negros is doubtful as Villamor is young. He is using unlimited promotion as a club to buy opposing leaders."[99] A submarine would bring an agent from Quezon around 8 July to Catmon Point. At the end of June fifty Japanese ships upset SWPA's timetable by bombarding Dumaguete and landing four hundred troops at Tolong on Negros. Villamor postponed his departure but still asked SWPA to confirm Abcede as 7th MD commander, assign Ausejo to Fertig, and place Gador on inactive status "for the sake of unity in Negros."[100] SWPA agreed to the first two requests but decided to leave Gador alone for the time being.

On Panay, twenty-six-year-old Lieutenant Colonel Pedro Serran served as Peralta's G-2 and ran his intelligence network. SWPA observed: "There is good indication that his reports are reliable but that his sources are loosely organized and developed, and that little effort is being made to keep the financial accounts of the intelligence sector."¹⁰¹ Indeed, Peralta was spending a half a million pesos each month on intelligence. He had recently told SWPA: "Problem of money this district acute. Released one million pesos printed last month and all gone."¹⁰² At the PRS, Whitney worried: "How much of these funds are actually distributed for legitimate purposes and how much are dedicated to the creation of an overlordship that may later prove a harassing thorn in our side, is a matter for pure conjecture but, as Peralta himself points out in this radio, 'money talks.'"¹⁰³

SWPA suspected Peralta was building a power base.¹⁰⁴ He had sent two groups of agents to Luzon, Captain Alejandro P. Hontiveros with the 2nd Combat Team through Masbate and Lieutenant Colonel Enrique Jurado with 1st Combat Team through Mindoro.¹⁰⁵ By July Peralta had seven radios on Luzon in Batangas, Tarlac, Bataan, Corregidor, Lingayen, Pangasinan, and Cavite.¹⁰⁶ Yet according to SWPA, "Reports were infrequent and often considerably delayed.... Reports from central Luzon and Manila were exaggerated and sometimes were treated with reserve unless verified from other sources."¹⁰⁷ Still, Peralta had agents in the government, in Japanese installations, and on city street corners.¹⁰⁸ He reached into Masbate, Marinduque, Mindoro, and Palawan. He also continued to support Abcede on Negros and Blas Miranda on Leyte. Only Fenton on Cebu and Fertig on Mindanao escaped his influence.

SWPA needed Peralta to rein in Visayan compadre networks that undercut their distribution of supplies. Agents reported: "Supplies sent from SWPA are reported to have appeared in quantity on the black market and seldom reach the needy or those for whom the supplies were intended. ... Besides graft and sometimes strained relations with the civilians, the compadre system by increasing overhead personnel and depleting supplies seriously has further reduced the effectiveness of the organization, destroyed discipline almost entirely and at times immobilized the army."¹⁰⁹ Even so, the PRS would arm nearly 100 percent of guerrillas by mid-1944.¹¹⁰

In Puerto Princesa on Palawan, provincial inspector of the constabulary Major Guillermo Maramba had hidden in the hills with his family and other followers since the Japanese invaded. In June one of the Cobb brothers met with Maramba in Danlig, and they got into a heated argument. Cobb shot and killed Maramba and then tried to recruit his seventy-five armed constabulary members under executive officer Captain Pedro

Manigque.[111] U.S. Army intelligence described Manigque as a "weak character, congenial but not intelligent, and not respected by his men."[112] Even so, Manigque resisted the Cobbs.

On Palawan's north coast, guerrillas under former governor and Philippine army medical reserve Captain Higinio Mendoza suffered from dwindling supplies of equipment, men, and food. In January he merged with the Cobbs to form the Mendoza-Cobb group headquartered in Tinitian and began attacking collaborationists in the bureau of the constabulary.

Second Lieutenant Baldomero R. Garcia, a cousin of a lieutenant colonel in Peralta's command, hid on the west coast of Palawan until February 1943 when he joined Manigque as his executive officer. When Peralta officially recognized Manigque as Palawan commander in early June, Garcia charged Manigque with misuse of funds and won a vote to take command. The next month he promoted himself to first lieutenant and went to Peralta, who decided to keep Manigque in command. In October Peralta would form a special battalion with Garcia as executive officer, but this time Manigque refused to work with him and opposed the battalion. Garcia took Manigque captive in January 1944 and imprisoned him until the end of the war.

Peralta again reached into southern Luzon. In June Escudero sent his son Antonio with three hundred men to Panay seeking permission to organize all of Bicol. Peralta had offered to support anyone who could unite the 5th MD but hesitated to recognize Escudero. Unwilling to wait longer, Escudero declared himself a full colonel in command of all Bicol under authority from Straughn, and warned all others—that is, Peralta—that he would not tolerate interference in his area.

On Negros Siquijor, Major Cunanan placed his two guerrilla battalions under Ausejo's 75th Regiment and confronted the last of several attempted Japanese landings. A captured mine that his men placed in the channel sank an enemy transport at Larena. Although hundreds of soldiers may have drowned, the troops that got ashore dispersed the guerrillas. At Morgan's invitation, Cunanan left Second Lieutenant Eduardo Cornella in charge on Negros Siquijor and went to assume command of the 8th MD in Cebu and Bohol.[113] After several weeks of confusion, he retreated to assume duties as the headquarters commandant for the new 7th MD under Abcede.

Cebu was confusing enough without Cunanan. Fenton and James Cushing had about nine thousand men, half of them armed, and plentiful supplies, supported by another three thousand civilian volunteers. They had access to a literal shipload of food that had never made it to Corregidor because of the Japanese blockade. Yet for months Cushing battled malaria and the Japanese while an exhausted Fenton suspended all guerrilla offensive operations. The people became uneasy. SWPA noted: "Fenton was becoming more eccentric, his killings became more wanton, the lack of pay for his men and the constant Japanese raids caused further disaffection, and many men began to leave for other islands."[114] Fenton was overtly hostile to the popular governor, Hilario Abellana, who had escaped the Japanese to oppose puppet governor Jose Delgado. When Cushing left to recuperate on Negros, he sensed he was on a collision course with Fenton.[115]

LUZON, D572/R-477

On 30 June Tojo began his second tour of Manila with vice minister of Greater East Asian affairs Kenryo Sato and bureau of political affairs chief Kumaichi Yamamoto. The orchestrated throngs of a year earlier failed to materialize. "What is this?" Tojo asked his official reception committee. "This is quite a change from the last time I was here." Wachi lamely answered: "Perhaps it is because it is too warm."[116] Tojo met Laurel and the PCPI in the Manila Hotel and found them cool to his suggestion for a military alliance against the United States.

Stability and security still eluded the Japanese.[117] As July came to a close, the high command ordered a new campaign to end the resistance. They would begin in the Visayan area, deemed to be "the worst in the maintenance of peace and order."[118] The campaign aimed to secure all political centers, resources areas, and strategically and tactically important points by the end of 1943. The order prioritized "the breaking up of guerrilla bases, the destruction of enemy radio apparatus and extermination of enemy submarine bases," and noted that "special attention will be given to win the heart and mind of the people."[119] The Fourteenth Army, however, believed it lacked the numbers required to succeed in such a campaign.[120]

The time seemed opportune for the Japanese. With no signs of MacArthur's return, Ramsey noticed "a waning in the popular will to resist."[121] He thought people were beginning to believe the occupation was "irrevocable" and were demoralized by the broken economy.[122] This dissatisfaction, however, cut two ways. A Japanese Fourteenth Army report noted: "The population gradually turned against the Army because of the shortage of goods, the inflation of money, and above all, the stringency of food, clothing, and housing facilities. Hence, the hold on public opinion, which had been most carefully guided by the Army, was not easy to maintain."[123] The report ranked the areas of worst resistance: Panay, Cebu, Bohol, and Negros.[124]

The resistance hurt Japanese economic exploitation efforts. The Taiheiyo Kogyo company produced a respectable six thousand tons of high-grade manganese ore at the mines in Bani in southern Luzon, but guerrilla intimidation denied recruitment of enough longshoreman to ship the ore.[125] Taiheiyo's chief in the Philippines, Eijiro Namikawa, petitioned the JMA for 40,000 Filipino POWs held in army prisons. The JMA granted the POWs their freedom in exchange for their labor. Taiheiyo engineer Yoichiro Ikeda took 150 POWs from Cabanatuan, and they finished loading the ore in Bani on 29 August before being freed to return to their homes.[126]

In Benguet, the Mitsui mining company increased production of copper ore at the Mankayan copper mine from roughly 800 tons per day in January to a peak of 1,500 tons per day by June.[127] Through financial and material incentives—and Kempeitai coercion—the mine maintained between 4,600 and 5,500 workers guarded by Japanese troops.[128] The guerrillas aimed at more vulnerable points. By September only 52 of the mine's 402 vehicles remained in working order—creating a shipping backlog of 3,400 tons. The JMA sent fifty vehicles from its Manila motor pool and fifty more from the military to transport the stockpile. It also redirected spare parts from the military and Toyota motor industries, authorized the use of lower grade lubricating oil, and ordered retraining of Filipino vehicle operators.[129]

Still hoping religion could pacify the Filipinos, between May and October the JMA finalized a six-point strategy: (1) replace Archbishop O'Doherty with either Bishop Guerrero of Manila or Archbishop Reyes of Cebu; (2) replace all Caucasian priests with Filipinos; (3) move all Western clergy and missionaries to incarceration in Japan as quickly as possible; (4) lease church property for tenant farmers; (5) leverage an ongoing tenant uprising at the church-owned Buena Vista estate against the church; and (6) take control of private school curriculum.[130] Because Bishop Taguchi still opposed government interference with religious education, the JMA prepared to compromise on this one issue if the Vatican approved the removal of O'Doherty and the Caucasian priests. It would take until 6 January 1944 for the JMA to finalize its communique to the Vatican and two more days for Laurel to send a letter to Pope Pius XII requesting the appointment of Filipinos to the church hierarchy in the islands—too late to help the Japanese, but their work would have lasting impact on church reforms in the Philippines.

The JMA also hoped continued appeals to Asian identity could finally overcome Filipino resentments. In July it sponsored the Greater East Asian War Inquiry Commission staffed with diplomats, businessmen, politicians, and academics that issued a report "to expose the outrageous words and actions of the enemy nations, words and actions which violate all the principles of justice and humanity."¹³¹ The report cast the war as a "counteroffensive of the Oriental races against Occidental aggression" by the United Kingdom and the United States to deny Japanese power. The JMA disseminated the report across the Philippines.

In another promising but futile project, the JMA offered to expand the Philippine textile industry.¹³² It proposed to import 120,000 spindles and 4,800 looms to add to the 20,000 spindles used in the National Development Corporation textile mills. State agencies ran the mills through the Central Bank of the Philippines in a tangle of corruption and favoritism.¹³³ The Daiwa Boseki company brought 50,000 spindles and 1,800 looms from Japan, but Filipino elites resisted interference in their business and used shortages of fuel, transformers, and building materials to block expansion. When the JMA closed in October, so did the mill's reform enterprise.

Inflation undermined all the pacification efforts. On 15 July the JMA issued military ordinance number 15 to fix prices of prime commodities including cotton, cloth, matches, salt, tobacco, soap, and paper.¹³⁴ It followed with administrative ordinance number 10, which created the Philippine prime commodities distribution control association to ration commodities and prevent hoarding and black markets. Every Filipino had to register with a neighborhood association to receive ration tickets for prime commodities. Yet the Japanese military seized half of all textile commodities allocated to the private sector and corporations, although there was only one Japanese soldier to every twenty-five Filipinos.¹³⁵

In August a spontaneous display of Filipino loyalties rudely disproved Japanese claims of amity in the islands. Movie director Yutaka Abe staged a big-budget picture, *The Dawn of Freedom*, featuring the "liberation" of the Philippines to rally support for the Greater East Asia Co-Prosperity Sphere. General Kuroda, who was having an affair with an actress in the movie, supported the production and arranged for "thousands of American POWs to be trucked into Manila so they could suffer the humiliation of reenacting for the cameras their defeat of 18 months earlier."¹³⁶ Many more thousands of Manileños held an impromptu celebration at the sight of the Americans, screaming and rushing to touch the POWs. Police and troops aggravated the situation by brutally suppressing the crowd.

MINDANAO, D575/R-474

In July the Japanese reoccupied Misamis Occidental and Zamboanga's north coast and sent Fertig and his headquarters scurrying. "My soldiers run off with the greatest of ease," he complained.¹³⁷ Captain Jose Naranjo heroically delayed the enemy to keep the 10th MD forces from disintegrating, and Fertig reestablished his base at Lanao. Through "brutal headaches" and bouts of paranoia he rationalized, "It is only natural, I suppose, to place yourself in the position that you are No. 1 in the eyes of the enemy, and that their sole interest is to trap the leader."[138]

Chick Parsons arrived with three survivors of the Bataan Death March who escaped the Davao penal colony: Navy Lt. Cdr. Melvin McCoy, Army intelligence officer Maj. Stephen Mellnik, and former MacArthur staffer Army Lt. Col. William Edwin Dyess.[139] Fertig in turn surprised Parsons by presenting his brother-in-law, Capt. Tommy Jurika, who had also recently escaped a Japanese prison.

Fertig found Mellnik, McCoy, and Dyess "a bit stir crazy and apparently determined to continue on south."[140] Mellnik and McCoy asked for transportation for ten people to Australia. Fertig tepidly said he would ask SWPA. McCoy remembered, "I didn't expect him to fall over us, but he was downright hostile! Is he afraid we'll debunk his phony rank?"[141] On 18 June they got SWPA's reply: a submarine would arrive between 15 and 25 July to pick up Parsons, McCoy, Mellnik, and Dyess "at the specific direction of General MacArthur to obtain information on the treatment of American prisoners of war in Japanese hands."[142] After a harrowing hike, barely dodging Japanese patrols along the way, the men linked up with SS-202 *Trout* southeast of Olutanga Island for the trip to Brisbane.

NEGROS, D578/R-471

On 8 July SWPA relieved Villamor in Negros and approved Abcede as commander of the 7th MD. Anticipating his departure, Villamor held his September conference on organization, operations, and command. Gador refused to attend and threatened to disrupt Ausejo's organization before retreating to Bohol and the protection of his former subordinate, Ismael Ingeniero. In October Gador would receive a letter from SWPA directing him to relay reports through Abcede. This implied subordination. Gador chose instead to send his reports directly to SWPA, explaining that "he had come to Bohol after receiving a SWPA letter on Negros and that he was awaiting further instructions."[143] SWPA sent no reply. Gador would virtually disappear after the Japanese landed on Bohol in June 1944.

The Japanese stepped up raids on Negros' south coast from Dumaguete to Sipalay, attacked the farms of central Negros Occidental and Oriental, and conducted a terror campaign in the north. Abcede reported to SWPA: "The Japanese can do anything they want to on Negros."[144] He dispersed his men and supplies, established early warning systems, and instituted higher levels of secrecy.¹⁴⁵ Then the Japanese suddenly turned to central Panay, reaching Peralta's district headquarters by September and capturing and destroying large stocks of his supplies.

Despite these attacks, late on 9 July SS-202 *Thresher* under Skipper Hull delivered 500 pounds of supplies and 50,000 rounds of .30- and .45-caliber ammunition at Catamon Point. Before departing for Pearl Harbor, Hull put ashore the promised representative from Quezon, an agent "Gatbiala" in a major's uniform.¹⁴⁶ Villamor recognized him as Dr. Emigdio Cruz, Quezon's personal physician. Cruz assumed an alias, Major Suylan, for his incredible mission of going to Manila to somehow meet with Roxas, Rafael Alunan, Yulo, and any other leaders he could find.

Quezon had told him, "Cruz, this is a very tough job. Personally, I believe you have no chance to get through."¹⁴⁷ The AIB did not like the mission either, but Whitney and MacArthur approved it. Despite his misgivings, Villamor agreed to help Cruz. "Once in Manila he would try to determine if Vargas and his associates had really been won over [by] the Japanese," Villamor recalled. "Had they lost hope that America would ever redeem them? Did they believe that Japan would win? Had the people become pro-Japanese?"¹⁴⁸ Cruz would also try to explain Quezon's departure and the delay in the U.S. return. "Tell Vargas," Quezon had told him, "and tell all those whom you can safely see and talk to, that I give them my word Japan will lose this war. I know it. I have seen the almost infinite resources of America, and its enormous war production. The whole thing staggers the imagination. It is only a matter of time."¹⁴⁹

VISAYAS, D597/R-452

On the last day of July, SS-209 *Grayling* under Lt. Cdr. Robert M. Brinker delivered agents under Lieutenant Ireneo Ames with equipment and supplies for Peralta at Pucio Point.¹⁵⁰ Interestingly, SWPA G-2 recorded, "This shipment was intended mainly as a token of material support for the Panay guerrillas."¹⁵¹ On 23 August, now under Lt. Cdr. E. Olsen, *Grayling* delivered two tons to Pandan Bay, Panay. Four days later, the sub torpedoed and sank a transport, *Meizan Maru*, west of Mindoro—and then disappeared forever.¹⁵²

On 3 August a frustrated Villamor wrote to MacArthur: "Morale effectively undermined by threats, force propaganda, misunderstanding between friendly units and between army and civilians, sickness, activities of some puppets and the supposed kindness of Nips to 'misguided element.' If not immediately and effectively counteracted all semblance of resistance here will soon disappear."¹⁵³ Exhausted and feeling ignored, he added a proposal to gather six of his old Filipino pilots in Australia for a bombing raid on Tokyo.[154] That request went nowhere. On 15 August Villamor wrote to Quezon,

> If you only see us now you will see that our hearts are broken, our souls torn between love of liberty and love of dear ones who are dying for lack of medicines, food and shelter, and our minds confused by enemy propaganda and the enormous uncertainties of our daily lives. But with all that we aim to carry on till no human can do any more. Please tell America that over here we do not pray for victory, for victory is sure to come. Rather we pray that God may speed the day of their coming which shall also be our day of liberation from the tyrannical heels of the warlords of Japan.[155]

LUZON, D606/R-443

In early August the *Manila Tribune* printed Laurel's first interview as chairman of the PCPI. "The constabulary will be reorganized and strengthened to compel obedience of unruly elements. The force will be increased as needed to maintain order," he told Japanese and Filipino newsmen. "If necessary, the Nippon forces will be requested to extend assistance during the transition period."[156] The Japanese spent the next month conducting zoning operations in and around Manila.

The jungle telegraph suddenly flashed news of FAIT leader Colonel Hugh Straughn's capture on 5 August. Villamor saw a photo of the captured colonel in the *Rabuang Arudela* and heard him on the radio denouncing guerrillas as "trouble-makers and racketeers."[157] Fertig reported, "Tokyo radio is playing up the capture as that of the guerrilla leader of the Philippines. Jap like he was quoted 'I wish I could advise all my followers now hiding in the mountains to surrender.'"[158] A month later the Visayan newspaper *Shimbung* cited Straughn: "I organized a guerrilla band known as the Filipino American Irregular Troops which was nothing but a make believe organization and materially composed of bandits, outlaws and other dissatisfied elements without effective arms or weapons."[159] If Straughn chose his words in hopes of saving his former guerrillas from attack, they did not appreciate the favor. Rumors circulated that the colonel had been betrayed by Marking's guerrillas, but Panlilio recalled that when Marking heard of Straughn's capture, he openly wept and said, "I told him that peninsula was a pocket! I told him to come with us. I told him to get farther back. I told all of them. Why didn't they listen?"[160] Panlilio admitted, however, that she never liked Straughn.

Without their leader, the FAIT went their own way. The Hunters in Cavite ignored orders and continued to fight the Japanese, the Huks, Marking's guerrillas, and itself.[161] President Quezon's Own Guerrillas became an independent group in Batangas. About four hundred poorly armed FAIT men near Antipolo fell under a "Col. Elliot P. Ellsworth" who some said was General Vincente Lim. By May 1944 the Hunters and Marking's groups absorbed Ellsworth's FAIT (the Japanese would execute both Straughn and Lim). The capture of Straughn led Laurel to exclaim: "It will take two more years to put down Germany; it will take another three years to beat Japan, that is five years. In the meantime, we must keep peace and order to forestall pestilence and famine. We *must* liquidate all guerrillas."[162]

Success against the guerrillas made failure to end the famine more noticeable. By August, the National Rice and Corn Corporation's warehouses held only enough rice to feed Manila for one month.[163] With a new planting season at hand, Japanese agriculture plans were clearly in trouble.[164] Unfavorable weather, poor soil, and pests devastated rice and cotton cultivation. Price controls failed. The cost of rice remained somewhat stable only around Manila, and the price of meat spiked everywhere. Attempts to compensate with increased slaughter only reduced the number of animals available for farm work. Tight Japanese control of transportation and fuel further hampered the economy.

The wider war's demands exacerbated problems. After losing the 122nd Regiment to the Central Pacific, Fourteenth Army only maintained enough garrison battalions by incorporating second- and third-tier troops.[165] Late in the year the independent garrisons reorganized to create three independent mixed brigades in Mindanao and the Visayas built around six such battalions.[166] Still, Manuel Roxas passed word to Mona Snyder that Luzon held 50,000 Japanese soldiers and had become the main reserve area for the Southwest Pacific Army. She ventured to his home, where Roxas asked her to be his liaison to Ramsey.[167] The next month Mona informed Ramsey that Roxas believed the new republic would declare war on the United States. Ramsey dispatched runners to both Peralta and Fertig to rush this news to MacArthur.

Outside Manila, Bernard Anderson sent an American named Schaffer with Bim Manzano to arrange a meeting with Marking. Panlilio described the pairing of Marking and Anderson as "gunpowder and matchstick."[168] Marking suspected that the American officer wanted to take command of his 200,000 guerrillas. Instead, Anderson offered recognition. "Bullshit, recognition!" Marking told him. "Nobody has to give me permission to fight. I'd like to see anybody stop me!"[169] Anderson explained, "Recognition means bullets."¹⁷⁰ Urged by Panlilio, Marking grudgingly agreed to accept orders from MacArthur—but only MacArthur.

Anderson asked permission to rally soldiers still hiding in Marking's area. Marking and Panlilio thought any skulking soldiers just might respond to an American officer. Anderson and his officers then canvassed the *kaingin* (burned farm clearings) across the countryside and found numerous men willing to report for duty. "They were Americans again, doing important work," Panlilio wrote, "where in humiliation they had been mean, surly, ugly, all of a sudden in restored importance there was humility and friendliness—and gratitude."¹⁷¹

SOUTHERN LUZON, D606/R-443

Near Sorsogon, under pressure from Peralta, Lapus agreed to unite his 54th Regiment with Sandico's guerrillas to form the 56th Regiment. Sandico informed SWPA that Peralta offered him the military governorship of Bicol, but he refused because Escudero was still governor. Escudero then charged Lapus with unlawful declaration of martial law. Lapus embraced Peralta who, craving influence on Luzon, alternately encouraged Lapus, Zabat, and Escudero to unify Bicol.¹⁷²

Before the end of August, each of these three guerrilla leaders possessed a letter from Peralta acknowledging the bearer as the 5th MD commander. Thus Peralta increased his volume of intelligence at the cost of bloody competition among Bicol's guerrillas. Finally, Bernard Anderson sent Lieutenant Russell Barros to intervene. He found Lapus "anxious for a settlement," but Escudero refused any suggestion of agreement.¹⁷³ The competition for Bicol, stoked by Peralta, would continue to destabilize southern Luzon.¹⁷⁴

MINDANAO, D607/R-442

On 27 July Fertig wrote: "Morgan apparently thought that I would be going to Australia and had left Bowler in command. He would then take over. His latent anti-American jealousy came to the surface in his drunken speeches."¹⁷⁵ The situation festered. Two days later Morgan resigned from Fertig's command and began signing orders as "General of the Fighting Guerrilla," "C.O. of the Guerrillas," and Fertig's chief of staff.¹⁷⁶ Fertig accepted Morgan's resignation as of 30 July. Finally, on 4 August Fertig received a courier from Misamis Occidental with news that Morgan was assuming command of Mindanao and Sulu. Fertig confided to his diary, "Personal opinion is that it is a trial ballon [sic] to test my reaction."¹⁷⁷

After two more days, Fertig received a proposal from Morgan to meet at Kolambugan. Fertig thought him "nuts" and replied that any "conference would be held at my order."[178] Another three days passed, and Morgan sent a letter cataloguing his issues. Fertig ignored the letter but noted, "It boils down to his regret that he named me to command instead of assuming it himself."[179] At last the two men met on 11 August in Liangan. Morgan offered to leave Fertig in charge of the 10th MD if Fertig acknowledged him as commander of the field forces. "I did tell him exactly what I thot [sic] of his actions," Fertig wrote.[180] Morgan left the next morning. Fertig made a flurry of organizational changes, but Morgan was not included in them.

On 22 August a wearied Fertig sat in a hillside shack in Lanao gazing across the placid blue bay while listening to a radio station from Chungking playing Dinah Shore's "The One I Left Behind." He wrote in his diary, "Love and happiness seem far away so does War with the pleasant air of the hillside."[181] At that moment Morgan was setting up his command not far away in Misamis Occidental—hence Villamor's account that Morgan took thirty loyal men into the jungle to fight as loyal independent guerrillas.[182] Fertig explained, "The man is crazy 'insane' and will make trouble eventually I fear."[183] SWPA's log noted, "The situation threatened to become serious due to Morgan's violent attempt at mutiny."[184]

VISAYAS, D620/R-420

On Mindoro, Captain Esteban P. Beloncio finally merged his 250 guerrillas around Lake Naujan with Ruffy's Bolo battalion and started duty as Ruffy's executive officer. Peralta had no influence with Ruffy and may have been the source of SWPA's impression that Beloncio "was not well liked."[185] By the end of March 1944 Peralta succeeded in getting Jurado to convince Beloncio to break with Ruffy.

Meanwhile, the Japanese captured Harry Fenton's wife and children and offered to release them if Fenton and Cushing agreed to surrender. The two guerrillas refused. By now, however, they agreed on little else. When Cushing took his regimental commanders to Negros, he left secret orders with his executive officer, Lieutenant Richard Estrella, to arrest Fenton. Estrella held a conference with select commanders on 19 August to obtain their support, and they agreed Fenton had crossed a line when he had arrested and executed missionary priest Father Patrick Drumm.

On 2 September Cushing met with Villamor on Negros. Villamor notified MacArthur: "Cushing just arrived. States that their present situation requires immediate solution else total collapse Cebu forces inevitable. Claims that majority of forces will no longer obey Fenton whose life is in danger."[186] Villamor thought Cushing a "sacerdotal figure" and a "mild figure of a man."[187] He passed along the Cebu guerrillas' requests for immediate financial aid, the authority to issue money, and the ability to impose civil government.

Convinced by Parsons that both Fenton and Cushing were out of control, SWPA denied the requests. Matters came to a head on 15 September when Estrella arrested Fenton and his most loyal officers. Cushing would later claim he only expected Fenton's detention, but Estrella held a hasty court martial and executed Fenton and several of his aides.

LUZON, D622/R-427

In September Major General Sosaku Suzuki arrived as the new commander of the Army shipping headquarters in Manila. Convinced that the JMA needed to be more aggressive in purging pro-Americans from the Philippine government, he advocated greater use of anti-American Moros and Ganaps. Suzuki went to the 31st Garrison Unit commander and Great Asian Society board member Colonel Koreshige Inuzuka to propose a coup. Inuzuka hired a writer named Hayase to research and promote the Ganaps, but he resisted any overthrow of Filipino leaders.[188] Shortly thereafter, the Japanese high command sent Suzuki out of the country.

By this time Volckmann felt he had sufficient control to reorganize the USAFIP-NL in northern Luzon. He contacted Romulo Enriquez in Nueva Vizcaya Province, Robert Lapham in Pangasinan, Dennis Molintas northeast of Baguio, Parker Calvert northeast of Baguio, and George Barnett on the Ilocos coast. "We were still having trouble," he wrote, "contacting any unit north of us, and contact with Praeger had been completely lost."[189] Volckmann issued his "Reorganization Plan of 1943" establishing seven geographical districts in northern Luzon and directed each district commander "to organize a combat regiment generally along the lines of a Philippine Army regiment" and to emphasize intelligence collection and avoid confrontations with the Japanese.[190]

Praeger laid low through the summer in Ilocos Sur while the Japanese searched for his new headquarters.[191] Finally, on 30 August they captured Praeger with Lieutenant Arthur P. Furagganan and Staff Sergeant Earl J. Brazelton.[192] Some guerrillas thought they had been betrayed; others suggested that the fatigued officer was ready to surrender. Evidence indicates that the Japanese had been intercepting Praeger's radio for weeks, deciphering transmissions with a broken code.[193] A priest told another story to Blackburn: "Praeger had captured these Japanese. He was treating them according to the rules of land warfare. But, he was running out of food and medicine, so he decided that he couldn't adhere to those rules. So, he asked Father David to take the Japanese back to the commander in the town of Tuguegarao, down in the Cagayan Valley, which he did. The Japanese turned around and captured Praeger."[194]

Guerrillas spotted Praeger on display at Cabanatuan, obviously suffering from cruel treatment. Ramsey later recalled, "This was becoming more common: Guerrilla leaders were being paraded before the public after having been tortured beyond endurance and forced to make speeches denouncing the resistance and urging Filipinos to betray us."[195] Praeger withstood the treatment, so the Japanese executed him in November.

Volckmann tasked Blackburn to find any guerrillas in Benguet. "Well, every time I would send someone north," Blackburn commented, "the collaborators would cause their capture. They would take our man out and put him on a bamboo pole, tie his hands and feet like a pig, and take him to the town where he was ultimately executed."[196] He sent Thomas Quiocho and Herb Swick with a company to Apayao and Cagayan. They hid each day and traveled at night until, in a surprise attack, they seized "every public official, every policeman, and all of the public files" in both Kabugao and Ripang.[197] They found letters in which the mayor of Ripang described to Mountain Province governor Hillary P. Clapp how they caught guerrillas including Praeger—with lists of names of individuals "instrumental in this capture."[198] The guerrillas rounded up the individuals, allowed them to confess to Father David, and executed them in the city square.[199] Later, Blackburn asked Father David if they had made any mistakes. He answered, "I won't say that you made any mistakes, but, my son, I don't approve of your method." "Good enough," replied Blackburn.[200]

Volckmann began his next phase. "The new objectives were to get the guerrillas into camps," recalled Blackburn, "and get them organized with the ultimate objective being to be in a position to render the maximum effectiveness in support of the Americans when they returned to the islands."[201] Volckmann constructed company-sized camps far from populations. "This policy improved morale of both civilians and the military units, and also improved the discipline of the troops," he observed.[202]

Exasperated with part-time guerrillas, Volckmann set out to create full-time outfits.[203] He set up a general headquarters, USAFIP-NL, with a G-5 civilian affairs section in every district, regiment, and battalion to gain and maintain popular support. The regiments established field hospitals of six doctors and six to fourteen nurses, a dentist, and seventy enlisted personnel, augmented with civilians as necessary.[204] Blackburn strung up one hundred miles of telephone lines, powered by old hand-cranked commercial receivers retrieved from municipal buildings.[205] Eventually he even issued two newsletters relaying any good news gleaned from KGEI out of San Francisco—one tailored for the guerrillas, the other for civilians.[206] Volckmann next planned to: "One, take stern measures against spies and informers, i.e., their elimination; two, control the puppet officials; three, destroy the Japanese Bureau of Constabulary that was being put into the area; and four, gain the confidence of the people and restore their morale."[207]

MANILA, D628/R-420

Through the summer, Vargas traveled the islands exchanging 7 million pesos in Philippine occupation currency for the guerrilla scrip authorized by Quezon. He explained to Tanaka, "The possession of these [guerrilla] notes has a very great psychological effect on their holders and induces them to wish that the Government that authorized their issue should come back."[208] Vargas also requested that the JMA revoke its prohibition of the Filipino flag. "The restoration of this flag would enhance the faith of the Filipino people in Japan and the Imperial Japanese forces and will no doubt make them eternally grateful," he explained.[209] Finally, he asked the JMA to outlaw the Sakdals and Ganaps under the ban on political groups other than the KALIBAPI. Laurel, however, challenged Vargas on this issue because he wanted to continue using the Sakdals as informers.[210]

On 6 September the KALIBAPI assembly completed their draft constitution for an "independent" Philippines. The Japanese general affairs bureau worried that now all territories including India and Korea might push for independence.[211] They had compelled Burma to declare war against the United States and Britain as its price for independence and wanted a similar pact with the Philippines, but the new constitution included no such declaration. "To that," explained author Nicholas Tarling, "the activities of the guerrillas contributed, the Huks, the left-wing Chinese Hua Zhi, and above all those affiliated to the USAFFE."[212]

Laurel repeatedly argued that any alliance with Japan against the United States would split the Philippines, aid the guerrillas, and lead to civil war.[213] When pressed by Tojo, Laurel claimed that only popular leaders such as Quezon, Osmeña, and Roxas could deliver such an indecent declaration against a former benefactor.[214] He could only allow for a declaration of war "if feasible, as soon as possible."[215]

It was easy to argue that the collaborationist government had little popular support. Filipinos had been provoked in countless ways by the occupation. The experience of Adalia Marquez was typical.[216] On 27 August the Japanese arrested her husband, Philippine Civil Liberties Union leader and principal organizer of the underground Free Philippines, Antonio Bautista, at his law office. The officials had strong suspicions about his activities but no proof.

Adalia pursued every available avenue to see her husband before turning to a Filipina acquaintance named Linda who was living with a Kempeitai colonel as his mistress. Afterward, on the evening of 3 September, Adalia unexpectedly received instructions to report to the Fort Santiago prison at 0700 hours the next morning. She did not realize that the Japanese intended to use her to break her husband's will. She made arrangements for a neighbor to watch her children and arrived early at the prison. Adalia was left waiting outside until 0800 when guards escorted her to a room containing one table and one chair. They left her standing there.

After an indeterminate amount of time—there was no clock in the room—two men entered and identified themselves as Lieutenant Namiki and interpreter Fujiwara. They did not bring Bautista. Namiki sat in the chair and questioned Adalia about her husband's rank and role in the guerrillas. She claimed to know nothing, and in fact her husband had made certain that she knew as little as possible of these things. Around noon the two interrogators left her standing alone.

At about 1300 hours the two men returned. They presented Adalia with a poorly written letter supposedly composed by her highly educated husband. The letter read: "If you love our children, you must tell the truth, as I have already CONFESSIONED. Please, for the sake of our HOUSE, you must tell the truth because the Japanese Military POLISE is very magnanimous and they will let you go home after you are telling the truth."[217] Adalia recognized the forgery and assumed that the interrogators were desperately fishing for information.

When Adalia continued to plead ignorance of any guerrilla activities, Namiki began beating her with a heavy ruler. Panlilio described such beatings: "It began in the application of a ruler edgewise to the face and hands, aimed at the bone protrusions such as eyebrows, bridge of the nose, knuckles. It ended in simply pounding the victim to a jelly with a baseball bat or rifle butts."[218] Namiki screamed at Adalia, "This is the kind of treatment you deserve! You want to be like American girl—you want to wear pants, eh? Why do you wear pants!"[219] The harsh questioning continued well into the night. Finally, the two men left her curled up on the floor. Around 0400 hours on 5 September she awoke to the call of a distant rooster. She was alone.

Not until 2100 hours on 6 September did another person enter the room. Adalia recalled, "Then a white clad figure appeared at my door. A bowl of thin rice gruel was thrust toward me. 'Lugao, eat it quickly,' Fujiwara whispered."[220]

During the afternoon of 7 September Namiki and Fujiwara reentered the room and renewed the interrogation. They asked about Adalia's brother in the United States, indicating that they had done some homework on her family. Worried about her husband, her children, and herself, she came up with a plan. Clearly exhausted, she answered with lies laced with just enough exaggerated gossip to pacify them. It seemed to work. They appeared especially receptive to any gossip regarding Japanese officers and their interactions with Filipinos, particularly with women. After a while the two men again left Adalia alone.

Sometime the next day a Filipino boy brought Adalia another bowl of lugao, and that night Fujiwara shared a few rice cakes with her as she told him about Linda and the Japanese Kempeitai officer—she had become convinced that it was Linda who betrayed her husband.

Before sunrise, Namiki and Fujiwara returned carrying flashlights to wake Adalia and hear more about Linda. "I adlibbed enough material to fill a Sunday supplement scandal sheet," she recalled. "I began to suspect what I later found out to be actually the case. There were two cliques among the Japanese Military Police and they were terribly jealous of each other, one clique would do anything to discredit the other."[221]

Finally, after nearly two weeks of detention, Namiki released Adalia on 9 September at 0200 with orders to return at 0730 with a written report of all she knew about the guerrillas. She returned at the appointed time and was left waiting until 1200, when she was taken to a cell. Late that day she was released again with orders to come back at 0900 hours. When she returned to Fort Santiago, she was shown photos of suspected guerrillas to identify. She was released at noon. Four hours later she received a call telling her to expect a visit from Fujiwara at 1900 hours.

On the hour, the interpreter arrived at Adalia's home and demanded 10,000 pesos. He was almost crying as he explained that he had a wife and three children in Japan and they desperately needed money. Fujiwara told Adalia, "You understand, of course, why Lieutenant Namiki admires you so much—why he treats you the way he does? It is because of the way I interpret for you."[222]

On 11 September at 0700 hours, Adalia met Fujiwara on a bridge and handed him 5,000 pesos—all she could borrow. An hour before midnight on 12 September, she received another phone call telling her to meet Fujiwara in a hotel bar at 0300. At that meeting Fujiwara informed Adalia that she would begin working as an informer for the Japanese military police.

Despite all her efforts, she never saw her husband. He was later reported to have escaped and was never seen again.

AUSTRALIA, D633/R-416

Since June, the PRS reworked plans for "intelligence penetration separate from guerrilla consideration or support."[223] Gradually, however, they began to value the guerrillas. Villamor's HT-9 on Negros relayed for numerous short-range B3Z and ATR-4 radios in central Luzon, southern Negros, western Panay, and eastern Sorsogon, including traffic from Anderson, Merrill, and Ramsey.[224] Each night, when solar radiation abated, the bases sent their updates directly to SWPA. In August the PRS proposed a plan "to develop intelligence procurement through guerrilla sources south of 12°00' N"—the line dividing Mindoro and Luzon from the rest of the Philippines.[225]

Whitney got MacArthur to approve a plan from Parsons for SPYRON—an amalgamation of "Spy Squadron"—to shuttle supplies, communications, and agents into the islands.[226] Parsons hired his brother-in-law, Tommy Jurika. Army captain George Kinsler procured equipment for the guerrillas from civilian sources. Navy ensign William Hagans—born and raised in the Philippines—arranged forward bases for submarines. Navy lieutenant Lee Strickland arranged semi-forward bases. The Navy's Seventh Fleet sent Capt. A. H. McCollum to coordinate support. Commodore Jack Haines of Task Force 72 also worked closely with Parsons. "It was a novel arrangement to have Army officers working at Navy bases and vice-versa, and we were looked upon as mystery men," recalled Parsons.[227]

Whitney sought improved radios, equipment for extracting fuel from coconuts, and lightweight carbines for the jungle fighters. He prioritized orders for desperately needed supplies ranging from atabrine to shotgun shells. Finally, he sorted through special requests. What might seem unimportant to a general supply officer might be critical to a particular guerrilla—the PRS understood why Fertig needed soap, Pendantun needed polish, and Kangleon needed dentures.[228]

The AIB noted a broadcast from Wolfgang Kleinecke of the Nazi Transocean news organization from Berlin:

> The headquarters of a North American espionage ring in the Philippines, led by a 63-year-old Catholic American woman missionary, were eliminated in January of this year by the arrest of the ringleaders, it became known only now from Manila. The ring

numbered more than 100 North American, British, Chinese and Indian agents. Investigations have revealed that one Col. Evans before the outbreak of the G.E.A [Greater East Asia] War was head of the U.S. Secret Service in the Philippines, and had sent a man by the name of Charles Parson [sic] as his secret envoy to the Philippines to establish connections with 63-year-old Blanche Jurika, who ostensibly was a Catholic missionary in Manila, but who in fact led a corps of guerrillas. By the way, Jurika is the mother-in-law of Parson. Parson, himself, was charged with rigging up a far-flung espionage apparatus and with organizing guerrillas. Parson collected anti-Japanese elements and on Mindoro Island overlooking Manila Bay established a secret wireless station which kept in constant touch with Australia and America. Blanche Jurika was the ring leader of the organization. She was already before the war an active member of the U.S. spy service in the Philippines, while her elder son, Stephan Jurika, prior to the outbreak of the war was military attaché at the U.S. Embassy in Tokyo. It is reported that Stephan Jurika was directly in the lead of the air raid on Tokyo in 1942, and was aboard the U.S. aircraft carrier commanded by Doolittle. Also, Blanche Jurika's second son, Thomas, was discovered to be a spy.[229]

Of course, much of this report was inaccurate: there was no international ring of one hundred spies in Manila; Blanche Jurika was not spy; and Stephan Jurika was a naval intelligence officer aboard USS *Hornet* who briefed Doolittle's pilots, not one of his fliers. Yet the report indicated two items of interest: the Japanese knew of Chick Parsons, and they were concerned about him. It also raised questions about the source of the report.

MINDANAO, D645/R-404

On 13 September Fertig crowed, "Morgan is whipped.... Tate pulled away and left him out on a limb. The mutiny is done."[230] Fertig sent Cabili to Morgan in Misamis Occidental "with a proposal that will solve everything if accepted."[231] Believing Morgan dreamed of "a general amnesty," Fertig notified him that MacArthur needed him in Australia for vital coordination.[232] For about a month the new *Balao*-class submarine SS-287 *Bowfin* patrolled the South China Sea from Brisbane under veteran skipper Lt. Cdr. Joseph H. Willingham.[233] Before dawn on 29 September the boat delivered seven tons of supplies to Binui Point, Mindanao. Fertig sailed out on *Rubin IV* to meet them. "Beautiful deadly sight, silhouetted against the driving rain squalls that slithered down Malindang. Comdr. Wallingham [*sic*] met me on the bridge and we went below to clean linen, drip-o-later coffee, sandwiches and cookies."²³⁴ A separate launch came alongside with evacuees including Captain Tracy Tucker, Captain Leonard Minter, Lieutenant Francis Napolillo, Major DeWitt Glover, Major Paul Owens, Captain Samuel Graschio, Offret, Kuder—and Morgan.²³⁵ On his way to the sub, Fertig received a message from SWPA instructing him that Morgan, Tucker, and Minter were to be kept in Mindanao. "It was too late," he decided, "for the easiest solution of Morgan was to send him out."²³⁶ The 10th MD guerrillas delivered more than a ton of fresh fruit to the sub. "At 8:30 we cast off and there in that thin steel shell are some of my biggest problems," commented Fertig, "some friends, and my letters to my loved ones."²³⁷

NEGROS, D652/R-397

On 20 September Captain Sofio Bayron on Bohol relayed to Villamor word from an agent on Cebu named Santander indicating that the "whole island will be overrun."²³⁸ At Villamor's side, Cushing was highly agitated, threw up at least once, and appeared ready to use his .45-caliber pistol. The PRS told Villamor that the 8th MD would go to Fertig, who was to deputize Cushing to organize Cebu. SWPA still denied Cushing the authority to print money. Fertig or Gador, or perhaps both, were to provide him with funds. Villamor recalled the impact of this message: "Cushing was crushed. He began to tremble with anger."²³⁹

At that moment Villamor was distracted by Mauricio Guidote, who arrived in his camp claiming to be an agent sent by Roxas. His interest in Villamor's radio, his praise of the Japanese, the sudden appearance of Japanese planes, and his demands that they contact Governor Montelibano raised suspicions as to whether Guidote was actually a spy. Unable to contact Roxas to verify the man's bona fides, Villamor convened a board of senior officers to interrogate Guidote. After several hours, they determined that the man's story "appeared more and more phony."²⁴⁰ The board unanimously ordered Guidote shot, and a firing squad quickly carried out the sentence.

MANILA, D667/R-382

On 5 October Fourteenth Army commander General Tanaka visited the presidential palace in Malacañang. Vargas informed him of considerable USAFFE remnants that were causing trouble and still refusing JMA offers of amnesty. "This problem can be solved by the military authorities in two ways," he said, "either by sending sufficient troops to control the situation in the troubled provinces, or by authorizing the Executive Commission to organize, fully equip, and utilize the Constabulary for this purpose."[241] He recommended commissioner of the interior Benigno Aquino to command an armed Philippine Constabulary against the guerrillas.

A much different exchange occurred at 0933 hours on 14 October. Vargas repeated the words of the commander in chief of the Japanese army and declared: "Effective October 14th, 18th year of Military Administration throughout the occupied territory of the Philippines is terminated."[242] With those words Jose P. Laurel became president of the Second Philippine Republic as elected by the national assembly. Chief justice Jose Yulo administered the presidential oath while national heroes of forty years earlier, General Emilio Aguinaldo and General Artemio Ricarte, raised the Philippine flag as their national anthem played in public for the first time since the invasion. At 1730 hours the new president signed an alliance between the Philippines and Japan promising close "political, economic, and military" cooperation.

The Japanese Military Administration officially disbanded. Colonel Utsunomiya, the Fourteenth Army's deputy chief of staff and the JMA's director of the general affairs department, became the consular attaché to the new government. Philippines Cotton Growers Association chairman Shozo Murata, the highest-ranking civilian and supreme advisor to JMA, became ambassador plenipotentiary. Harvard-educated former executive of General Motors in Japan, Masakatsu Hamamoto, became special advisor to Laurel.[243]

In his inaugural address Laurel asked that "every living Filipino, including those in the mountains who still had some doubts," to "come down to help us."[244] That evening he departed for Tokyo with Vargas and Benigno Aquino. President Roosevelt broadcast his denunciation of the "puppet government" as born in "fraud and deceit" and added, "I wish to make it clear that neither the former collaborationist 'Philippine Executive Commission' nor the present 'Philippine Republic' has the recognition or sympathy of the Government of the United States. No act of either body is now or ever will be considered lawful or binding by this government."[245]

Four days later, Laurel called a special session of the assembly to address the country's economic crisis.[246] Under the new constitution the Japanese companies retained their exploitation rights. The Japanese also still oversaw all fuel, transportation, media, and treasury operations. The new Philippine government had no choice but to comply with Japanese policies, especially in the area of law and order. Only the guerrillas interfered with their control.[247]

"At the time the Philippines declare their independence," the Japanese military stated, "guerrillas will be looked on as traitors who continue to disturb the peace in the Philippines, but the ones who repent their misdeeds and renew their allegiance to the Japanese Forces will not be punished."[248] Laurel took the opportunity to offer a new amnesty to those "who may be responsible for crimes and offenses of sedition, illicit association, engaging in guerrilla activities or aiding and abetting those so engaged or spreading false rumors and for all crimes and offenses political in nature committed heretofore against the laws of the Philippines."[249] The assembly unanimously approved the amnesty and ratified the alliance with Japan. All those receiving amnesty, however, had to pass a thirty-day "rejuvenation course" designed to "infuse into their misguided hearts a true and lasting understanding of Asiatic brotherhood."[250]

8

A Dangerous Game
October 1943–May 1944

MINDANAO, D682/R-367

"Granting independence to the puppet administration in 1943 did not reduce anti-Japanese feeling," historian Saburo Ienaga observed. "Many Filipino men joined organized guerrilla units, but the whole populace—old and young, men and women—cooperated with the resistance."[1] This was certainly true on Mindanao, where Fertig formed new units—mostly under American officers. After Lieutenant Villarin raised the 112th Provisional Battalion in the Augusan Valley and southern Surigao, Fertig sent American lieutenant Anton Haratik to assume command. U.S. Army Air Corps lieutenant Owen P. Wilson wandered out of the jungle near Caraga, and Fertig sent him to command the 111th Provisional Battalion in Frank McGee's new 106th division. First Sergeant Javito Pedraya had killed the previous commander, a Captain Asis, for attempting to surrender, but Wilson kept Pedraya as his executive officer.[2]

Gumbay Piang joined Fertig in September to lead the 119th Regiment. The Japanese had held him in house arrest in Cotabato to appease the Moros, and when inspectors checked on him, he would point to a "Gumbay Piang, Prisoner of War" sign over his door. Learning they had discovered evidence that he was still a guerrilla, Piang fled to join his men full time.

Farther south, Kwok's guerrillas attacked the Japanese in Borneo, drove them out of Jesselton, and held the town for forty-eight hours. A robust Japanese counterattack dispersed his men. Guerrilla Lim King Fatt was later able to contact the 10th MD, but the Japanese reportedly killed Third Lieutenant Kwok in January 1944.³

LEYTE, D683/R-366

On 21 October SWPA approved Parsons' designate Kangleon as commander of Leyte's guerrillas. Fertig sent him Navy lieutenant (junior grade) I. D. Richardson as a liaison officer with radio operators Lt. Joseph St. John and Lt. Truman Hemingway to tie into the 10th MD net. From his camp in Jaro, Lieutenant Colonel Balderian agreed to merge his guerrillas with Kangleon's organization as the 95th Regiment.

A guerrilla leader in east central Leyte, Colonel Antonio C. Cinco, had reportedly served as a Japanese informer until they discovered that he had been a USAFFE soldier. Threatened with execution, he escaped to rally guerrillas and joined Kangleon as his 1st Battalion, 85th Regiment commander. The Lang-Jain group, with Lieutenant Jose Nazareno on Panaon Island, agreed to become Kangleon's 94th Regiment.

Ciriaco Centino and his son Isabelo had each assumed the rank of major to lead guerrillas for Balderian in the northeast towns of Jaro, Pastrana, and Palo. USAFFE First Sergeant Filemon Pabilona broke from Centino to form his own command around San Miguel, Babatngon, Alangalang, and Tacloban. Eventually, Pabilona joined Kangleon as a lieutenant colonel in command of the Second Battalion, 95th Regiment. Technical Sergeant Felix Pamanian organized guerrillas near Mount Capoocan in northern Leyte. He absorbed a group under USAFFE captain C. Corpin from Biliran. Kangleon also recruited the Pamanian Group as the 3rd Battalion, 95th Regiment and promoted its leader to lieutenant colonel.

Not all the guerrillas on Leyte were willing to follow Kangleon. Brigadier General Blas Miranda, commanding the formidable Western Leyte guerrilla warfare force from Palompon to Baybay, hated collaborators and anyone like Kangleon who had surrendered. A history of the U.S. Army stated: "He killed many former prisoners, whom the Japanese had released, on the pretext that they were spies."⁴ Peralta offered to recognize Miranda as the commander of Leyte and Samar, apparently unaware that Parsons (and Fertig) had tapped Kangleon for that role.

Reports of Blas Miranda's supposed "inconsistent response to the Japanese" enraged Kangleon.⁵ With SWPA's backing, he ordered Miranda to subordinate his command in the name of MacArthur. If he refused, Kangleon promised that his 92nd Division "would force . . . Miranda to join us."⁶ Miranda refused. In August, Kangleon attacked the Western Leyte Guerrilla Warfare Force in western Leyte. After three months of battles,

Kangleon ordered Miranda's officers to report to his 92nd Division headquarters, but none came.

Finally, during a December typhoon, reinforced Japanese units launched precise attacks against Miranda's main and regimental headquarters in Albuera, Palompa, Merida, and Baybay. He dispersed his men and sent his chief of staff, Marcos Soliman, to see Peralta.[7] Kangleon seized the opportunity to finish off Miranda. He attacked and overwhelmed the Western Leyte Guerrilla Warfare Force and absorbed the remnants into his new 96th Regiment, bringing the 92nd Division to more than three thousand men.

NORTHERN LUZON, D685/R-364

On Luzon, Blackburn recalled, "Throughout the north there were independent bands which were going to do their own thing, including out-and-out banditry. If we were going to do the things that Volckmann wanted to do, we had to 'command' and keep these scalawags from stirring things up."[8] They sent emissaries to round up the strays. In October they brought Dennis Molintas and Bado Dagwa into the USAFIP-NL.

Volckmann ordered his guerrillas to collect radios and parts and find someone who could turn them into a working transmitter. They gathered the parts at his headquarters, where a 300-foot waterfall powered a captured 220-volt generator. Volckmann remarked, "A search through North Luzon failed to turn up a single individual with the required skill."[9] Finally, agents in Manila found Timoteo Sinay and Crespo Hernandez, technicians who believed they could build a working radio.

In the meantime, Blackburn recalled, "We cultivated a system of SS agents, secret service agents, who were planted in the barrios and towns."[10] Frustration with informers led to unorthodox strategies. Blackburn discovered that details of guerrilla activities in Tuao quickly found their way to the Japanese. He arrested leaders of the area's three most prominent families—the feuding Sanchez, Casabang, and Rodriguez clans—on suspicion of trading information to the Japanese. Blackburn promised his detainees that he would kill them if Japanese attacks continued. "It stopped, just like that," he noted. "Bang, we had no problems."[11]

VISAYAS, D689/R-360

To prepare for MacArthur's return, SWPA would conduct forty-one submarine missions and more than fifty insertions in the Philippines between April 1943 and January 1945 and would deliver more than 12,080 tons of supplies to the guerrillas.¹² By 27 October 1944 the AIB and PRS would have 134 radio stations in the islands: 46 on Mindanao, 23 in Panay, 21 in Luzon, 13 on Negros, 11 on Leyte, 6 on Mindoro, 5 on Palawan, 3 each on Cebu and Samar, and 1 each on Bohol, Masbate, and Tawi Tawi.[13]

MacArthur helped the PRS obtain one of the Navy's largest, and oldest, submarines. After a fifteen-day refit by Submarine Division Eighty-One, the thirteen-year-old SS-167 *Narwhal* under Cdr. F. D. Latta departed Brisbane on 23 October.[14] It carried eleven Filipino-American graduates of the Tabragalba guerrilla school, and Parsons led a team of four officers and six enlisted men from the 978th Signal Services Company.[15] Among the ninety-two tons of supplies *Narwahl* carried were 1.2 million atabrine tablets and 800,000 quinine pills.[16] "The principle [sic] medicine needed is for amoebic dysentery," McGee had radioed. "Next is local anaesthetic [sic], calcium, sulfa drugs etc."[17]

Meanwhile, Peralta sent Lieutenant Garcia back to Palawan in October with operations officer Major Pablo Muyco. The two obtained agreements from the island's guerrilla leaders, except Manigque, to join in a 6th MD Palawan Special Battalion under Muyco with Garcia as executive officer. Within a few months the battalion spanned Palawan, with 57 officers and 954 men—about 300 armed—and men on the nearby islands of Balabac, Cagayancillo, Busuango, Culion, Coron, Cuyo, and Agutaya. They also covered Dumaran Island with at least two agents in every town. Within a year these guerrillas were well integrated into SWPA's network.

Later that month Cushing returned to Cebu after having received little help during his trip to Negros.[18] He found Estrella in command after the hasty execution of Fenton. Mysteriously, some P150,000 from Fenton's treasury had disappeared. More disturbing, some officers accused Estrella of accepting P60,000 from the Japanese to arrange Cushing's arrest. Alarmed, Cushing declined an invitation from Fertig to go to Mindanao to discuss Cebu.

MANILA, D696/R-353

Just after sunset on 3 November SS-225 *Cero* under Capt. "Swede" Momsen, then leading America's first submarine wolf pack with SS-235 *Shad* and SS-208 *Grayback*, rendezvoused with Bernard Anderson north of Manila. Momsen unloaded twenty tons of supplies, two intelligence officers, six radio operators, a two-man weather team, and a demolition team of two officers and four enlisted men.[19] *Cero* then departed for refit at Midway.

In the capital, Laurel secretly put a radio in the Malacañang Palace.[20] Constabulary General Francisco brought him radio expert Captain Angelo P. B. Frago from the Japanese-run PIAM station (the old KZRH) to operate the post. Every night Frago listened to international radio and had Lieutenant Ciriaco Quinto prepare synopses for Laurel. They kept the radio secret to prevent the Japanese from knowing what Laurel knew. The Kempeitai, tipped by a captured guerrilla, eventually arrested Frago but failed to break him before Laurel secured his release.

On 5 and 6 November Laurel went to Tokyo, where regional leaders were attending the greater East Asia conference. Chang Ching-hui of Manchukuo, Prince Wanwaithayakon of Thailand, Wang Ching-wei of China, and Ba Maw of Burma joined Laurel in celebrating "Pan-Asian idealism and the demise of white colonial rule in Asia."[21] Prior to the conference, Laurel met with Tojo to say that freedom for his country—and all Asia—depended on Japan's success in the war and added, "If the Asian people become aware of this fact, they will naturally cooperate with Japan in her task of liberating her East Asian brothers."[22]

Laurel, like the other delegates, agreed to make a speech, yet he alone declined to submit his text in advance for official review. In his speech he said, "One billion Asians will never again become victims of Western exploitation. . . . Although the Philippines is a newly born, small, and feeble country, we are prepared to devote all the spiritual and material elements of the country to victory in the Greater East Asia War."[23] However, when the Japanese offered to send 220 "advisors" to assist Laurel and his government, the new president demurred. He reasoned that "we are afraid it would give the impression that the Philippine government is a puppet regime."[24] Tojo reassessed Laurel as "useful" but not "cooperative."[25]

At home, Laurel faced another failed rice harvest and famine. The occupation authorities found they could buy spies and turncoats "for twelve pesos and six liters of rice."[26] Magsaysay recalled, "My men did not surrender as a result of the rice offers. But I knew that the offers had a demoralizing effect among them."[27] Because the TVGU could not feed its "guerrilla reservists," they were sent home but remained ready to mobilize when needed.[28] Offensive action was left to small, specially trained units such as the Bagong Sirang Society assassination squad.[29] The guerrillas also employed greater numbers of women to make rattan *bakya* sandals, soap, and other products to sell in local markets to raise money for food.[30] Some organizations, such as the Hua Zhi and the Hunters, even signed mutual aid agreements to get through the famine.[31]

AUSTRALIA, D600/R-350

On 20 October the submarine SS-288 *Cabrilla* had been hunting enemy ships on its first war patrol when Cdr. Douglas T. Hammond received a change in orders.³² He altered course to pick up four people, including Villamor, from Doog Point, Negros.³³ Abcede now led the 7th MD, while Ed Andrews served as nominal head of Villamor's intelligence net and Benedicto secretly operated the Planet net invisible to the guerrillas.³⁴ Fertig despised Andrews for supporting Morgan. SWPA thought Andrews well experienced but noted, "He is sensitive to his mixed blood and when things are not going to his personal tastes, often jumps to the conclusion that he is being discriminated against [because] of this."³⁵

Villamor arrived in Freemantle, Australia, on 6 November to debrief a panel of six SWPA officers led by MacArthur's psychological operations chief, Brig. Gen. Bonner F. Fellers. Villamor reported that in the Philippines, "The morale of the troops and the people appears on the surface to be high. Actually, it is built on a very shaky foundation which crumbles every time the Japs start a campaign in a particular area."³⁶ The panel wanted to know if MacArthur's "lay low" orders hurt the guerrillas. "In other words," asked Maj. C. A. "Archie" McVittie, "if they were not permitted to pull these ambushes, do you believe that they would be able to hold them together as a unit?"³⁷ Villamor said he thought the units could hold together.

News arrived that the Japanese had again burned Bell's camp. This time the professor and his family barely escaped capture. He had enough. Bell called SWPA and asked for a submarine to remove civilians from Negros, including his family and him. Villamor asked to return to Negros to resume command of his net.³⁸ Whitney, however, had doubts about Villamor—and Andrews.³⁹ On 6 December he notified MacArthur: "There is convincing evidence before us (Parsons—H. L. Meider) to the effect that Villamor, upon his return to Negros, became politically ambitious—Meider says that he now envisions himself as Quezon's successor as President of the Philippines—and under such circumstances it would be difficult for him to confine employment of such a net to military rather than political purposes."⁴⁰ Whitney wanted to turn the Negros net over to Abcede.

VISAYAS, D706/R-343

In late November new Japanese attacks along the east coast of Panay reached Tablas Island and, a week later, Sibuyan Island. They drove into the Romblon Islands in December and the Aklan area in January and February. "This was the most thorough-going and ruthlessly destructive campaign of all," SWPA noted. "Loss of life and civilian property was exceptionally heavy but this only further embittered the people against the

Japanese."⁴¹ Later intelligence would show that the Japanese had "carefully observed guerrilla activity and radio traffic, even breaking some coded and ciphered messages" prior to their attack.⁴²

Peralta's chief of staff Relunia decided to streamline the 6th MD and formed seven semiautonomous combat teams that relied on the division only for supply and administration. He gave the teams special units but kept S-2 liaisons under district command. SWPA noticed the result: "The products of Peralta's intelligence network has [sic] been vastly detailed and exceptionally voluminous."⁴³ Unfortunately, the agents did not always grasp SWPA's intelligence priorities.

After spending two days attacking Japanese ships and evading destroyers, *Narwhal* slid silently on her electric motors through a moonlit night on 13 November to within 1,600 yards of the beach on Butuan Bay in Mindoro.⁴⁴ At its closest point Mindoro was just eight miles from Luzon across the Verde Island passage that Parsons wanted under observation. He went ashore in a rubber raft escorted by a Filipino soldier. Spotting an anchored *batel*, Parsons made a snap decision to requisition the craft to ferry supplies from the sub. He climbed aboard, only to awaken Japanese army sentries on deck. Parsons took a bayonet to the chin as he escaped overboard while gunfire erupted behind him.⁴⁵ Once ashore, he linked up with local guerrillas and got his chin bandaged until he could get it properly stitched back aboard *Narwhal*.

The next day the enemy *batel* sailed away. At 1815 hours skipper Latta moored on the starboard side of the guerrilla schooner *Dona Juana Maru* and unloaded forty-six tons of supplies along with a coast watcher team under Major Lawrence H. Phillips for the Verde Island and Apo East passes.⁴⁶ Parsons was supposed to have put Phillips' team ashore on an isolated section of coast but instead chose to land them at Paluan, where he had an associate.⁴⁷ It would prove to be a bad decision.

Narwhal rendezvoused with Fertig and ferried him to Naspit Harbor on 15 November. "The expected sight brought us relief—the largest sub in the world," wrote Fertig. "Enroute to the pier, we grounded but by blowing down the aft we floated clear and tied up at the pier. The only case in our history where one of the naval craft moored at a pier in enemy occupied area."⁴⁸ A local band playing *Anchors Aweigh* greeted Latta's boat. Fertig recalled, "Sandwiches and coffee in the ward room. Letter from home with pictures of Mary and the girls. Gee, I was homesick."⁴⁹

The guerrillas offloaded another forty-six tons of supplies, along with Parsons and five agents, under the gaze of two guests. "Kangleon and Ingeniero were much impressed by their visit to sub," Fertig noted. "Now to send them home with some supplies will complete their trip and cement their loyalty."[50] The Leyte and Bohol leaders could hope for similar support. At midnight Latta departed with thirty-two evacuees, including members of Bulkeley's famous PT boat crew along with eight women, two youngsters, and two-year-old Steven Cryster.[51] "In the forward torpedo room, Steven solemnly bit into his first pieces of bread. 'Cake mommy,' he said."[52] *Narwhal* departed for Darwin, arriving on 22 November.[53]

Narwhal's return posed a problem: what to do with the civilian evacuees? Conferring with the American Red Cross, Whitney decided to commandeer the Stathalan Hotel in Caloundra, seventy miles north of Brisbane. As the G-2 reported: "This housed 30 to 60 people at various times and was seldom empty for more than a few days at a time from early November 1943 until it was closed in August 1944."[54] SWPA G-2 interviewed the evacuees at the hotel while Alice Thompson of the Red Cross prepared them for return to the United States. The remote location helped preserve secrecy. "Approximately 250 persons were processed at Caloundra," SWPA noted, "and much valuable information was accumulated for use of occupation forces and for dealing with post-occupation problems such as guerrilla recognition (Luzon), emergency currency, recovered personnel, and claims."[55]

After three days of refit, *Narwhal* returned to sea. At dusk on 2 December Latta began unloading ninety tons of supplies, three Army officers, and ten enlisted men in Butuan Bay on the northeast coast of Mindanao at Cabadbaran.[56] One member of Charlie Smith's team, radioman Bob Stahl, recalled two hundred natives with a small band greeting them with *Anchors Aweigh*, despite Japanese forces being only ten miles away in garrisons at Nasipit and Cabadbaran. "They're as scared of us as we are of them," one of Fertig's men assured Stahl. "We whipped their asses lots of times, and they leave us alone."[57] Parsons, seven evacuees, and ten tons of bananas departed on the sub before dawn the next morning.[58]

Three days later *Narwhal* picked up another nine evacuees "with great haste" from Alubijid Bay about 120 miles to the west at Misamis Oriental.[59] A Navy history reported, "Latta stepped up the four engines to 17 knots as the submarine left this bay—the place had an unhealthy look."[60] Over the next three days he picked up nine more people from Negros and Mindanao—and sank the Japanese merchant *Himeno Maru* with gunfire off Camiquin Island—before returning to Darwin on 11 December.

Meanwhile, on 23 November Phillips radioed SWPA from Mindoro: "Increased activity against guerrillas in general. Expect meet with Majors Jurado, Ruffy, and Valencia to talk about guerrilla difficulties."[61] The previous May, Peralta had sent Lieutenant Enrique L. Jurado to organize Mindoro, where former constabulary Major Ramon Ruffy and Captain Esteban

Beloncio competed for leadership.⁶² Two days later Phillips—without authority from SWPA—encouraged Ruffy to assume the role of 4th MD commander, independent from Peralta. On 26 November they all reconvened in Mamburao and came away with an understanding that Ruffy would take command with Beloncio as his executive officer.

Not until 13 December did Phillips get a reply from SWPA: "Your mission is one of secret intelligence, and while it is desired that you extend friendly cooperation to local guerrillas and loyal residents, your participation in their affairs to any greater extent could tend to compromise the success of that mission and should be carefully avoided."⁶³ Peralta responded by sending Jurado back to Mindoro reinforced with men from his 1st Combat Team, who claimed to be on a mission to observe the Verde Island passage and establish a base for the penetration of Luzon.

BOHOL, D719/R-330

Ignoring several more senior officers, Ismael Ingeniero, leader of the Behind the Clouds guerrillas, assumed the rank of major and claimed command of all Bohol's guerrillas. "This may have caused friction within the command," reported SWPA, "and there are indications that Ingeniero maintained a close surveillance of these men lest they attempt to assume command."⁶⁴ The new major named his new organization "Boforce" and placed its headquarters near Carmen. SWPA agents reported: "The organization was run in a military manner with some formality, and guards and sentry posts were frequently on highways. Discipline was reported as good."⁶⁵ Yet SWPA also noted, "Despite this outward show the military efficiency of the organization was questionable. And little action was taken against the enemy other than occasional ambushes and the gathering of intelligence."⁶⁶

Ingenerio added a women's auxiliary service to sew clothing and raise money to sustain operations. Local attorney G. Lavilles ran a unit newspaper, *Bolos and Bullets,* which became popular reading on Bohol. Ingenerio even claimed command of the 8th MD, which included Cebu, and extended his intelligence network to Cebu City. In December SWPA would officially recognize Ingeniero as commander of the Bohol area—but not Cebu—and sent him supplies and a radio.

Politics challenged the Boforce leader. The next June, only the unexpected arrival of senator Carlos P. Garcia disrupted a plot by some officers to overthrow and kill Ingeniero. He fled to Panay shortly before Japanese forces landed on 23 June and seized the island. SWPA later learned senior inspector Muego of the puppet constabulary had provided the Japanese with complete Boforce rosters prior to their arrival.⁶⁷

NEGROS, D719/R-330

On 26 November Ed Andrews reported that Quezon's physician had returned to Negros from Manila.[68] Incredibly, the doctor had met with Roxas, minister of agriculture and natural resources Rafael Alunan, chief justice Jose Yulo, PCPI second vice president and director general Ramon Avanceña, and others.[69] He found all of them—and all the generals—still loyal to Quezon. Cruz thought that KALIBAPI secretary general Pio Duran, who had given his children Japanese names before the war, competed with General Artemio Ricarte for the occupiers' favor, but minister of public works and communications Quintin Paredes, "whose prewar business connections with the Japanese made him suspect," was still loyal.[70] Cruz cautioned, however, that Jorge Vargas "had become helpless" under the Japanese, and like Benigno Aquino, Benigno Ramos, and Pio Duran, he sought appointment to higher positions within the occupation government.[71] "Independence is a joke," he added. "Ninety-eight percent of people and government employees are true and loyal."[72]

Cruz managed to drop in unannounced to surprise his wife in Manila. She was shocked, he recalled, "but after praying for a few minutes to the Image of our Holy Virgin, she became composed. She was speechless, keeping a tight hold on me and trying to convince herself that I was not a product of her imagination."[73] All too soon, he had to say his goodbyes and began his long journey back to Quezon in the United States.

On 20 December Andrews sent a multipart message to SWPA requesting recognition, promotion, and the authority to promote his people and establish financial contacts across the islands. Nine days later SWPA replied: "It is desired you report to commander Seventh Military District [Abcede] for duty."[74] Learning of this, Villamor became very upset. More than a decade later he searched archives to learn why Planet was subsumed and concluded: "These channels were Filipino manned and guided. The new channels developed were all under American leadership."[75] He surmised that Whitney was a racist and commented, "Andrews was no 'bobo,' no undesirable, although Whitney would have treated him like one."[76]

Three years after the war Willoughby also reviewed the Philippine guerrilla intelligence operations and remarked: "Regarding Maj. Villamor's mission to Negros to establish an intelligence net, it is now known that he assembled one of the most active and best connected of any intelligence group gathered in the Philippines. The potential was enormous but largely unrealized."[77] The G-2 concluded that Villamor's contacts, especially in Manila, were under the impression they were talking to SWPA. In practice, however, they were talking to Villamor, and when he left, they were talking to no one. Except for contacts who found other conduits to pass information, SWPA had to start from scratch. This was the cost of the AIB's highly compartmentalized designs. The G-2 study concluded: "This tendency to ignore experience and existing organizations is one of the less creditable characteristics of the otherwise brilliant intelligence enterprise in the Philippines."[78]

Villamor's accusation of racism ignores several pertinent factors. While Whitney and others were more comfortable with professional U.S. Army officers (who were white) manning key command and control nodes in the islands in preparation for MacArthur's return, the case of Negros does not support claims of racism. Whitney in fact recommended that a Filipino—Abcede—take over Villamor's net.[79] Villamor's sense of frustration was also not unique: Americans like Fertig, Volckmann, and Lapham shared his feelings of persecution by SWPA.[80]

SOUTHERN LUZON, D742/R-325

In November Turko and Padua nominated Zabat for command of Bicol. A few weeks later, Mayor Velasco of Libon delivered an offer of amnesty from the Japanese to Zabat if he would cease operations. The colonel used the offer to obtain pledges of loyalty from lieutenants Sandico, Francisco Lelis, and I. M. Capayas. Peralta's representative Colonel Serran told Zabat that if he could get Miranda, Lapus, Escudero, and Flor to join him, Peralta would recognize him as commander of the 5th MD. Then Sandico renounced his "forced" pledge to Zabat (although he told Lelis and Capayas to stay with the colonel), and Zabat failed to recruit Lapus, Escudero, and Miranda.

Before leaving Panay for Bicol on 9 December, Miranda agreed to merge his TVGU into Lapus' 54th Regiment. The Japanese then conducted a two-week zonification campaign in Tancong Vaca. "A sidelight to this," wrote Barrameda, "was the rumor at the TVGU headquarters that at the height of the Japanese 'bandit-zone' operation, some VTG men tried to betray the location of Miranda's camp to the Japanese."[81] After a year away, Miranda finally returned to the TVGU on Christmas Eve with fourteen soldiers and a shipment of weapons from Peralta.[82]

CENTRAL LUZON, D743/R-306

In late November Ramsey received an invitation to visit Brigadier General Lim, who was under house arrest in Manila. The invitation to discuss unifying all Luzon guerillas meant travelling into the capital, where Kempeitai chief Nagahama had raised the bounty on Ramsey to half a million pesos. Nevertheless, he felt Lim was worth the risk and crossed Japanese lines in a railroad boxcar secured by Claro Camacho. Swiss national Walter Roeder, technical director of the Manila Gas Company, posed as a collaborator while secretly supporting the guerrillas. Using photographs taken by Major Jorge Joseph and assisted by eighteen-year-old Pacifico Cabral, Roeder had false identification papers waiting for Ramsey when he entered the city in a sedan on 20 December. With these papers, Ramsey spent the days before Christmas traveling openly and coordinating covertly with resistance leaders, usually with Ramona Snyder at his side.

On Christmas day Ramsey met a Czech consul named Schmelkis, who informed him that a Filipino claiming to be "Agent CIO-12" had arrived in Manila by submarine and wanted to meet.[83] The man's bona fides seemed valid, Schmelkis said, but he thought it strange that he said Ramsey had come to Manila to assassinate General Lim. Perplexed, Ramsey had Schmelkis tell CIO-12 that he had left to deal with a Huk ambush of some of his guerrillas. Word soon came from Roxas that Nagahama reported Ramsey was in Manila, and Baba knew he had left to deal with Huks who had killed some of his men. Clearly, CIO-12 was a conduit to the enemy. The Kempeitai spent nine days searching for Ramsey, who was hiding in Roeder's gas company compound guarded by more than one hundred Japanese soldiers. At that moment the Japanese announced an end to their amnesty offers: "After 25 January 1944 any American found in the islands, whether un-surrendered soldier or civilian, will be executed without trial."[84] Peralta reported that on Panay, the Japanese executed thirteen Americans, including women and children.

Marking's guerrillas returned to their old Sulok camp, where they received a holiday visit from prominent Manila social worker Asunción A. "Lola" Pérez.[85] She conveyed Roxas' tearful reply to Marking's offer of refuge: "I am old and sick. I cannot carry arms. I would be a burden. Here in another way, I fight."[86] Interestingly, Pérez relayed Roxas' request to Marking: "Do not shoot Laurel again."[87] Rather than deny involvement, Marking insisted on the appropriateness of the attack. Pérez said Roxas feared that killing Laurel or any other member of the government would just deliver more radical collaborationists into office and added, "Seriously, Laurel has changed. He was always a Filipino, a good Filipino. . . . He may not love the Americans, but he does love his own people."[88]

Pérez explained, "The way it is, the Japs use Laurel, and so do Roxas and the loyal men behind Roxas."[89] She provided a strong defense of the Philippine president:

> It is a dangerous game that Laurel is playing. In front of the Japanese, he and Roxas disagree just enough to invite the Japanese

to take Laurel's advice instead of Roxas's, and it is really Roxas's advice they take through Laurel. Laurel cannot move around too much. He is forever surrounded by the Japanese. But Roxas has connection that keep him informed of the real state of affairs, and so he puts into Laurel's mouth the words that will not only annul the endeavors of the enemy but also inform the people of the real intentions of the Japanese.[90]

VISAYAS, D746/R-303

On 23 December Charles Smith took a coast watcher team from Mindanao north toward Leyte Gulf and Manila Bay. With him were medical officer Capt. James "Doc" Evans and Cpl. Bob Stahl. He traded Doc Evans, who replaced Capt. Armato Arietta as the 10th MD medical officer, for Lieutenant (formerly Private) Robert Ball. Pennsylvanian Lt. Elwood Royer—who knew how to operate a .50-caliber machine gun—also joined Smith. The bulk of Smith's team were nine Filipinos from the First and Second Filipino Infantry Regiments in California.[91] Sixteen-year-old Rodriques had learned to cook from Smith's wife, Kathryn, and served as his man Friday. Smith's bodyguard, Catalina, had sailed with him on *Or Else* to Australia and had been a coast watcher at Davao for Fertig. Two others sent by Fertig, Ochigue and Madeja, were veteran guerrillas known for their courage and loyalty. Finally, there was teenager Frederico, long-time aide-de-camp and something of an adopted son to Ball.[92]

Smith established stations on the Bondoc Peninsula, Masbate Island, Cebu City, Samar, and central Luzon.[93] Travelling aboard a seventy-foot sailboat they called *Malaria*, Ball, Smith, and Stahl arrived in Guiuan Bay on Samar on 27 December. Three days later Ball and Stahl set up radio station MACA (for the way MacArthur initialed papers) and were soon sending reports to Fertig's station KUS for relay to Australia.

Smith discovered that Major Manuel Vallie controlled southern Samar, while Captain Pedro Merritt dominated the north. Neither would cooperate with the other. While placing Sergeant Cardenas to watch the west coast, Smith shuttled between the two guerrillas, hoping to work out an alliance. Meanwhile, Ball, Royer, and Stahl left Sergeant Herreria operating a small radio at Pambujan Sur and headed farther north on 3 January. After Stahl set up another post, Vallie arrived with several local politicians. Stahl let them listen to news from San Francisco and observed, "Seeing us—real, live Americans who had come from Australia—and hearing the news of the Allied offensive in New Guinea and other islands in the south brought tears of joy to their eyes! They had been waiting for General

MacArthur to send THE AID, and it had finally arrived."[94] The natives held a party where Vallie shared a hidden stash of Coca-Cola mixed with stateside whiskey.

The agents needed two generators to operate their heavy fifty-watt radio, but one quickly broke down. Mrs. Emma McGuire, the Filipina widow of an American mestizo mine operator at Borongan, led them to a diesel engine and a 10-kilowatt, 110-volt generator.[95] The largest part weighed more than five hundred pounds and had to be carried by four cargadores. The guerrillas recruited twenty men each day to tote the generator, which was dubbed "McGuire's Monster." In the interim, they enjoyed several days of Mrs. McGuire's cooking and visits from Dr. Arturo Victoria.

NORTHERN LUZON, D748/R-301

In December runners informed Volckmann of the executions of Thorp, Straughn, and Barker in Fort Santiago. Undaunted, he dreamt of expansion: "I planned to move west over into western Benguet or eastern La Union province to set up a new headquarters."[96] Expansion meant friction. Lapham, now wearing colonel's rank, had guerrillas across Nueva Ecija and Pangasinan.[97] He believed that SWPA was tired of intra-guerrilla disputes: "CPT Bartolomeo Cabangbang issued a memo to all unit commanders on Luzon to stop our petty squabbling."[98] SWPA changed the way it sent communications. "Thereafter, SWPA directives were addressed to [Bernard] Anderson, Volckmann, and me en masse," Lapham recalled, "as if it made no difference whether we were together or separate or some subordinated to others."[99]

USAFIP-NL's contacts with former 11th Division members in the constabulary began to pay dividends. Sergeant Pedro Dunuan gathered intelligence for the guerrillas while working as a clerk in a Japanese garrison. Constabulary Captain Emiliano Dunuan agreed to arrest suspected collaborationists on charges of aiding the resistance with "evidence" provided by the guerrillas. A sympathetic judge in Augarrine sent the suspects to a jail in Bontoc under Japanese escort. "Now, if the guy was real bad," explained Blackburn, "we'd ambush that patrol to Bontoc and get rid of him. If the Constabulary couldn't handle it, we would do it quietly, and the Constabulary would cover it up."[100]

Volckmann operated from his new Camp Seven on a mountainside overlooking the Taboy Valley. There he observed cultural differences between the tribe he had just left and the one he now lived among: "The dances in general portray the differences in the characteristics of the two peoples.

The Benguet in general is even-tempered, modest and peace loving, while the Ifugao is more impatient and is hot-tempered and a fierce individual fighter."[101] Effective public relations policies grew from such observations.

Blackburn, who claimed to have cured an infected heel by walking on it until it got better, suffered yet another violent spell of malaria.[102] Nurse Spessard brought him blood medicine called *salvisand* found in a burned-out sawmill. "I felt that malaria was a blood weakener, at least that is my hypothesis," he recalled, "and since we had the damn stuff, I said, 'Why not try it?' So, she shot it everywhere but in the vein, and my damn arm swelled up and looked like a baseball bat. I never had so much pain. I couldn't use that arm for two weeks."[103]

Things were tough all over. Ramsey thought Filipino morale in Manila was perilously low.[104] After much consideration, he jettisoned his Maoist cadre organization and restructured the East Central Luzon Guerrilla Force's 30,000 guerrillas into five regimental military districts based around Manila, Bataan, Bulacan, Pampanga, and Pangasinan-Tarlac.[105] He renamed his force the East Central Luzon Guerrilla Area (ECLGA).

Eugenio Lopez, from a wealthy family on Panay, waited out the war in his summer home in Baguio on Luzon and surreptitiously supplied guerrillas. "Simultaneously, however," noted Alfred McCoy, "he cultivated a warm social relationship with the local Japanese command, hosting frequent parties for the most senior officers."[106] In December Franco Vera Reyes arrived in Baguio posing as an American intelligence colonel sent by MacArthur. He had used this con to get money from the Manila underground and delivered Rafael R. "Liling" Roces Jr., industrialist Juan Miguel Elizade, and Del la Rama shipping manager Enrico Pirovano to the Kempeitai.[107] Reyes enticed Congressman Ramon Mitra and Colonel Manuel Enriquez to meet "resistance members" at Baguio's Tropicana Restaurant. Walking in, however, Reyes recognized Lopez, the restaurant's owner, and instantly left. Lopez had also recognized Reyes as a con man he had encountered before the war. Fearing a trap, he alerted Enriquez, who quickly accepted Laurel's personal standing offer of amnesty, and Mitra, who hastily agreed to a Kempeitai request to serve as mayor of Baguio.[108]

MINDANAO, D753/R-296

In December Fertig reported, "Radio contact has been made and maintained direct with Australia. Plenty of good dope to them."[109] The Japanese had forced Fertig to move his headquarters from Lanao to the Augsan Valley, where he decided to form a separate A Corps with four divisions under Bowler.[110] The Japanese then issued a proclamation that any American in Mindanao, or anyone helping an American, faced execution. "True to their word," recalled Virginia Hansen Holmes, "particularly when they found a guerrilla, American or Filipino, the Japanese forces immediately executed him, usually by beheading."[111] Public spaces seemed to sprout collections of heads on stakes.

In June 1942 Davao constabulary Captain Claro B. Laureta had taken thirty men from Camp Victor to the Lubugon River where they protected about four thousand refugees. The 110th Division recruited Laureta's outfit, and within a year he commanded its 130th Regiment in Misamis Oriental.[112]

Fertig reassigned 105th Division Lt. Col. Ciriaco Mortera—described as capable but not particularly aggressive—to be adjutant general of A Corps in January and gave the 105th to fifty-four-year-old Lieutenant Colonel Hipolito Garma, former chief of constabulary under General Sharp.[113]

The Japanese 16th Division attributed the public disorder on Mindanao to hunger: "Lack of rice and corn makes the people worry too much about the food situation. It becomes the main topic of the day among the residents here."[114] Senator Ozámiz told Parsons that the Kempeitai had withdrawn from many towns, and without them the Chinese merchants running the black markets had priced rice at P1,000 per bag to both ensure profits and humiliate the Japanese.[115] The JMA countered by redistributing rice through the neighborhood associations. They also paid laborers five scrip pesos per day and a bag of rice, a fivefold increase of prewar wages. Ozámiz described the "Mickey Mouse money" as worthless: "A man may buy a woman for a night, he may gamble, hoping to treble his stake and so purchase something on the black market. Otherwise there is nothing to buy. Inflation is advancing rapidly."[116]

The Japanese outlawed prewar Philippine currency but accelerated inflation by floating two million pesos in occupation scrip and printing more every day until there was far more money than the value of goods available. Only in guerrilla areas where Quezon authorized the printing of currency were prices under control. "Not only is there no inflation in the unoccupied sections," Parsons reported, "but also there is no black market or profiteering. Ceiling prices are rigorously maintained and anyone endeavoring to profit by the situation is dealt with by the guerrilla chiefs."[117]

MacArthur tried to further damage the Japanese administration by spurring inflation. SWPA sent Peralta $500,000 in U.S. $100 bills in July. The next month they sent another P1 million into the islands. Parsons brought back samples of the latest Philippine invasion currency (known as *apa*) to counterfeit. In December 1943 he slipped into circulation another P500,000 of artificially aged counterfeit currency.[118] By the end of the month, Washington delivered ten million more artificially aged pesos to fund guerrilla operations.¹¹⁹ "However," a postwar study noted, "P10,000,000 was only a 'drop in the bucket' compared to the tremendous amount of currency printed by the Japanese themselves; it would have made no appreciable difference to the economic system in the Philippines."¹²⁰

Ozámiz informed Parsons that the Japanese had a $50,000 bounty on his head, dead or alive.¹²¹ Parsons had one question: had he any news about his mother-in-law, Blanche Jurika? Yes, he was told, she had been arrested and sentenced to thirty-five years in prison.¹²²

One night Parsons sailed from Mindanao on one of Fertig's interisland supply craft. Before dawn the wind fell, stranding him eight miles from his destination.¹²³ A Japanese patrol craft passed within one hundred yards as the Filipino crew pretended to mend a fishing net carefully placed to hide their radio and supplies while the well-tanned Parsons, in native costume, manned the tiller. Any attempt to move from the enemy boat would have brought an instant fusillade. The Japanese apparently saw nothing of concern and continued on their way.

LUZON, D754/R-295

Between 31 December and 3 January Laurel reorganized his government to address rising hunger.¹²⁴ He summoned Luzon's absentee landowners to Malacana and told them, "We have to get rice. If necessary, we must compel planters to sell to [government agencies]. We will strengthen the constabulary to keep peace and order and if the constabulary can't do it, I will ask the Japanese Army to help me."¹²⁵ Four days later he told his advisors: "If necessary, we have to sacrifice one third of our people in order to save the other two thirds."¹²⁶

The next day Laurel issued proclamation number 10, calling all students, KALIBAPI, and religious groups to contribute to food production.¹²⁷ After touring Laguna, Batangas, and Tayabas, education commissioner Claro Recto reported, "The recent food shortage as well as the present hardships suffered by the people are due mainly to the activities of the guerrillas, who hinder food production."¹²⁸ Laurel established the food administration under Jose Sanvictores. To curb the black market, the administration asserted the National Rice and Corn Corporation's monopoly on rice and banned citizens from bringing it into Manila. The corporation, however, had become so poorly regarded that Laurel replaced it with the Filipino-run National Rice Granary.¹²⁹ It rationed rice at one-quarter pound per person per day but soon cut that amount in half.¹³⁰ Because special courts, drafts of manpower, and confiscation failed to impact the famine, Laurel set up a long-range economic planning board.¹³¹

At this time, the Japanese sent Ricarte back to Tokyo amid rumors that he planned a coup against Laurel (they would bring him back in April). A worried high command instructed the Fourteenth Army: "The attitude of the Filipinos must be watched closely to see whether any sign of enemy operation against the Philippines appears. The guerrilla bands will rise against our forces in full strength just before the enemy invades the Philippines, and attack railways, communication, bridges, airbases, harbors and munition camps."[132]

VISAYAS, D761/R-288

Ramsey received word of another supposed SWPA agent who arrived by submarine and wanted to meet near Manila. This one carried instructions from MacArthur and a radio. Despite his suspicions, Ramsey decided to investigate. "There was little more I could accomplish in Manila," he noted, "and, given the surveillance, a meeting with General Lim was out of the question."[133] On 7 January he and Roeder left the city on bicycles to see their visitor. Manila district chief of staff Colonel Patricio Gonzalez (also known as Pat Gatson) waited in a suburban house with the PRS agent, Sergeant Ben Harder, who informed Ramsey that Major Phillips on Mindoro had a radio for him.[134] Ramsey decided to make the long trek across Manila Bay, down southern Luzon, over the interisland waterways, and on to Mindoro where Ruffy and Beloncio maintained their uneasy alliance, with 6th MD's Jurado lurking nearby.

On 15 January Ramsey left Manila. Gatson arranged passage through the fractious guerrilla territories of southern Luzon. An area under "General Ernie" was particularly worrisome. "Tishio Ernie had been a renegade for years," Ramsey explained, "and neither the prewar government, nor the Japanese had been able to suppress him."[135] The old bandit warred against Japanese and guerrillas alike but accepted a truce long enough to let Ramsey, Gatson, and four bodyguards pass. General Ernie even staged a beating and summary execution of several suspected spies to impress the ECLGA commander.[136]

Peralta had sent American Sgt. Charles Hickok to nearby Marinduque to organize transit between Panay and Luzon. He suddenly sent Sofronio Untalan to Marinduque as a captain to command Company M of Lieutenant Garcia's 60th Infantry Regiment. Untalan had surrendered in July 1942 but later jumped parole. Hickok thought Untalan "not very intelligent and not reliable under pressure" and was incredulous to see him return.[137] The two clashed, and Hickok left.[138]

SWPA also received reports of problems on Masbate Island where constabulary Captain Manuel Donato had led guerrillas with promises of support from a group under Captain Juan Villaojada (Jesus Arazaga) and his brothers. Peralta sent Major Vincente Tansiongco and Captain Leon Gamboa to get control of Masbate as a stepping-stone to Luzon.[139] Gamboa returned to Panay with his cohort of 130 guerrillas after leaving Tansiongco to oversee the radio communication and weekly courier runs between Bicol, Samar, Leyte, Masbate, and Panay. Tansiongco, however, irritated Donato, who reached out to Zabat in Bicol for support. Coincidentally, Villaojada broke with Donato and began attacking his people.

SWPA became alarmed by reports that Tansiongco, Gamboa, and several other Masbate leaders met with puppet government and Japanese officials on 23 January. They agreed to a truce until Villaojada was captured or killed, after which they would meet again and Tansiongco would surrender to the Japanese. "This is an interesting sidelight on the enemy pacification program," MacArthur's staff noted. "It likewise shows the weakness of the Masbate guerrillas."[140]

Things appeared even worse on Samar, where Japanese forces captured and imprisoned Pedro Arteche and his brother Melecio in Tacloban. A military escort took Pedro to a church in Catbalogan so he could beg his assembled neighbors to cooperate with the Japanese. Instead, he urged the parishioners never to surrender. Pedro was dragged away and never seen again.[141]

LUZON, D769/R-280

In Camarines Sur, Lapus ended nearly three months of self-exile to persuade Miranda to end TVGU cooperation with Zabat and join Peralta's 6th MD. Miranda agreed, and the TVGU became the 3rd Battalion of Lapus' 54th Infantry Regiment. Then guerrillas under Captain Natividad Mata, claiming to be with FAIT under Marking, resurfaced in TVGU country near Bagotayog. Unaware of Miranda's return, Mata requested a conference with Aureus in Tatlong Parang. Miranda sent a delegation under a Lieutenant Sibulo to meet Mata. They were redirected to Basiad Bay, at the border of Camarines Norte. A second patrol under Lieutenant Leonardo Golpe followed. Neither patrol ever found Mata.

Closer to Manila, the Hunters linked up with guerrillas under Colonel Ramirez. When the Japanese captured Ramirez, the Hunters tried unsuccessfully to coordinate with the Huks, Thorp, and Straughn. "They lost thousands of members in counter guerrilla operations launched by the Japanese," claimed Panlilio, "yet throughout 1943 they continued to expand, at one time cooperating with Marking's Guerillas, then with Colonel Ramsey's East Central Luzon Sector guerrillas, and later with the 6th

Military District force of Peralta on Panay."¹⁴² Reinforced by FAIT survivors in early 1944, the Hunters began openly fighting with both Marking and the Huks, causing Bernard Anderson to intervene. They also sent Captain Leonardo Aquino to Bataan and Zambales to develop intelligence contacts that he organized into four hundred poorly armed men in a branch outfit called the Cavite Hunters.

Marking also developed branch organizations, including the Texans in Cavite and Dunging's Mountain Corps in Rizal. By January he claimed to have 200,000 guerrillas. He sent Serense to Manila to form a guerrilla intelligence division from six hundred handpicked men and women from seventeen regiments.¹⁴³ The division ran mail, collected food and supplies, mapped enemy locations, transported people, and conducted surveillance and spying. Their couriers took the name "Pony Express," and their escape teams became the "Underground Railroad."

VISAYAS, D782/R-267

The PRS continued to expand its radio network. Sergeant Crispolo Robles and Sergeant Anciento Manzano set up MAA on 28 January on Bondoc Peninsula on Luzon. The next day, Sergeant Restituto Besid, Private Querubin Bargo, and Private Andres Savellano opened station MAB on Masbate to relay reports from the Sibuyan Sea. Soon after, Sergeant Gerardo Sanchez and Sergeant Daniel Sabado had station MAD operating on Cebu.

On 5 February *Narwhal* under skipper Latta unloaded forty-five tons at Libertad, Panay, and Parsons met Peralta for the first time.¹⁴⁴ He was surprised to see the colonel commanded 12,000 well-organized and disciplined men.¹⁴⁵ He also noted the influence of Governor Confesor. Peralta professed complete loyalty to MacArthur, and Parsons promised him recognition and aid. *Narwhal* picked up six evacuees and two days later arrived at Balatong Point, Negros, to unload forty-five tons and pick up twenty-eight men, women, and children to take to Australia.¹⁴⁶

CENTRAL LUZON, D786/R-263

After his arrest in the Nacoco store in Baguio and imprisonment in Manila, Manuel Enriquez had been released in October under the general amnesty. He reorganized guerrillas in Mountain Province and acquired a transmitter from Manila. Captain Ali Al-Raschid, chief of police of Baguio and a former Philippine army officer, supervised his communications from Baguio. In late 1943 an agent arrived at Enriquez's headquarters claiming that Villamor had sent him to obtain a 14th Infantry Regiment roster.

The guerrillas gave him their roster before realizing he was the swindler Franco Vera Reyes working for the Japanese. Fearing their security had been irreparably compromised, Enriquez met with his top lieutenants and got them to agree that some of them should surrender to the Japanese. The rest fled to join other guerrillas. A raid on the Nacoco store rounded up the rest of Enriquez's men. In February the Japanese would capture Enriquez.

For most guerrillas, capture seemed less a danger than starvation. "Suddenly there was little left to eat in the land," recalled Panlilio. "With hunger came another pale horseman, disease—with them both came the short tempers which almost undid us all. . . . The guerrillas and civilians alike clawed for food, the starving from the starving."[147] Marking's agents reported how the Japanese pretended to address the famine: twenty-one ships departed Manila with rice for Tokyo, but one turned back to Manila to appear as if it were delivering rice.[148] The people watched prices skyrocket. The cost of a 56-kilogram *cavan* of rice rose from about P7 in 1941, to P30 in late 1942, P70 in mid-1943, P250 by mid-1944, nearly P4,000 by December, and P12,000 in 1945.[149] Average wages rose from P1.3 to about P4 per day in worthless currency. Panlilio added, "The Japs were demanding almost more than the harvest, and most of the seasonal crops had already been gathered in, but there was still *palay* [husked rice] in the fields and, left in peace, the people could sneak enough of their own on the side to live through a while longer."[150]

NORTHERN LUZON, D795/R-254

On New Year's Day 1944 Haliaps near Volckmann's headquarters reported a stranger lurking near local trails. The guerrillas picked him up, and under Blackburn's interrogation, the man confessed to being a spy for the Japanese. Guerrillas summarily executed the interloper.[151]

Volckmann toured his camps. Gualberto Sia organized about four thousand men from McGuire's remnants near Olongapa and Botolan and attached them to Anderson in Tayabas. On 10 February Volkmann left Ifugao for Counselor Tammicapao's Camp Seven on the eastern side of the Taboy Valley. Eleven days later he reached Parker's First District camp in Benguet and decided to make it his new headquarters. Captain Alipio Cubas' 1st Battalion of the 121st Infantry in the Second District impressed him with his hospital and dental office. They held reveille and taps each day with American and Philippine flags. The women's auxiliary service organized plays, dances, and social events. "No wonder the morale of this unit was so high," Volckmann remarked. "Soldiering in Ifugao had never been like this!"[152]

The USAFIP-NL commander directed George Barnett to send some of the 121st Infantry north through Abra into Ilocos Norte and find Ablan's guerrillas. All earlier attempts had failed. Patrick O'Day went with K and M companies and made contact with a guerrilla commander east of Laoag. Days later Barnett suffered a major Japanese attack. "O'Day determined that he was not going to be run out of the area," Volckmann noted, "and, suspicious of this local leader, detailed agents to watch him closely."[153] O'Day met the guerrilla leader and demanded he lay down his arms. When he attempted to flee, O'Day shot him down along with several of his men. Volckmann explained, "It turned out that the Japs, in order to protect the Laoag area which included the largest Japanese air base in the North Luzon, had cleverly organized and armed groups of natives who posed as guerrillas."[154]

O'Day appeared hardened by the experience. From late August into September he conducted a "reign of terror and atrocity" to purge Ilocos Norte of any suspected "Japanese collaboration faction."[155] Lapham recalled, "His main interest seemed to be pursuit of a vendetta with another group headed by CPT Fermin Bueno. The feud was resolved only when O'Day raided Bueno's camp, captured Bueno and some of his men, and had them flogged."[156]

Barnett's men identified a collaborator living next to a nearby Japanese garrison. The guerrillas snuck in at night and executed the man. "I don't know how they did this under the noses of the Japanese," Blackburn reported, "but they put him up on the flagpole right in front of the Japanese garrison. The next morning the Japs found him hanging there. Well, that town cleared up in short order."[157] Blackburn concluded: "If you could eliminate spies almost in the presence of the Japs, then nobody is going to continue being a collaborator."[158]

To the occupiers, the guerrillas seemed to be everywhere. Japanese police detained Senator Ozámiz, Laurel's chief of the games amusement division, after he resigned on 11 February and discovered he carried a letter from Parsons to Roxas.[159] The Kempeitai rounded up twenty-nine Filipinos in Manila associated with Ozámiz.[160] (SWPA G-2 later learned this all resulted from an agent on Mindoro who observed Phillip's landing and traced his subsequent contacts.[161])

Kempeitai chief Nagahama took three truckloads of military police to see Laurel and demand Roxas' immediate arrest. Laurel's son alerted the palace guards, and a tense situation developed. Laurel refused Nagahama, saying, "If you insist on arresting Roxas, you must get orders from the High Command. You are a mere subordinate and I refuse to deal with you."[162] Nagahama departed but promised that he would get Roxas. Laurel rushed to Ambassador Murata and Masakatsu Hamamoto to persuade Kuroda to block Nagahama.

The multiplying guerrillas seemed to herald MacArthur's return.[163] On 12 February the imperial army headquarters accepted that battle was inevitable and declared, "The Philippine operation will be a decisive battle with the main American force."[164] In other words, they intended to defeat, not bleed, the U.S. forces. Geography dictated their next steps: they needed to (1) blockade the main straits to prevent submarine transits; (2) build defenses for islands and harbors; (3) watch the coasts; (4) capture "enemy radios and the sectors in which the guerrillas are in operation"; and (5) organize an anti-sub task force.[165]

MINDANAO, D800/R-249

Lt. Adolph Sternberg Jr. of the U.S. Army Air Corps joined Fertig after being bedridden with a tropical skin disease for more than a year with Laureta's force near the Libuganon River. Fertig sent him back to Davao as a liaison between the 130th Regiment and the 110th Division. Once there, he received eighty men to form a special intelligence detachment near Matlivas. SWPA later reported, "LT Sternberg's intelligence activities in the Davao area have been quite valuable."[166]

On 15 February *Narwhal* arrived at Darwin and transferred thirty-four refugees from the Philippines to an Army tug before docking. After a day of resupply and refit, the sub headed back to the Philippines with Lt. Col. Ernest McClish and Maj. Clyde Childress. Guerrillas failed to rendezvous in Tawi Tawi, so Latta sailed on to Mindanao. On 2 March *Narwhal* entered the mouth of the Augusan River to deliver McClish and Childress with seventy tons of supplies at Naspit. After spotting a prearranged signal on Cabadbaran Beach at 1850 hours, Latta sent the officers forward on a rubber boat. The river proved too rough for the guerrillas' barge, however, so Latta brazenly sailed upriver through the moonless night. Warrant Officer Walter Wallace awaited with twenty-nine servicemen and eight civilians awaiting evacuation.[167] Wallace wrote: "Hats were thrown into the air, we kissed and hugged each other, we shouted and cheered, and cheered and shouted, until no one had any breath left to shout and cheer longer."[168] By 0230, despite the difficult conditions, the supplies were with Fertig, and the evacuees (plus Parsons) were on the sub.[169]

The next day in the Sulu Sea, Latta engaged and damaged the 560-ton *Karatsu*, the river gunboat formerly known as USS *Luzon*. On 5 March *Narwhal* returned to Tawi Tawi, this time to Bohi Gansa, despite contrary currents between the beach and reefs. Captain Hamner came out with two small boats to receive the remaining twenty tons of supply. Latta inflated his four rubber boats and broke open all cases of carbines to ease transfer. Even with ten evacuees assisting, the delivery was incomplete when three Japanese destroyers arrived and forced *Narwhal* to escape. Exiting the bay, Latta closely passed several native sailboats, one of whose crew repeatedly bowed before they broke into celebration at seeing the skipper's white face.

The next day *Narwhal* attacked and sank a transport before suffering its most intense depth charge assault of the war. "Hatch wheels spun, lights went out, fuses blew," the skipper recalled, "the port annunciator splintered in a symmetrical sunburst design as the escort crossed directly overhead between #2 and #3 charges."[170] Latta completed his last patrol with *Narwhal* and transferred his passengers to the Australian navy tug *Chinampa* at Darwin on 11 March before heading to Fremantle for refit and a change of commanders. He finished his tour as one of the unsung heroes of the Philippine resistance.

VISAYAS, D802/R-247

On northeast Samar, Charles Smith found a new home for radio station MACA in makeshift huts in Palapag Mesa. Using a one-hundred-foot antenna stretched between trees along a 1,300-foot peak, Ball had them back on the air in the second week of February. The team established alternate radio sites with caches of fuel, equipment, and money in case the Japanese forced them to flee. With inexperienced Morse code operators, Ball and Stahl had to personally monitor the weak signals through heavy earphones in daily shifts from 0600 to 2200 hours.[171] Stahl recalled, "So many stations—Army, Navy, and civilian—communicated on our assigned frequencies that the interference was, at times, horrendous."[172] Slowly they learned to wait until interfering signals abated, pick out the weaker MACA net communication, and vary the signal's pitch to distinguish it from the other noise.

Smith took Stahl with him to confront the contemptuous Captain Merritt in Catubig. They had the impression that "Merritt would go with the side that did the most for him, and he hadn't yet heard the Japanese offer."[173] Stahl said of Merritt, "He was much larger than any Filipino I had yet seen. His skin color and Negroid facial features belied any Filipino heritage. Filipinos are brown. He was black."[174] Received with a fiesta, Stahl noticed that neither Merritt nor Smith drank any alcohol, and their discussion grew bitter. "Finally, Smith stood up and slid his hand down to his pistol," Stahl reported. "I stood up and cocked my tommy gun. 'Listen to me, you *black bastard*!' Smith shouted, 'I'm in control of this island. If you do anything to try to stop me, or help the Japs stop me, I'll cut your balls off and ship them back to Africa!'"[175] Not one of Merritt's men moved. From that day forward, Merritt gave Smith very little help but gave him no trouble, either. Even so, the confrontation said as much about the racial biases of the actors as it did about the nature of intra-guerrilla power politics.

Meanwhile, Ramsey hacked through jungle, sailed past a Japanese destroyer in an early morning mist, rode horse carts escorted by unfamiliar guerrillas, and fought typhoon-whipped waves on his three-hundred-mile journey to Mindoro in search of a radio. When "outcast in some barrio, or buried deep in the jungle," he despaired, but he concluded that "the guerrilla movement had grown far beyond a job, and its goals and ideals had surpassed duty's ability to explain them.... Guerrilla struggle, I began to realize, had altered not only my understanding of tactics but also my whole concept of the nature of war, from that of a conflict fought by the rules with conventional weapons to one fought by instinct, with faith and devotion above all."[176]

Most importantly, Ramsey grasped an indefinable principle of successful guerrillas: "I was no longer merely *with* the Filipino people, I was *of* them.... Their struggle had become my struggle, and their liberation, inevitably, would be mine as well."[177] Guerrillas could not win over the people until they were first won over by the people. They had to fight for the people—for the people's values—before the people would fight for them.

Ramsey, like others, also realized that there was no one set of values among the guerrillas and people across the islands. As Lapham had noted: "Some such bands were led by Americans, but an overwhelming majority in all them were Filipinos whose motives were varied: hatred of the Japanese enemy, a desire to plunder, sheer fear, or some combination of these."[178] The people did share one interest: MacArthur's return. "MacArthur was reality," Ramsey reported, "the long, unfailing cable that bound us to the outside world."[179]

On 21 February Bernard Anderson notified Lapham that he had not heard from Ramsey since November. Two weeks later Anderson issued an order to all ECLGA guerrillas bequeathing northern Nueva Ecija, Pangasinan, Tarlac, and northern Tayabas to Lapham.[180] When Ramsey returned, Lapham recalled, "Ed raised no protest against this action; indeed he never made trouble of any kind for me."[181] The transfer nevertheless irked Volckmann.

Ramsey made it to Mindoro near Bongabong in March. "I was impressed with Ruffy's camp," he recalled. "It was large and well organized, with a kind of permanence I didn't usually associate with guerrilla forces. Rows of well-built thatch-and-nipa barracks stood on streets edged in stone."[182] Ruffy had with him twenty-three officers and six hundred men, a local government, a volunteer home guard, and Phillips providing liaison with SWPA. Phillips, however, had taken Ramsey's radio to his base on the opposite side of the island.

Ramsey found an unexpected visitor waiting for him: Peralta's man Jurado. The ECLGA commander was unaware that Peralta had tried to recruit Ruffy and that Phillips had recommended SWPA appoint Ruffy as 4th MD commander.[183] Ramsey also met Phillip's executive officer, Captain R. Galang, who entered the tug-of-war over Ruffy. Ramsey just wanted a radio.

"We have heard rumors that Phillips' camp was raided," Ruffy reported, "and since then I have had no radio contact with him. No one knows if he escaped or is even alive."[184] Ramsey waited ten days before a half-naked and clearly exhausted Warrant Officer B. L. Wise of Phillips' group stumbled into Ruffy's camp. He told of a Japanese raid near Naujan that killed or drove off his team and captured their radio.[185] Phillips and Wise wandered the jungle for weeks before they ran into a Japanese patrol that killed Phillips. Wise then spent a month struggling back to Ruffy.

Years later, the Army learned that when Parsons changed Phillips' landing spot, he delivered him to the enemy. Japanese agents had reported: "Maj. Phillips, WO Wise, and six Filipinos landed on Paluan, Mindoro with equipment. They brought small wireless sets to mountains north of Paluan Town on that island and reported details concerning ship movements to Maj Phillips until 15 February this year."[186] After observing Phillips' contacts, a patrol sent into Mount Calavite caught the team off guard and eventually killed Phillips.[187]

As Ramsey dejectedly prepared to return to Luzon, Peralta sent word that he had arranged for a submarine delivering supplies to southern Mindoro to take Ramsey back to Australia. "It was tempting, it was tantalizing," Ramsey recalled. "But I knew I could not leave."[188] Only after he declined the offer did Ruffy reluctantly show him another cable: "MacArthur to Ramsey: Request that you return to Luzon to command your resistance forces. [signed MacArthur]."[189] Ramsey realized Peralta was aware of this order and yet still tried to get him to leave the Philippines. Ramsey gathered his entourage and left for Luzon. Soon afterward, Peralta encouraged Beloncio to break from Ruffy, and their combined Bolo battalion collapsed.[190] Wise returned to Australia but would insist on returning to the Philippines to reestablish Phillips' coast watching station. He would be lost with the submarine SS-197 *Seawolf* when it was sunk on its way to Mindoro.

MANILA, D823/R-226

By now Peralta had an extensive intelligence network in Manila organized as the 43rd Division under Captain Ricardo Perez. The division's four regiments supported sabotage missions conducted by a special unit with a reported one thousand members under I. B. Fernandez.[191] In early 1944, however, Japanese agents would uncover the unit and capture most of its agents.

On 9 March Major General Shiyoku Kou (Hong Sa-ik), an ethnic Korean, arrived in Manila fresh from command of the 108th Infantry Brigade in China to assume command of all POW camps in the islands.[192] The outrages committed under his name contributed to a Filipino saying: "The Koreans committed more atrocities than the Japanese" (*Mas malupit ang mga Koreano kaysa mga Hapon*).[193] As historian Lydia N. Yu-Jose noted, however, unlike in China, the Japanese used few Korean troops in the Philippines.[194]

When the U.S. Navy began raiding Palau, the imperial general headquarters again reassessed the Philippines.[195] One general likened it to "the pivot on a fan."[196] The war was advancing between Palau, New Guinea, and the Philippines, and labors to defend the area began at once. The imperial headquarters detailed an expeditionary group staff under Lieutenant General Sosaku Suzuki to "improve Army equipment and head efforts being made to bring about cooperation in operations for the protection of the sea lanes."[197]

Meanwhile, a report from the army section of imperial general headquarters insinuated that the JMA had been too complacent with the Filipino elites: "In the Philippines, even after independence, pro-American ideas are still widespread and stubbornly upheld within every social strata and class, and cannot be extracted."[198] The planners concluded, "It is impossible to fight the enemy and at the same time suppress the activities of the guerrillas."[199] Rumors of a coup raised suspicions between Filipinos and Japanese in Manila.[200]

The Japanese feared that both their soldiers and the Filipinos had become lax and "thus were apt to become careless in their work which attached importance to military administration."[201] Furthermore, they found that preoccupation with guerrillas distracted from defenses "which needed revision to meet the changes in the conditions."[202] They needed to concentrate on transportation, manpower, and equipment.

Japanese planners expected that an American return to the Philippines would begin on Mindanao. In March, Major Yamajo Chotoku, Fourteenth Army intelligence section, Manila branch, requested the imperial general staff send agents—"preferably a Haji"—to coordinate "Moro operations" against Americans.[203] The general staff forwarded the request to the Greater Japan Islam Association, which promised a three-man survey team.[204] The imperial army staff also ordered the transfer of the Southern Army general headquarters from Singapore to Manila to strengthen strategic points by July.[205] They planned to place a division in the Surigao-Cagayan area, another in the Davao-Cotabato area, and a third in the Palawan and Sulu Islands and determined that four more divisions were needed for defense.[206]

Japanese planners also calculated forces needed to fight guerrillas. They categorized two types of antiguerrilla missions to be conducted while fighting MacArthur: first, the protection of installations including "railway, roads, bridges, communication, harbor installations, airbases, mines, factories, and munition dumps"; and second, the maintenance of "order in the districts."[207] Experience in Manchuria and China led them to calculate that they would need "about 24 garrison battalions."[208] The planners noted: "The strength on hand added up to only a field division (the 16th Division) and four independent mixed brigades (the 30th through 33rd Brigades, a total of 24 battalions). It was concluded that six divisions must be dispatched immediately."[209]

PANAY, D834/R-215

Before dawn on 20 March Lt. Cdr. Robert I. Olsen maneuvered the submarine SS-240 *Angler* to a point eight miles south of a rendezvous point off Libertad in northern Panay with orders to pick up ten people.[210] According to historian Theodore Roscoe, "About 0900 a crowd of people was seen walking behind the tree line on the beach, and an hour later the prescribed signals were hoisted in the palms along the water's edge." *Angler* remained submerged until sunset, surfaced at battle stations, and approached to within one thousand yards of the beach.[211] Lieutenant Colonel Cerilo Garcia, Peralta's First Combat Team commander, arrived on a *banca* to tell Olsen there were fifty-eight people, including sixteen women and children, awaiting departure—a number almost equal to all the sailors on the sub.

On the twelve-day run back to Darwin, the boat's entire crew—minus the torpedo watch standers—berthed in a cramped aft battery compartment. Olsen placed the male evacuees in the aft torpedo room, females in the forward torpedo room. "CPO quarters were inhabited by one woman with a two months old baby, one pregnant woman (8 months), one seriously ill girl (worms—temperature 104 degrees) and two elderly women," he noted. "Ship was immediately infested with cockroaches, body lice, and hair lice. A large percentage of the passengers had tropical ulcers plus an odor that was unique in its intensity."[212]

The sailors watched their passengers rapidly devour all food passed their way. Skipper Olsen had to put his crew and guests on rations of two meals per day with soup at midnight. "Habitability forward of the control room resembled the 'Black Hole' of Calcutta, a condition which resulted from children urinating and spitting on the deck, body odors, and 47 persons sleeping forward of the control room," Olsen added.[213] *Angler* reached Freemantle on 9 April.

SOUTHERN LUZON, D839/R-210

Charles Smith reached Bicol and reported to SWPA that he "had the foundation of a good intelligence net started and that he had given Lapus financial assistance."[214] That support undermined Turko's ongoing efforts to recruit Lapus into a unified force under Zabat and thereby denied Zabat's chance to win Peralta's recognition as 5th MD commander.[215]

Filipinos had by now lived with the war for more than eight hundred days. "Like Manila and other population centers," Barrameda wrote, "Naga had since settled into a somnolently placid and economically squeezed acceptance of the bored enemy, the underground movement only momentarily and not often breaking through the tranquil surface of mixed disquiet and grey despair."[216] In late February the Japanese in Naga sent a delegation of Filipinos led by governor Andres Hernandez and judge Gabriel Petro to negotiate with the TVGU. Miranda, Aureus, and others met them in San Gabriel, Pamplona. The negotiators presented Hitomi's "sit-it-out" argument: "The war was between Japan and America. There was no reason for the Filipinos and the Japanese to continue fighting each other."[217]

Miranda asked the Japanese to demonstrate their sincerity by disarming *rondas* (vigilantes) under Geronimo San Jose and Teodoro Rey in Sipocot in the next two weeks. Barrameda described the *rondas*: "They professed no love for the guerrillas, served the political interests of the Japanese invaders who tolerated their extra-legal existence, robbed and abused civilians and claimed they were maintaining law and order."[218] When the Japanese failed to act, Miranda sent a detachment under Lieutenant Sibulo to Awayan to disarm Rey's group. San Jose reacted violently, assaulting Sipocot and Malinao, wounding many civilians, and sending many more to the Tara prison. Sibulo then turned his patrols against San Jose.

The Japanese responded by arresting Aureus' sisters and other TVGU relatives and sending them to Tara as hostages for the return of Rey's weapons. They also sent twenty soldiers and forty constabulary troops to burn down the TVGU barracks in Tila and an ordnance post in Malinao. On 25 March Miranda ordered his men to return the sixteen rifles taken from Rey to the Japanese in Quitang. When the authorities still did not free his sisters as promised, Miranda went to the Ateneo de Naga building—the city hall. The Japanese released his sisters and arrested Miranda. Just before his execution, however, assisted by Tom Kilates and other double agents, Miranda escaped and returned to the TVGU.

With Japanese support, San Jose began a two-week campaign in early April of brutal raids in the Libmanan-Sipocot area. Zabat seized the opportunity to send some of Padua's Camp Isarog II guerrillas with Turko's men into Sibulo's TVGU area. Zabat then ordered Turko "to whip Miranda into line."[219] Warned of these moves, Sibulo managed to keep his B Company intact through September while Zabat's men conducted ten attacks against the Japanese, apparently to draw local popular support from the TVGU. The Japanese responded by torturing and beheading citizens in the area through mid-October.

CEBU, D845/R-204

Following Fenton's execution and the Japanese attack in January, James Cushing began rebuilding his organization on Cebu. SWPA recognized him as 8th MD commander, sent him supplies, and established direct radio contact in March. Cushing eventually organized 5,687 men with 2,700 mixed arms divided into the 85th, 86th, 87th, and 88th Regiments. He wanted Bohol added to his district, but Fertig and Abcede also claimed that island.

The last day of March began what MacArthur termed "one of the most dramatic incidents of the war."[220] Just after sunset, two four-engine Kawanishi HSK2 flying boats left besieged Palau for Davao, Mindanao.[221] Aboard one was Admiral Mineichi Koga, Yamamoto's successor as commander of the Japanese combined fleet. His chief of staff, Rear Admiral Shigeru Fukudome, flew separately with fourteen staff officers and a leather case in a sealed box containing Koga's plans for decisive naval operations. Updated copies of "Combined Fleet Secret Operations Order No. 73" and "A Study of the Main Features of Decisive Air Operations in the Central Pacific" were bound in a red cover marked with a Z. Only a month earlier, the imperial general staff had approved the "Z plan" for defense against advancing U.S. forces.

A violent storm brought down Koga's plane and all its passengers. Fukudome's plane changed course for Manila but, running low on fuel, tried for Cebu instead and wound up ditching into the Bohol Strait about two hours after midnight. Thirteen of the twenty-five passengers survived and managed to swim the two-and-a-half miles to Cebu by dawn.[222]

Spotting Cebu City about six miles to their north, the survivors decided to swim up the coast to that city's Japanese garrison. At about 1100 hours, however, fishermen from Magtalisay captured Fukudome and ten of his companions. The two others grabbed a canoe and continued to Cebu City. As the natives took their captives toward Basak, Japanese airplanes began circling overhead.

U.S. signals intelligence decoded an emergency message from the Japanese high command in Tokyo alerting field commanders that Admiral Koga had gone missing with some important documents. Cebu City garrison commander, Lieutenant Colonel Seiichi Onishi, sent two thousand soldiers to search the island. They were ruthless, leaving burnt villages and slaughtered inhabitants in their wake. Some soldiers released boxes into the waters near the crash site to see where they might drift ashore. The boxes floated to Magtalisay.[223] In fact, early on 3 April Magtalisay villagers Pedro Gantuangoko and Rufo "Opoy" Wamer found a box containing documents and hid it from passing Japanese patrols. They passed the box to local guerrilla Corporal Norberto "Berting" Varga just before the Japanese arrived to burn their homes.[224]

On 8 April Cushing reported the crash and survivors to SWPA, along with his worries about the intense Japanese search. Whitney offered to transport the prisoners to another island, but Cushing thought that would be too difficult as three prisoners were badly hurt and Fukudome was litter-bound with a fever of nearly 104 degrees. The guerrillas had already killed one captive who had tried to escape. Fukudome's aide, Commander Yuji Yamamoto, spoke enough English to convince the guerrillas that the admiral was General Twani Furomei, commander of Macassar, Celebes. After talking with the "general" (who spoke English), Cushing became suspicious.

The next day Japanese patrols closed in, and Cushing asked SWPA to remove the prisoners immediately, but it would take three days for his request to reach the high command. Meanwhile, Cushing deserted his base and took twenty-five guerrillas and their captives to Kamungayan, where he learned that the Japanese had taken more than one hundred Filipinos as hostages to swap for the prisoners. Along their way a Japanese patrol, supported by aircraft, intercepted the group and killed two guerrillas and a nurse. Cushing decided it was time to negotiate.

Late that night Cushing sent two guerrillas and two prisoners to Onishi with an offer to release all his prisoners if the Japanese would end their violent campaign. At the same time, he desperately tried to contact SWPA for guidance. Onishi terminated negotiations and demanded the immediate release of all the prisoners. Near midnight Cushing radioed SWPA of his decision, but two more days would pass before they got his message.

At noon on 10 April the two sides completed their exchange. Onishi told Cushing, "I expect to see you again in the battle field someday."[225] Too late, SWPA informed Cushing of a scheduled submarine rendezvous to pick up the prisoners. Onishi's troops were back on the warpath three days later, but with orders to avoid attacks on civilians. Fukudome arrived in Tokyo before the end of the month.

Cushing's surrender of the prisoners upset some senior officers in SWPA. By some accounts, MacArthur was so irritated that he demoted Cushing to private.[226] Whitney, however, admired Cushing's service and thought "he and his followers merit all assistance reasonably possible."[227] Whitney would get him "reinstated" after the war.[228]

On 13 April Cushing reported some more important-looking Japanese documents delivered by Gantuangoko and Opoy Wamer, including maps "showing airbases, naval bases, wireless stations, emergency landing fields, triangulation points, heights, and other control symbols" in the Philippines, Palau, French Indochina, Hainan Island, and South China.[229] After consulting with Whitney, on 15 April Cushing put the documents into five empty mortar shell cartons and sent them with Captain Celso C. Enriquez and Herb Ritter to Ed Andrews in Culipapa, Negros. Two weeks later, Cushing received two more batches of documents and sent one to Andrews and the second to Fertig in an attempt to catch a submarine.

Reports that the Japanese on Cebu were offering P50,000 for documents lost in the crash raised eyebrows at SWPA. On 4 May Andrews received the first documents. Three days later SWPA chief of staff Sutherland got the Navy to divert SS-291 *Crevalle* from a patrol in the South China Sea off Borneo to pick up evacuees from Negros.[230] Whitney got Abcede to oversee transfer of the documents. At dusk on 11 May *Crevalle* arrived at Basay and recovered twenty-eight women and children from Tolong, Negros. Abcede personally handed skipper Francis David Walker Jr. a wood box for MacArthur.

Crevalle left after two hours, remaining surfaced as much as possible for faster travel to Australia. Three days later the boat was damaged by a depth charge attack north of Celebes. Walker changed course from Freemantle to Darwin and made port on 19 May. Commander X. M. Smith, the commanding officer of the U.S. naval base in Darwin, retrieved the box. After another six hours the captured documents completed their 1,800-mile journey to SWPA at Brisbane.

By 21 May the documents were with Colonel Sidney F. Mashbir of the Allied Translation and Interpreter Section (ATIS). After two more days Mashbir distributed mimeographed copies of the twenty-two-page Translation Number 4, "Z Operation Orders," with the first two copies going to Gen. George C. Marshall and MacArthur. Within five days Mashbir added the twenty-nine-page translation of "A Study of the Main Features of Decisive Air Operations in the Central Pacific" along with ATIS Limited Distribution Translation Number 5 of the remaining documents.[231]

MacArthur tried without success to relay the intelligence by radio to Pacific Fleet Commander Adm. Chester Nimitz.[232] The Seventh Fleet director of intelligence, Capt. Arthur McCollum, then sent hard copies of the documents to Nimitz's intelligence chief Captain Layton at the joint intelligence center, Pacific Ocean area, at Pearl Harbor, and he quickly passed it to Nimitz. The admiral ordered copies sent immediately to "all flag officers assembling in the Marshalls," including Adm. Raymond Spruance and Adm. Marc Mitscher as they prepared for operations in the Marianas.[233]

Meanwhile, on 22 May Cushing radioed SWPA to report that the Japanese naval commander in Cebu, Takeshi Watanabe, had spread leaflets addressed to Cushing demanding that all documents and items from the crash site be turned over to the mayor of San Fernando by noon on 30 May. Cushing wrote to Wanatabe denying any knowledge of documents but added that local fisherman reported seeing a *banca* take a satchel out of the water and head off toward Bohol. The Japanese sent a three-thousand-man detachment to search Bohol.[234] At the deadline, the Japanese stepped up attacks and took Cushing's headquarters by surprise. Three days later, Cushing radioed SWPA that Japanese patrols had burned local villages and had his battered band on the run. By that evening, however, all remaining captured documents were in Andrews' hands, and Whitney promised Sutherland a submarine to retrieve them within ten days.

9

The Return
May 1944–August 1945

LUZON, D846/R-203

As the Japanese rushed to secure Luzon, Marking's guerrillas fell under attack in Rizal Province. Patrols circled the guerrillas in an area two miles long and half a mile wide. After concentrating fires into that area, they attacked from all sides. "For four hours, the Japs had bombed and strafed, shelled and mortared and sniped, combed the grass and bayoneted," Panlilio recalled. "Against four hundred of us plus a score of prisoners and the weaponless, they had pitted eighteen hundred troops, a cavalry detachment, six planes, three mountain guns and, near the highway, a tank."[1] The hungry and tired guerrillas barely managed to escape to Sampaloc.[2]

A raid on the USAFIP-NL's 66th Infantry killed 1st Lt. Grafton Spencer. He had survived serious illnesses and numerous encounters with the enemy to become a competent and popular guerrilla leader, only to fall victim to two guerrillas who broke under torture.[3] Warned in advance, Spencer overestimated the time it would take enemy patrols to reach him. When they did, he sent men scurrying with his papers while he and two others provided covering fire before he was shot and captured. "The Japs tried to extract information from their prisoners, and Spencer underwent severe torture," reported his men, "but to each question he merely answered with a broad grin. The Japs finally could stand no more, bayonetted him to death, and moved off with the two Filipino prisoners."[4]

On 6 April Lapham finally announced that he was assuming command of the Second Military District. Some months later, Lapham recalled, he received a letter from Volckmann "to complain that I was intruding on his territory, a matter he hoped would be straightened out after his report reached Australia."[5] Three weeks later Volckmann sent another letter charging Lapham with exceeding his authority in Nueva Vizcaya.[6] Lapham later explained, "I had laid claim to it, tongue in cheek, only because Anderson had told me it was within my domain and because I knew that doing so would irritate Volckmann."[7] Volckmann did not take the matter lightly and threatened Lapham with either a court martial or an attack.[8] Ramsey ended the bickering when he returned to Luzon, passing through burnt huts and tortured inhabitants all along his earlier route. "What was more," he wrote, "the raid had been led personally by General Baba."[9] The population now feared helping the guerrillas.

Blackburn also found that the Japanese had turned much the population when he moved to reclaim the northern Fourth District. "However," Volckmann wrote, "with the able help of Herb Swick and an outstanding Filipino officer, Major Joaquin Dunuan, and with great determination, Don gradually extended control north through Kalinga and Apayao."[10] They would organize eight thousand guerrillas with seven thousand more in reserve and five thousand in support duties.

MANILA, D849/R-200

"For the Filipinos, the year was the most critical not only because of the thousands of arrests and executions perpetrated by the Japanese, but also because of the scarcity of food and medicine," Agoncillo chronicled. "There was a slackening in the buy and sell trade, and the law of supply and demand was taking its toll: hundreds of people were dying of hunger."[11] On 8 April Laurel at last convinced Roxas to accept the chairmanship of the new Economic Planning Board to curb the black market and reform the rationing system.[12]

Laurel also established the Labor Recruitment Agency to secure laborers for the Japanese. In a radio address on 16 April he promised 40,000 Filipinos to build defenses against a U.S. invasion.[13] Almost no one volunteered. In Davao, the governor ordered the neighborhood associations to draft five workers per district. Author Terami-Wada Motoe explained, "This phenomenon was due to growing dissatisfaction among the people with the Japanese occupation, bad working conditions, fear of guerrilla reprisals, and effective guerrilla propaganda."[14]

As the islands moved from depot to front line, the Japanese Supreme Southern Army headquarters began moving to Manila.[15] The imperial general headquarters instructed: "We must destroy the enemy before they gain a foot-hold on land, if possible at sea with the air force which has great maneuverability and can begin operations on a large scale at anytime and anywhere."[16] To do this, they would transform the islands into a giant air base. Unfortunately for Japan, the Supreme Southern Army staff would not complete their move until September.[17]

The imperial general staff stood up two headquarters in the Philippines: the Fourteenth Area Army Command in Manila, and the Thirty-Fifth Army Command in Cebu. The 30th Division went to Mindanao. More than ten thousand men came from other fronts to Manila but, recalled Japanese staff officers, "the majority of them were compelled to remain there due to the shortage of sea transportation."[18]

The Fourteenth Army planned to "suppress the guerrillas with as small a group of men as possible and defend the Philippines with the greater part of its force."[19] To fight the guerrillas, they made available four brigades and parts of two active divisions, a force thought small enough not to detract from the preparation of air bases, munition dumps, and defenses.[20] In May a planning section from the imperial headquarters under Major General Tsuchio Yamaguchi arrived to oversee the construction of seventy airfields, but the plan would fall short of expectations because of problems with labor, equipment, and weather.[21] In addition, the U.S. Navy upset supplies, and guerrillas disrupted everything else.

Japanese officers noted, "The guerrillas became more and more active and not a single day passed without the Army having to take some action against them by dividing many units to protect arms, ammunition, fuel and other supplies, railway and communication centers."[22] The army was just spread too thin. They decided "to maintain a state of order only in the districts which were important to carry out the defense operations, namely main cities, air bases and their vicinity, important harbors, sectors along the railways and the main roads."[23] The rest was left to the guerrillas—and MacArthur.

Guerrillas targeted supplies and communications. Japanese staff noted that "the shortages of the supplies tended to worsen the state of order. The situation went from bad to worse when more and more of the inhabitants began to disobey our orders."[24] Concerned about a general insurgency in support of a U.S. invasion, the Kempeitai stepped up repression.

Meanwhile, on 17 April Benigno Aquino led a "gratitude mission" to Tokyo accompanied by chief justice Jose Yulo, minister of finance Antonio de las Alas, director-general of the KALIBAPI Camilo Osias, and others.[25] Laurel secretly charged de las Alas and Osias to seek economic help while Aquino received the First Order of Merit with the Grand Cordon of the Rising Sun from the emperor—his second award from the Japanese—and announced, "Quezon is a puppet; final victory will be Japan's."[26]

Ironically, such displays helped blind the Japanese to the roots of resistance. In May a Filipina named Nina tended to wounded soldier Itsuro Horiguchi in a Manila hospital. Her kindness attracted him, and when she spoke, he recalled, "My heart leapt with joy, and I responded to her."[27] Once when they were alone, they talked of life under the occupation. "Freedom taken away, the lack of goods, the poverty of life, the brutality of military police, hatred towards Japanese soldiers," Horiguchi recalled her litany of complaints. "She concluded by asserting strongly, 'MacArthur will certainly return and save us.' But I was one of those hated Japanese soldiers. My blood ran backward, my lips trembled, and I glared at her. If it hadn't been firmly forbidden, I would most likely had knocked her down."[28] His was the attitude of the Japanese in general.

VISAYAS, D875/R-174

On 31 March the Allied Air Forces requested three weather posts and a net control station on Mindanao.[29] Charlie Smith on Samar already "had several pre-war Philippine weather observers and enough equipment to furnish weather observations."[30] He sent his first weather reports on 14 April. The next month the Allied Air Forces placed a special weather net control station in New Guinea and sent weather teams under Warrant Officer Lucien V. Campeau to Fertig for Lanao, the Agusan Valley, and Zamboanga City.[31] Later teams went to Mindoro in June and central Luzon in August.

Smith also reported Escudero's eviction of Lapus from Sorsogon, raising questions about Lapus' claims of popular support. The Japanese then chased Lapus to Masbate and back to Sorsogon, where he asked Smith for either P500,000 or the authority to print his own money. He had sent a similar request to Peralta, who chose not pass it to SWPA. Smith forwarded the request, but SWPA rejected it. Lapus turned to Ed Andrews on Negros with promises to send his intelligence through him and not Smith. Exasperated, Smith arranged a conference with Lapus and Escudero, but they failed to iron out their differences.[32] G-2 noted: "The situation between the two was so antagonistic and confused that Smith felt he could not rely on either completely."[33] Ultimately, he established his own radio station in Sorsogon.

On 15 May new skipper Lt. Cdr. Jack C. Titus sailed *Narwhal* out of Darwin for the Philippines.[34] Nine days later he delivered twenty-five tons of supplies and twenty-two men to Alusan Bay in Samar.[35] Three U.S. Army Air Corps meteorologists—Sgt. William Richardson, Cpl. William Becker III, and Pfc. Jerry Pascua—set up a weather station on the east coast. Becker set up another with Sergeant Raymundo Agcaoili and Private Isaac Aguila at Sorsogon, Luzon. Stahl recalled, "They had to move frequently, for making weather observations required that they release hydrogen-filled balloons into the air daily to determine wind currents. Obviously, this activity drew attention to their location and aroused Japanese interest."[36]

After a failed attempt to link up with guerrillas near Sanco Point, *Narwhal* delivered eight more men and seven tons to Fertig at Tukuran with a second stop with eight men and forty-five tons to Bowler.[37] On 9 June the boat returned to Darwin before heading out again the next day. After shelling oil tanks in the Netherlands East Indies, on 20 June *Narwhal* delivered four men and ninety-two tons of supplies to Tukuran. On the way home, Titus damaged the oil tanker *Itsukushima Maru* in the Sulu Sea.

LUZON, D890/R-159

Ramsey reached Manila to find that the Japanese had arrested dozens of ECLGA agents. "For the second time," he lamented, "our Manila network had been stripped."[38] Colonel Sanchez, Hukbalahap 8th Region commander, reported that in December Thorp, Noble, Moses, Praeger, and Barker had been forced to dig their graves in the old Chinese cemetery and were beheaded. None had betrayed the guerrillas. Barker's death hit Ramsey especially hard. "He was only one of over twenty-five hundred guerrilla fighters who had so far lost their lives," he observed, "and though he was closer to me than the others, and his face was clearer in my mind, I allowed him to take his place among them in my memory."[39]

The emotional toll added to the physical stress of malaria, malnutrition, and exhaustion. Ramsey collapsed. After more than a week recovering in the home of a Catholic priest in San Mateo, an answer to his prayers arrived in the form of Modesto Castandeda (also known as Captain Casey), who brought a radio from the PRS. Castandeda had travelled one thousand miles from Negros in four months. Ramsey wrote, "We were back in the wider war, in touch with the world."[40]

Communication meant life, but staying alive required medicine. The USAFIP-NL staffed two relatively well-supplied field hospitals with six doctors and six nurses in each. "Well, with the area being as large as it was," Blackburn recalled, "I had to take those hospitals and split them up."[41] The largest, at Manauan, was "a structure with a thatched roof and floors, containing an emergency room, operating room, and several wards" with sixty beds.[42] Volckmann described his Second District hospital as "the best I had seen anywhere. They constructed patients' beds that could serve as stretchers to carry the patients quickly."[43] When the Japanese destroyed the hospital in June, the guerrillas safely fled with all patients, staff, and supplies.

Guerrillas offered medical assistance to civilians to cement relations. Blas Miranda's Western Leyte guerrilla warfare force surgeon Dr. Domingo C. Veloso, for example, organized a hospital at San Jose that became a local "health-giving oasis."[44] Modern U.S. counterinsurgency doctrine recognizes the centrality of "civilian-military unity."[45] Medical aid helped create that unity. "Later on, when the people recognized that we were consolidating our area, they began trying to move out of the Jap areas and into ours," Blackburn added. "We set up places for them to live, gave them seed, and a piece of land that was designated for them by the mayor of the town."[46]

Unity with SWPA proved more elusive. In early March, Roxas sent Colonel Narciso Manzano from Manila to Fertig with a request that SWPA appoint him as "coordinator of intelligence of Luzon."[47] On 20 March SWPA instructed Fertig to keep Manzano in Mindanao. On 14 April they authorized Manzano to develop Luzon intelligence for Fertig. At the end of May Fertig asked for a submarine to take Manzano to Luzon. On 24 July SWPA arranged a submarine for his transit, but two days later they cancelled it. SWPA arranged for and cancelled a second submarine in August. Finally, on 1 September the PRS permanently assigned Manzano to Fertig. The G-2 later compared this "baffling" case of Manzano to those of Villamor and Andrews, "a promising potential, with extraordinary background, unexploited due to the refusal to grant centralized operational control in intelligence matters and a total and irritating division of authority."[48]

VISAYAS, D901/R-148

On Samar on 24 May Charlie Smith loaded two bancas with men and equipment from *Narwhal*. He sent one team under Lieutenant Vincente Labrador and Lieutenant Carlos Ancheta to Ball on Baler Bay.[49] A second group under Bob Stahl headed for the Bondoc Peninsula in southern Luzon to link up with Sergeant Crispolo Robles and establish "an alternate NCS [net control station] should MACA be lost to the enemy."[50]

The banca crews relied on a large-scale 1933 *United States Coast and Geodetic Chart of the Philippines Islands* and a 1940 *Socony-Vacuum Oil Company Road Map*. By sheer luck, Stahl landed very near Robles' base on 30 May. The next day he established radio station S3L near Patabog and radioed Smith: "Chased en route but arrived ok."[51] Smith now connected four stations on Samar, one in Cebu, one in Masbate, two in southern Luzon, and two more in central Luzon.[52]

As fast as SWPA could emplace radios, the Japanese tried to take them down. They virtually besieged both Smith's MACA station on Samar and Fertig's KUS on Mindanao. Stahl recalled: "I had agents losing their radios—or worse, being captured. I had stations coming on the air, only to disappear and never be heard again. I had really important ship sightings that I could not get through to GHQ because the Japanese were jamming my signals."[53]

In Bontoc, Stahl was called to meet a native general in a nearby schoolhouse. About twenty men in ragged uniforms with bolos and pistols provided a chilly reception. With a show of pomp, "Lieutenant General" Guadencio V. Vera was introduced as "Commander in Chief and Judge Advocate of the Tayabas Guerrilla Vera's Party!" Stahl remembered: "He was about five feet, two inches tall, exceedingly thin, gaunt, sunken cheeked, hollow eyed. His teeth were much too large for his mouth, giving him a constant snarl. His eyeballs were very large, adding to his proper appearance as the madman he was."[54] Vera—the man who had executed the TVGU's Lieutenant Vicente Villa nearly two years earlier—welcomed Stahl and proclaimed, "The United States Army and the Philippine Army may have surrendered, but *we* did *not* surrender!"[55] As proof of his power, Vera produced Americans George McGowan, Eldred Sattem, and Chester Konka, who had escaped internment and wandered into Vera's hospitality. McGowan warned Stahl that Vera was going to kill them all.

Vera would later explain how he had led his people into the hills and added, "We would be a guerrilla army. But with no money we soon became bandits in order to survive."[56] Stahl recalled, "More than one hundred men, women and children living in a jungle camp where every call of nature was handled as an animal would—drop it anywhere and don't even cover it catlike! . . . The stench was unbearable."[57] Yet Stahl needed to stay in their area. Thinking fast, he forged a message from MacArthur to Vera praising him as an important guerrilla leader, asking him to support Stahl and the coast watchers, and promising to send guns as soon as possible. Stahl observed, "The scheme worked! Moral: When you're dealing with a nut, think like a nut."[58]

VISAYAS 911/R-138

On 5 June *Nautilus*, under Cdr. George A. Sharp Jr., transported ninety-two tons of supplies to Tukuran.[59] Seventeen days later the sub delivered another ninety-two tons and four men to Balatong Point, Negros, and picked up seventeen evacuees. On 9 July Sharp entered the Amsay River in Mindoro to deliver twenty-two men and twelve tons of supplies.

After a run to Bohol was cancelled, he delivered two men and thirty tons of supplies to Lagoma, Luzon. Finally, on 16 July he recovered the last of the sensitive documents and two packages from Balatong Point, Negros.

Meanwhile, on 8 June, Lt. Cdr. Marshall H. Austin sailed *Redfin* (SS-272) to Ramos Island near Palawan to deliver an observation team of six guerrillas under Sergeant Amando S. Corpus and twenty-five tons of gear.[60] Two weeks later the team made its first radio contact with SWPA. At 2200 hours on 13 August they saw a vessel transiting the Balabac Strait explode.[61] U.S. Navy Task Force 71 identified the vessel as SS-250 *Flier*. Eight of the thirteen sailors who got off the sinking sub made it to Mantagule Island, where natives found them.[62]

The U.S. Navy concluded that *Flier* had hit a floating mine. Weeks earlier, Palawan guerrillas under Dr. Higinio Acosta Mendoza Sr. had relayed word from three sailors in the Puerta Princesa prison camp of the sinking of their boat, *Robalo* (SS-272), two miles west of Palawan by a mine.[63] The Navy radioed Corpus: "Results thus far are disappointing and immediate improvement in your intelligence coverage and reports is desired and expected."[64] He took the reprimand hard. Two days later, Sergeant Carlos S. Placido notified SWPA that his team leader had shot himself through the heart.

SWPA general headquarters issued Staff Memorandum 18 on 5 June announcing the end of the PRS's semi-independent status.[65] For three months the G-2 had worked on recommendations to bring all staff sections into the Philippine operations in preparation of MacArthur's return.[66] SWPA assigned the "direction of guerrilla activities" to G-3, intelligence to G-2, and supply to G-4 (see map 9.1).[67] The PRS became a subordinate part of G-3.

SAMAR, D921/R-128

On 15 June the United States began a monthlong battle for Saipan that cost Americans almost 3,500 killed and 10,000 wounded. The Japanese lost 24,000 soldiers killed in battle and 5,000 more to suicide. Another 22,000 Japanese civilians died, mostly by suicide. Japanese leaders embraced their example as inspiration for future sacrifice. Tokyo papers popularized a *Time* magazine article describing young women hurling themselves over cliffs to avoid falling into American hands. Haruko Taya Cook and Theodore F. Cook noted, "Such awe-filled 'enemy' reports were presented by Tokyo as clear-evidence of the glory of civilian sacrifices, and portrayed as proof of the 'pride of the Japanese woman.'"[68]

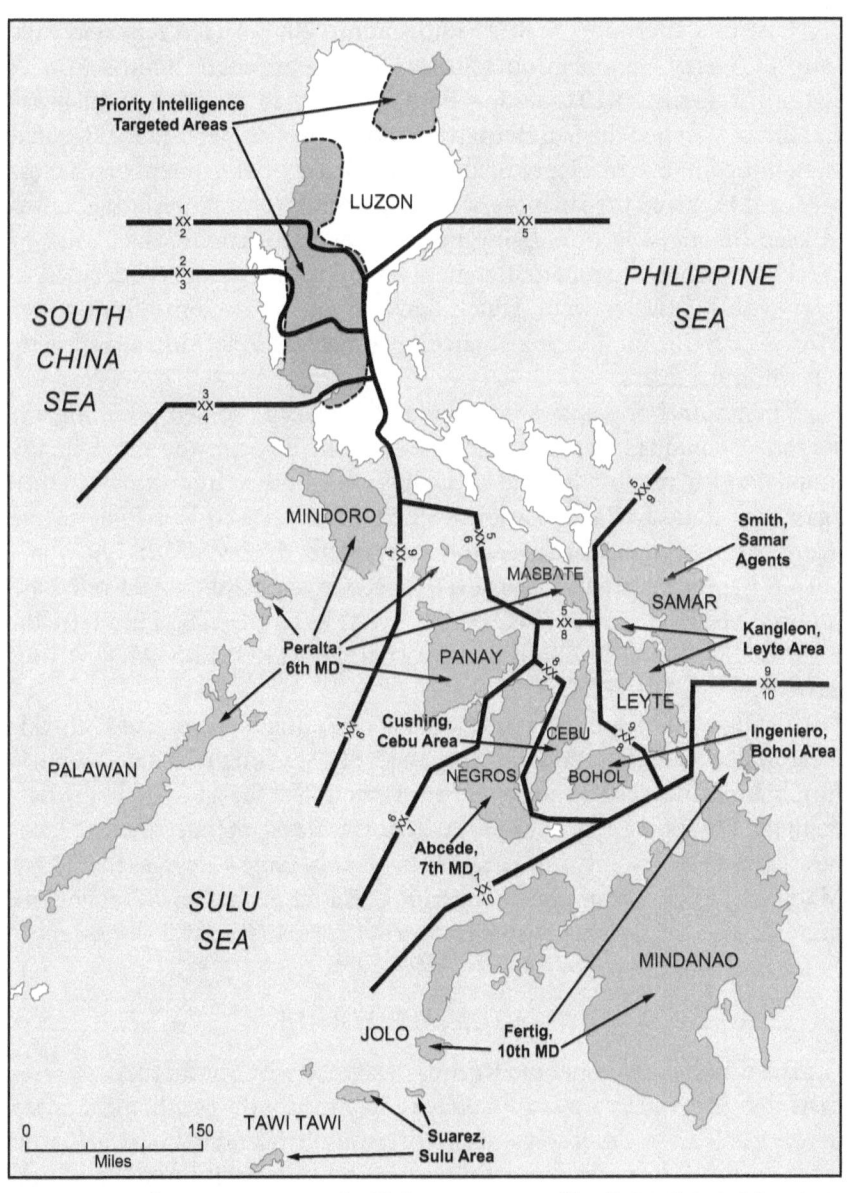

MAP 9.1. Intelligence coverage in the Philippines, reported by SWPA G-2, 27 May 1944

Late that afternoon, Stahl's radio station S3L detected repeated calls from Lt. Gerry Chapman on southern Luzon for either Smith's MACA station or Fertig's KUS station—both conduits to SWPA.⁶⁹ Stahl knew Chapman watched the San Bernardino Strait, and his persistence signaled something important. He recalled, "I had no idea of the content of his message, but I noticed the Japanese 'jamming'—sending out interfering noises to keep his message from being heard—was more intense than usual."⁷⁰ Piecing together Chapman's fragmentary transmissions, Stahl decided to relay with his twelve-watt "Dutch Set." He got no response from either MACA or KUS. Stahl took a chance to contact KAZ in Australia directly but without success.

Then somebody answered. "Suddenly, I heard someone calling my station. I couldn't read the caller's ident, but through the din I finally understood a request for me to change to another frequency."⁷¹ Once again, the Mackay Radio station KFS in San Francisco had come to the guerrillas' rescue. KFS relayed the message to KAZ via KUS on Mindanao. Chapman's dispatch journeyed 22,600 miles. Stahl then decoded the report: "GOING EAST TWO SMALL PATROL BOATS, TEN CRUISERS, THREE BATTLESHIPS, ELEVEN DESTROYERS AND NINE AIRCRAFT CARRIERS."⁷²

Chapman had spotted a Japanese fleet heading to attack the Fifth U.S. Fleet under Adm. Raymond A. Spruance. His warning reinforced reports from submarine pickets and helped Spruance defeat the Japanese in the Battle of the Philippine Sea.⁷³ On 19–20 June U.S. naval aircraft sank five Japanese carriers and twenty capital ships. In what became known as the "Great Marianas Turkey Shoot," vastly superior U.S. aircraft shot down roughly six hundred enemy airplanes, virtually destroying Japanese naval air power.

MANILA, D931/R-118

Fourteenth Army commander Kuroda disagreed with Southern Army forecasts that the Americans would attack Luzon from the south and wanted to move at least one division and two brigades to defend for an attack from the east.⁷⁴ The dispositions would remain the 16th Division on Leyte and the 30th Division in northeast Mindanao, with the newly formed 32nd Independent Mixed Brigade (IMB) in Northern Luzon, the 33rd IMB in Southern Luzon, the 31st IMB in the Visayas, and the 30th IMB on Mindanao. Sixty percent of the new air bases were reported complete.

On 25 June Japanese officers in dress uniforms came to Fort Santiago. "Something somber dominated the atmosphere," Adalia Marquez recalled.⁷⁵ They organized forty prisoners into two groups with picks and shovels, chained together at the ankles and tied with ropes at the wrists. The first group contained Chinese prisoners. American captain George Harrison led the second group. The prisoners marched out of the fort at 1430 hours. Adalia recalled, "I had to look. Those noble men, with heads held high, marched on.... I saw men whose kind make history."[76] Four and a half hours later Lieutenant Yamada led the guards back alone. Yamada had been kind to Adalia and her children, so she dared to ask him if the stronger men had shot the rest. "No," he answered, "that is where I came in. You know, I am greatly honored by this. Those people who are gone were all first-class men. I had the honor to shoot them!"[77]

The guards were sworn to follow two codes of conduct dating from 1882 and 1941. Both derived from the code of *bushido* that supposedly emphasized self-discipline and tolerance, compassion, and justice.[78] Yet the codes also demanded blind obedience to superior officers who represented the emperor. As Yuki Tanaka explained: "To despise men who had surrendered rather than fight to the death became a first step toward justifying reckless violence against them."[79]

Under this guidance, the camps became hell for prisoners. Don Willis recalled, "The men became walking skeletons on our food ration, about ten ounces (a large sardine can scoop) of *lugow*, a watery rice, and *kangkong*, a plant which grew in the ditches around camp."[80] Prisoners waited hours for a dripping water hose, often to be shooed away at the last minute. An observer at the Campas prison reported: "Men lie on the floor in agony, moving their bowels where they lie, soaking in that unclean stench because there is not enough water to wash it away. Flies ravage the sick and the dying. Outside the barracks, the dead are piling up like sandbags."[81]

When George Harrison arrived at Fort Santiago in April 1944, the guards starved him for ten days, beat him, fed him, and then starved him again. They hauled him before an interrogator who used Adalia Marquez as an interpreter. The interrogator placed food before Harrison as an inducement to talk. Harrison ate greedily, then pretended not to remember anything. "The interrogator jumped up and sat on Harrison's stomach, bouncing up and down while raining blows on Harrison's head until Harrison began to vomit blood," Adalia testified.[82]

Harrison had suffered a common torture: "Tie up a man, force his mouth open under a faucet, fill him full of water, then kick him and beat him in the stomach!"[83] The Japanese also employed the sun cure: "The victim was tied to a stake in the full heat of the sun with a sentinel to prod him with a bayonet to keep his face up and his eyes opened full in the sun's direct rays."[84] Panlilio reported, "The Japs, to amuse themselves, would tie the victim's penis, scrotum, or both and lead him around like a dog on the leash, yanking it, laughing hilariously at the pain it provoked."[85] Others reported: "Suspected guerrillas had lighted matches thrust under their fingernails and white-hot irons applied to their genitals. Women came in for especially cruel treatment, including rape and mutilation."[86]

Few prisoners saw signs of kindness in their guards, but Adalia detected hints of humanity. A turnkey named Wada, she noted, "was not a strict guard. He swore at the prisoners like five drunkards all in one, but he was inclined to be kind, even allowing his charges to gossip and joke with him."[87] Willis recalled a Lieutenant Okubo at Cabanatuan who was transferred with him to the Davao penal colony. "He would always ask, 'How awe you, Lieutenant Weeus?'" he remembered and added, "I intended to use him if I could as he seem to take a liking to me."[88]

SWPA sought to aid the prisoners. After he escaped Davao in July 1943, Stephen Mellnik was whisked to Washington to meet a secret organization, MIS-X, dedicated to helping U.S. prisoners in enemy hands. They interrogated him for help in communicating with prisoners in the Philippines.[89] Mellnik returned to SWPA and on 11 December submitted a memorandum to the G-2 on developing contacts in Davao and Cabanatuan.

In February MIS-X officer Lieutenant Harold A. Rosenquist assigned to SWPA agreed to go to the Davao penal colony, but the G-2 stopped him.[90] Whitney finally approved his mission on 26 March, over the objections of the PRS who feared trespassing on Fertig's territory. A month later the PRS notified Fertig that Rosenquist "has been placed on temporary duty with your command for the purpose of acting as your advisor in the planning of assistance to prisoners of war in your military area."[91] SWPA did not know that on 1 March, Fertig had sent Lieutenant Robert Spielman, another Davao escapee, to contact the prisoners.[92] Spielman linked up with the prisoners on 19 March and passed them a few supplies, which the guards discovered eight days later. Captain Mark Wohlfeldt then led ten POWs in a desperate escape, but patrols recaptured and severely punished four of the escapees.

Unaware of all this, on 1 June *Nautilus* put Rosenquist ashore at Turkuran, and the lieutenant made his way to Major Claro Laurenta's guerrilla headquarters in Kapatangan. Laurenta got him to Fertig's headquarters on 23 July. Assigned a team of guerrillas, Rosenquist reached the Davao penal colony in early August—only to discover it empty.

SWPA later learned that on 6 June the Japanese had marched the camp's 1,250 prisoners blindfolded and tied together to Lasang Pier in Davao.[93] Six days later they crammed the prisoners aboard the merchant freighter *Eire Maru* for Zamboanga, where they transferred 750 of them to *Shinyo Maru* bound for Manila. U.S. submarines SS-256 *Hake*, SS-241

Bashaw, and SS-263 *Paddle* were waiting to intercept a Japanese fleet reportedly gathering at Tawi Tawi.[94] Notified by Allied Naval Forces of a troop ship in their area, *Paddle* attacked *Shinyo Maru* on 7 September. Only 82 prisoners made it to shore.[95] This was not an isolated incident: of the 126,000 Allied prisoners transported in 156 voyages on 134 unmarked Japanese vessels, 21,000 were killed by U.S. planes and submarines.[96]

After the war, MacArthur's G-2 section reviewed Rosenquist's mission to Davao and concluded: "It is now known also that the guerrillas with a little assistance might have removed most of the PW safely had the project been organized while the opportunity presented itself."[97]

CENTRAL LUZON, D933/R-116

Preparing for MacArthur's return, the Japanese high command authorized "punitive actions in order to maintain public peace and order" against the "very powerful and active" Philippine guerrillas.[98] Manila newspapers reported on 11 July the arrest of 120 guerrillas, including priests and nuns. "They have not dared to touch priests and women religious till now," commented Pacita Pestano-Jacinto. "But the Japanese no longer have the time or patience to play ball even with religious elements."[99]

Ramona Snyder fled the capital to join Ramsey at his new headquarters at Balagbag.[100] He had built six nip huts for troops with a larger one as his mess hall and hospital. A separate small hut served as Ramsey's home. An escaped POW, Marine corporal Jimmy Carrington, oversaw security with two .50-caliber machine guns salvaged from a wrecked U.S. fighter plane. Lieutenant Colonel Leopoldo Guillermo emplaced radio station LRT behind Ramsey's camp on "Signal Hill."[101] MacArthur connected to Ramsey through Ed Andrews' net control station NAL on Negros. Ramsey passed intelligence from ECLGA intelligence chief in Manila, twenty-nine-year-old Lieutenant Colonel Liberato "Obie" Bonoan, that Laurel had supplied 250,000 laborers to the Japanese.[102] Ramsey also began distributing a newsletter, *The Voice of the Misguided Elements*. "They were in great demand as the only available source of outside information," he said, "and people read and reproduced them at the risk of their lives."[103]

The ECLGA tried to harass the enemy. "Operatives would pour cane sugar into the gas tanks of planes and vehicles, set fire to depots, or attack military convoys in the countryside," Ramsey reported.[104] He wanted more substantial operations. Roeder answered his call with an explosive device made of two six-inch lead cylinders welded together, match heads, and black powder in one end and the other filled with sulfuric acid, separated by thin copper sheathing. "The sulfuric acid eats through the copper plate until it reaches the matches," Roeder explained. "It ignites them, and they in turn explode the powder."[105] With these time-delayed detonators, Ramsey prepared for a sabotage campaign in mid-July.

MANILA, D946/R-103

On 10 July the United States started bombing Tokyo, and the Imperial Army Headquarters considered the best places to shift troops for the final "Shogo" or "Victory Operation": Formosa, the Philippines, the Kurile Islands, and Honshu.[106] Ten thousand troops—including many wounded—were shipped from the Southern Area to Manila and caused a chaotic buildup. The Southern Army therefore established a new 1st Field Replacement Hospital to educate, train, supply, and house those men with an eye to using them in defense of the Philippines.[107]

Reinforcements arrived as shipping allowed: the 26th Division in July and August, the 8th Division in August and September, and the 2nd Tank Division. The army also formed several new divisions: the 103rd Division in Northern Luzon; the 105th in Southern Luzon; the 102nd in Visayas; and the 100th in Mindanao.[108] These were reinforced by newly raised IMBs: the 54th IMB in Zamboanga and the 55th in central Luzon. The 58th IMB reached the Philippines in early July. Two others completed arrival in October. Like MacArthur, they realized they had too few troops to defend all possible invasion beaches in the Philippines. Moreover, Saipan demonstrated that U.S. naval gunfire and airpower could destroy positions on beaches. The Fourteenth Army therefore decided to execute an inland defense of the Philippines.[109]

The U.S. Navy strangled the Japanese forces in the Philippines "When I was in Manila for repairs in the summer of 1944 and learned of the heavy submarine losses of ships crossing the Bashi Straits from Formosa to Luzon," a Japanese merchant captain recalled, "I and my associates began to fear the war was beginning to be lost."[110] The JMA requested a shipment of 100,000 drums of fuel. By the end of September only 40,000 had arrived—and air raids promptly destroyed 37,000 of those.[111]

The Japanese army confiscated three thousand motorcars in the islands, half from Manila, further debilitating the economy. A third of the vehicles went to airfield construction.[112] In July Matsui Kozan closed the Mankayan copper mine because the ore could not be transported. Manager Yoshimichi Ozaki explained: "Impassable steep roads, decrepit vehicles and lack of replacement parts, uncooperative Filipino drivers, destruction of roads by torrential seasonal rain, and anti-Japanese guerrilla activities."[113] Matsui Kozan desperately advertised for two hundred mechanics and two hundred truck drivers—"a state of affairs not at all unrelated to guerrilla activities."[114]

To combat the guerrillas, the Japanese prioritized the elimination of their radios. Filipinos began noticing boats carrying strange arrays of antennas. When these "Chinese clotheslines" appeared off the Bondoc Peninsula, Stahl recalled, "I suspected that these were crude radio-direction-finding rigs seeking a fix on our station. My concern was great enough that we ceased radio operations for several days until they moved away, shifting our radio relay network to one of the other net stations."[115]

Japanese frustration grew. A greater Japan Islam Association survey team of Jingo Okamoto, Masato Owada, and Harukaze Furukawa arrived in Manila too late to make a difference.[116] Lieutenant Shigenobu Mochizuki of the department of information published guidance for using schools to eradicate Western ideals and align popular loyalty to Japan.[117] He built the New Philippines Cultural Institute—the Tagaytay Educational Corps—forty-five miles southeast of Manila to mold future Filipino leaders. The first class of sixty handpicked Filipino POWs learned the Japanese spirit of self-sacrifice and the evils of American individualism and materialism. "Indeed," Lydia Yu-Jose observed, "the memories that remained in the minds of the graduates of this institute were patriotism and the discipline he enforced."[118] Before his guidance was published or his first class graduated, however, in May 1944 guerrillas killed Mochizuki in an ambush in Cavite. Without him, the institute closed. His graduates absorbed a sense of patriotism, but their nation was the Philippines.[119]

LUZON, D943/R-106

On 6 July 4,300 Japanese troops died on Saipan in the largest banzai charge of the war. The next day, Laurel broadcast, "No right-thinking Filipino should allow the re-conquest of the Philippines. We must bear in mind our commitments as an ally of Japan."[120] Behind closed doors, however, he told Filipino and Japanese officials that he would rather quit as president than declare war on the United States.[121] The Japanese again considered replacing Laurel with Ricarte.

Meanwhile, Ramsey had his men place as many of Roeder's new pipe bombs as possible throughout Manila in the weeks prior to 15 July. After 0100 hours that morning, the bombs began erupting. The main Japanese fuel depot at Tanque burst into flames. Railroad tanker cars in the Manila yards exploded. Oil tanks in the Philippines Manufacture Company convulsed into an inferno. At dawn a ten-thousand-ton tanker in the harbor rippled in brilliant flames caused by a bomb in a fifty-gallon oil drum loaded the previous day.¹²² The blast ignited several vessels anchored next to the ship. "The Japanese, taken completely by surprise, had dashed about the city trying to determine what had happened," Ramsey reported. "Roeder's unpredictable fuses had been an inadvertent asset, imposing a randomness on the explosions that made it impossible for the Japanese to coordinate a response."¹²³ Baba closed Manila, stepped up food confiscations, and began a new wave of arrests. A handful of Ramsey's saboteurs were caught and punished severely. Nonetheless, follow-on strikes would burn Piers 5 and 7 in the South Port and destroy a steamer in the Pasig River.¹²⁴

The Huks quickly claimed credit for Ramsey's bombings. Conflicts with them were by now quite common. "A typical fight with the Huks developed once in 1944 up in the Sierra Madre," Lapham noted, "when they ambushed one of our patrols that was protecting Filipino *cargadores* carrying supplies sent to us from Australia."¹²⁵ Tensions increased. "Early in the war," Lapham explained, "disputes within and between guerrilla groups had been mainly over what our duties were and what our policies should be, much complicated by our rivalry for access to food and arms, all exacerbated by personal grudges. By 1944 we were quarreling mostly over jurisdiction: who should rule whom."¹²⁶

Anderson tried to intervene, but he had little influence with the Huks. His influence with the Hunters had weakened when he gave them a radio. He also lost face with Marking when he ordered him not to retaliate against Japanese attacks near Infanta, and Panlilio complained that "the people whose houses had been burned all along the lower river said, under their breath, 'Cowards! Big talkers!'"¹²⁷ Anderson had SWPA send supplies and three radio operators to placate Marking.¹²⁸

Sixty miles farther south in Bulacan Province, the Japanese confiscated harvests and brutally molested women. Mayor Alfredo Cruz Eraña asked Philippine army captain Alejo Santos to organize guerrillas to protect the people. With support from prominent citizens near his base in Victory Hills, Santos organized eight regiments of the Bulacan Military Area guerrillas: *M*, Ponce, Republic, Mountain, Buenavista, Biyák-na-Bató, Kákarong, Valenzuela, and Batatè.¹²⁹

SOUTHERN LUZON, D957/R-92

Lapus angered Zabat by using P8,000 from Charles Smith to purchase cooperation from Flor. SWPA believed that although Zabat "aroused considerable animosity in other leaders of the district," he led Bicol's most powerful group with up to one thousand armed men around Albay.¹³⁰ Zabat charged Flor with spying for the Japanese and Lapus of trying to forcibly recruit his subordinate Molintas. On 21 July he sent ninety men to attack Lapus' base at Monito. Lapus fled to Albay and requested that SWPA immediately recognize him as commander of the 5th MD, claiming that his 54th Regiment had 2,600 armed men with a full division in reserve. Bernard Anderson's agent Barros confirmed that Lapus' troops were the "most military" he had seen in Bicol.[131]

On the Bondoc Peninsula, Stahl grew critically short of supplies and had to seek aid from Vera. Expecting the same ragtag group of bandits he saw in May, he was surprised by Vera's new camp. "It was different," Stahl wrote. "There were no soldiers lolling about doing nothing.... Everyone in sight seemed to be engaged in a chore of one sort or another."[132] Vera had changed too. "No longer was he a braggart, a boor, a horse's ass," Stahl noted. "He appeared to be interested in preparing to fight a war rather than in killing his family's political enemies and robbing civilians."[133] Like many Filipinos, Vera had set out to lead his people against the Japanese without realizing the enormity of the task. To professional soldiers, he and his men had appeared woefully inept, but they were tough, smart, and determined. Given time, they adapted.

Vera stunned Stahl by saying, "I have thought a lot about our first meeting. I was going to wipe out your little group and take your guns. You did not fool me with your message to General MacArthur and his answer to me."[134] Yet the "message" had saved Stahl, for Vera could not dismiss it without confirming that the Americans took him lightly. He wanted their respect. "You also ended my career as a bandit," Vera continued, "for no one would take me seriously any longer. I had to change my army into a real guerrilla army."[135] Vera had created a well-trained and disciplined force of about one thousand men with no assistance from SWPA.[136]

VISAYAS, D957/R-92

On 20 June *Narwhal* delivered four men and ninety-two tons of supplies to Peralta at Lipata Point, Panay.[137] With Japanese garrisons three-and-a-half miles south and thirteen miles north, Peralta supplied enough boats to the transfer—a quick chore, but his men refused to load them to the full. After sharp words and further delays, at 0400 hours skipper Titus jettisoned the last fifteen tons of supplies, ordered the guerrillas to swim fuel drums ashore, and pushed about twenty of Peralta's men overboard for refusing to leave his boat. Despite leaving four sailors ashore, *Narwhal* departed with fourteen evacuees.[138]

To replace Phillips' defunct station on Mindoro, SWPA sent a PRS team under Commander George F. Rowe with orders to develop communication with central Luzon, watch the Manila Bay approaches, collect weather data, and give air warnings.[139] Early on 10 July *Nautilus* delivered

Rowe with twenty-two men and twelve tons of supplies on the Amaay River. Better trained "in the operation of technical equipment" and "better equipped than any other party," Rowe was on the radio net within eight days with air, weather, and radar observations.[140] With new high-powered cameras and film equipment, they photographed shipping lanes, installations, and captured enemy documents. Rowe also kept out of the dispute between Ruffy and Jurado.

At the same time, the Japanese unexpectedly withdrew all their forces except one small garrison from nearby Bohol. Ingeniero's deputy, Captain Estaban Bernido, reassembled his Boforce guerrillas. Ingeniero would return by early September and dispatch agents to Cebu, Negros, and Leyte in search of arms, ammunition, and a radio.

HAWAII, D962/R-87

Filipino faith in MacArthur's return was not well founded in Washington: The chiefs of staff had concluded that their best strategy to end the war was to bypass the Philippines for Formosa. They realized, however, that MacArthur was intent on fulfilling his promise. Gen. George C. Marshall therefore warned him, "We must be careful not to allow our personal feelings and Philippine political considerations to override our great objective, which is the early conclusion of the war with Japan."[141] MacArthur insisted on making his argument to the president.

On 26 July Roosevelt arrived in Honolulu aboard the cruiser USS *Baltimore*. MacArthur had already arrived after a twenty-six-hour flight from Brisbane. The president immediately summoned the general. MacArthur returned to his temporary quarters at Fort Shafter and complained to his staff that Roosevelt had only wanted a photograph for his reelection campaign.[142]

The next day, after dinner at the Holmes estate, the president and his commanders discussed routes to Japan. Nimitz spoke first and, supported by staff and visual aids, argued to skip the Philippines for Formosa. He won points on geography, logistics, and other military principles. When he finished, MacArthur stood alone before a map without notes and reviewed America's failure in the Philippines, his own embarrassment, and his promise to return.[143] He noted that Filipinos, unlike Formosans, had historical connection to the United States and were in fact actively fighting the Japanese as part of the U.S. effort. Unlike the Formosans, they would support a U.S. invasion. MacArthur also warned of the political costs of bypassing the Philippines: "We would admit the truth of Japanese propaganda to the effect that we had abandoned the Filipinos and would not shed American blood to redeem them; we would undoubtedly incur the open hostility of that people; we would probably suffer such loss of prestige among all the peoples of the Far East that it would adversely affect the United States for many years."[144] He closed with a word of counsel: "I feel also that a decision to eliminate the campaign for the relief of the Philippines, even under appreciable military considerations, would cause extremely adverse reactions among the citizens of the United States."[145]

Roosevelt declared a recess to talk alone with the general. "Seizing the initiative," Alfred Castle wrote, "MacArthur used his political trump card. Reminding the president that this was a reelection year, he argued that abandoning 7,000 starving POWs and 17 million Filipino Christians would turn public opinion against him."[146] The candidate understood.

The group reconvened the next morning at 1030 hours. At about noon the president waved his hand and said he had heard enough. He would allow MacArthur to retake the Philippines and instructed Nimitz to support him. The fact of Filipino resistance had proved decisive to MacArthur's argument.

LUZON, D969/R-80

Ball sent a radio with Lieutenant Carlos Ancheta and Sergeant Pete Luz to Volckmann to tie the USAFIP-NL into the Ball-Smith-SWPA net. "This was one of the most thrilling moments I experienced during my guerrilla days in the Philippines," Volckmann exclaimed. "Radio contact with SWPA, lost since March 1943, was re-established! We again had hopes of receiving help from the outside world."[147] Communications, however, brought a torrent of requests from others. Lapham recalled that in the last six months of 1944, "I constantly received 'orders' and 'suggestions' from Anderson, Volckmann, Merrill, and the agents of several different Filipino guerrilla leaders."[148] Volckmann asked SWPA for supplies and was surprised to learn that an officer with fifteen men and fifteen tons of supplies had already landed in Ilocos Norte and was heading his way. It took two weeks for USAFIP-NL scouts to find Lieutenant Valera, who had made a "blind landing" after the sub's skipper had to run from Japanese warships.

Information flowed; supply did not. Lapham received his radio from Ball in May and between 17 and 28 July coordinated with SWPA for his first supplies. They finally decided on a spot on Dibut Bay on the east coast of Luzon, five miles of steep hills and dense jungle from the Japanese garrison at Baler.[149] The PRS planned a mission under Parsons, and in early August SWPA approved it. Lapham went to the rendezvous area seven weeks early to oversee Lieutenant Aquino's Squadron 103 as they built rafts and rehearsed the signal plan for linkup.[150]

On 2 August a news bulletin flashed across the islands: "President Quezon of the Philippines died this morning August 1 at Saranac Lake, New York. Sergio Osmeña has succeeded to the presidency."[151] Mrs. Osmeña, with her family in Baguio, feared that the Japanese would take her and her children hostage. She asked the USAFIP-NL to move them into the mountains under guerrilla protection. Volckmann passed the request to Osmeña, who replied that his family should stay in place. Volckmann informed the new first lady over her vehement protests.

On 12 August Titus steered *Narwahl* out from Fremantle with forty-five passengers.[152] Seventeen days later Lapham's men anxiously watched Dibut Bay. He recalled, "Then, early in the evening, the sub suddenly rose right out of the sea like a gigantic whale—between me and the shore! I was simultaneously thrilled and dumbfounded. The thing looked like a battleship."[153] Parsons and Private Courtney Whitney—the colonel's son—came ashore in a rubber raft. The next day at 1600 hours, skipper Titus returned to unload twenty-three passengers and ten tons of supplies "by the expedient handling and direction of Commander Parsons."[154]

The men used ropes to guide bamboo rafts to and from the sub while Lapham shared ham sandwiches and coffee with the skipper in the boat's mess. He remembered, "Days later I found that part of our cargo was a delicious new kind of army chow called K rations. I didn't know that most GIs called their contents dog biscuits and other colorful, often vulgar, names. To me, after so many months of a guerrilla diet, even the Spam tasted like prime T-bone steak."[155] Lapham suddenly thought: "What in the hell am I going to do with all this stuff?"[156]

At 1856 hours on 1 September *Narwhal* arrived at the Magnac River farther south, recovered Parsons and Whitney, and unloaded another twenty men and ten tons of supplies.[157] John M. Kerrey of the 228th Signal Operations Company fell into the water and drowned, but the sub took aboard four evacuees.[158] After a stop in Cateel Bay the next day to pick up one man and some mail, Titus headed south and made Darwin on 10 September.

On the Magnac River, Parsons delivered supplies to Bernard Anderson. To the west, Barros ran a station on Ragay Gulf with about sixty former Philippine Scouts provided by Miranda. Having promised to send Barros arms, Anderson sent a courier instructing him to send men to Basiad Bay. Twenty men under Captain Leonardo Golpe and Lieutenant Eulogio Castañeda left Miranda's area on 25 September and returned on 13 October with twelve M-1 carbines, three submachine guns, three tommy guns, and assorted supplies.¹⁵⁹ With that, what Lapham had requested in May arrived in guerrilla hands five months later.

Anderson also sent Barros an unusual low-wattage radio powered by a hand-cranked generator for a new coast watcher station. Barros sent an operator to Stahl to coordinate codes and procedures. After several days without hearing from the new station, Stahl decided to sail across the bay and find out what was wrong. "Naturally, I had an ulterior motive," he explained. "He had supplies—food, I should hope. Perhaps even cigarettes!"¹⁶⁰

After a perilous sail across the bay, a climb hundreds of yards up a sheer cliff, and a hike along a difficult jungle trail, Stahl and Eldred Sattem followed guide Pablo Montalvo into Barros' "Ohio Headquarters." There they met American Ted Suttles, a former employee of the Camarines Norte mining company recently freed by guerrillas from the Naga prison. Barros explained that his operators "might be good code clerks, but what's the good of that if they can't get the damned radio going?"¹⁶¹ Stahl realized the operators had not been properly trained. From his experience with the bicycle-powered "Dutch Set," he knew that a transmitter and receiver would drift off frequency if the person cranking the generator did not maintain a steady pace. After some practice, they perfected the proper pedal rate to maintain contact with station S3L.

The nets were now humming. On 29 August Volckmann radioed to SWPA: "D-Day missions have been assigned within this command as follows: to destroy all enemy lines of communication; to harass, delay, and destroy all troop and supply movements; to destroy enemy supply dumps, truck parks, troop concentrations, and command posts: to prevent enemy from securing locally food supplies, construction materials, labor, means of transportation."¹⁶² He only awaited orders to attack. SWPA sent no reply.

MANILA, D992/R-57

On 22 July a general with more than forty years' service, Kuniaki Koiso, replaced Tojo as prime minister with instructions from the emperor "to carry on the war as effectively as possible and then at some point to prepare the groundwork for peace."¹⁶³ Koiso believed the best window for negotiation with the Americans had opened with the battle of Guadalcanal and closed with Japan's defeat at Saipan. Any settlement now rested on the upcoming battle for the Philippines. "If Japan won even one engagement in the battle," Akira Iriye explained, "it could then prepare for a truce arrangement."¹⁶⁴

To this end, the Southern Army changed the premise of its plans: "the Philippines Operation would not be a defensive but a decisive operation."¹⁶⁵ They were out to force a settlement. The army "decided to launch the attack before the enemy forces attempt a landing on any part of the Philippines."[166] The Southern Army labeled their new offensive plan *Sho Ichigo*—"one opportunity."

The *Manila Tribune* on 21 July optimistically boasted: "There is one thing we can definitely say without reservation and that is that the defense of the Philippines is complete."[167] Actually the army did not begin final preparations for defense until mid-August.[168] Even then, shortages challenged their efforts; less than one-third of promised weapons, ammunition, supplies, and vehicles had arrived.[169] Troops rescued at sea and recuperating in Manila hospitals were pressed into the line after a short training period with captured weapons—"but after August, even these weapons were no longer obtainable."[170]

A malaria outbreak hampered preparations. At Fort Santiago, a guard named Fukumoto explained to Adalia Marquez that it was brought by people who had come down from the mountains. "From this," she recalled, "I gathered that there were many guerrillas who had surrendered as a result of the pacification campaign conducted by the Japanese-run Department of Justice."[171] Adalia and her children were released from Fort Santiago, but others were less fortunate: in August U.S. Army MSgt. Richard Sakakida witnessed the executions of up to forty people charged of involvement with guerrilla activities.[172] He distinctly recalled one being an elderly woman named Mrs. Blanche W. Jurika—Parsons' mother-in-law.

Rumors of U.S. planes bombing Davao stirred the islands, and on 6 September two thousand Huks assaulted the Japanese base on Mount Arayat sixty miles south of Manila. Mayor Leon Guinto responded: "No hostile acts against the Republic and the Imperial Japanese Army and Navy will be tolerated. I weigh my words when I solemnly declare that the consequences of such hostile acts will be fatal!"[173] Two days later U.S. bombers conducted their heaviest raid yet on Davao.[174]

MINDANAO, D1,007/R-44

Ali Dimaporo, a Muslim from Lanao, was drafted into USAFFE in October 1941. As a 10th Infantry Division third lieutenant he organized a Bolo battalion but surrendered in May 1943. In July he was released from the Camp Keithley prison in exchange for a promise to fight Moro guerrillas. Provided with thirty armed men, Dimaporo traveled Misamis Oriental delivering speeches, collecting arms, and protecting traders. He also secretly provided guerrillas "food, money, shelter and ammunition."[175] Finally Captain Ishima, the Japanese commander in Malabang, arrested Dimaporo on suspicion of aiding guerrillas but released him for lack of evidence.

On 24 June Dimaporo commanded a twenty-six-man detail protecting workers on the Malabang-Parang road while Ishima and twelve Japanese soldiers watched nearby. During lunch, Dimaporo slaughtered Ishima and his soldiers. From then on, he fought as a guerrilla. The attack was a part of a trend of collaborators seeming to suddenly turn against the Japanese.[176]

In early September the Japanese began moving more troops to Mindanao.[177] Fertig was worried: "The food situation is extremely critical. If we are not run out of here, we have enough fuel for 80 days. There is only food for 10 days. Our only chance of survival will be for the Nips not to press us too hard. Again our future is in God's hands."[178] The 25,000 Japanese troops in Surigao and 80,000 in Davao deliberately confiscated all the food they could find.

Japanese troops relocated from Surigao to Cagayan and defenses in South Bukidnon. Another five thousand soldiers from Naspit, followed by Japanese women and children, joined them in Cagayan, despite harassment from Fertig's 110th Infantry Regiment. The moves left a 550-man garrison in Hinataun, 700 in Surigao, and possibly 2,000 in Agusan. They completely withdrew across the Agusan River by mid-month and vacated the Davao penal colony.[179] The units at Camp Keithley would secretly retreat in early October, link up with the battalion at Iligan, and move to Davao. They would also vacate Damaslan and Iligon to concentrate 35,000 troops "between Digos, Pikit, and Velencia."[180]

As U.S. carriers struck Davao, Surigao, Cagayan, and Bukidnon, Fertig became optimistic. "After nearly two weary years of battle," he believed, "the tide has turned. It should run to flood without serious opposition. I wanted to be home when the Aspens turn but impossible. Maybe by Christmas."[181] On 13 and 14 September the Navy hit Cebu, Leyte, Panay, and Negros. A week later, they bombed Legaspi.[182] Fertig wrote, "Box score thru 20 Sept. is 701 planes destroyed 176 ships sunk or damaged. Jap airforce practically driven from Mindanao, Davao, Sarangani Bay and Zambo hit almost daily."[183]

On 14 September *Narwhal* departed Australia on its fourteenth war patrol with forty-one passengers. After dropping off thirty-five men and thirty-five tons of supplies near Kiamba, *Narwhal* fought heavy rains to rendezvous with guerrillas off Balingasag and deliver three men and twenty tons of supplies.[184] Guerrilla captain Chandler Thomas met the sub to arrange the pickup of four stretcher-bound guerrillas down the coast in Siari Bay.[185] On 29 September skipper Titus found the landing site a poor one due to currents, shoals, and exposure but nevertheless sent out two rubber boats with petty officers to retrieve the four wounded men. To their surprise, eighty-two evacuees came out to board *Narwhal*. Eighty were POWs who survived the sinking of *Shinyo Maru*.[186] Thomas had been correct, however, in that only four were litter cases.[187] The overloaded *Narwhal* lost power on her rear planes and was stuck in diving posture to 170 feet before emergency procedures brought her to the surface just as a Japanese aircraft arrived overhead. The boat made it to Mios Woendi on 5 October.

Meanwhile, photographic reconnaissance by carrier raids in September convinced Halsey that the Japanese were weak in the central Philippines.[188] The joint chiefs authorized MacArthur "to occupy Leyte, by-passing Mindanao, with Nimitz's forces joining in the attack."[189] Of course, when they had met in July and the president asked, "Douglas, where do we go from here?" MacArthur had replied, "Leyte, Mr. President, then Luzon!"[190]

PANAY, D1,029/R-20

By now Peralta had six combat teams spanning Panay with radios and couriers connecting to Bohol, Samar, Leyte, Luzon, and Masbate. Peralta's agents on Luzon reported from city street corners, government offices, and Japanese bases.[191] "The object," the PRS explained, "has been to introduce an element of competition between agents and to cross check information received."[192] Competition meant friction. SWPA observed, "Shifting support, failure to thoroughly examine the facts in disputes and the resultant hasty decisions, often cited by junior and inexperienced officers, have aggravated the local political situation on those islands."[193]

Peralta reported 22,600 guerrillas with 8,000 arms of various types and about 160 rounds of ammo per weapon. Over two years SWPA had delivered 350 tons of supplies to Panay including "carbines, assorted machine guns, tommy guns, a few mortars, etc."[194] Peralta's men confined the Japanese to garrisons at San Jose (Antique), Santa Barbara, Iloilo City, and Capiz. The situation seemed to make Panay an ideal choice as a base for MacArthur's return, but geography said otherwise. Leyte would make a better stepping-stone to Luzon.

MANILA, D1,005/R-46

On 21 September from a window of Saint Rita College, young Isabela Yumol watched airplanes approach Manila. "Then the air-raid siren started to blare out loudly," she recalled, "and I see small white puffs of smoke in the sky. The two bodied airplanes move so fast none of the white puffs is hitting them."[195] The last American fighters over the Philippines were outclassed by the Japanese Zeros.[196] The new P-38 Lightning fighters over Manila were superior in every measure and heralded quantitative and qualitative advantages in weapons and systems that would shock the Japanese and guerrillas alike.[197]

Robin Prising watched from a rooftop in Santo Tomas prison: "Out of the massy surge of clouds, the American bombers came, tier upon tier of them, flying high, flying low, and earth shaking armada of aeroplanes, glistening silver-white in the sun as they rode the air."[198] Guerrillas reported "especially gratifying" battle damage in the first two days of raids on Manila with up to three thousand Japanese casualties and 90 percent of military installations hit, with some forty to sixty vessels sunk in Manila harbor.[199] Outside the city, Marking remarked on how moved he was by this display of power. A deputy answered, "Today is not the wonder of it. The wonder, Marking, is how you pulled through last year. The wonder is how you kept on fighting."[200]

Six days into the bombing, Laurel—with the unanimous consent of his cabinet—declared war against the United States and Great Britain. Lichauco noted in his diary a popular sense that Laurel had saved the elected assembly from having to vote for war against America, something their new constitution required. "Laurel may yet prove to be one of the true heroes in our struggle against the Japanese invaders," he wrote. "Of course, no one takes his statement seriously."[201]

Laurel also let loose the Ganaps and the Makapili. They collected one sack of rice for each guerrilla head but, Abaya noted, "No salary was provided for these 'patriotic' soldiers. Hence an open incentive for looting."[202] To be sure, the collaborators found little reward for their efforts. Adalia Marquez observed: "No matter how faithfully they worked for the Japanese, when they outlived their usefulness they were done away with."[203] She recalled a boy named Hilario who accidentally stole a Japanese general's briefcase. Military police captain Eda rounded up sixty-four people. "They were condemned not for participation, not for guilt by association, but by accident of location," Adalia explained. "Even those informers who had helped the Japs get their men were still behind bars. It was common to hear, 'What is the use? Be on the Japs' side, they imprison you. Go against them, they do the same. Might as well be against them!'"[204]

On 29 September the submarine SS-197 *Seawolf* under Lieutenant Commander Alfred Marion Bontier reached Manus on eastern Samar to deliver personnel and supplies. After exchanging radar signals with *Narwhal* on 3 October, she disappeared with all hands—possibly sunk by friendly fire.[205] By now the U.S. Navy had forced the Japanese to abandon the shipping lanes from Davao to Halmahera and Manila to Saigon. By November they would drop the lanes from Miri to Manila, from Singapore and Soerabaja to Balikpapan, and from Manila to Ormoc and Davao.²⁰⁶ The Ishihara Sangyo company reduced operations at the Larap mine to minimal production for local pig iron foundries.²⁰⁷ The entire mine would shut down on 18 December.

Philippine rice production had fallen by 73 percent since 1941.²⁰⁸ Japanese commanders confiscated food on Luzon to deny it to guerrillas. At the same time, Abaya reported, "Many landlords amassed fortunes selling rice to our Jap guests at fantastic prices. . . . the poor went hungry. . . . *Rice at two thousand pesos a* cavan *and still shooting up!*"²⁰⁹ Starvation wracked the resistance. Ramsey recalled, "Through October and November we began eating monkey, birds, and the indigenous *kamoting kahoy*, a pasty wild tuber. We were all losing weight, and by mid-November I was dangerously thin and debilitated."²¹⁰

The Japanese were busily concentrating their remaining aircraft and naval vessels in the Philippines in hopes of destroying an invading U.S. fleet. Southern Expeditionary Army Group commander General Viscount Hisaichi Terauchi arranged for General Tomoyuki Yamashita to take command of the Fourteenth Area Army. The imperial headquarters ordered him to prepare to fight the decisive battle on Leyte.²¹¹

Yamashita arrived in Manila on 6 October.²¹² He had a reputation as a highly effective commander who "inspired strong loyalty and affection in his men."²¹³ Though deeply involved in the "February 26 incident," the failed coup attempt in 1936, he went on to conquer the impregnable British citadel of Singapore and earn the sobriquet "the Tiger of Malaya." He had since spent most of the war in semi-exile in Manchukuo and China.

Yamashita convened a meeting of his division commanders "where he elucidated the important elements of the operational plan."²¹⁴ He emphasized traditional battle spirit and said units "must fight the battle on Luzon with the utmost effort."²¹⁵ Yamashita anticipated a decisive battle in defense of Luzon's naval bases and airfields and reorganized his 262,000 men into the 152,000-man Shobu group under his command in north Luzon, the 80,000-man Shimbu group under Lieutenant General Shizuo Yokoyama around Manila, and the 30,000-man Kembu group under Major General Rikichi Tsukada near Bataan. They were to fight delaying actions and withdraw into inland strongholds. Yamashita planned to declare Manila an open city.²¹⁶

Assessing the guerrilla threat, Yamashita confessed to chief of general affairs Utsunomiya, "I had no idea how bad the peace and order situation is in the Philippines."²¹⁷ He blamed the staff, called Utsunomiya a "lazy official" (*dara-kan*), accused chief of staff Major General Takaji Wachi of spoiling the Philippine elites, and pointedly asked Ambassador Murata, "How could you have spent nearly three years here and let this happen?"[218]

On 11 October Yamashita ordered the "subjugation" of "armed guerrillas."[219] He declared: "Those who stand against the Japanese Army must be regarded as their enemies. In the Philippines today, the war has come to the situation of kill or be killed."[220] He approved an idea advocated by Koreshige Inuzuka and Tomoji Kageyama to arm loyal Filipinos.[221] The Fourteenth Area Army Headquarters tasked an eighty-one-man special construction unit (*Tokubetsu Kosaku Tai*) under Major Sato to organize and train a volunteer Filipino army to fight against guerrillas and any invasion forces.[222]

Meanwhile, the Japanese rounded up anyone suspected of supporting guerrillas. Adalia Marquez was one. The day Yamashita arrived in Manila, one of her former guards, Kawata, warned her to leave town quickly or be arrested again and sent back to Fort Santiago. This time she would not return.[223] Adalia gathered her children and fled to family in Bucawe.

Ramsey, who now claimed 45,000 members (7,000 armed) in his ECLGA, learned Charles Putnam had been captured and beheaded. The Japanese also executed Pat Gatson in Fort Santiago. Ramsey then had his own brush with death—from appendicitis. ECLGA guerrillas abducted Dr. Teng Campa to conduct an appendectomy, and he secured a black market vial of spinal anesthetic.[224] When it turned out to contain only water, Ramsey sedated himself with Tanduay rum. After five days of delirium and intermittent comas, Campa told Ramsey, "Your hospital is a joke. You need a surgeon."[225] The doctor volunteered to stay for the remainder of the war.[226]

The Japanese pressed Laurel for more laborers, and his administration issued a report to explain why Filipinos did not—and would not—respond: language barriers, poor wages, harsh working conditions, forced relocations, separations from family, and starvation.[227] The report concluded: "The anti-Japanese guerrilla efforts to prevent people from applying for work in Japanese projects, which this report does not mention, must have contributed to the difficulties in procuring labor encountered by military-commissioned mineral resource development projects."[228]

Several newly arrived Fourteenth Army staff officers proposed to assassinate Laurel and asked Benigno Ramos and Ricarte for support. Older hands on the staff reacted with alarm and stopped the plot.[229] Ambassador Shozo Murata, President Laurel's interpreter Masakatsu Hamamoto, and Colonel Utsunomiya continued to support Laurel and fought against attacks on the Philippine elite.[230]

HOLLANDIA, D1,032/R-17

MacArthur's staff began considering the Philippine guerrillas in their future operations. On 30 September SWPA G-3 Maj. Gen. Stephen J. Chamberlain wrote to chief of staff Sutherland: "Our guerrilla forces have never burdened themselves with keeping or protecting Japanese captives and have not infrequently submitted them to severe methods of torture."[231] He wanted MacArthur to broadcast to the guerrillas (and the Japanese) that SWPA treated prisoners according to the laws of war, and it expected all others to do the same. The next day Sutherland answered: "Desperate men who fight outside the rules of land warfare cannot be expected to apply those rules unilaterally. I know of no case in history where it has been done. For these reasons I do not concur in the promulgation of the proposed directive."[232] The planners decided that the guerrilla units would fall under SWPA forces in their areas and "be required to abide by the established rules of land warfare."[233]

Parsons reported to Sixth U.S. Army commander Lieutenant General Walter Krueger in Hollandia and learned that MacArthur would invade Leyte on or about 20 October.[234] Like most others, he had assumed MacArthur would strike Mindanao first. Instead, Fertig would harass the Japanese there while Charlie Smith assisted diversionary landings on Samar.[235] Not until the end of September, however, did the Samar guerrillas name Smith as their overall commander.[236]

Krueger informed Parsons that MacArthur and Osmeña wanted to move natives from the invasion beaches to minimize danger to Philippine civilians but feared such action would tip off the Japanese. They decided to send one trusted agent into the area prior to the invasion to devise some way to move the locals without alerting the Japanese. That trusted agent would be Parsons.

Parsons, of course, would need Kangleon's help, but the island's other guerrillas remained at odds. Pedro Merritt's 1,800-man unit—reflagged as the 93rd Division—still refused to work under Kangleon. Because Merritt reportedly exploited the local government and people, Major Manuel Valley refused to join him and added his 1,200 men on Samar to Kangleon's ranks. Captain Luciano Abia joined his constabulary troops to Valley. Colonel Juan Causing gave his guerrillas on Leyte to Kangleon and agreed to become his chief of staff.

Parsons had to get to Kangleon's headquarters somewhere near the Leyte capital of Tacloban. A submarine insertion, however, would take too long and would draw too much attention. He would have to go by air. With MacArthur's authority, he went to Seventh Fleet commander Vice Admiral Thomas C. Kinkaid, who reluctantly provided a PBY Catalina Black Cat flying boat specially equipped for night operations. Parsons then went to the fleet commander of aircraft Rear Admiral Frank D. Wagner to schedule a flight with a special crew for a "destination to be designated by the above-named Parsons."[237] He returned to Hollandia, where Sutherland informed him that Army intelligence had sent Lt. Col. Frank Rawolle to join the mission. The Army was not going to rely solely on a naval officer.

MacArthur ordered all guerrillas to acquire "reliable—specific information" on the enemy.[238] SWPA's whole staff had specific requests. "As a result," Ramsey recalled, "his demands on us for intelligence became more insistent and pointed."[239] Lapham remembered MacArthur sent several messages with "specific instructions to survey the whole area we controlled, make every possible advance preparation for combat, and plan in detail an extensive program of sabotage to be put into effect when orders came from Australia."[240] SWPA thought the guerrillas provided "a good picture of what they would meet after their landing."[241]

In one example of the guerrillas' collection effort, Lapham recalled,

> At various times we reported 2,000 to 3,000 Japanese troops accompanied by 200 Philippine Constabulary men and 2,000 drums of gasoline at various places on Luzon; 3,000 enemy troops at Urdaneta with four small tanks; 10,000 Japanese in the hills south of Paladapad; 15,000 more along the National Highway; 4,000 more near a certain barrio; 500 in one place; 800 in another, and 15,000 in a third along Dingalan Bay; a division and half along the Zambalese coast, three more divisions in Pampanga, and 1,500 PC nearby, though perhaps half of these were really pro-American; 3,000 ground troops aboard fourteen transports off Port San Fernando, and 200 Nip engineers at Mahoag; fifty Japanese guarding the supply depot at Damortis in the railway warehouse north of the station, plus 100 who guarded an ammunition dump at Batac barrio school, 400 infantrymen at Rosario, 900 troops and one mountain gun at Binalonan, 5,000 troops and some guns in a nearby convent, and 2,000 more in Inbac.[242]

SWPA saturated the islands with agents. In early October Stahl learned of a new radio station in his area on the Bondoc Peninsula. He said, "They weren't anxious to tell me what they were doing although they admitted they knew of the existence of station S3L and had been told to relay through my station in an emergency."[243]

SWPA also wanted information on the Huks. Guerrillas in north and central Luzon reported on Huk locations, strengths, and leaders. Lapham recalled, "We emphasized that they were loyal to neither Japan nor America because they were true Communists who would try to seize power at the end of the war; that they probably had more troops in reserve; and that when they were not actively making trouble for us, they devoted much effort to plundering civilians."[244]

LEYTE, D1,040/R-9

After threading around Japanese spotting stations and radar sites early on 12 October, Parsons' flying boat searched through a moonless rain for one of the three planned insertion points on eastern Leyte until, low on fuel, they had to return to base. He then received a note from Whitney: "Kangleon on west coast. Does not believe he can get across for several days, due to heavy enemy interference. Recommend your trip be delayed as long as possible."[245] Parsons tried again that night.

The first pilot needed rest and opted for the copilot seat on the second attempt. Flying just above the waves, they again ran the gauntlet between Homonhon and Dinagat Islands before setting down on the water near Tacloban. Worried about a nearby Japanese airfield and guns on the highlands above the beach, the flying boat kept its engines running while Parsons and Rawolle launched themselves and their rubber raft out a side window. In less than a minute they were paddling toward shore as the plane flew out of sight.

As their raft tangled on a reef, the two Americans watched a light approaching from shore. Rawolle grabbed his carbine, but the habitually unarmed Parsons called out to those approaching to fetch a boat. The tense moment passed when two native fishermen arrived with a canoe. Half the town of Cavite celebrated the arrival of Parsons and Rawolle, and a retired Navy mess attendant prepared a hearty feast for them. The officers slept soundly until early on 14 October when two guerrillas with a boat took them to one of Kangleon's radio stations, where they sent a message to SWPA: "Party arrived safely—Parsons."[246] They then sent the boat to get Kangleon.

That evening Parsons informed Kangleon that MacArthur knew the Japanese had 24,000 men on Leyte and in a few days U.S. airpower would strike their garrisons. He planned heavy naval and air bombardments of Tacloban, normally home to 30,000 Filipinos. Fearing for their safety, he wanted Kangleon to move the people before 16 October and keep them hidden for one week. Without hesitation, Kangleon said it would be done.[247]

The next day Kangleon informed Parsons that the Japanese had abandoned Tacloban, and he asked that the Americans spare it from bombing.[248] Parsons relayed the request but could not be certain SWPA had even received the message. He learned that the Japanese had imprisoned Kangleon's children in Tacloban and suggested that they had time to liberate them. Kangleon refused to risk men and possibly tip off the Japanese to the impending invasion.

On 15 October the U.S. Navy conducted heavy air raids on Luzon at Naga and Sipocot. "Two days later," wrote Barrameda, "another massive morning air raid, this time in Pili, fueled the anger of the Japanese in the garrison there, and they massacred no less than 50 men, women and children that afternoon in Barrio Agdangan in the town of Baao."[249] Early the next day the Japanese left Panaon, leaving only civilians in the area targeted for heavy bombing. Parsons again radioed to spare the town. His messages had been received and debated. "We had to decide whether the Japs were playing a game in withdrawing from Tacloban before the bombing started," noted Whitney. "They might have returned after the barrage—and that would have been tragic for the American lads on the beach."[250] MacArthur and Osmeña ordered SWPA to redraw its bomb lines to spare Tacloban and Panaon.

That day SWPA ordered all the guerrillas in the Philippines to attack in support of the impending invasion. "The guerrillas rose up against our forces everywhere," a Japanese officer recalled, "and even attacked our garrisons due to the small number of men stationed there."[251] Lapham recalled, "We blasted bridges, cut communication lines, knocked holes in highways, ambushed truck convoys, attacked enemy garrisons."[252] Fertig's guerrillas attacked fortifications in Misamis City with 400 men armed with 200 Enfield rifles, submachine guns, automatic rifles, and three 81-mm mortars with 150 rounds.[253]

For several days, the U.S. Navy swept for mines and surveyed beaches on Leyte. On 17 October teams from the 6th Rangers seized several small islands off Tacloban. SWPA ordered the guerrillas to prepare for the landing of the Sixth U.S. Army. On 20 October at 0600 hours, the U.S. Navy opened fire on beaches near Tacloban. Four hours later Lt. Gen. Walter Krueger's Sixth U.S. Army went ashore. In the X Corps sector at 1330 hours, MacArthur waded back onto Philippine soil. To a waiting microphone, he said, "People of the Philippines, I have returned!"[254]

Parsons established a communication center on Kreuger's flagship, and MacArthur recognized Kangleon as the Leyte area commander.[255] Krueger instructed his commanders that "guerrillas not be given missions beyond their capabilities," limiting them to reconnaissance, outposts, guard duties, and guides.[256] Historian M. Hamlin Cannon added, "These men frequently operated and patrolled in enemy-held territory and brought the Americans valuable information on Japanese movements and dispositions."[257] MacArthur ordered all guerrillas not yet under U.S. Army units to harass Japanese movements and intensify intelligence collection. It was soon clear that they could do much more.

As A. Frank Reel, an attorney later assigned to Yamashita, recalled,

> It is impossible to comprehend the speedy re-conquest of the Philippines by the United States forces without an understanding of the part played behind the lines by the guerrillas.... Bridges were destroyed, wires were cut, military vehicles were wrecked. Japanese night patrols would fail to return to their bases—the soldiers would eventually be found dead, their heads and other important organs removed by bolo knives. Ambush, demolition, assassination, occasionally open combat, became the nocturnal activity of over a hundred thousand men who had secreted themselves in the hills and mountain slopes and who were supplied with food and information by other more loosely organized groups of men, women and even children in the villages below.[258]

Frightening reports reached Yamashita: "Guerrillas had hacked half-drowned sailors to pieces as they struggled to shore on the southern coasts of Luzon.... guerrillas had murdered innocent Japanese civilian women and children."[259] Patrols discovered machine guns and grenades on the perimeter of Yamashita's headquarters in Fort McKinley and a bomb buried under the officers' mess.[260] Reel concluded: "It is little wonder that Japanese soldiers felt that practically the entire population of provincial areas had sprung to arms against them, that the placid Filipino 'civilians,' who smiled at them by day, were treacherously murdering them by night."[261] Krueger even sent Parsons on a gunboat from Seventh Fleet to link up with guerrillas at Malitbog and Massin to attack Japanese garrisons and secure southern Leyte.[262]

Despite the debut of kamikaze attacks, between 23 and 26 October the U.S. Navy defeated several Japanese fleets in the Battle of Leyte Gulf, but mistaken and exaggerated reports led the Imperial General Headquarters to believe they had won and cut off MacArthur on Leyte.[263] Yamashita received orders to shift 34,000 troops to Leyte to finish off the Americans.[264]

Early on 30 October Volckmann's guerrillas moved the seven members of Mrs. Osmeña's family from Baguio. Two miles out, a friendly constabulary falsely reported their car passed through his checkpoint toward Manila. The 66th Infantry then led the Osmeñas up the mountain trails, carrying the first lady and her pregnant daughter-in-law in chairs, while others dumped their car over a cliff. "The entire plan worked out without a mishap," Volckmann recounted.[265]

Guerrillas on Luzon under Major Romulo Manriquez recovered Yamashita's defense plans from a crashed Japanese transport plane near Nueva Vizcaya on 30 November.[266] By that time Blackburn ordered his guerrillas to go on the offensive, and they began driving the Japanese from the west side of the Cagayan River near Tuso.[267]

On New Year's Day SWPA ordered all guerrillas on Luzon: "Beginning at dark on Fourth January proceed to destroy targets assigned by the Headquarters."[268] Since 29 November Lapham's men had fought six engagements—three against the Huks.[269] Now, he activated all seventy of his squadrons and wrote, "Before that first night was over, practically every one of our squadrons managed to get into at least one or two fights with the Japanese."[270]

On 9 January seventy U.S. Navy warships put 175,000 men of Sixth Army ashore on the Lingayen Gulf beaches despite kamikazes sinking or damaging thirteen ships.[271] As they advanced, Ramsey's ECLGA reported Yamashita moving the Shobu group's 152,000 soldiers inland. Other guerrillas spotted Yokoyama's 80,000-man Shimbu group moving from Manila to Bicol and Tsukada's 30,000-man Kembu group taking positions around Clark Air Field, the Bataan Peninsula, and Corregidor.[272] Lapham noted that "a particularly sharp-eyed lookout" reported Yamashita in a convoy heading north through Nueva Ecija at 1300 hours on 3 January.[273]

The guerrillas scouted and provided intelligence, conducted diversionary attacks, harassed lines of communication, and blocked movements. Colonel Robert Connolly's 21st Rangers coordinated with Blackburn to capture Aparri.[274] The guerrillas took the town on their own and Blackburn boasted, "The Americans never did provide much assistance."[275] When the 38th Division reached the San Marcelino airstrip, they found Captain Ramon Magsaysay's guerrillas had secured the field three days earlier.[276] When rains washed out MacArthur's hastily constructed airfields around the Lingayen Gulf, Volckmann provided his inland airfields on Poro Point.

One Army history noted, "[Sixth Army] units had been fortunate enough to find bridges and fordable crossings almost everywhere they went."[277] It was not fortune, it was the guerrillas. They knew the best routes, avoided obstacles, and even built bridges and roads.[278] During the 24th Division's fight on Kilay Ridge in late October, officers discovered their maps were inaccurate and "relied on the service of Filipino guides" for their rest of the campaign.[279]

To be fair, the guerrillas also demonstrated some shortcomings. They routinely inflated enemy estimates. In November they reported five thousand enemy troops in Carigara when the actual numbers were far fewer.[280]

Their reports indicated the Japanese held the Bataan Peninsula with 13,000 men when Yamashita left only 4,000 there, leading MacArthur to unnecessarily commit 35,000 men to the peninsula.

Gradually, many guerrillas assumed conventional warfighting roles. A postwar study noted, "The USAFIP-NL was a critical part of the Sixth Army campaign in northern Luzon in some of the most vicious and toughest fighting in the southwest Pacific theater."[281] The Sixth Army provided Volckmann with the 308th Bomb Wing and forward air controllers.[282] He also received an artillery battalion for operations in the Bessang Pass near Cervantes.[283] His men conducted large-scale conventional attacks on dug-in Japanese positions with the help of a 24th Marine Air Group radio van to direct air and artillery support.[284]

Near Puerto Princesa, Palawan, on 14 December the Japanese forced 150 prisoners into trenches flooded with gasoline and set them on fire, gunning down anyone trying to flee. Still, eleven escaped, including Pfc. Eugene Nielsen, who reported to U.S. Army intelligence on 7 January. Three weeks later Lapham warned Sixth Army that the Japanese were about to massacre another five hundred POWs at Cabanatuan. Krueger's G-2, Colonel Horton White, tasked the 6th Ranger Battalion under Lieutenant Colonel Henry Mucci to liberate the camp. On 30 January, with help from Alamo Scouts and Lapham's guerrillas, they freed 522 POWs, including 492 Americans while guerrilla Captain Juan Pajota and 250 of his men blocked Japanese reinforcements.

SWPA Captain George Miller got the Hunters and Marking's guerrillas to cooperate in the Rizal–Eastern Laguna Command to do the "demolition and sabotage work which paved the way for the liberation of Manila."[285] Ramsey's ECGLA cleared out six hundred Japanese soldiers from the fishpond area outside Manila and guided the U.S. 37th Infantry Division to the capital.[286]

At 1835 hours on 3 February the 1st Cavalry Division reached Manila and was greeted by two guerrillas. The skeptical Americans "subjected the senior of the two, Captain Manuel Colayco, to intensive interrogation."[287] Other guerrillas raced ahead to warn residents "to lock and barricade your front doors and close your front windows. Do not go out, or even look out, whatever it is you might hear. The safest place is the middle of your houses."[288] Colayco guided the soldiers past mines to Santo Tomas, where he was killed by a grenade thrown by a Japanese sniper. The U.S. soldiers rescued more than four thousand captives from the prison.

Yamashita declared Manila an open city, but Rear Admiral Sanji Iwabuchi decided to fight to the death there with 16,000 marines and 5,000 soldiers.[289] Residents reported that the Japanese trucked old men to a church in Calamba and strangled them, massacred two thousand citizens around the capital, and killed one thousand more in Lipa.[290] A witness recalled: "On the slightest provocation and, frequently, for no reason at all, Japanese marines would open fire or throw hand grenades onto groups of helpless civilians and, in this manner, countless Filipinos perished."[291] Iwabuchi's men "plundered, raped, and murdered" civilians in the Itramuros district until they were overrun.[292] "The Japanese attitude," another wrote, "put quite simply was: 'If you are not with us, you are against us.' They thus declared that all Filipinos, including women and children, found inside the battle area were to be considered guerrillas and exterminated."[293]

On 27 February MacArthur announced the liberation of the capital. Fertig observed, "Manila has ceased to exist. Someone said that they are simply pushing the rubble into the bay to make ramps [on] which cargo could be unloaded."[294] Lapham recalled that "human waste was scattered everywhere, both outdoors and in what was left of buildings. Anywhere one looked there was decomposing human bodies covered with flies and emanating a paralyzing stink."[295] The battle had killed almost 100,000 Filipinos and thousands of American soldiers—"even MacArthur could not bring himself to organize a victory parade."[296]

Yokoyama launched counterattacks east of Manila but by 17 May the 43rd Division, "aided by guerrilla forces and air strikes that delivered the heaviest concentration of napalm ever used in the Southwest Pacific," beat them back.[297] For the Japanese, life in the mountains became a horror. "Passing through the jungle, I reached a hill. As far as I could see there were dead bodies, clothed only in dirty, worn loincloths," soldier Takamaro Nishihara recalled. "A fellow soldier whose name I didn't know came crawling over to me. Taking off his clothes he bared his pointed rear end. It had become bluish-green. 'Buddy, if I die, go ahead and eat this part,' he said, touching his scrawny rear end with his bony finger."[298]

Meanwhile, I Corps pushed northeast from Manila. The 33rd and 37th Divisions, "with the aid of air strikes and guerrilla harassment, wore down the defenders until they were on the verge of starvation."[299] They captured Baguio on 27 April. Americans encircled the remaining Simbu group in Bicol near Lake Taal and then cut to the east coast. While the 11th Airborne Division isolated the peninsula, the 1st Cavalry Division, "with substantial support from guerrilla units," turned north to seize Infanta by 25 May.[300]

Meanwhile, the fight turned to the Visayas. The Japanese had withdrawn their 1st Division from Leyte to Cebu but found "most of the inhabitants in the neighborhood of the area where the Division was to be quartered seemed to have moved out guided by the guerrillas."[301] Eighth

Army's Americal Division under Major General William Arnold landed on 26 March against little resistance. "Together with Cushing's guerrillas," a report noted, "they killed any Japanese who turned to fight."[302]

On 29 March Eighth Army invaded Negros. The Japanese 354th Independent Infantry Battalion held its position for fifty-two days on what would become known as Dolan Hill. Kokubo Sakurai recalled, "Maggots hatched in our bandages, writhing on our flesh and exuding a foul stench. Food supplies were cut off.... Hunger gnawed at people's spirit. There were those who ate human flesh."[303] In an eight-week campaign, the Americans lost 370 dead and 1,025 wounded and killed more than 4,000 Japanese in battle, another 3,300 Japanese died from starvation and disease; 6,000 would surrender at the end of the war.[304]

General Robert L. Eichelberger sent a 164th Infantry battalion to Bohol near Tagbilaran. "Assisted by the local guerrilla force, the battalion pushed inland, located the defenders, and by the end of the month had cleared the island of active Japanese resistance at a cost of seven men killed."[305]

On 18 May General Rap Brush's 40th Division landed on Panay west of Iloilo, twenty-seven days after MacArthur had declared the Visayas secured. An Army history noted, "There they were greeted by Col. Macario L. Peralta's Filipino guerrillas drawn up in parade formation, and General Eichelberger recalled in his memoirs how the guerrillas stood 'stiff in starched khaki and resplendent with ornaments.' The strong guerrilla force of 23,000 had secured most of the island, except the area immediately around Iloilo where 2,750 Japanese were ensconced."[306]

On Mindanao, the Japanese combined strong defenses with the challenging geography but faced severe shortages of supplies and transportation. As Stephen Lofgren observed: "Further complicating life for the Japanese was a vibrant guerrilla force led by Col. Wendell W. Fertig."[307]

Eichelberger divided Major General Franklin Sibert's X Corps to land the 24th Division near Malabang on 17 April to secure an advance airfield and the 31st Division farther south near Parang on 22 April to secure Highway 1 to Davao. Before the first landings, however, Fertig reported that his guerrillas—with support from Colonel Clayton Jerome's Marine aviators from guerrilla airfields at Dipolog—had driven off the Japanese and secured Malabang and its airfield.[308] Eichelberger changed plans, and by 3 May the 24th Division entered Davao City and began a fierce two-month fight for the city.

That day the 31st Division reached the northern end of the Japanese line of communication with Davao City. Following Fertig's advice, Eichelberger limited operations on the trail to a reconnaissance-in-force and sent the division north.[309] The reconnaissance covered the line in eighteen days. The 24th Division, with Fertig's guerrillas, renewed its attack on 17 May. Lofgren noted: "Beginning on 29 May, the 19th Infantry and Filipino guerrillas caved in the Japanese eastern flank, seizing the town of Mandong on 15 June and the eastern bank of the Davao River, which flows from north to south into Davao City."[310] The Japanese 100th Division retreated. The 24th Division lost 350 men killed and 1,615 wounded; the Japanese had lost about 4,500 killed.[311]

On 22 June Fertig attended a gala dinner with Admiral Halsey, Adm. Lewis Combs, Adm. Robert Carney, and Adm. Arthur Dewey Struble and General Eichelberger, Gen. Frederick Irving, Gen. Andrew Bruce, and Gen. Clovis Byers. He relished their praise for the guerrillas: "Admiral Halsey remarked that the shipping report on the movement of the Jap fleet in June 1944 helped to catch them off guard."[312] When the Eighth Army relieved the Sixth Army on 30 June, Eichelberger told MacArthur all Japanese organized resistance had ended.

The Japanese lost nearly all of their 230,000 military personnel on Luzon, while the Americans reported 10,380 killed, 36,550 wounded, and more than 93,400 noncombat casualties in the return campaign.[313] General Yamashita surrendered with about 50,000 of his men only after the close of hostilities on 15 August. On Mindanao, the Japanese lost more than 10,000 killed in combat, about 8,000 more noncombat deaths, and some 22,000 who surrendered, while U.S. forces lost 820 killed and 2,880 wounded.[314]

10

Conclusion
Legacies

THE YEARS OF WAR AND RESISTANCE permanently altered the fortunes of the Philippines, Japan, and the United States. Despite MacArthur's reestablished influence, the United States had lost the Philippines, first to the Japanese and then to the Filipinos. The Japanese had learned the hard lesson that neither their military power nor their imperialist rationale was sufficient to pacify conquests and secure their ambitions for empire. Filipinos, on the other hand, emerged from the occupation with a framework for nationhood and a belief that they had paid for independence with their blood.

How much did the Philippine guerrillas contribute to the defeat of Japan? Operations in the islands had reportedly cost the Japanese 498,600 casualties during the course of the war.[1] Their conquest in 1941–42 accounted for 11,225 casualties, and the Allied invasion in 1944–45 inflicted 419,912 more (with 80 percent due to starvation or disease).[2] These numbers leave 67,463 Japanese casualties suffered during the occupation. Assuming a high 80 percent nonbattle casualty rate would still leave roughly 13,500 Japanese casualties from combat against the guerrillas.[3] The Philippine guerrillas may therefore have cost the Japanese somewhere between one understrength division (13,500 men or 23 infantry battalions) to roughly four-and-a-half full divisions (67,500 men or nearly 113 battalions).

A loss of even 67,500 soldiers, however, would not have had a critical impact on the overall Japanese war effort. The Japanese army began the war with fifty-one divisions (twenty-seven in China and twenty-four for the Pacific).[4] A loss of 67,500 men would have constituted a significant 17 percent of this early force, but during the war the Japanese army grew to 5 million men and 145 divisions. They garrisoned the Philippines with no more than twenty-four infantry battalions, about one first line division.[5] Throughout the war, losses and garrisons in the Philippines cost the Japanese about 1 to 4 percent of their final army strength.

The guerrillas may not have defeated the Japanese, but they arguably denied them the fruits of victory. They contributed to a significantly lower transfer of goods and payments from the Philippines to Japan than from any other occupied Southeast Asian territory.[6] Iron ore exports to Japan, for example, fell to just 10 percent of prewar levels.[7] Guerrilla coast watchers helped sink nearly eight hundred Japanese vessels in Philippine waters.[8] Most importantly, their fight inspired a wider resistance by the general population throughout the islands.

The existence of the guerrillas also discouraged meaningful collaboration. Japanese General Akira Muto had served in China, Singapore, Sumatra, and the Netherland East Indies before arriving in the Philippines. He recalled that "in all other colonial areas occupied by the Japanese during the war the conquerors found the native populations to be acquiescent, if not co-operative. Only in the Philippines did they encounter fanatical resistance, despite the Japanese device of setting up an 'independent' government in the islands, which government had formally declared war on the United States."[9] Eighty thousand Southeast Asians from India, Malaya, and other countries served in pro-Japanese military forces, but Laurel used the guerrillas to argue that forcing Filipinos to serve in an army against the United States would lead to civil war.[10]

Perhaps the guerrillas' most important contribution was in enabling MacArthur to convince President Roosevelt to allow him to return to the Philippines and deliver a crushing blow on the Japanese.[11] The Japanese had hoped to wage such a costly battle that the Americans would be persuaded to negotiate an end to the war, but MacArthur enjoyed decisive advantages in airpower, artillery, and logistics.[12] "Another reason for success," noted Lofgren, "was the great assistance that organized Filipino guerrilla forces provided."[13] With the guerrillas' support, MacArthur inflicted nearly 20 percent of all combat deaths suffered by the Japanese during the entire war.[14] Another 115,755 Japanese soldiers surrendered—more than twice the number who surrendered in all their other campaigns.

Despite MacArthur's victory, the Philippines were no longer a U.S. possession. As Charles Smith told Fertig in late May, the new commonwealth government was "definitely interested in running American capital out of the Philippines, that Independence is an accomplished fact; that this is no place for the American after it is all over."[15] Some American guerrilla leaders presented SWPA with plans for incorporating their insurgent organizations into a new Philippine army, but SWPA accepted only a few units—under Filipino commanders.[16]

In fact, the American guerrillas were too enfeebled to continue in command. Blackburn, for example, had battled malaria for "nearly the whole damn war."[17] Volckmann departed for an assignment in Washington but "spent more time at Walter Reed Army Hospital than he did at the Personnel Division offices."[18] Worn down by malaria, dysentery, anemia, malnutrition, and "general nervous collapse," Ramsey weighed ninety-three pounds, and doctors ordered him to desk duty at Sixth Army headquarters.[19] One morning in May 1945, he collapsed and had to be hospitalized. A day after returning to his desk, he noticed his vision blurring as his hand began shaking. He recalled, "The spirit dissolved within me. It was coming, and there was nothing I could do about it except to withdraw into that pinpoint back in my brain from which I watched in safety while my nervous system fell to pieces again."[20] One by one, the American guerrilla leaders went home.

Even the U.S. officers who most completely embraced the Filipinos' cause would find no place in the new Philippine army or government. The Filipinos were determined to form their own administration. The years of resistance had transformed their weak confederation into a people who shared a national vision and a desire to govern themselves. Moreover, they believed they had paid a heavy cost for the right to try.

Filipinos had lost as many as 900,000 civilians and 57,000 soldiers.[21] U.S. Army records counted 131,028 Americans and Filipinos "murdered, starved and tortured to death in the Philippines."[22] Manila suffered damage only comparable to that seen in Warsaw, and only Berlin and Stalingrad exceeded Manila's 100,000 citizens killed in battle.[23] More than 200,000 residents were left homeless. Real per capita income had been cut by half.[24] As Collingham observed, "It was not uncommon to see the corpses of those who had starved lying in the streets."[25] The survivors, especially in Manila, were left greatly dependent on their new government and U.S. aid.

Many Filipinos appeared to have dodged such sacrifices, but collaboration came in shades of gray. MacArthur had defined disloyalty as acts that impeded "the services of USAFFE officers or men who have continued to resist."[26] In practice, judgment of treason was not so simple. In early October 1944 "hula hula dancer" Judy Geronimo tried to pass a letter from local guerrillas to Eugenio Lopez, who only knew her as "very close friends of the Japanese military police."[27] He declined the letter, saying it "would first have to be cleared by the Kempeitai."[28] Two weeks later, the Kempeitai arrested, tortured, and interrogated Geronimo. She later testified, "I was taken to Bining, Mountain Province on 16 October, by three Japanese soldiers, where I was shot and buried. The Japanese then left, and some Igorots took me to the hills and took care of me."[29]

In April 1945 Geronimo lodged charges of treason with the U.S. Counter Intelligence Corps against Eugenio Lopez. They learned that throughout the war, he published the pro-Japanese daily paper *Panay Sho-Ho* in Iloilo while his brother Fernando maintained a string of casinos in Iloilo City under Japanese protection. Yet the brothers had also maintained contact with guerrillas through Captain Patricio Miguel and Captain Alfredo Gestoso "who helped Fernando escape from the city at the war's end and later protected him from collaboration charges."[30] Like many others, the Lopez brothers worked both sides of occupation and maintained their place after the war.[31] Numerous resistance veterans believed the Americans and returning Filipino elites considered those who had remained and worked with the Japanese to be "the real heroes of the occupation."[32]

The development of the guerrilla resistance also undermined those most dedicated to the overthrow of Filipino elites—the Hukbalahaps. Personally instructed by Mao's veterans, the Huks followed the three phases outlined in Maoist revolutionary doctrine: organization, guerrilla warfare, and decisive conventional operations.[33] MacArthur's promise to return, however, undercut any development of third phase conventional forces capable of overthrowing either a Japanese or a Philippine government. As Colleen Woods noted, the subsequent reestablishment of prewar elites created "a deeply unequal colonial society and a government that would disproportionately serve the interests of the wealthiest or most politically connected class of Filipinos."[34] The Huks were left on the outside of power, doomed to carry on a futile revolt after the war.

It is important to note that this dynamic of the Philippine resistance challenges the canon of postwar analyses of guerrilla warfare derived from Maoist revolutionary warfare. Other than the Huks, the Philippine guerrillas did not embrace social revolution. As Joe Barker had noted, "Our job isn't to start a revolution, it's to prepare for MacArthur's invasion. We're military men, not politicians."[35] They engaged in the kind of nonrevolutionary guerrilla warfare described by Carl von Clausewitz as "a general insurrection within the framework of a war conducted by the regular army, and coordinated in one all-encompassing plan."[36] In the Philippines, that regular army was the U.S. Army, and the all-encompassing plan came from MacArthur.

The guerrilla war decided many other long-running Philippine political contests. Ambitious figures eliminated rivals for power. Ramon Durano, for example, used Fenton to execute his political adversaries on Cebu and emerged as a dominant postwar figure. Fermin Caram on Panay tried to use the Japanese to take down his rivals. Guerrilla groups outmaneuvered and outfought rivals to establish local political authority that replaced the traditional power of kinship networks. Through contact, recognition, and supplies, MacArthur skillfully shaped this competition to empower reliable old-order Filipinos such as Ruperto K. Kangleon on Leyte over more radical competitors such as Blas E. Miranda.[37] Through Thorp, Volckmann, Ramsey, and others on Luzon, he isolated the Huks. By supporting Fertig, he prevented Moros from seizing power on Mindanao. A mosaic of empowered guerrilla groups arose to form a national framework.

MacArthur prevented any single guerrilla leader from assuming supremacy across the Philippines and thereby handed this emergent national power structure to the returning prewar elites and their allies who had remained behind. He emplaced Nacionalista stalwart Sergio Osmeña Jr. as president of the new Philippines. In 1946 MacArthur's agent Manuel A. Roxas became president at the head of the Liberal Party. In 1953 former guerrilla Ramon Magsaysay won back the presidency for the Nacionalistas. That party retained the presidency when Carlos P. Garcia, a Boforce guerrilla, followed him in office. Liberal Diosdado Macapagal, a former collaborationist aide to Laurel, won the presidency in 1961, but four years later Ferdinand Marcos assumed the office and would retain power largely on his mythic reputation as a guerrilla leader. He finally fell from power in 1986 by a revolt led by Corazon Aquino, collaborator Benigno Ramos' daughter-in law.

All these native leaders routinely courted the bloc of guerrilla veterans and their kin, yet U.S. government recognition long eluded many guerrillas.[38] Approximately 1.3 million Filipinos claimed to have served in more than 1,000 guerrilla units, but the U.S. Army recognized only 260,715 guerrilla from 277 units.[39] (An estimated 33,000 guerrillas died during the war.[40]) The claim of guerrilla veteran status by 7.8 percent of the total population may have seemed extreme, but the Army's recognition of only 1.6 percent of the population as guerrilla veterans appears low when one considers that about 11 percent of Americans served in the U.S. military during the war, and their country had not been occupied.[41] While some no doubt submitted false claims in hopes of obtaining veterans' benefits, the vast majority had likely supported the guerrillas in some manner, and many of them were no doubt ignored for reasons of routine bureaucratic inefficiency. Their sacrifice demands recognition. This book is an effort to tell their story.

Notes

CHAPTER 1. INTRODUCTION

1. Matt K. Matsuda, *Pacific Worlds: A History of Seas, Peoples, and Cultures* (Cambridge: Cambridge University Press, 2012), 61.
2. Alfred W. McCoy, "'An Anarchy of Families': The Historiography of State and Family in the Philippines," in *An Anarchy of Families: State and Family in the Philippines*, ed. Alfred W. McCoy (Madison: University of Wisconsin Center for Southeast Asian Studies, 1993), 1, 10.
3. Brian Fegan, "Entrepreneurs in Votes and Violence," in McCoy, 51. See also Richard J. Kessler, *Rebellion and Repression in the Philippines* (New Haven, Conn.: Yale University Press, 1989), 15.
4. Kessler, 7.
5. Kenichi Goto, *Tensions of Empire: Japan and Southeast Asia in the Colonial and Postcolonial World* (Athens: Ohio University, 2003), 7.
6. Walter LeFeber, *The Clash: U.S.-Japanese Relations Throughout History* (New York: W. W. Norton and Company, 1990), 61.
7. Al Raposas, "Japanese Involvement in the Philippines," *Filipino Historian International*, 16 December 2012.
8. Grant K. Goodman, "'A Flood of Immigration': Japanese Immigration to the Philippines, 1900–1941" (Lawrence: University of Kansas Center for Digital Scholarship, 2011), 3.
9. Sandra Wilson, "The 'New Paradise': Japanese Emigration to Manchuria in the 1930s and 1940s," *The International History Review* 17, no. 2 (May 1995): 249.
10. George A. Malcolm, *The Commonwealth of the Philippines* (New York: D. Appleton–Century Company, 1936), 357.
11. Max Boot, *The Savage Wars of Peace: Small Wars and the Rise of American Power* (New York: Basic Books, 2002), 115.

12. John E. Koehler, "Review: *The Huks: Philippine Agrarian Society in Revolt*, by Eduardo Lachia," *Economic Development and Cultural Change* 23, no. 1 (October 1974): 188.
13. Alvin H. Scaff, *The Philippine Answer to Communism* (Stanford, Calif.: Stanford University Press, 1955), 7–10. See also Benedict J. Kerkvliet, *The Huk Rebellion: A Study of Peasant Revolt in the Philippines* (Berkeley: University of California Press, 1977), 31.
14. Kessler, 30; Kerkvliet, 98.
15. Luis Taruc, *He Who Rides the Tiger: The Story of an Asian Guerrilla Leader* (New York: Frederick A. Praeger, 1967), 13. See also Kerkvliet, 37.
16. Nicholas Tarling, *A Sudden Rampage: The Japanese Occupation of Southeast Asia, 1941–1945* (Honolulu: The University of Hawaii Press, 2001), 162.
17. Manuel Quezon, *The Good Fight* (New York: D. Appleton-Century Company, 1946), 151–52.
18. Lydia N. Yu-Jose, *Japan Views the Philippines, 1900–1944* (Manila: Ateneo de Manila University Press, 1992), 68–69.
19. Military History Section, Headquarters, Army Forces Far East, "Political Strategy Prior to Outbreak of War, Part II," 24 October 1950, National Archives II, Japanese Monographs, monograph 146, record group (RG) 550, box 21, 15–16 (henceforth, "Japanese Monographs").
20. Goto, 21.
21. Satoshi Ara, "Food Supply Problem in Leyte, Philippines, During the Japanese Occupation (1942–44)," *Journal of Southeast Asian Studies* 39, no. 1 (February 2008): 31–32.
22. Ara, 33.
23. "Outline of the Empire's National Policy to Cope with the Changing World Situation." See Military History Section, Headquarters, Army Forces Far East, "Political Strategy Prior to Outbreak of War, Part III," Japanese Monographs 147, 28.
24. Tarling, 74.
25. S. C. M. Paine, *The Wars for Asia, 1911–1949* (Cambridge: Cambridge University Press, 2012), 182.
26. Meirion Harries and Susie Harries, *Soldier of the Sun: The Rise and Fall of the Imperial Japanese Army* (New York: Random House, 1991), 291.
27. Military History Section, Headquarters, Army Forces Far East, "(Japanese) Political Strategy Prior to Outbreak of War, Part IV," Japanese Monographs 150, 73–74.
28. Japanese Monographs 147, 46.

29. Japanese Monographs 150, 10–12.
30. Paine, 182.
31. Terada Takefumi, "The Religious Propaganda Program for Christian Churches," in *The Philippines Under Japan: Occupation Policy and Reaction*, ed. Ikehata Setsuho and Ricardo Trota Jose (Manila: Ateneo De Manila University Press, 1999), 217–18.
32. Goto, 90.
33. Louis Morton, *The Fall of the Philippines: The War in the Pacific* (United States Army in World War II) (Washington, D.C.: U.S. Army Center of Military History, 1989), 21.
34. Japanese Monographs 147, 46.
35. Japanese Monographs 147, 9.
36. Tarling, 76.
37. Japanese Monographs 150, 12.
38. See Steven E. Clay, "U.S. Army Order of Battle 1919–1941," updated by Leo Niehorster and Mark Boland, in "World War II Armed Forces—Orders of Battle," http://niehorster.orbat.com/013_usa/_41_usarmy/philippines/_usaffe.htm.
39. "Interview with Brigadier General Donald D. Blackburn, USA Retired," 29 December 1982, U.S. Army Heritage and Education Center, Donald D. Blackburn Papers, 1916–1983, box 1, 24 (hereafter "Blackburn interview").
40. Blackburn interview, 30.
41. Russell W. Volckmann, *We Remained: Three Years Behind the Enemy Lines in the Philippines* (New York: W. W. Norton and Company, 1954), 5.
42. Douglas MacArthur, *Reminiscences* (New York: McGraw-Hill, 1964), 105.
43. Marvin A. Kreidberg and Merton G. Henry, *History of Military Mobilization in the United States Army, 1775–1945* (Washington, D.C.: Department of the Army, 1955), 434.
44. The AMT even issued a circular suggesting the formation of twelve-man squads as the basis for combat. Scaff, 22. See also Teodoro A. Agoncillo, *The Fateful Years: Japan's Adventure in the Philippines, 1941–1945*, vol. I (Quezon City: R. P. Publishing Co., 1965), 663.
45. Japanese Monographs 150, 19.
46. Japanese Monographs 147, 51.
47. Japanese Monographs 150, 21.
48. Japanese Monographs 150, 89.
49. Japanese Monographs 150, 24.
50. Japanese Monographs 150, 30.

51. Japanese Monographs 150, 56.
52. Japanese Monographs 150, 58.
53. Harries and Harries, 339–40.
54. Harries and Harries, 50.
55. Harries and Harries, 50–51.
56. Harries and Harries, 52.
57. Japanese Monographs 150, 46.
58. Japanese Monographs 150, 49.
59. Military History Section, Headquarters, Army Forces Far East, "Philippines Operations Record, Phase I Monograph No. 1," 24 October 1950, National Archives II, Japanese Monographs, RG 550, box 21, 10.
60. Japanese Monographs 1, 26.
61. Japanese Monographs 1, 30–31.
62. Ikehata Setsuho, "Mining Industry Development and Local Anti-Japanese Resistance," in Setsuho and Jose, 129–30.
63. Setsuho, 130–31.
64. Japanese Monographs 1, 30–31.
65. Japanese Monographs 1, 26.
66. Japanese Monographs 150, 97.
67. Japanese Monographs 150, 99.
68. Japanese Monographs 150, 100.
69. Japanese Monographs 150, 101.
70. John W. Dower, *War Without Mercy: Race and Power in the Pacific War* (New York: Pantheon Books, 1986), 205–6.

CHAPTER 2. A TIME TO DIE

1. Isabel Yumol Jennings, *Changing Tides: World War II Occupation and Independence in the Philippines* (Buffalo Gap, Tex.: State House Press, 2016), 3.
2. Edwin Price Ramsey and Stephen J. Rivele, *Lieutenant Ramsey's War: From Horse Soldier to Guerrilla Commander* (Washington, D.C: Brassey's Books, 1990), 38.
3. Morton, 69.
4. Morton, 88.
5. Adalia Marquez, *Blood on the Sun: The Japanese Occupation of the Philippines* (Manila: Create Space Independent, 2014), 3.
6. Carlos P. Romulo, *I Saw the Fall of the Philippines* (New York: Doubleday, Doran, and Company, 1943), 22.
7. A. V. H. Hartendorp, *The Japanese Occupation of the Philippines*, vol. I (Manila: Bookmark, 1967), 62.

8. Morton, 98. See also MacArthur, 123.
9. Romulo, 55.
10. Blackburn interview, 36.
11. Ramsey and Rivele, 46.
12. Marquez, 4.
13. Parsons had two uncles who had remained after the Spanish-American War. See Travis Ingham, *Rendezvous by Submarine: The Story of Charles Parsons and the Guerrilla-Soldiers in the Philippines* (Garden City, N.Y.: Doubleday, Doran, and Company, 1945), 20–23.
14. Ingham, 35.
15. Quezon, 194.
16. Quezon, 196–98.
17. Parker had Brig. Gen. Vincente Lim's 41st Division and Brig. Gen. Albert Jones' 51st Division. Morton, 109.
18. Blackburn interview, 45, 47–48.
19. Morton, 109.
20. Jose V. Barrameda Jr., *In the Crucible of an Asymmetrical War in Camarines Sur 1942–1945 (The Story of the Tangcong Vaca Guerrilla Unit)* (Manila: National Historical Institute, 2007), 6.
21. Quezon described Roxas as "one of our most able." Quezon, 201.
22. Quezon, 202.
23. Quezon, 214.
24. Barrameda, 7.
25. Barrameda, 8.
26. Barrameda, 13.
27. Boayes was nicknamed "Turko" for his Syrian descent.
28. Teodoro A. Agoncillo, *The Fateful Years: Japan's Adventure in the Philippines, 1941–1945,* vol. II (Quezon City: R. P. Garcia Publishing Company, 1965), 701.
29. Robert Lapham and Bernard Norling, *Lapham's Raiders: Guerrillas in the Philippines 1942–1945* (Lexington: University Press of Kentucky, 1996), 95.
30. Lapham and Norling, 702.
31. Bob Stahl, *You're No Good to Me Dead: Behind the Japanese Lines in the Philippines* (Annapolis, Md.: Naval Institute Press, 1997), 109.
32. Stahl.
33. Barrameda, 10.
34. Barrameda, 11.
35. Barrameda, 24.
36. Donald H. Willis and Reyburn Myers, *The Sea Was My Last Chance: Memoir of an American Captured on Bataan in 1942 Who Escaped in*

1944 and Led the Liberation of Western Mindanao (Jefferson, N.C.: McFarland and Company, 1992), 125.
37. Stahl, 6.
38. Ramsey and Rivele, 37.
39. Ramsey and Rivele, 42.
40. Ramsey and Rivele, 45. See also Morton, 69.
41. Morton, 507–8.
42. Paul P. Rodgers, *The Good Years: MacArthur and Sutherland* (New York: Praeger Publishers, 1990), 106.
43. Morton, 508.
44. Morton.
45. Volckmann, 6.
46. Blackburn interview, 49.
47. Volckmann, 19. See also Mike Guardia, *Shadow Commander: The Epic Story of Donald D. Blackburn, Guerrilla Leader and Special Forces Hero* (Philadelphia: Casemate, 2011), 13.
48. Bernard Norling, *The Intrepid Guerrillas of Northern Luzon* (Lexington: University Press of Kentucky, 1999), 83.
49. Morton, 135–36.
50. Agoncillo, vol. II, 656.
51. War Department Technical Manual 11-227, *Radio Communication Equipment* (Washington, D.C.: Government Printing Office, 10 April 1944), 25.
52. Volckmann, 15–16.
53. Barrameda, 134.
54. General Headquarters, Southwest Pacific Area, Military Intelligence Section, General Staff, "Guerrilla Resistance Movements in the Philippine," 31 March 1945, National Archives II, Philippines Archive Collection, RG 407, box 255, 23 (hereafter "Guerrilla Resistance Movements").
55. William D. Chalek, *Guest of the Emperor: 1941 to 1945 in the Philippines Surviving the War, and as a POW, Bataan Death March, Cabanatuan, Davao Penal Colony, The "Hell Ships"* (Lincoln, Neb.: Writers Club Press, 2002), 40–60.
56. "Guerrilla Resistance Movements," 23.
57. Norling, 16.
58. Volckmann, 34–35.
59. Ramsey and Rivele, 63.
60. Ramsey and Rivele, 70.
61. William Manchester, *American Caesar: Douglas MacArthur, 1880–1964* (Boston: Little, Brown and Co., 1978), 241.

62. Quezon, 212.
63. Romulo, 60–61.
64. Tarling, 163.
65. Hartendorp, vol. I, 192.
66. Jennings, 5.
67. Pacita Pestano-Jacinto, *Living with the Enemy* (Pasig City, Philippines: Anvil Publishing, 1999), 11.
68. George Hicks, *The Comfort Women: Japan's Brutal Regime of Enforced Prostitution in the Second World War* (New York: W. W. Norton and Company, 1995), 126–27.
69. Hernando J. Abaya, *Betrayal in the Philippines* (New York: A. A. Wyn, 1946), 22.
70. Quezon, 226.
71. Abaya, 22.
72. Jesus Villamor with Gerald S. Snyder, *They Never Surrendered: A True Story of Resistance in World War II* (Quezon City, Philippines: Vera-Reyes, 1982), 46.
73. Romulo, 99.
74. Villamor, 46.
75. Manchester, 245.
76. Marquez, 7.
77. Marquez, 7–8. See also Agoncillo, vol. II, 685.
78. Marquez, 7.
79. Japanese Monographs 1, 309.
80. Yung Li Yuk-Wai, *The Huaqiao Warrior: Chinese Resistance Movement in the Philippines 1942–45* (Hong Kong: Hong Kong University Press, 1995), 115.
81. Yuk-Wai, 135–37. The report is cited from Uladarico S. Baclagon, *The Philippine Resistance Movement Against Japan, 10.12.1941–14.6.1945* (Quezon City: Munoz Press, 1965), 301. The supply of rifles is not mentioned in the "Affidavit of Shih I-sheng" in National Archives II, Philippine Archive Collection, 407/323/106-1. Unsubstantiated sources reported that on 18 December USAFFE supplied the US-CVP with six hundred Springfield rifles.
82. Also known as the Kang Chu. Yuk-Wai, 94.
83. Japanese Monographs 1, 308–9.
84. Jennings, 8.
85. Yay Panlilio, *The Crucible: An Autobiography by Colonel Yay, Filipina American Guerrilla*, ed. Denise Cruz (New Brunswick, N.J.: Rutgers University Press, 2010), 89. For details on the destruction of the bridges, see Morton, 209.

86. Panlilio, 96.
87. Agoncillo, vol. II, 692.
88. He also mimeographed a newsletter to counter propaganda and expose collaborators. Marquez, 192.
89. Romulo, 46.
90. Pestano-Jacinto, 14.
91. Wallace Edwards, *Comfort Women: A History of Japanese Forced Prostitution During the Second World War* (North Charleston, S.C.: Absolute Crime Books, 2013), 78.
92. Hicks, 126.
93. Maria Rosa Henson, *Comfort Woman: A Filipina's Story of Prostitution and Slavery under the Japanese Military* (New York: Rowman and Littlefield Publishers, 1999), 23–26.
94. Lancelot Lawton, *Empires of the Far East: A Study of Japan and of Her Colonial Possessions of China and Manchuria and the Political Questions of Eastern Asia and the Pacific*, vol. I (London: Grant Richards, Ltd., 1912), 722, 724.
95. T. Fujitani, *Race for Empire: Koreans as Japanese and Japanese as Americans During World War II* (Berkeley: University of California Press, 2011), 371. See also Edwards, 7, 25, and Frank Gibney (ed.) and Beth Cary (trans.), *Senso: The Japanese Remember the Pacific War: Letters to the Editor of Asahi Shimbun* (London: M. E. Sharpe, 2007), 81.
96. Yuki Tanaka, *Hidden Horrors: Japanese War Crimes in World War II* (Boulder, Colo.: Westview Press, 1996), 99.
97. Edwards, 77.
98. Henson, xvi.
99. Henson.
100. Villamor, 120.
101. Lapham and Norling, 106.
102. Quezon, 292.
103. Barrameda, 72.
104. Quezon, 250.
105. Japanese Monographs 1, 88.
106. Quezon, 236.
107. Quezon, 239.
108. Quezon, 239–40.
109. Pat Minch, "1LT Grafton Jacob 'Spence or Budd' Spencer," findagrave.com, http://www.findagrave.com/cgi-bin/fg.cgi?page=gr&GRid=56753681.
110. Abaya, 31.

111. Yu-Jose, 157.
112. Japanese Monographs 1, 104.
113. Agoncillo, vol. I, 424.
114. Japanese Monographs 1, 120.
115. Quezon, 241.
116. Ingham, 34.
117. William Wise, *Secret Mission to the Philippines: The Story of "Spyron" and the American-Filipino Guerrillas of World War II* (Lincoln, Neb.: iUniverse.com, 2001), 43.
118. Barrameda, 12.
119. Barrameda, 13.
120. Hartendorp, vol. I, 8, 11.
121. Hartendorp, vol. I, 11.
122. Horan's accounts are from "Dairy [sic] of Col Horan," National Archives, Philippine Archives Collection, RG 407, box 258. The radio was probably the Bureau of Post radio at Suyoc. See also "Geography of Luzon, June 1942," MacArthur Archives, Papers of Courtney Whitney, RG 16, box 68.
123. Norling, 50.
124. Volckmann, 30.
125. Agoncillo, vol. II, 656.
126. Romulo, 106.
127. Romulo, 111.
128. Romulo, 652.
129. Miguel Ver, diary, 15 May 1942, Philippine Diary Project, https://philippinediaryproject.wordpress.com/tag/miguel-ver/.
130. Agoncillo, vol. II, 687.
131. Romulo, 38.
132. Barrameda, 13, 14.
133. Barrameda, 14.
134. Quezon, 290.
135. Quezon, 291.
136. Jonathan Black, "Jose P. Laurel and Jorge B. Vargas: Issues of Collaboration and Loyalty during the Japanese Occupation of the Philippines," thesis, Claremont McKenna College, 2010, 4.
137. Tarling, 164.
138. Quezon, 292.
139. Tarling, 167.
140. Abaya, 26.
141. Hartendorp, vol. I, 196.
142. Quezon, 293-94.

143. See John M. Gates, "The Pacification of the Philippines," in *U.S. Army and Irregular Warfare*, http://www3.wooster.edu/history/jgates/pdfs/fullbook.pdf.
144. Lapham and Norling, 13.
145. See Herminia S. Dizon, "Complete Data Covering the Guerrilla Activities of the Late Colonel Clade A. Thorp," National Archives II, Philippine Archive Collection, RG 407, box 258. See also Lapham and Norling, 13.
146. Morton, 500.
147. Lapham and Norling, 11.
148. Military Intelligence Section, General Staff, General Headquarters, United States Armed Forces Pacific, *Intelligence Activities in the Philippines During the Japanese Occupation*, vol. II, Intelligence Series, 10 June 1948, 1, in Russell W. Volckmann Papers, box 1, Center for Military History (hereafter "Intelligence Activities").
149. Allison W. Ind, *Secret War Against Japan: The Allied Intelligence Bureau in World War II* (Philadelphia: McKay Co., 1958), 104.
150. "Intelligence Activities," 2.
151. Lapham and Norling, 14.
152. Lapham and Norling, 18–19.
153. "Intelligence Activities," 2.
154. Panlilio, 104.
155. Tarling, 132.
156. Barrameda, 14–15.
157. Joyce C. Wilson, *Japan's Greater East Asian Co-Prosperity Sphere in World War II, Selected Readings and Documents* (London: Oxford University Press, 1975), 80.
158. Wilson, 79.
159. Japanese Monographs 1, 26.
160. Morton, 501.
161. Goto, 54.
162. Goto.
163. Agoncillo, vol. I, 426.
164. Villamor, 55.
165. Satoshi Nakano, "Captain Hitomi's 'Goodwill' Mission in Luzon and Panay, 1942–43: A Logic of Conciliation in the Japanese Propaganda in the Philippines," draft paper prepared for 13th IAHA Conference, Sophia University, Tokyo, 5–9 September 1994, 5.
166. Ramsey and Rivele, 147.
167. Marquez, 19.
168. Willard H. Elshrec, *Japan's Role in South-East Asia Nationalist Movements* (Cambridge, Mass.: Harvard University Press, 1953), 160.

169. Ed Cray, *General of the Army: George C. Marshall, Soldier and Statesman* (New York: Cooper Square Press, 1990), 284.
170. Nakano, 47.
171. Nakano, 4.
172. Nakano, 7.
173. Agoncillo, vol. II, 649.
174. Volckmann, 37.
175. Quezon, 256.
176. Morton, 353–54.
177. George W. Baer, *One Hundred Years of Sea Power: The U.S. Navy, 1890–1990* (Stanford, Calif.: Stanford University Press, 1993), 211.
178. Taruc, 21.
179. Agoncillo, vol. II, 666.
180. Leon Trotsky, "On the United Front (Material for a Report on the Question of French Communism)," in *The First Five Years of the Communist International*, vol. II (London: New Park, 1974), chapter 8.
181. Taruc, 21.
182. Rodgers, 212–14.
183. Villamor, 55.
184. Quezon, 266.
185. Tarling, 166.
186. Quezon, 267.
187. Quezon, 269.
188. Six months later, Marking removed Vargas from his list of targets for assassination. Panlilio, 176.
189. Volckmann, 138–39.
190. Yuk-Wai, 80.
191. Yuk-Wai, 99, 100.
192. Agoncillo, vol. II, 667.
193. Edgar Snow, *Red Star Over China* (New York: Grove Press, 1978), 283.
194. Snow, 282–87.
195. Snow.
196. Snow, 288.
197. Quezon, 56.
198. Romulo, 178.
199. John Costello, *The Pacific War 1941–1945* (New York: Quill, 1982), 212.
200. Merle Miller, *Ike the Soldier: As They Knew Him* (New York: G. P. Putnam's Sons, 1987), 341.
201. Quezon, 281.
202. Ricardo T. Jose, "Governments in Exile," *Asian and Pacific Migration Journal* 8, nos. 1–2 (1999), 181.

203. Forrest C. Pogue, *George C. Marshall, Interviews and Reminiscences for Forrest C. Pogue*, ed. Larry I. Bland (Lexington, Va.: George C. Marshall Research Foundation, 1991), 609.
204. Ramsey and Rivele, 70.
205. John Boyd Coates, ed., *Preventive Medicine in World War II*, vol. IV, *Communicable Diseases: Malaria* (Washington, D.C.: Department of the Army, 1963), 505.
206. See Leon I. Warshaw, *Malaria: The Biography of a Killer* (New York: Rhinehart and Co., 1949), 245, and Coates, 505.
207. Coates, 506–7.
208. See John A. Glusman, *Conduct Under Fire: Four American Doctors and the Fight for Life as Prisoners of the Japanese, 1941–1945* (London: Penguin Books, 2005).
209. Coates, 503–4.
210. Ramsey and Rivele, 71.
211. Willis and Myers, 27.
212. Richard P. Strong, *Stitt's Diagnosis, Prevention, and Treatment of Tropical Diseases*, vol. II (Philadelphia: The Blakiston Company, 1944), vol. I, 444–54; vol. II, 1051.
213. Harries and Harries, 374.
214. Lapham and Norling, 43.
215. Abaya, 43.
216. Lapham and Norling, 98.
217. Abaya, 25.
218. Abaya.
219. Romulo, 191.
220. Stahl, 92.
221. Vina A. Lanzona, *Amazons of the Huk Rebellion: Gender, Sex and Revolution in the Philippines* (Madison: University of Wisconsin Press, 2009), 121.
222. Agoncillo, vol. II, 668.
223. Leonard Davis, *Revolutionary Struggle in the Philippines* (New York: St. Martin's Press, 1989), 63n.
224. Lanzona, 121–22.
225. Morton, 502.
226. Morton, 501.
227. Rodgers, 213.
228. Manchester, 256.
229. Manchester, 502.
230. Manchester, 254–63.
231. Ronald H. Spector, *Eagle Against the Sun: The American War with Japan* (New York: Vintage Books, 1985), 117.

232. Spector, 118.
233. Cray, 297.
234. Costello, 211.
235. Winston Churchill, *The Second World War: Their Finest Hour* (Boston: Houghton Mifflin Company, 1949), 108.
236. Manchester, 251.
237. Cray, 297.
238. Villamor, 58.
239. Quezon, 298–99.
240. Morton, 388.
241. Ramsey and Rivele, 76.
242. Romulo, 230.
243. MacArthur, 145.
244. MacArthur.
245. MacArthur.
246. Ramsey and Rivele, 77.
247. Pestano-Jacinto, 41.

CHAPTER 3. THE DEATH MARCH

1. Goto, 40.
2. Tojo on 14 March. Tarling, 133.
3. Goto, 66.
4. Goto, 55.
5. Raymond Lamont-Brown, *Kempeitai: Japan's Dreaded Military Police* (Gloucester, UK: Sutton Publishing, 1998), 122.
6. Lamont-Brown, 75, 126.
7. Pestano-Jacinto, 28.
8. Panlilio, 12.
9. Juan Escandor Jr., "Village Won't Forget Guerrillas," *Inquirer Southern Luzon*, 14 March 2012.
10. Barrameda, 15.
11. Barrameda, 11, 20–21.
12. Barrameda, 11.
13. Barrameda, 20–21.
14. Norling, 148.
15. Norling, 15.
16. Agoncillo, 650.
17. Volckmann, 37.
18. Hicks, 126.
19. Worse for Gertrude, after the war her husband disowned her and took her two children away. Garrick Utley, "Philippine Women Seek

Apology and Retribution from the Japanese Years after World War II," *NBC Nightly News*, 3 April 1993.
20. Hicks, 124.
21. Theresa Kaminski, *Angels of the Underground: The American Women Who Resisted the Japanese in the Philippines in World War II* (New York: Oxford University Press, 2016), 44.
22. Hartendorp, vol. I, 194.
23. Hicks, 124. See also Barrameda, 72.
24. Hicks.
25. Hartendorp, vol. I, 194.
26. Hicks, 127.
27. Pestano-Jacinto, 166.
28. Felmar Castrodes Fiel, "The Martyrdom of Bishop Finnemann," 30 March 2009, http://williamfinnemannsvd.blogspot.com.
29. Diary, "Message Traffic Intelligence Summaries Later Conference," 6 January 1943, Wendell W. Fertig Papers, box 1, Center for Military History (hereafter Fertig diary).
30. The Pen Corps first appeared in China. Yu-Jose, 166.
31. Yu-Jose, 166–67.
32. Yu-Jose, 167.
33. Lapham and Norling, 19.
34. Lapham and Norling, 18–19. Lapham recalls the radio arriving on 20 March, but Dizon sets the date in May.
35. Lapham and Norling, 19.
36. Ricardo T. Jose, "The Rice Shortage and Countermeasures During the Occupation," in Setsuho and Jose, 202.
37. Lizzie Collingham, *The Taste of War: World War II and the Battle for Food* (New York: Penguin Press, 2012), 235–36.
38. Malcolm, 254.
39. Jose, "The Rice Shortage and Countermeasures During the Occupation," 201.
40. Hartendorp, vol. I, 193.
41. Yu-Jose, 158.
42. Setsuho and Jose, 134–37.
43. Setsuho and Jose, 159.
44. Setsuho and Jose, 162.
45. Takefumi, 239.
46. Quezon, 296.
47. Takefumi, 241.
48. Romulo, 81.
49. Jennings, 26.

50. Kerkvliet, 12.
51. See Lanzona, 122. Vincente Lava took over for Taruc as head of the communist party.
52. "Guerrilla Resistance Movements," 12. See also Blackburn interview, 88–89.
53. Agoncillo, vol. II, 672.
54. Taruc, 23.
55. Lapham and Norling, 139.
56. Davis, 37.
57. Lapham and Norling, 132.
58. Collingham, 243.
59. Taruc, 22.
60. Two squadrons formed a battalion and two battalions a regiment. Taruc, 22.
61. Agoncillo, vol. II, 675.
62. Lapham and Norling, 132.
63. Lapham and Norling.
64. Taruc, 23.
65. Willis and Myers, 164.
66. Lapham and Norling, 132.
67. Yuk-Wai, 90.
68. Others thought this Huk was Alejandrino. Lapham and Norling, 21.
69. Blackburn interview, 89.
70. Blackburn interview, 18.
71. Romulo, 231.
72. Morton, 501.
73. Morton, 502.
74. Ramsey and Rivele, 80.
75. Ramsey and Rivele, 78.
76. Frank Hewlett, "Battling Bastards of Bataan," International War Veterans' Poetry Archives, http://www.iwvpa.net/hewlettf/index.php.
77. Rodgers, 214.
78. Stenographer Rodgers later asked: "Who can say that the troops would have suffered more than they did in prison camps?"
79. Sylvia L. Mayuga, "Wit at War," *Philippine Inquirer*, 27 February 2016.
80. Blackburn interview, 227.
81. Ramsey and Rivele, 84.
82. Ramsey and Rivele.
83. Lapham and Norling, 24.
84. Blackburn interview, 71.
85. Blackburn interview, 67.

86. Volckmann, 45.
87. Blackburn interview, 71.
88. Mike Guardia, *American Guerrilla: The Forgotten Heroics of Russell W. Volckmann* (Philadelphia: Casemate, 2010), 42.
89. Volckmann, 53.
90. Blackburn interview, 69.
91. Panlilio, 42, 3.
92. Panlilio, 158.
93. Stahl, 64, 76–77.
94. Willis and Myers, 80–81.
95. Ramsey and Rivele, 252.
96. Willis and Myers, 80.
97. Stephen Mellnik, *Philippine Diary, 1939–1945* (New York: Van Nostrand Reinhold Company, 1969), 248.
98. Keats, 28.
99. Keats.
100. Volckmann, 57.
101. Blackburn interview, 71.
102. Blackburn interview, 79.
103. Blackburn interview.
104. Volckmann, 114–15.
105. Mary Ellen Condon-Hall and Albert E. Cowdrey, *The Medical Department: Medical Service in the War Against Japan* (United States Army in World War II: The Technical Services) (Washington, D.C.: U.S. Army Center of Military History, 1998), 360.
106. Ramsey and Rivele, 103.
107. Ramsey and Rivele, 104.
108. Ramsey and Rivele, 94.
109. Blackburn interview, 77. Some guerrilla memoirs, such as Volckmann's, refer to the Fassoth brothers as Faussetts.
110. Guardia, *American Guerrilla*, 78.
111. Villamor, 76; Hartendorp, vol. I, 425–32; see also "List of POW Camps in the Philippine Islands," http://www.west-point.org/family/japanese-pow/Camps-Philippines.htm.
112. Pestano-Jacinto, 36.
113. Harries and Harries, 315–16.
114. Blackburn interview, 75–76.
115. Blackburn interview. The ships carried 4,852 well-trained and battle-tested troops of the Kawaguchi detachment.
116. Morton, 503.
117. Morton, 505.

118. Morton, 503–5.
119. Japanese Monographs 1, 276.
120. Morton, 506.
121. "Guerrilla Resistance Movements," 34.
122. Villamor, 89.
123. Villamor.
124. Japanese Monographs 1, 281.
125. Japanese Monographs 1.
126. Japanese Monographs 1.
127. Japanese Monographs 1, 229–30.
128. Nakano, 4.
129. Nakano, 230.
130. U.S. Department of State, *Foreign Relations of the United States: Diplomatic Papers*, 1942 (General; British Commonwealth; the Far East), vol. I, doc. 789, "Memorandum by the Under Secretary of State (Welles) to the Adviser on Political Relations (Hornbeck)," 11 April 1942, https://history.state.gov/historicaldocuments/frus1942v01/d789.
131. U.S. Department of State, doc. 790, "Memorandum by the Adviser on Political Relations (Hornbeck) and the Chief of the Division of Far Eastern Affairs (Hamilton) to the Under Secretary of State (Welles)," 14 April 1942, https://history.state.gov/historicaldocuments/frus1942v01/d790.
132. Lapham and Norling, 26–27.
133. Lapham and Norling, 26.
134. Lapham and Norling.
135. Ramsey and Rivele, 160.
136. Lapham and Norling, 27.
137. Morton, 507.
138. Japanese Monographs 1, 276.
139. Morton, 507.
140. Morton.
141. Morton.
142. U.S. Department of State, doc. 790.
143. U.S. Department of State, doc. 793, "Memorandum by President Roosevelt to the Secretary of State," 22 April 1942, https://history.state.gov/historicaldocuments/frus1942v01/d793.
144. See memorandum, "Summary History of Organization of A.I.B.," 25 January 1943, NARA II, Philippine Archives, RG 496, box 469.
145. "Summary History of Organization of A.I.B."

146. Correspondence between Commander E. A. Feldt, Navy Office, Commonwealth of Australia, and Ind through April 1942 indicates how desperately the Allied Intelligence Bureau searched for field radios unavailable in country. See Whitney Papers, RG16, box 68.
147. Ingham, 38.
148. Ind, 145.
149. U.S. Department of State, doc. 792, "The Chief of Staff (Marshall) to the Acting Secretary of State," 20 April 1942.
150. Villamor, 62.
151. Villamor.
152. Barrameda, 26–27.
153. Hartendorp, vol. I, 135.
154. Hartendorp.
155. Hartendorp, 133.
156. Barrameda, 26–27.
157. Barrameda, 32.
158. Barrameda, 32–36.
159. Ramsey and Rivele, 98.
160. Lapham and Norling, 22.
161. Volckmann, 57.
162. Volckmann, 60. "I thought Guerrero had a lot of guts," Blackburn remarked. Blackburn interview, 76.
163. Demson disappeared on 5 May. Guardia, *American Guerrilla*, 55.
164. Morton, 510.
165. Morton. A battalion of the 10th Independent Garrison Regiment had already relieved the detachment.
166. Morton, 508.
167. These were units under Lt. Col. Russell J. Nelson augmented by constabulary troops. Morton, 510.
168. Japanese Monographs 1, 277.
169. Morton, 515–16.
170. Agoncillo, vol. I, 375.
171. Goto, 68.
172. Agoncillo, vol. I, 351–52.
173. Yu-Jose, 160–61.
174. Agoncillo, vol. I, 352.
175. Villamor, 75.
176. As late March 1943 only 1,227 of 8,724 elementary schools had reopened and only 267,977 of 1,324,335 students had enrolled. Agoncillo, vol. I, 434.
177. Japanese Monographs 1, 270.

178. Morton, 518.
179. Rodgers, 214.
180. Japanese Monographs 1, 272–79.
181. Richard Connaughton, John Pimlott, and Duncan Anderson, *The Battle for Manila* (Novato, Calif.: Presidio Press, 1995), 49.
182. Alfred W. McCoy, "Rent Seeking Families and the Philippine State: A History of the Lopez Family," in McCoy, ed., 472.
183. "Guerrilla Resistance Movements," 48.
184. "Guerrilla Resistance Movements," 6.
185. "Guerrilla Resistance Movements," 102.
186. "Guerrilla Resistance Movements," 103.
187. Abaya, 24.
188. Villamor, 144.
189. "Guerrilla Resistance Movements," 97.
190. "Guerrilla Resistance Movements," 98.
191. Keats, 131.
192. Keats.
193. Keats.
194. "History of the Mindanao Guerrillas," 5, http://www.west-point.org/family/japanese-pow/Guerrillas/History%20of%20the%20Mindanao%20Guerrillas.pdf.
195. "History of the Mindanao Guerrillas," 88.
196. Ind, 3. At the same time SWPA lost contact with Capt. Ralph Praeger on Luzon. Volckmann, 90.

CHAPTER 4. ALONE

1. Also identified as Mr. Dreishcer. John Keats, *They Fought Alone* (New York: Pocket Books, 1965), 6–10. See also http://www.lanbob.com/lanbob/FP-AGOM/FP-AGOM-TM.htm.
2. Keats, 6.
3. Japanese Monographs 1, 278.
4. Harries and Harries, 313.
5. Agoncillo, vol. II, 657. See also Blackburn interview, 127.
6. Agoncillo, vol. II, 654.
7. Guardia, *American Guerrilla*, 101, and Volckmann, 32.
8. Mellnik, 248.
9. Stahl, 63.
10. Pestano-Jacinto, 85.
11. Lapham and Norling, 74.
12. United States Army Forces in the Philippines, Northern Luzon. Volckmann, 129.

13. Blackburn interview, 165–66.
14. Mellnik, 244.
15. Ramsey and Rivele, 98.
16. Ramsey and Rivele, 100.
17. Ramsey and Rivele, 110.
18. Ramsey and Rivele, 102–3.
19. Agoncillo, vol. II, 691.
20. "Guerrilla Resistance Movements," 31.
21. Abaya, 44.
22. Jennings, 33.
23. Pestano-Jacinto, 17.
24. Dower, 46.
25. Lapham and Norling, 106–7.
26. Villamor, 120.
27. Panlilio, 166.
28. Willis and Myers, 109.
29. Villamor, 85.
30. Villamor.
31. Villamor, 99.
32. "Guerrilla Resistance Movements," 69, 74. See also "Intelligence Activities," 13.
33. Kawashima Midori, "Japanese Administrative Policy Towards the Moros in Lanao," in Setsuho and Jose, 111.
34. Yuk-Wai, 104.
35. Guardia, *American Guerrilla*, 55.
36. After the war, the Army denied reimbursements to Bill Fassoth: "You were not authorized to incur expenses for which you seek reimbursement; it was a voluntary act on your part which does not create any obligation, legal or implied, on the part of the United States to reimburse you." Malcom Decker, From Bataan to Safety: The Rescue of 104 American Soldiers in the Philippines (Jefferson, N.C.: McFarland and Company, 2008), 1. Martin Fassoth was captured by the Japanese in 1943 and served out the war as a POW.
37. Decker, 1.
38. Volckmann, 62.
39. Blackburn interview, 79.
40. Guardia, *American Guerrilla*, 57–58.
41. Blackburn interview, 83.
42. The meals lacked the vitamin B needed to combat beriberi. Volckmann, 65.
43. Blackburn interview, 80.

44. Japanese Monographs 1, 284.
45. Japanese Monographs 1, 308.
46. Japanese Monographs 1, 292.
47. Japanese Monographs 1, 297.
48. Wise, 51.
49. Ingham, 38.
50. "Guerrilla Resistance Movements," 81.
51. "Intelligence Activities," 19.
52. Villamor, 128.
53. Villamor.
54. Kaminski, 241.
55. Lapham and Norling, 66.
56. Agoncillo, vol. II, 695.
57. Agoncillo, vol. I, 407.
58. Agoncillo, vol. I, 111.
59. Lapham and Norling, 36.
60. Yuk-Wai, 91–92.
61. Davis, 38. See also Lapham and Norling, 133.
62. Davis, table 8, 84.
63. Davis, 93.
64. Agoncillo, vol. II, 673–74.
65. Lapham and Norling, 129.
66. Ramsey and Rivele, 115.
67. Lapham and Norling, 134.
68. Lapham and Norling, 98, 133.
69. Lapham and Norling, 33.
70. Hampton Sides, *Ghost Soldiers: The Epic Account of World War II's Greatest Rescue Mission* (New York: Doubleday, 2001), 128.
71. Sides, 34.
72. Carlos P. Romulo and Marvin M. Gray, *The Magsaysay Story* (New York: The John Day Company, 1956), 45.
73. Barrameda, 142.
74. Barrameda, 143.
75. Agoncillo, vol. II, 709.
76. Agoncillo, vol. I, 120.
77. Robert J. Hanyok, "The Necessary Invention: The Cryptologic Effort by the Philippine Guerrilla Army, 1944–1945," *Cryptologic Almanac*, 13 September 2014, http://documents.theblackvault.com/documents/nsa/cryptoalmanac/The_Necessary_Invention.pdf.
78. Ind, 119.
79. "Guerrilla Resistance Movements," 46–50.
80. Ind, 37.

81. Major General Courtney Whitney, "MacArthur's Rendezvous with History," *Life*, 15 August 1955, 49. Breuer noted the Java stationed picked up the message on 10 July; Whitney recalled receiving the message 20 July.
82. William B. Breuer, *MacArthur's Undercover War: Spies, Saboteurs, Guerrillas, and Secret Missions* (New York: John Wiley and Sons, 1995), 46. See also Norling, 96.
83. Whitney, 49.
84. MacArthur, 202–3.
85. Volckmann, 139. Note Volckmann said Nakar received MacArthur's response on 29 June.
86. Stahl, 18–19.
87. Stahl.
88. See Memorandum, "A.I.B., ADMINISTRATIVE ADJUSTMENTS," 16 April 1943, NARA II, Philippine Archives, RG 496, box 473.
89. Rebecca Robbins Raines, *Getting the Message Through: A Branch History of the U.S. Army Signal Corps* (Washington, D.C.: U.S. Army Center of Military History, 1996), 290.
90. Breuer, 47.
91. "Intelligence Activities," 5.
92. Ind, 101.
93. Jose, "The Rice Shortage," 203.
94. Malcolm, 241, 251.
95. Villamor, 187.
96. Jose, "The Rice Shortage," 203. The initial ration was 1 *ganta*, or 1,200 grams per day.
97. Collingham, 235.
98. Collingham, 75.
99. Jose, "The Rice Shortage," 203.
100. Nagano Yoshiko, "Cotton Production under Japanese Rule, 1942–1945," in Setsuho and Jose, 178.
101. The policies were: "Outline for Implementing Projects for Increasing Cotton Production in the Philippines," "Outline for Implementing Projects for Cotton Cultivation in the Philippines for the Year 1942," and "Outline for Projects to Increase Cotton Production in the Philippines."
102. Yoshiko, 181.
103. Nakano, "Captain Hitomi's Goodwill Mission," 4.
104. Blackburn interview, 101.
105. Satoshi Nakano, "Appeasement and Coercion," in Setsuho and Jose, 47.

106. Nakano, 48.
107. Midori, 112.
108. "Guerrilla Resistance Movements," 90.
109. Keats, 21.
110. Keats.
111. Midori, 112.
112. Keats, 59.
113. Midori, 97.
114. Keats, 131.
115. Keats, 81.
116. Keats, 82–83.
117. Mellnik, 254.
118. Mellnik, 255.
119. Stahl, 33.
120. Villamor, 86.
121. Villamor, 82.
122. "Guerrilla Resistance Movements," 70.
123. "Guerrilla Resistance Movements," 71.
124. Lapham and Norling, 79.
125. Mellnik, 244.
126. Lapham and Norling, 80–81.
127. Barrameda, 65.
128. Blackburn interview, 153.
129. Panlilio, 18.
130. Panlilio.
131. "Yay furnished the necessary rein to Marking's extravagant enthusiasm," Agoncillo, vol. II, 693.
132. "Guerrilla Resistance Movements," 19.
133. Panlilio, 58.
134. Agoncillo, vol. II, 691.
135. Jennings, 37.
136. Pestano-Jacinto, 67.
137. Pestano-Jacinto.
138. Ara, 63.
139. Hartendorp, vol. I, 453.
140. Blackburn interview, 141.
141. Blackburn interview.
142. According to Blackburn, O'Day "was a civilian engineer and an unsavory character," Blackburn interview, 123.
143. Volckmann, 79–80.

144. Che Guevara, *On Guerrilla Warfare* (New York: Frederick Praeger, 1961), 58.
145. Brian McAllister Linn, *The Philippine War, 1899–1902* (Lawrence: University Press of Kansas, 2000), 90, 148, 286, 298. See also Brian McAllister Linn, *Guardians of Empire: The U.S. Army and the Pacific, 1902–1940* (Chapel Hill: University of North Carolina Press, 1997), 16.
146. Malcolm, 385.
147. Blackburn interview, 135–36.
148. See Antonietta P. Ebol, "The Philippine Malaria Vectors," Republic of the Philippines Department of Health, http://www.actmalaria.net/IRW/IRW_Philippines.pdf.
149. Centers for Disease Control and Prevention, "Malaria Information and Prophylaxis, by Country," *Health Information for International Travel 2016 (CDC's Yellow Book)*, http://www.cdc.gov/malaria/travelers/country_table/p.html.
150. Warshaw, 9, 10–14, 16.
151. Office of Scientific Research and Development, *Advances in Military Medicine: Science in World War II*, vol. I, ed. E. C. Andrus et al. (Boston: Little, Brown and Company, 1948), 668.
152. World Health Organization report in *Denguematters*, "Issue 7—Dengue in the Philippines," http://www.denguematters.info/content/issue-7-dengue-philippines. See also Strong, vol. II, 905.
153. Strong, vol. II, 916.
154. Strong, vol. I, 444–54.
155. Strong, vol. I, 447.
156. Strong, vol. I, 454.
157. Strong, vol. II, 1,038.
158. Warshaw, 9.
159. See Ramsey and Rivele, 138.
160. Blackburn interview, 82.
161. Ramsey and Rivele, 138.
162. "Record of Operations in the Philippines, Part II," Japanese Monographs 3, 5.
163. Gibney, 104.
164. Edward J. Drea et al., *Researching Japanese War Crimes Records: Introductory Records* (Washington, D.C.: National Archives and Records Administration for the Nazi War Crimes and Japanese Imperial Government Records Interagency Working Group, 2006), 31–32.
165. Setsuho, 159.
166. They scavenged equipment including two six-hundred-horsepower diesel generators from local gold mines. Setsuho, 146.

167. Setsuho, 141.
168. Setsuho, 147.
169. Yoshiko, 182.
170. Yoshiko, 157.
171. "Guerrilla Resistance Movements," 35.
172. "Intelligence Activities," 18.
173. Scott A. Mills, *Stranded in the Philippines: Professor Bell's Private War Against the Japanese* (Annapolis, Md.: Naval Institute Press, 2009), chap. 9.
174. "Guerrilla Resistance Movements," 74. See also "Intelligence Activities," 19.
175. "Guerrilla Resistance Movements," 57.
176. Lapham and Norling, 39.
177. Blackburn interview, 86.
178. Guardia, *American Guerrilla*, 58–59.
179. Blackburn interview, 85.
180. Volckmann, 67.
181. Volckmann misidentifies Calyer as Colonel Cayler.
182. Blackburn interview, 86–87.
183. Guardia, *American Guerrilla*, 63.
184. Lapham and Norling, 37.
185. Blackburn interview, 86.
186. Volckmann, 69–70.
187. Blackburn interview, 90.
188. Guardia, *American Guerrilla*, 64.
189. Ingham, 48–49.
190. Ind, 145.
191. John P. Finnegan, "U.S. Army Signals Intelligence in World War II: An Overview," in *U.S. Army Signals Intelligence in World War II: A Documentary History*, ed. James L. Gilbert and John P. Finnegan (Washington, D.C.: U.S. Army Center of Military History, 1993), 11.
192. Ingham, 48–49.

CHAPTER 5. ISLANDS AT WAR

1. Lapham and Norling, 49.
2. Blackburn interview, 95.
3. Blackburn interview, 98.
4. Volckmann, 80.
5. Guardia, *American Guerrilla*, 73.

6. Volckmann, 84.
7. Volckmann, 85.
8. Volckmann, 35–36.
9. Volckmann, 145.
10. Satoshi, 28.
11. Five remaining members of the religious section stayed in Manila at the University of San Tomas seminary.
12. Takefumi, 226.
13. Ramsey and Rivele, 136.
14. Ramsey and Rivele, 100.
15. Ramsey and Rivele.
16. Ramsey and Rivele, 112–13.
17. Ramsey and Rivele, 129.
18. Villamor, 75.
19. Ramsey and Rivele, 116.
20. Ramsey and Rivele, 116–25.
21. Lapham and Norling, 40.
22. Lapham and Norling, 44.
23. Lapham and Norling, 45.
24. Abaya, 44.
25. Agoncillo, vol. II, 654.
26. Breuer, 47.
27. Volckmann, 139.
28. "Summary History of Organization of A.I.B."
29. "Guerrilla Resistance Movements," 41.
30. Lapham and Norling, 41.
31. Lapham and Norling, 43.
32. Boayes did not join Miranda in July as SWPA thought. Barrameda, 146.
33. Barrameda, 148.
34. Barrameda, 147.
35. Midori, 113.
36. Keats, 131.
37. "Guerrilla Resistance Movements," 95–96.
38. Japanese Monographs 3, 123.
39. "Guerrilla Resistance Movements," 94.
40. "Guerrilla Resistance Movements," 95.
41. "Guerrilla Resistance Movements," 39.
42. Morgan was also known as William Morgan and Morgan Morgan.
43. Virginia Hansen Holmes, *Guerrilla Daughter* (Kent, Ohio: Kent State University Press, 2009), 73.
44. Keats, 89.

45. Keats, 102–4.
46. "Guerrilla Resistance Movements," 89.
47. Keats, 123.
48. "Guerrilla Resistance Movements," 93.
49. Mellnik, 259.
50. Keats, 127.
51. Mellnik, 259.
52. Mellnik, 261.
53. Mellnik, 160.
54. Mellnik.
55. Mellnik, 180.
56. Spector, 466.
57. Ramsey and Rivele, 141.
58. Volckmann, 133.
59. Volckmann.
60. Ramsey and Rivele, 142.
61. Lapham and Norling, 49.
62. Lapham and Norling, 50.
63. Lapham and Norling, 130.
64. Lapham and Norling, 131.
65. Parsons' observation. Ingham, 108.
66. Ingham, 169.
67. Romulo, 203.
68. Villamor, 185.
69. Willis and Myers, 106.
70. William R. Nelson, cited in *Japanese Infantry Weapons,* vol. I, ed. Donald B. McLean (Forest Grove, Ore.: Normount Armament Company, 1966), 2.
71. Romulo, 198.
72. B. David Mann, "Japanese Defense of Bataan, Luzon, Philippine Islands 16 December 1944–4 September 1945," *Journal of Military History* 67, no. 4 (2003): 1151.
73. Tanaka, 208.
74. Yutaka Yokota, "Volunteer," in *Japan at War: An Oral History,* ed. Haruko Taya Cook and Theodore F. Cook (New York: The New Press, 1992), 309.
75. Harries and Harries, 428.
76. Suzuki Murio, "As Long as I Don't Fight, I'll Make it Home," in Cook and Cook, 131.
77. Quezon, 284.
78. Holmes, 115.

79. Panlilio, 33.
80. In 1940 the Japanese army had 910,000 regular troops and 380,000 reservists; in 1943 they had 1,502,000 regular soldiers and 2,295,000 reservists. See table 11.2, "Regular Army and Reserve Troop Numbers, 1937–1945," in Edward J. Drea, *Japan's Imperial Army: Its Rise and Fall, 1853–1945* (Lawrence: University Press of Kansas, 2009), 235.
81. Lapham and Norling, 89.
82. Stahl, 122.
83. Lapham and Norling, 89.
84. Lapham and Norling, 90.
85. Ramsey and Rivele, 252.
86. Murio, 134.
87. Gibney, 143.
88. Stahl, 122.
89. Barrameda, 162.
90. Panlilio, 111.
91. Panlilio, 130.
92. Barrameda, 57.
93. Panlilio, 73.
94. Villamor, 88–89.
95. Villamor.
96. Tanaka, 204.
97. Brian Hardesty, "Japanese Counterinsurgency in the Philippines: 1942–45," *Small Wars Journal* (29 April 2009), 6.
98. Tanaka, 204.
99. Panlilio, 33.
100. "Intelligence Activities," 5.
101. "Intelligence Activities."
102. Supreme Commander for the Allied Powers, *Reports of General MacArthur* (Washington, D.C.: U.S. Army Center of Military History, 1994), 300.
103. "Intelligence Activities," 8–9.
104. "Guerrilla Resistance Movements," 75.
105. Villamor, 66–67.
106. See "Commando Unit for Operation on the Island of Mindanao," Villamor to Ind, 19 November 1942, in Whitney Papers, RG 16, box 63.
107. Ind, 106.
108. The author thanks Ian O'Toole, curator of the Kurrajong Radio Museum, for his expertise on the operation of wartime radios, especially the 3BZ and ATR-4.
109. Ind, 121.

110. "The 3BZ Coast Watchers Wireless Set," VK2DYM Military Radio and Radar Information Site, http://www.qsl.net/vk2dym/radio/3BZa.htm.
111. Note from Ind to Lieutenant Commander Quere, n.d., Whitney Papers, RG 16, box 68.
112. Steven Shapiro and Tina Forrester, *Hoodwinked: Outwitting the Enemy* (Buffalo, N.Y.: Annik Press, 2004), 64.
113. "'PLEVEN' Party—General Report," from Ind to A.C. of S., G-2, 27 April 1943, Whitney Papers, RG 16, box 63.
114. Ind, 110, 122. Ind claims the transmitter was fifty watts, but the manifest claims eighty watts.
115. Villamor described Quinto's set as a modified ATR4 transmitter combined with a Dutch-built NEI receiver. Villamor, 70. See also "Bob B. Glenn? Jr. (*sic*)" to Villamor, 24 December 1942, Whitney Papers, RG 16, box 68.
116. The Hallicrafter Co., *Technical Manual for Model HT-9 Radio Transmitter* (Chicago: Hallicrafters, 1946).
117. Theodore Roscoe, *United States Submarine Operations in World War II* (Annapolis, Md.: United States Naval Institute, 1949), 266.
118. "Intelligence Activities," 19.
119. "Intelligence Activities," 19–20.
120. Fujitani, 97.
121. Only one Nisei, Hawaiian-born Clarence S. Yamagata, worked full time for the Allied Translation and Interpreter Section Central Bureau. James C. McNaughton, *Nisei Linguists: Japanese Americans in the Military Intelligence Service during World War II* (Washington, D.C.: Department of the Army, 2006), 245.
122. Blackburn interview, 104.
123. Agoncillo, vol. II, 658–59.
124. Volckmann, 88.
125. Blackburn interview, 107.
126. Volckmann, 89.
127. Norling, 170. See also "Intelligence Activities," 6.
128. Whitney, 49.
129. Breuer, 48.
130. Guardia, *American Guerrilla*, 80.
131. Blackburn interview, 107–8.
132. Volckmann, 90.
133. Guardia, *American Guerrilla*, 79.
134. Volckmann, 92.
135. Blackburn interview, 109.
136. Volckmann, 96.

137. Volckmann, 97.
138. Nakano, "Captain Hitomi's Goodwill Mission," 8.
139. Nakano.
140. Blackburn interview, 109.
141. Hicks, 125.
142. Hicks.
143. Scott Walker, *The Edge of Terror: The Heroic Story of American Families Trapped in the Japanese-Occupied Philippines* (New York: Thomas Dunne Books, 2009), chap. 9. See also "Intelligence Activities," 12.
144. SWPA believed KFS responded to Peralta in the clear. Whitney, 49. See also "Intelligence Activities," 12.
145. Breuer, 47.
146. Villamor, 69.
147. Parsons began working on a plan to go to Peralta. Ingham, 50.
148. "Intelligence Activities," 54.
149. Villamor, 69.
150. Villamor.
151. "Intelligence Activities," 12.
152. Walker, chap. 9.
153. "Intelligence Activities," 17.
154. MacArthur, 203–4.
155. Message, 17 December 1942, in "Intelligence Activities," 16.
156. Memorandum, Ind to Merle-Smith, 19 November 1942, Whitney Papers, RG 16, box 63.
157. "Intelligence Activities," 16.
158. "Guerrilla Resistance Movements," 60.
159. Hartendorp, vol. I, 110. See also "Guerrilla Resistance Movements," 71.
160. Blackburn interview, 108.
161. Lapham and Norling, 52.
162. Lapham and Norling, 53.
163. Lapham and Norling.
164. Ramsey and Rivele, 127.
165. Barrameda, 43–44.
166. Barrameda, 23.
167. Barrameda, 48.
168. Setsuho, 158.
169. Volckmann, 125.
170. Tarling, 162.
171. Panlilio, 46.
172. Panlilio.
173. Panlilio.
174. Pestano-Jacinto, 105.

175. Fertig diary, 6 January 1943.
176. Villamor, 75.
177. Agoncillo, vol. I, 364.
178. Pestano-Jacinto, 57.
179. Agoncillo, vol. I, 364.
180. Lapham and Norling, 99.
181. Pestano-Jacinto, 133.
182. Tarling, 167. See also Agoncillo, vol. I, 365.
183. Anna Kluge, "Today She Wrote a Story that Will Never Be Published," *Tampa Bay Times*, 9 September 1956, 7.
184. Volckmann, 102.
185. Volckmann, 115.
186. Volckmann, 117.
187. Volckmann, 105.
188. Blackburn interview, 134.
189. Blackburn interview, 114.
190. Blackburn interview, 136.
191. Blackburn interview, 137.
192. Elmer N. Lear, "The Western Leyte Guerrilla Warfare Forces: A Case Study in the Non-Legitimation of a Guerrilla Organization," *Journal of Southeast Asian History* 9, no. 1 (March 1968): 75.
193. Lear.
194. Rafael Omega's affidavit. Ara, 48.
195. "Intelligence Activities," 12.
196. "Guerrilla Resistance Movements," 65.
197. Barrameda, 103.
198. MacArthur, 203.
199. Breuer, 47.
200. Mao Tse-Tung, *On Guerrilla Warfare* (New York: Praeger Publishers, 1961), 98.
201. Lapham and Norling, 30–31.
202. Keats, 209.
203. Lapham and Norling, 31.
204. Villamor, 70. Note that MacArthur (*Reminiscences*, 204) ends the message with "I am coming."
205. Villamor.
206. Villamor, 101.
207. Villamor.
208. Lapham and Norling, 77.
209. Lapham and Norling, 178.
210. Lapham and Norling, 179.
211. Ramsey and Rivele, 264.

212. Romulo and Gray, 48.
213. Volckmann, 126.
214. Romulo and Gray, 49.
215. Volckmann, 72.
216. Ramsey and Rivele, 264.
217. Ramsey and Rivele.
218. Barrameda, 87.
219. Barrameda, 52.
220. Alan J. Levine, *Captivity, Flight, and Survival in World War II* (Westport, Conn.: Praeger; 2000), 68–71.
221. "Intelligence Activities," 5–6.
222. Villamor, 70.
223. See "Commando Unit for Operation on the Island of Mindanao," Villamor to Ind, 19 November 1942, in Whitney Papers, RG 16, box 63.
224. See *Reports of General MacArthur: The Campaigns of MacArthur in the Pacific*, vol. I, prepared by General Staff (Washington, D.C.: U.S. Army Center of Military History; reprint 1994), plate 86, 306.
225. Villamor, 72.
226. Ramsey and Rivele, 145.
227. Ramsey and Rivele, 146.
228. Baba is misidentified by Ramsey and others as General Masao Baba, who was in Sumatra.
229. Lapham and Norling, 99.
230. Tarling, 170.
231. Lapham and Norling, 57.
232. Levine, 72.
233. Keats, 185.
234. See Hamner's tale in Bob Stahl, *Fugitives: Escaping and Evading the Japanese* (Lexington: University Press of Kentucky, 2001), 99–125.
235. Levine, 72.
236. "Intelligence Activities," 12.
237. "Guerrilla Resistance Movements," 96–97.
238. Fertig diary, 6 January 1943.
239. Fertig diary.

CHAPTER 6. THE AID

1. Lapham and Norling, 53.
2. Ramsey and Rivele, 152.
3. Ramsey and Rivele, 148.

4. Agoncillo, vol. II, 653. See also MacArthur, 204.
5. Agoncillo, vol. II.
6. Toshimi Kumai, *The Blood and Mud in the Philippines: Anti-Guerrilla Warfare on Panay Island*, trans. Yukako Ibuki, ed. Ma. Luisa Mabunay and Ricardo T. Jose (Iloilo City, Philippines: Malones Printing and Publishing, 2009).
7. Nakano, "Captain Hitomi's 'Goodwill' Mission," 52–53.
8. Nakano.
9. Nakano.
10. Fertig diary, 13 January 1943.
11. Breuer, 51. See also "Report by Mr. J. A. Hammer" to Major Allison W. Ind, 18 January 1943, Whitney Papers, RG 16, box 68.
12. Barrameda, 164.
13. *Reports of General MacArthur*, 300.
14. "Intelligence Activities," 13.
15. Ind, 122.
16. Villamor, 79.
17. Villamor, 79fn.
18. "Guerrilla Resistance Movements," 75.
19. Villamor, 85.
20. Lapham and Norling, 93.
21. Lapham and Norling, 76.
22. Lapham and Norling, 86.
23. "Guerrilla Resistance Movements," 75.
24. Fertig diary, 19 February 1943.
25. Villamor, 86–87.
26. Villamor.
27. Villamor.
28. "Intelligence Activities," 17.
29. Villamor, 88.
30. The response was received on 10 January 1943. Villamor, 88.
31. "Guerrilla Resistance Movements," 68.
32. Memorandum, Ind to Merle-Smith.
33. Villamor, 123.
34. Fertig diary, 15 January 1943.
35. Breuer, 54.
36. "Guerrilla Resistance Movements," 91–92.
37. "The Philippines Never Surrendered," *Cavalcade of America* radio show, 30 April 1945, written by playwright Arthur Miller, identified Kuder as Edward. See https://www.oldtimeradiodownloads.com/drama/the-cavalcade-of-america/the-philippines-never

-surrendered-1945-04-30. See also an article of the same title written by Edward M. Kuder and Pete Martin and passed to the Bureau of Public Relations by Gen. George C. Marshall. See https://www.marshallfoundation.org/library/digital-archive/to-ben-hibbs/. The article also appeared in the *Saturday Evening Post* 217, issue 37 (10 February 1945), 20.
38. "Guerrilla Resistance Movements," 91–92.
39. Keats, 189–92. MSF was the Mindanao-Smith-Fertig signal only Smith and Fertig knew.
40. Keats, 191.
41. MacArthur, 204.
42. Keats, 183.
43. Japanese Monographs 3, 6.
44. Satoshi, 23.
45. Ramsey and Rivele, 148.
46. Romulo and Gray, 57.
47. Romulo and Gray.
48. Tarling, 135.
49. Tarling.
50. Nakano, "Hitomi's Goodwill Mission," 37.
51. Motoe, 71.
52. Marcial P. Lichauco, *"Dear Mother Putnam": A Diary of the War in the Philippines* (Washington, D.C.: publisher unknown, 1949), 76.
53. Lichauco, 77.
54. Panlilio, 21.
55. Panlilio, 24.
56. Panlilio, 26.
57. Villamor, 92.
58. Villamor, 93.
59. Villamor, 67.
60. Villamor, 96.
61. S. C. M. Paine, *The Wars for Asia, 1911–1949* (Cambridge: Cambridge University Press, 2012), 125.
62. Panlilio, 161.
63. Agoncillo, vol. I, 368.
64. Agoncillo, vol. I, 370.
65. According to Blackburn, Villamor saw this article and "accepted it at face value." Blackburn interview, 161.
66. Fertig diary, 11 February 1943. See also Abaya, 44.
67. Yoshiko, 182.
68. Eighty percent of the cotton grew on Luzon, seven percent in Negros. Yoshiko, 184.

69. Yoshiko, 186–87.
70. Keats, 193.
71. Villamor, 96.
72. "Orders from MacArthur," Headquarters U. S. F. North Luzon in the Field, 10 February 1945, National Archives II, Philippines Archive Collection, RG 407.
73. Keats, 193.
74. Keats, 195.
75. Keats, 196.
76. "Intelligence Activities," 15.
77. "Intelligence Activities," 18.
78. "Guerrilla Resistance Movements," 103.
79. Hargis Westerfield, "125th Infantry Regiment (Moro): The Sulu Guerrilla Story, Part I," *41st Division Filipino Infantry Jungleer*, March 1997, 16–24.
80. "Guerrilla Resistance Movements," 104.
81. Pestano-Jacinto, 123.
82. Norling, 191.
83. Message to "All Guerrilla Leaders" in USAFIPS from Colonel Martin Moses, 10 February 1943, National Archives II, Philippine Archives Collection, RG 407, box 248.
84. Norling, 190.
85. Panlilio, 80–82.
86. Agoncillo, vol. II, 676.
87. Lapham and Norling, 127.
88. "Guerrilla Resistance Movements," 84.
89. Ingham, 48–49.
90. Wise, 77.
91. Larry S. Schmidt, "American Involvement in the Filipino Resistance Movement on Mindanao During the Japanese Occupation, 1942–1945," master's thesis, Command and General Staff College, Fort Leavenworth, Kans., 1982, 171.
92. "Intelligence Activities," 54.
93. Fertig diary, 21 February 1943.
94. See "Tambor," https://uboat.net/allies/warships/ship/2912.html.
95. Fertig diary, 5 March 1943.
96. Keats, 200–202.
97. Fertig diary, 19 February 1943.
98. Keats, 208.
99. Keats, 205.
100. Keats.
101. Fertig diary, 23 February 1943.

102. Keats, 207.
103. Keats, 219. See also "Intelligence Activities," 90.
104. Manchester, 379.
105. Fertig diary, 16 May 1943.
106. Lichauco, 33.
107. Keats, 214.
108. Keats, 215.
109. Lapham and Norling, 115.
110. Villamor, 97.
111. Villamor.
112. Jose S. Arcilla, "Tomas Confesore's [sic] Letter to Fermin Caram," *Philippine Studies* 44, no. 2 (Second Quarter 1996): 250–56.
113. Arcilla.
114. Arcilla.
115. Arcilla.
116. Arcilla.
117. Pestano-Jacinto, 185.
118. Nakano, "Hitomi's Goodwill Mission," 54.
119. Nakano, 54.
120. Nakano, 9.
121. Nakano, 8–9. Hitomi believed that Governor Caram had pressed the JMA to end the relocation plan.
122. Villamor, 189.
123. Villamor.
124. Barrameda, 153.
125. Only the intervention of Padua's executive officer saved Dianela from execution, Barrameda, 141–42.
126. Barrameda, 154.
127. Barrameda, 156.
128. Villamor, 126.
129. Mellnik, 259.
130. Fertig diary, 16 March 1943.
131. Villamor, 99.
132. Villamor, 100.
133. YuHico added: "He claims your face has given you away. The people have deduced your mission," Villamor, 101.
134. Villamor, 104.
135. Lapham and Norling, 77.
136. Marquez, 17.
137. Panlilio, 177.

138. Jennings, 45.
139. Villamor, 102.
140. Volckmann, 125.
141. Volckmann, 116.
142. Volckmann, 136.
143. Ind, 147.
144. The coconut fuel provided fewer BTUs than diesel but still burned clean and true. Ingham, 63–64.
145. Ingham, 160.
146. "Intelligence Activities," 35.
147. Keats, 208.
148. Ingham, 68.
149. Wise, 95.
150. Note Travis Ingham identifies the Lang and Peters guerrillas as based at Ormoc and Tacloban. Ingham, 70–71.
151. "Intelligence Activities," 18.
152. Kangleon began: "Apparently it is not the time for a soldier to rest," Ingham, 75.
153. "Intelligence Activities," 18.
154. Lear, 76–78.
155. Lear, 83.
156. Norling, 181.
157. Norling, 199.
158. Willis and Myers, 94. See also "Intelligence Activities," 13.
159. This was termed a "wearing-out policy." Andrew J. Birtle, *U.S. Counterinsurgency and Contingency Doctrine 1860–1941* (Washington, D.C.: U.S. Army Center of Military History 2001), 113–14.
160. Keats, 208–9.
161. Norling, 181–84.
162. Message to "All Guerrilla Leaders" in USFIPS from Col. Martin Moses and Col. Arthur Noble, 20 March 1943, National Archives II, Philippine Archives Collection, RG 407, box 248.
163. Breuer, 52–54.
164. Ind, 127.
165. "Andy had good men," noted Yay Panlilio, "for the good are magnets for those of the same metal," Panlilio, 157.
166. Barrameda, 71.
167. Hartendorp, vol. I, 453.
168. Hardesty, 3–4.
169. Omuri had arrived in Leyte in October 1942. Ara, 67.

170. Lapham and Norling, 55.
171. Panlilio, 29.
172. Panlilio.
173. Agoncillo, vol. II, 653.
174. Volckmann, 139.
175. Blackburn interview, 133.
176. Villamor, 106.
177. Peralta relayed these plans to YuHico. Villamor, 104.
178. Villamor, 105. See also Fertig diary, 12 April 1943.
179. Villamor.
180. "Intelligence Activities," 70.
181. Ramsey and Rivele, 170.
182. Lapham and Norling, 58.
183. Lapham and Norling.
184. Barrameda, 73.
185. Ramsey and Rivele, 170.
186. The daughters selected Paz Caguia as their president, and their officers included Ezperanza Dañgalan, Modesta Pancho, Rosario Sicad Peña, Maria Lareza Uy Abitria, and Soledad Uy-Boco.
187. Kaminski, 225. See also Claire Phillips and Myron Goldsmith, *Agent High Pockets: A Woman's Fight Against the Japanese in the Philippines* (American History Classics, 2017), 112.
188. Villamor, 187.
189. Willis and Myers, 101.
190. Panlilio described Díaz as "a tomboy, but so gracious of heart she gave no offense nowhere," Panlilio, 30.
191. Panlilio, 26.
192. Panlilio, 104.
193. Panlilio, 154.
194. Ramsey and Rivele, 125.
195. Lapham and Norling, 105–6.
196. Barrameda, 75.
197. Guerrilla Doyle Decker reported the Huk bounty on Ramsey. Lapham and Norling, 139, 58.
198. Willis and Myers, 101.
199. Willis and Myers, 97.
200. Willis and Myers, 151.
201. Stahl, 43.
202. Keats, 285.
203. Villamor, 125.
204. Villamor, 102.

205. Stahl, 138.
206. Fujitani, 372.
207. Yu-Jose, 161–62.
208. Yu-Jose.
209. Panlilio, 163.
210. Agoncillo, vol. II, 699. See also Panlilio, 107.
211. Panlilio, 111.
212. Blackburn interview, 120.
213. Blackburn interview, 121.
214. Guardia, *American Guerrilla*, 96.
215. Blackburn interview, 121.
216. Setsuho, 148.
217. Abaya, 32.
218. Abaya.
219. Motoe, 73.
220. Villamor, 107.
221. Villamor.
222. Villamor, 108.
223. Villamor.
224. Blackburn interview, 145.
225. Michael Cullinane, "Patron as Client: Warlord Politics of the Duranos of Danao," in McCoy, 170.
226. Cullinane, 169.
227. Cullinane.
228. Blackburn interview, 145.
229. "Intelligence Activities," 12–13.
230. "Intelligence Activities."
231. "Guerrilla Resistance Movements," 104.
232. After contact with Parsons, Kangleon had reached out to Fertig for support.
233. Villamor, 139.
234. Villamor, 138–40.
235. Villamor, 139.
236. Villamor, 140.
237. See "PLEVEN Party–General Report."
238. Sometimes identified as Frank Magee, Ingham, 82.
239. Ingham, 95.
240. "Guerrilla Resistance Movements," 93.
241. Wise, 104.
242. Fertig diary, 3 May 1943.
243. Wise, 94.

244. Wise, 95.
245. Ingham, 94–97.
246. Ingham, 97.
247. Keats, 223.
248. Keats, 225.
249. C. Parsons, "Certificate," 23 July 1945, Basilio J. Valdes Digitized Collection, Presidential Museum and Library, Manila, Philippines, https://archive.org/stream/certificate-lt-colonel-jose-ozamiz-july-23-1945/BVC-0467-072345-CSPA#page/n0/mode/1up.
250. Ingham, and Wise after him, place this meeting as late in 1943. Cuezon places it in late May 1943. See Mar L. Cuezon, "Senator Jose Ozámiz, the Forgotten Hero," City of Ozamis website, http://ozamizcity.com/JoseOzamiz.htm.
251. Wise, 140. See also "Intelligence Activities," 55.
252. Kaminski, 219–20. See also Villamor, 187–88.
253. Hartendorp, vol. II, 242.
254. Ingham, 162.
255. Ingham, 164.
256. Parsons, "Certificate."
257. Pestano-Jacinto, 125.
258. Nakano, "Hitomi's Goodwill Mission," 23.
259. Tarling, 168.
260. Fertig diary, 7 May 1943.

CHAPTER 7. DIVISIONS

1. Villamor, 112–13.
2. "Guerrilla Resistance Movements," 76. Montelibano had gathered money and food with Mata for local guerrillas.
3. Villamor, 117, 119.
4. Villamor, 123.
5. "Guerrilla Resistance Movements," 72.
6. Ramsey and Rivele, 121.
7. Ramsey and Rivele, 152.
8. Ramsey and Rivele, 163.
9. Volckmann, 145.
10. Volckmann, 118.
11. Kuroda said that "in politics there should be no room for excessiveness or bullying." Setsuho and Jose, 30.
12. Barrameda, 90.
13. Harries and Harries, 434.

14. Goto, 151.
15. Pestano-Jacinto, 168.
16. Goto, 162.
17. Villamor, 125.
18. Japanese Monographs 3, 29 October 1946.
19. Villamor, 125.
20. Breuer, 114.
21. *Reports of General MacArthur*, 298–302.
22. "Intelligence Activities," 29.
23. MacArthur, 205.
24. The 978th Signal Service Company became active on 1 July 1943. Raines, 290. See also Whitney's search for better radios in Breuer, 114.
25. "Intelligence Activities," 34.
26. Memorandum for Record, Chief of PRS to Controller AIB, 29 May 1943, Whitney Papers, RG16, box 63.
27. MacArthur, 205.
28. "Intelligence Activities," 30.
29. "Intelligence Activities."
30. Memorandum, "Request for Dispensary," Philippine Regional Section, 20 August 1943, Whitney Papers, RG16, box 68.
31. Letter of Transmittal—Philippine Section Personnel Training, LTC Allison W. Ind, 5 May 1943, Whitney Papers, RG16, box 68. Evidence suggests the camp population never went much beyond six hundred trainees.
32. The trainees spent 3.5 hours on judging distances; 8.5 hours each on map and compass reading; 10 hours on first aid; 21 hours on weapons training; 29.5 hours on ship and aircraft recognition; 30.75 hours on signals and Morse code; and 47.25 hours on physical training and unarmed combat. Whitney Papers, RG16, box 68.
33. See "Trout" at https://uboat.net/allies/warships/ship/2916.html. G-2 reported the departure date as 23 May. "Intelligence Activities," 27. See also Roscoe, 272.
34. Memo to Colonel Merrill-Smith, AIB, 28 March 1943, Whitney Papers, RG16, box 68, 1.
35. "First message from Maj. Hamner is dated 24 June 1943." "Intelligence Activities," 5.
36. "Intelligence Activities," 28.
37. Roscoe, 272.
38. "Intelligence Activities," 28.
39. "Intelligence Activities," 28–29.
40. Blackburn interview, 79.

41. Blackburn interview, 90.
42. Lapham and Norling, 190.
43. Volckmann, 69–70.
44. Villamor, 130.
45. Lear, 76.
46. Villamor, 130.
47. Lapham and Norling, 83.
48. Lapham and Norling, 86.
49. Panlilio, 193.
50. See Walter Rundell Jr., *Military Money: A Fiscal History of the U.S. Army Overseas in World War II* (College Station: Texas A&M University Press, 1980).
51. Lapham and Norling, 153.
52. Anderson took the money in September 1944. Lapham and Norling, 84–85.
53. Lapham and Norling, 82–83.
54. Willis and Myers, 64.
55. Willis and Myers, 83.
56. Lapham and Norling, 83.
57. Blackburn interview, 159.
58. Panlilio, 57.
59. Stahl, 43.
60. Willis and Myers, 28.
61. Stahl, 43–44.
62. Willis and Myers, 63.
63. Willis and Myers, 63–64.
64. Stahl, 124–25.
65. Blackburn interview, 127–28.
66. Ramsey and Rivele, 130.
67. Volckmann, 88.
68. In Zambalese, Volckmann said: "I was sure that in this country we had at least half a chance," Volckmann, 79–80.
69. Marquez, 14.
70. The others in the party were Dr. Nicanor Jacinto, Dr. Leoncio B. Monzon, Dr. Nicanor Reyes Sr., and Aurelio Montinola Sr.
71. Agoncillo, vol. I, 379.
72. Agoncillo.
73. Pestano-Jacinto, 164.
74. Blackburn interview, 123.
75. Volckmann, 119.
76. Blackburn interview, 128.

77. Blackburn interview.
78. Guardia, *American Guerrilla*, 100.
79. Fertig diary, 7 June 1943. See also "Guerrilla Resistance Movements," 90.
80. Fertig diary, 7 June 1943.
81. Fertig diary, 25 June 1943.
82. "Guerrilla Resistance Movements," 98.
83. Fertig diary, 13 June 1943.
84. Fertig diary.
85. Fertig diary, 20 June 1943.
86. Ingham, 98–102.
87. Tarling, 168–69.
88. Villamor, 191. See also Tarling, 169.
89. Jose, "The Rice Shortage," 204.
90. Agoncillo, vol. I, 383.
91. Abaya, 31.
92. Abaya, 32.
93. Villamor heard nothing from the guerrillas in Albay or Sorsogon. Abaya, 24.
94. "Intelligence Activities," 27.
95. Villamor, 136.
96. "Intelligence Activities," 27.
97. Barrameda, 155, 158–59.
98. Padua got districts 2 and 5, Aureus got 1, 3, and 4. Barrameda, 140.
99. Fertig diary, 22 June 1943.
100. Fertig diary.
101. Serran was a former first lieutenant in the intelligence section of the 61st Division. "Guerrilla Resistance Movements," 49.
102. Memorandum, General Headquarters Southwest Pacific Area Allied Intelligence Bureau, Subject: Philippine Operations, 27 May 1943, Whitney Papers, RG16, box 65, 1.
103. Memorandum, General Headquarters Southwest Pacific Area Allied Intelligence Bureau, 3.
104. Memorandum, General Headquarters Southwest Pacific Area Allied Intelligence Bureau, 48.
105. "Intelligence Activities," 36.
106. Captain Teodorico Haresco in Batangas; Lieutenant Porfirio Bretana near Fort Wint on Manila Harbor; Lieutenant Ludovico Pablico near Manila; Lieutenant Maximo Basco around Tarlac and Pampanga; Sergeant Elesco Pugne in Bataan and Corregidor; Sergeant B. Martinez in Lingayen and Pangasinan; and Sergeants Aurelio

Parrenas and Enrique Magalona in Cavite. "Intelligence Activities," 54.
107. "Intelligence Activities."
108. "Guerrilla Resistance Movements," 66.
109. "Guerrilla Resistance Movements," 49–50.
110. Only about 60 percent of guerrillas had arms in early 1943. Willis and Myers, 92.
111. See Trish Muyco-Tobin, "Her Name Means Light," in *Wells of Wisdom, Grandparents and Spiritual Journeys*, ed. Andrew J. Weaver and Carolyn L. Stapleton (Eugene, Ore.: Resource Press, 2005), 51.
112. "Guerrilla Resistance Movements," 64.
113. Fertig diary, 23 June 1943.
114. "Guerrilla Resistance Movements," 36.
115. "Guerrilla Resistance Movements," 102.
116. Agoncillo, vol. I, 384.
117. Japanese Monographs 1, 309.
118. The directive was the "The Outline of the Plan for Subjugative [sic] Operations in the Philippines." Japanese Monographs 1, 8.
119. Japanese Monographs 1, 8–9.
120. Japanese Monographs 3, 11.
121. Ramsey and Rivele, 174.
122. Ramsey and Rivele.
123. Japanese Monographs 1, 10.
124. Japanese Monographs 1, 11.
125. The production number is from 2 July 1943. Setsuho, 153.
126. Many Filipino POWs reported to a mine in Bohol managed by Nihon Kogyo.
127. Setsuho, 141–43.
128. The company town was home to only ten thousand people. Setsuho, 150.
129. Guerrilla Bado Dangwa worked diligently to counter each of these steps. Setsuho, 142.
130. This was a forty-six-page paper: "Policy Towards Philippine Roman Catholicism," Takefumi, 235.
131. Dower, 59.
132. Yoshiko, 188–91.
133. See Cheng-Tian Kou, *Global Competitiveness and Industrial Growth in Taiwan and the Philippines* (Pittsburgh, Pa.: University of Pittsburgh Press, 1995), 115–16.
134. Yoshiko, 192–94.
135. At this time there were 16 million Filipinos to 630,000 Japanese troops in the islands. Yoshiko, 193.

136. Connaughton et al., 60.
137. Fertig diary, 3 July 1943.
138. Fertig diary.
139. Ingham, 114.
140. Fertig diary, 30 May 1943.
141. Fertig diary.
142. "Intelligence Activities," 93.
143. "Guerrilla Resistance Movements," 72.
144. "Guerrilla Resistance Movements," 77.
145. "Guerrilla Resistance Movements."
146. Roscoe, 272.
147. Villamor, 149.
148. Villamor, 154.
149. Villamor, 155.
150. See "Grayling" at https://uboat.net/allies/warships/ship/2921.html. Roscoe identified the skipper as Lieutenant Commander J. E. Lee. Roscoe, 272.
151. "Intelligence Activities," 21.
152. Roscoe, 273. See also John Alden, *The Fleet Submarine in the U.S. Navy: A Design and Construction History* (Annapolis, Md.: Naval Institute Press, 1979), 252. See also Norman Friedman, *U.S. Submarines Through 1945: An Illustrated Design History* (Annapolis, Md.: Naval Institute Press, 1995), 285–304.
153. Villamor, 178.
154. Villamor, 179.
155. Villamor, 180–81.
156. Abaya, 35.
157. Villamor, 181–82. Villamor is also the only source to identify 5 August as the date of Straughn's capture.
158. Fertig diary, 7 August 1943.
159. Straughn was quoted in the article "Guerrilla Activities in P. I. Futile." Florinda d. F. Mateo, "The Philippine Guerrilla Movement and Counterpropaganda During World War II," *Plaride: A Philippine Journal of Communication, Media, and Society* 3, issue 2 (August 2006): 80–81.
160. Panlilio, 133.
161. Lapham and Norling, 92.
162. Laurel to a group of women from the KALIBAPI on 11 August. Abaya, 37.
163. Jose, "The Rice Shortage," 207.
164. Jose, 197.
165. Twenty-two to twenty-three battalions. The 122nd Regiment had two battalions of the former 65th Brigade. Japanese Monographs 3, 39.

166. Levies would bring the number of independent mixed brigades to four in early 1944. Japanese Monographs 3.
167. Ramsey and Rivele, 176.
168. Panlilio, 153.
169. Panlilio, 155.
170. Panlilio, 156.
171. Panlilio, 160.
172. Barrameda, 137.
173. Barrameda, 122.
174. Barrameda, 129.
175. Fertig diary, 27 July 1943.
176. Fertig diary, 31 July 1943.
177. Fertig diary, 4 August 1943.
178. Fertig diary, 6 August 1943.
179. Fertig diary, 10 August 1943.
180. Fertig diary, 11 August 1943.
181. Fertig diary, 22 August 1943.
182. Villamor, 140.
183. Fertig explained, "Morgan violated his agreement by notifying men on the other side to follow his orders until friction with me was settled." Fertig diary, 22 August 1943.
184. "Guerrilla Resistance Movements," 90.
185. "Guerrilla Resistance Movements," 62.
186. Cushing brought with him his regimental commanders: Lieutenant Colonel Olegario Baura, Captain Abel Trazo, and Captain Rogaciano Espiritu. Villamor, 196–97.
187. Villamor, 196.
188. Inuzuka chafed under Fourteenth Army policies. Together, Inuzuka and Hayase would produce a pamphlet in April 1944 lauding the Ganaps and Ramos. Motoe, 75–76.
189. Volckmann, 122.
190. "Except that the three rifle battalions consisted of four rifle companies instead of the usual three." Volckmann, 124.
191. Norling, 213, 199.
192. West Point Association of Graduates, Cullum No. 11167, http://apps.westpointaog.org/Memorials/Article/11167/.
193. Norling, 227.
194. Blackburn interview, 170–71.
195. Ramsey and Rivele, 173.
196. Blackburn interview, 149.
197. Blackburn interview, 150.
198. Blackburn interview, 151.

199. Villamor, 183.
200. Blackburn interview, 151.
201. Blackburn interview, 129.
202. Volckmann, 124–25.
203. Blackburn interview, 129.
204. Volckmann, 124.
205. Blackburn interview, 167.
206. Guardia, *American Guerrilla*, 110.
207. Guardia, 129.
208. Abaya, 33.
209. Abaya, 33–34.
210. Abaya, 35–36.
211. Fujitani, 61.
212. Tarling, 170.
213. Goto, 91.
214. Tarling, 170.
215. Goto, 90.
216. Marquez, 22.
217. Marquez.
218. Panlilio, 165.
219. Marquez, 23.
220. Marquez, 25.
221. Marquez, 28.
222. Marquez, 33.
223. "Intelligence Activities," 34.
224. Ind, 199.
225. Ind, 35.
226. Ingham, 135.
227. Ingham.
228. Ingham, 139–40.
229. "Intelligence Activities," 52–53.
230. Fertig added: "Tate is Oc. Misamis doing some harassing and trying to clear up the mess made under Morgan's orders," Fertig diary, 1–10 and 13 September 1943.
231. "Guerrilla Resistance Movements," 95.
232. Fertig diary, 17 September 1943.
233. See "Bowfin" at https://uboat.net/allies/warships/ship/3033.html.
234. Fertig diary, 29 September 1943.
235. According to Lapham, Fertig used Davao prison camp escapee and American pilot Lt. Samuel Grashio to get Morgan on the submarine. Lapham and Norling, 110.
236. Fertig diary, 29 September 1943.

237. Fertig diary.
238. Villamor, 199.
239. Villamor, 200.
240. Villamor, 205.
241. Abaya, 34.
242. Eighteenth year of Syowa—or Showa—the eighteenth year of Hirohito's reign. Agoncillo, vol. I, 393.
243. Masakatsu worried that there was not "even one pro-Japanese" in the highest levels of the new Philippine government. Nakano, "Hitomi's Goodwill Mission," 29.
244. Tarling, 169.
245. Abaya, 47–48.
246. Yu-Jose, 163.
247. Jose, "The Rice Shortage," 206.
248. Japanese Monographs 3, 12.
249. Agoncillo, vol. I, 399.
250. Pestano-Jacinto, 71.

CHAPTER 8. A DANGEROUS GAME

1. Saburo Ienaga, *The Pacific War 1931–1945* (New York: Random House, 1978), 172.
2. Fertig diary, 6–7 October.
3. "Guerrilla Resistance Movements," 105.
4. M. Hamlin Cannon, *Leyte, The Return to the Philippines* (U.S. Army in World War II, War in the Pacific) (Washington, D.C.: U.S. Government Printing Office, 1954), 16.
5. Ara, 41.
6. Cannon, 17.
7. Lear, 89–90.
8. Blackburn interview, 132.
9. Volckmann, 156.
10. Blackburn interview, 133.
11. Blackburn interview, 176–77.
12. See "Guerrilla Submarines" at http:// www.west-point .org / family /japanese-pow/Guerrillas/Guer-Subs.htm, and Seventh Fleet Intelligence Center, "Submarine Activities Connected with Guerrilla Organizations," https:// www.history. navy.mil/content/ history/nhhc /research/library/online-reading-room/title-list-alphabetically/s /submarine-activities-connected-with-guerrilla-organizations.html.
13. Memorandum titled "C.W.," 1 November 1944, Whitney Papers, RG 16, box 65.

14. Office of Naval Records and History, Ships' Histories Section, Navy Department, "History of USS *Narwhal* (SS 167)," Naval District Washington Microfilm Section, microfilm reel H108, AR-229-76, available at https://www.scribd.com/doc/176290597/SS-167-Narwhal-Part1, 7. See also Douglas E. Campbell, *Save Our Souls: Rescues Made by U.S. Submarines During World War II* (Morrisville, N.C.: Lulu Press, 2016), 300–303.
15. "Narwhal."
16. "Narwhal"; Condon-Hall and Cowdrey, 357.
17. "LTC F. D. McGee, Headquarters, 109th Division, Cotabato Sector, to C.O. 109th Division, 20 October 1943," 3. National Archives.
18. "Guerrilla Resistance Movements," 37.
19. "Guerrilla Resistance Movements."
20. Agoncillo, vol. I, 409.
21. Dower, 6.
22. Goto, 92.
23. Goto, 91.
24. Goto, 68.
25. See table 4-1, "Relationships of Four Southeast Asian Leaders with Japan," in Goto, 99.
26. Barrameda, 82.
27. Romulo and Gray, 58.
28. Barrameda, 77.
29. Barrameda.
30. Barrameda, 81.
31. Yuk-Wai, 92.
32. See "Cabrilla" at uboat.net, https://uboat.net/allies/warships/ship/3034.html.
33. Michael Sturma, *Fremantle's Submarines: How the Allied Submarines and Western Australia Helped to Win the War in the Pacific* (Annapolis, Md.: Naval Institute Press, 2015), 73.
34. "Intelligence Activities," 79.
35. "Guerrilla Resistance Movements," 76.
36. Villamor, 225.
37. Villamor, 214.
38. Villamor, 246.
39. Major H. L. Meider reported, "He is a personable young man but violently anti-American," Villamor, 242.
40. Villamor, 243–44.
41. "Guerrilla Resistance Movements," 47.
42. "Intelligence Activities," 30.
43. "Intelligence Activities."

44. "History of USS *Narwhal* (SS 167)," 8. The naval history incorrectly identified "Butuan Bay" as "Puluan Bay."
45. Ingham, 146.
46. "Intelligence Activities," 5.
47. "Intelligence Activities," 38.
48. Fertig wrote, "The job was done but the mental strain had been terrific," Fertig diary, 15 November 1943.
49. Fertig diary.
50. Fertig diary, 17 November 1943.
51. "Intelligence Activities," 94.
52. "Intelligence Activities."
53. See also Campbell, 302–3.
54. "Intelligence Activities," 94.
55. "Intelligence Activities."
56. See Roscoe, 274, and "Intelligence Activities," 39–40.
57. Stahl, 31.
58. Campbell, 303.
59. "History of USS *Narwhal* (SS 167)," 8. See also Campbell, 303–4.
60. Roscoe, 274.
61. Phillips concluded: "Will then advise recognition status," "Intelligence Activities," 36.
62. According to SWPA: "Peralta had appointed Maj. Ruffy CO on Mindoro under the Panay Command," "Intelligence Activities."
63. "Intelligence Activities," 36–37. Guerrilla relations would deteriorate as Japanese harassment of Phillips intensified.
64. "Guerrilla Resistance Movements," 81.
65. "Guerrilla Resistance Movements," 80.
66. "Guerrilla Resistance Movements," 81.
67. "Guerrilla Resistance Movements."
68. "Intelligence Activities," 7.
69. See "Second Philippine Republic," Malacanang Palace Presidential Library, http://malacanang.gov.ph/5235-70th-anniversary-of-the-second-philippine-republic/.
70. Panlilio, 177.
71. General Headquarters United States Army Forces, Pacific, *Intelligence Activities in the Philippines during the Japanese Occupation*, vol. II (Tokyo: General Headquarters Far East, 1948).
72. Villamor.
73. Connaughton et al., 64.
74. Villamor, 249.
75. Villamor, 284.

76. Villamor, 243, 249–50.
77. "Intelligence Activities," 22–23.
78. "Intelligence Activities," 27.
79. Abcede even shared Villamor's suspicion of American biases and Fertig's prejudices. "Intelligence Activities," 87.
80. Villamor, 241.
81. Barrameda explained, "Such was the paranoia of the times," Barrameda, 149.
82. Barrameda, 162.
83. Ramsey and Rivele, 199.
84. Ingham, 182.
85. Panlilio, 171.
86. Panlilio, 173.
87. Panlilio, 174.
88. Panlilio, 175.
89. Agoncillo, vol. II, 697.
90. Agoncillo.
91. Stahl, 47–48.
92. Stahl.
93. "Intelligence Activities," 39–40.
94. "Intelligence Activities," 58.
95. "Intelligence Activities," 62–63.
96. Blackburn would remain in Ifugao as commander of the 7th District and the 11th Infantry. Volckmann, 140.
97. Lapham and Norling, 68.
98. Lapham and Norling, 70, 117.
99. Lapham and Norling.
100. Blackburn interview, 139.
101. Blackburn interview, 138.
102. Condon-Hall and Cowdrey, 360.
103. Blackburn interview, 119–20.
104. Lapham and Norling, 60.
105. Ramsey and Rivele, 177.
106. McCoy, "Rent Seeking Families and the Philippine State," 473.
107. McCoy.
108. McCoy, 474.
109. Fertig diary, 11–15 December 1943.
110. Holmes, 79.
111. Holmes, 113.
112. "Guerrilla Resistance Movements," 97.
113. "Guerrilla Resistance Movements," 88.

114. Ara, 70–71.
115. Ingham, 163.
116. Ingham, 164–65.
117. Ingham, 166.
118. "Intelligence Activities," 21.
119. The counterfeit money was in 10,000 P50 notes, 500,000 P10 notes, 600,000 P5 notes, and 1.5 million P1 notes.
120. "Intelligence Activities," 21–22, fn35.
121. Wise, 140.
122. Ingham, 166.
123. Ingham, 172.
124. Agoncillo, vol. I, 404.
125. Abaya, 39.
126. Abaya, 40.
127. Ara, 71.
128. Abaya, 46.
129. Hartendorp, vol. II, 105.
130. Jose, "The Rice Shortage," 208.
131. Ara, 71.
132. Japanese Monographs 3, 40–41.
133. Ramsey and Rivele, 204.
134. Harder had not brought a radio. Phillips was still with Ruffy at Naujan. Ramsey and Rivele, 205.
135. Ramsey and Rivele, 214.
136. Ernie was "certainly not my idea of an officer," Ramsey later wrote. Ramsey and Rivele, 217–18.
137. "Guerrilla Resistance Movements," 59.
138. Untalan met the constabulary chief on Marinduque, Lieutenant Rudolpho Tescon.
139. "Guerrilla Resistance Movements," 56–57.
140. "Guerrilla Resistance Movements," 58.
141. Charo Nabong-Cabardo, "The Arteches in History," Samar News.com, 29 August 2007.
142. Villamor, 184.
143. Panlilio, 194.
144. "History of USS *Narwhal* (SS 167)," 9. See also "Narwhal" at uboat.net.
145. Ingham, 155.
146. See Roscoe, 369.
147. Panlilio, 196.
148. Panlilio. The ship was turned around at Olongapo.

149. Rice sold for between P3,000 and P5,000 by December 1944. Collingham, 243.
150. Panlilio, 187.
151. Guardia, *American Guerrilla*, 114.
152. Volckmann, 147.
153. Volckmann, 153.
154. After O'Day broke the Japanese operation and opened the area, Volckmann sent Robert Arnold to organize it as his Third District. Volckmann.
155. Nakano, "Hitomi's Goodwill Mission," 51.
156. Lapham and Norling, 109.
157. Blackburn interview, 144.
158. Blackburn interview.
159. Parsons commissioned Ozámiz as a lieutenant colonel. Agoncillo, vol. I, 411.
160. See Cuezon.
161. "Intelligence Activities," 56.
162. Agoncillo, vol. I, 414.
163. Japanese Monographs 3, 12.
164. Japanese Monographs 3, 31.
165. Japanese Monographs 3, 13, 18.
166. "Guerrilla Resistance Movements," 101.
167. "History of USS *Narwhal* (SS 167)," 9.
168. See Campbell.
169. Campbell identified twenty evacuees.
170. "History of USS *Narwhal* (SS 167)," 10.
171. Stahl, 70.
172. Stahl.
173. Stahl, 75.
174. Stahl.
175. Ochigue and Catalina also held Browning automatic rifles at the ready. Stahl.
176. Ramsey and Rivele, 222–23.
177. Ramsey and Rivele, 223.
178. Lapham and Norling, 103.
179. Ramsey and Rivele, 226–27.
180. Anderson signed the order: "Bernard L. Anderson, Capt, Infantry, U.S. Army Commanding," Lapham and Norling, 118.
181. Lapham and Norling, 119.
182. Bill Sloan, *Undefeated: America's Heroic Fight for Bataan and Corregidor* (New York: Simon and Schuster Paperbacks, 2012), 303.

183. "Intelligence Activities," 37.
184. Ramsey and Rivele, 231.
185. SWPA G-2 recorded the warrant officer's name as B. L. Wise ("Intelligence Activities"), but the West Point database on American guerrillas in the Philippines identifies him as 2nd Lt. David Wise (http://www.west-point.org/family/japanese-pow/Guerrillas/Guerrillas-List.htm).
186. From Japanese intelligence reports of 17 February to 7 March 1944. "Intelligence Activities," 37.
187. Ramsey and Rivele, 39.
188. Ramsey and Rivele, 234.
189. Ramsey and Rivele.
190. Beloncio took with him the A, C, and D companies to the 6th MD. Ruffy, left with B Company, fled to central Mindoro and rebuilt his force to about three hundred to four hundred men.
191. "Guerrilla Resistance Movements," 67.
192. Kou was a distinguished officer and would be promoted to lieutenant general in October.
193. Lydia N. Yu-Jose, "The Koreans in Second World War Philippines: Rumor and History," *Journal of Southeast Asian Studies* 43, no. 2 (June 2012): 324.
194. Yu-Jose.
195. Japanese Monographs 3, 48.
196. Japanese Monographs 3.
197. Japanese Monographs 3, 25.
198. The Army section's report was titled "Recent Conditions in the Philippines," Nakano, 27.
199. Japanese Monographs 3, 41–42.
200. Sven Matthiessen, *Japanese Pan-Asianism and the Philippines from the Late 19th Century to the End of World War II* (Lieden, The Netherlands: Koninklijkew Brill, 2016), 199–200.
201. Japanese Monographs 3, 19.
202. Japanese Monographs 3.
203. Midori, 109.
204. Midori.
205. Japanese Monographs 3, 45.
206. Japanese Monographs 3, 43.
207. Japanese Monographs 3.
208. Japanese Monographs 3.
209. Japanese Monographs 3, 44.
210. Roscoe, 369. See also "Angler" at uboat.net, https://uboat.net/allies/warships/ship/2986.html.

211. Roscoe.
212. Roscoe, 370.
213. Roscoe.
214. "Guerrilla Resistance Movements," 31
215. Zabat ordered Captain Garcia to bring Miranda to heel, but Garcia never tried. Barrameda, 162.
216. Barrameda, 91.
217. Barrameda, 94.
218. Barrameda, 23.
219. Barrameda, 108.
220. MacArthur, 205.
221. See Greg Bradsher, "The Z Plan Story: Japan's 1944 Naval Battle Strategy Drifts into U.S. Hands," *Prologue Magazine* 37, no. 3 (Fall 2005).
222. "Guerrilla Resistance Movements," 38.
223. See Bradsher.
224. Dirk Jan Barreveld, *Cushing's Coup: The True Story of How Lt. Col. James Cushing and His Filipino Guerrillas Captured Japan's Plan Z and Changed the Course of the Pacific War* (Havertown, Pa.: Casemate Publishers, 2015), 160.
225. Barreveld.
226. Peter T. Sinclair II, "Men of Destiny: The American and Filipino Guerrillas During the Japanese Occupation of the Philippines," master's thesis, Command and General Staff College, 20 December 2011, 50–51.
227. Villamor, 265.
228. John Toland, *The Rising Sun: The Decline and Fall of the Japanese Empire, 1936–1945* (New York: Random House, 1970), 480.
229. Barreveld, 161.
230. See "Crevalle" at uboat.net, https://uboat.net/allies/warships/ship/3037.html.
231. *Intelligence Activities*, 62 fn11b.
232. E. B. Potter, *Nimitz* (Annapolis, Md.: Naval Institute Press, 1976), 296.
233. Potter.
234. Potter, 176.

CHAPTER 9. THE RETURN

1. Panlilio, 205.
2. Panlilio, 217.
3. See Minch.

4. Volckmann, 149.
5. Lapham and Norling, 120.
6. Lapham and Norling.
7. Lapham and Norling.
8. Lapham and Norling.
9. Ramsey and Rivele, 237.
10. Volckmann, 151.
11. Agoncillo, vol. I, 415.
12. Four days later Roxas was playing golf with General Kuroda, Admiral Oka, and Ambassador Murata at Malacana Park. Abaya, 40.
13. Abaya, 40–41.
14. Terami-Wada Motoe, "The Filipino Volunteer Armies," in Setsuho and Jose, 71.
15. "Record of the Philippine Operation, Preparations made by the 14th Army Gp. For the Military Operations in the Philippine Islands from July 1944 to the End of November 1944," Monograph No. 4, Japanese Monographs, 18 October 1946, National Archives II, RG 550, box 7, 1.
16. Japanese Monographs 3, 48.
17. Japanese Monographs 3, 56.
18. Japanese Monographs 4, 13.
19. This was Fourteenth Army Operation Plan Number 11. Japanese Monographs 4, 53.
20. Japanese Monographs 4, 2. See also Japanese Monographs 3, 53.
21. Japanese Monographs 3, 51–52. Top priority for new airfields went to Manila, Clark, Lipa, Bacolod, Leyte, Davao, and Malaybalay.
22. Japanese Monographs 3, 52.
23. Japanese Monographs 3.
24. Japanese Monographs 3.
25. Agoncillo, vol. I, 416.
26. Abaya, 44–46.
27. Gibney, 146–47.
28. Gibney, 150–51.
29. "Intelligence Activities," 45.
30. "Intelligence Activities," 46.
31. "Intelligence Activities."
32. "Guerrilla Resistance Movements," 33.
33. "Guerrilla Resistance Movements," 89.
34. "History of USS *Narwhal* (SS 167)," 11.
35. Stahl, 79. See also General Headquarters Southwest Pacific Check Sheet, 18 May 1944, Whitney Papers, RG16, Box 68.
36. General Headquarters Southwest Pacific Check Sheet.

37. General Headquarters Southwest Pacific Check Sheet. Leaving at 2200 hours that evening, the boat ran aground but managed to get back to Darwin with no apparent damage. "History of USS *Narwhal* (SS 167)," 11.
38. Ramsey and Rivele, 238.
39. Ramsey and Rivele, 241.
40. Ramsey and Rivele, 243.
41. Blackburn interview, 155–56.
42. Condon-Hall and Cowdrey, 360.
43. Volckmann, 147.
44. Lear, 76.
45. Department of the Army, U.S. Army Field Manual 3-24/Marine Corps Warfighting Publication 3-33.5, *Counterinsurgency* (Washington, D.C.: Headquarters Department of the Army, 2006), 69.
46. Blackburn interview, 155–56.
47. "Intelligence Activities," 67, 85.
48. "Intelligence Activities," 67, fn4.
49. Labrador and Ancheta had with them Staff Sergeant Cipriano Miguel, Sergeant Pete Luz, Corporal Agrifino Duran, and Corporal Rudolph Santos.
50. Stahl took along Staff Sergeant Gerado Nery, Sergeant Jack Montero, Corporal Eddie Holgado, Corporal Julio Advincula, and two young civilians as bodyguards. Stahl, 79.
51. Stahl, 89–90.
52. "Intelligence Activities," 41.
53. Stahl, 90.
54. Stahl, 92.
55. Stahl, 92–93.
56. Stahl, 119.
57. Stahl, 104.
58. Stahl, 95–96.
59. See "Nautilus" at uboat.net, https://uboat.net/allies/warships/ship/2957.html.
60. See "Redfin" at uboat.net, https://uboat.net/allies/warships/ship/3018.html. The PRS had been planning this mission with an all-Filipino team of agents under First Sergeant Amando S. Corpus. "Intelligence Activities," 42–43.
61. "Intelligence Activities," 43.
62. Commander J. D. Crowley, Lieutenant J. W. Liddell, Ensign A. E. Jacobsen, Chief Radio Technician G. A. Howell, and Motor Machinist's Mate 3 E. R. Baumgart made it ashore together and later found

Quartermaster J. D. Russo, Fire Controlman 3 D. P. Tremaine, and Motor Machinist Mate 3 W. B. Miller. Roscoe, 356.
63. Roscoe, 348.
64. "Intelligence Activities," 43.
65. "Intelligence Activities," 58.
66. Memorandum to Chief Supply Officer, Deputy Controller AIB, 22 April 1944, Whitney Papers, RG16, box 68.
67. "Intelligence Activities," 58.
68. Cook and Cook, 339.
69. Stahl, 100.
70. Stahl, 100.
71. Stahl.
72. Stahl, 101.
73. See, for example, E. B. Potter, *Admiral Arleigh Burke* (Annapolis, Md.: Naval Institute Press, 1990).
74. Japanese Monographs 4, 3.
75. Marquez, 132.
76. Marquez.
77. Marquez, 133.
78. The prison guards memorized the *Imperial Code of Military Conduct* (*Gunjin Chokuron*) issued in 1882 and the *Japanese Service Code* (*Senjinkun*) of 1941. Tanaka, 207.
79. Tanaka, 208.
80. Willis and Myers, 27.
81. Pestano-Jacinto, 45.
82. Marquez, 118–19.
83. Volckmann saw this form of torture used against the people of Kiangan. Guardia, *American Guerrilla*, 111.
84. One day of the sun cure meant a day or two of blindness and possible permanent damage. Panlilio, 166.
85. Panlilio.
86. Ramsey and Rivele, 137.
87. Marquez, 118–19.
88. Willis said of his guard: "He even asked me to make a sketch of him, which I did." Willis and Myers, 37.
89. "Intelligence Activities," 59.
90. John D. Lukacs, *Escape from Davao: The Forgotten Story of the Most Daring Prison Escape of the Pacific War* (New York: NAL Caliber, 2011), 342–43.
91. Lukacs, 60.
92. Lukacs.
93. Lukacs, 343.

94. Roscoe, 366.
95. See "Roster of Allied Prisoners of War believed aboard *Shinyo Maru* when torpedoed and sunk 7 September 1944," http://www.west-point.org/family/japanese-pow/ShinyoMaruRosterJPW.html.
96. Lukacs, 343.
97. "Intelligence Activities," 60.
98. Japanese Monographs 4, 9.
99. Pestano-Jacinto, 217.
100. Ramona Snyder maintained her contacts through couriers.
101. Ramsey and Rivele, 248.
102. Abaya, 39.
103. Ramsey and Rivele, 254.
104. Ramsey and Rivele, 255.
105. Ramsey and Rivele, 256–57.
106. Harries and Harries, 433.
107. Japanese Monographs 4, 9.
108. The 61st Independent Mixed Brigade also arrived in September, and the 58th IMB arrived in November. Japanese Monographs 4, 7.
109. Japanese Monographs 4, 4.
110. Roscoe, 360.
111. Japanese Monographs 4, 47.
112. Japanese Monographs 4, 48.
113. Setsuho, 142.
114. Setsuho.
115. Stahl, 101.
116. Midori, 109.
117. *Practical Outline for an Education and Enlightenment Movement in the Philippines: Guidelines and Concrete Proposals.* Terami-Wada Motoe, "Lt. Shigenobu Mochizuki and the New Philippine Cultural Institute," *Journal of Southeast Asian Studies* 27, no. 1 (March 1996): 104–23. See also Yu-Jose, *Japan Views the Philippines*, 164–65.
118. Yu-Jose, 165.
119. Yu-Jose.
120. Abaya, 41.
121. Abaya, 50.
122. Connaughton et al., 67.
123. Ramsey and Rivele, 260.
124. Connaughton et al., 67.
125. Lapham and Norling, 135.
126. Lapham and Norling, 121.
127. Panlilio, 228.
128. Panlilio, 229.

129. Agoncillo, vol. II, 684.
130. "Guerrilla Resistance Movements," 28.
131. "Guerrilla Resistance Movements," 31.
132. Stahl added, "He had, as Mayor Medenilla had said, cleaned up his act," Stahl, 118.
133. Stahl.
134. Vera told Stahl: "I want to get back at the Japanese for what they have done. After all, I am a Philippine Scout!" Stahl.
135. Stahl, 119.
136. Stahl, 159.
137. Stahl. On 10 June, *Narwhal* departed Darwin on her eleventh war patrol.
138. Campbell identified 15 evacuees.
139. "Intelligence Activities," 45.
140. "Intelligence Activities."
141. Villamor, 258.
142. Alfred L. Castle, "President Roosevelt and General MacArthur at the Honolulu Conference of 1944," *The Hawaii Journal of History* 38 (2004): 169.
143. Tarling, 120.
144. Villamor, 258.
145. Villamor.
146. Castle, 172.
147. Volckmann, 157.
148. Lapham and Norling, 115.
149. Lapham and Norling, 150.
150. "Intelligence Activities," 58.
151. Abaya, 49.
152. See "Narwhal" at uboat.net.
153. Lapham and Norling, 152.
154. "History of USS *Narwhal* (SS 167)," 12.
155. Lapham and Norling, 153.
156. Lapham and Norling.
157. The Magnac was referred to as the Masanga in the official records.
158. The evacuees were former tank sergeant Captain Rudolph O. Bolstad (LGAF), Captain Charles L. Naylor (LGAF), Private First Class Wilbur B. Jellison, and Lieutenant Wilbur J. Lage. Campbell.
159. Barrameda, 164.
160. Stahl, 128.
161. Stahl, 130.
162. Stahl, 159.

163. Akira Iriye, *Power and Culture: The Japanese-American War 1941–1945* (Cambridge, Mass.: Harvard University Press, 1981), 177.
164. Iriye, 178.
165. Japanese Monographs 4, 12.
166. Japanese Monographs 4, 13.
167. Lichauco, 174.
168. Japanese Monographs 4, 2.
169. Japanese Monographs 4, 47.
170. Japanese Monographs 4.
171. Marquez, 85.
172. Wise, 155.
173. Abaya, 51.
174. Japanese Monographs 4, 21.
175. G. Carter Bentley, "Mohamad Ali Dimaporo: A Modern Maranao Datu," in McCoy, 246.
176. Midori, 114.
177. Fertig diary, 19 October 1944.
178. Fertig diary, 5 August 1944.
179. Fertig diary.
180. Fertig diary, 19 October 1944.
181. Fertig diary, 9 September 1944.
182. Japanese Monographs 4, 21.
183. Fertig diary, 25 September 1944.
184. See "Narwhal" at uboat.net.
185. "History of USS *Narwhal* (SS 167)," 14.
186. The 82 men are identified in Campbell.
187. Fertig diary, 19 October 1944.
188. Roscoe, 369.
189. Tarling, 107.
190. Potter, *Nimitz*, 317.
191. Tarling, 66.
192. "Guerrilla Resistance Movements," 66.
193. "Guerrilla Resistance Movements," 48.
194. "Guerrilla Resistance Movements," 55.
195. Jennings, 51.
196. David Donald, ed., *The Complete Encyclopedia of World Aircraft* (New York: Orbis Publishing, Ltd., 1997), 290–91, 647.
197. The P-38Ls could fly up to 414 miles per hour and up to 40,000 feet. Donald, 581.
198. Connaughton et al., 67.
199. Lapham and Norling, 166; Japanese Monographs 4, 21.

200. Panlilio, 235.
201. Lichauco, 182.
202. Abaya, 57.
203. Marquez, 111.
204. Marquez, 142.
205. A prewar sub, *Seawolf* won thirteen battle stars during the war on its fifteen war patrols. See "Narwhal" at uboat.net.
206. Roscoe, 360.
207. Setsuho, 147.
208. Davis, 40.
209. Abaya, 51.
210. Ramsey and Rivele, 290.
211. Tarling, 107.
212. Agoncillo, vol. I, 422.
213. Harries and Harries, 339–40.
214. Japanese Monographs 4, 23.
215. Japanese Monographs 4, 24.
216. Japanese Monographs 4, 108.
217. Nakano, "Appeasement and Coercion," 41.
218. Nakano.
219. A. Frank Reel, *The Case of General Yamashita* (Chicago: University of Chicago Press, 1949), 105–6.
220. Barrameda, 114.
221. Motoe, "The Filipino Volunteer Armies," 79.
222. Motoe.
223. Marquez, 186.
224. Ramsey and Rivele, 269.
225. Ramsey and Rivele.
226. Volckmann, 85.
227. Setsuho, 152.
228. Setsuho, 152.
229. Motoe, "The Filipino Volunteer Armies," 78.
230. Nakano, "Appeasement and Coercion," 10. Smith reported having approximately 8,500 men (two-thirds with prewar training) but without trained officers.
231. General Headquarters Southwest Pacific Area Check Sheet, G-3 to Chief of Staff through G-2, 30 September 1944, Whitney Papers, RG16, box 65.
232. General Headquarters Southwest Pacific Area Check Sheet, Chief of Staff (U/S) to G-3, 1 October 1944, Whitney Papers, RG16, box 65. Still, men like Volckmann and Blackburn got into legal troubles after

the war and had to defend former guerrillas for "eliminating spies and saboteurs." Guardia, *Shadow Commander*, 135.
233. Guardia.
234. Ingham, 161.
235. Wise, 146.
236. "Intelligence Activities," 40. SWPA only confirmed Smith as commander on Samar on 4 October.
237. Ingham, 204.
238. Letter, Major H. C. Page to Colonel Frank D. McGee, 29 September 1943, National Archives II, Philippine Archives Collection, box 248.
239. Ramsey, 285.
240. Lapham, 163.
241. See *Reports of General MacArthur*, 195.
242. Lapham and Norling, 163–64.
243. Stahl, 133.
244. Lapham and Norling, 166.
245. Ingham, 210.
246. Ingham, 216.
247. Kangleon also agreed to Parsons' request to have all his radios stand by every hour. Ingham, 219–20.
248. Ingham, 223.
249. Barrameda, 169.
250. Ingham, 227.
251. Japanese Monographs 3, 56.
252. Lapham and Norling, 168.
253. Willis and Myers, 104.
254. Charles Robert Anderson, *Leyte: The U.S. Army Campaigns of World War II* (Washington, D.C.: U.S. Army Center of Military History, 1994), 12.
255. MacArthur instructed Kangleon: "I desire that you establish and maintain direct communication with this headquarters at your earliest opportunity and thereafter you keep me informed of major developments involving enemy movement, dispositions and other activity within your area and observation," Anderson, 17.
256. Cannon, 257 fn16.
257. "General Krueger made the guerrillas a part of his armed forces, and they became a source of additional strength to the Sixth Army," Cannon, 204.
258. Reel, 105–6.
259. Connaughton et al., 67.
260. Connaughton et al.

261. Reel, 105–6.
262. Ingham, 231.
263. Anderson, 19.
264. Anderson, 19–20. See also Drea, 243, and Cannon, 314.
265. A month later the president had a grandchild born in the 121st Infantry's field hospital. In January 1945 the whole clan reunited at MacArthur's headquarters at Dagupan. Volckmann, 161.
266. Guardia, *American Guerrilla*, 124.
267. Blackburn interview, 158.
268. SWPA had issued its sabotage plan by message on 29 November 1944. Lapham and Norling, 167.
269. Lapham and Norling, 160.
270. Lapham and Norling, 168.
271. On 6 January a kamikaze sank minesweeper DMS-12 *USS Long*. Between 4 and 10 January, kamikazes sank or damaged forty-five U.S. and allied ships in Philippine waters. See "USA Ship Losses 1945," WW2 Cruisers, at https://www.world-war.co.uk/warloss_895usa.php3.
272. Dale Andradé, *Leyte: The U.S. Army Campaigns of World War II* (Washington, D.C.: U.S. Army Center of Military History, 1996), 6.
273. Lapham and Norling, 164.
274. *Reports of General MacArthur*, 291.
275. Blackburn interview, 190.
276. Cannon, 179.
277. Andradé, 12.
278. Blackburn interview, 189.
279. Cannon, 228, 348, 250.
280. Cannon, 179.
281. Grant E. Jerry, "All Those Who Remained: The American-led Guerrillas in the Philippines, 1942–1945," master's thesis, Command and General Staff College, 4 December 2014, 34.
282. Sinclair, 53.
283. Volckmann, 216.
284. Volckmann, 198.
285. Agoncillo, vol. II, 701.
286. Agoncillo.
287. Connaughton et al., 67.
288. Jennings, 78.
289. Harries and Harries, 436. See also Andradé, 14.
290. These rumors dated from 12 to 25 February 1945. Jintaro Ishida cited by Seth Mydans, "Japanese Veteran Writes of Brutal Philippine War," *The New York Times*, 2 September 2001.
291. Lichauco, 214.

292. Harries and Harries, 436.
293. Connaughton et al., 107.
294. Fertig diary, 24 February 1945.
295. Lapham and Norling, 189.
296. Harries and Harries, 436.
297. Andradé, 25.
298. Collingham, 299.
299. Andradé, 25.
300. Andradé.
301. "Record of the Philippine Operation, Preparations, Vol. 3, Part 2, Record of 35th Army Operations (Leyte Area), Vol. 47," Monograph No. 6, Japanese Monographs, 144.
302. Japanese Monographs 6, 20.
303. Gibney, 152–53.
304. Stephen Lofgren, *Southern Philippines: The U.S. Army Campaigns of World War II* (Washington, D.C.: U.S. Army Center of Military History, 2008), 18.
305. Lofgren, 21.
306. Lofgren, 16.
307. Lofgren added: "The guerrillas were prepared to participate actively in future actions."
308. Lofgren.
309. Lofgren, 29.
310. Fertig diary, 17 May 1945.
311. Lofgren, 29.
312. Fertig diary, 22 June 1945.
313. Andradé, 30. Connaughton et al. claimed that between January and August the Japanese on Luzon had lost 255,795 soldiers, and another 125,755 surrendered. The Americans lost 10,380 killed and 36,550 wounded. Connaughton et al., 204.
314. Lofgren, 32.

CHAPTER 10. CONCLUSION

1. The Australia-Japan Research Project cites the Senshi Sosho (the official military history of Imperial Japan). Australia-Japan Research Project, http://ajrp.awm.gov.au/ajrp/AJRP2.nsf/530e35f7e2ae7707ca 2571e3001a112d/e7daa03b9084ad56ca257209000a85f7?Open Document.
2. The total casualties for the invasion and return come secondhand from the Senshi Sosho through Wikipedia. Total losses during the invasion were: 4,130 killed, 6,808 wounded, 287 missing. Total

regional casualties during the Allied return: 498,600 (Army, 377,500; Navy, 121,100).
3. Finding a battle/nonbattle casualty rate for the Japanese army is problematic. Required statistics do not exist. In most battles in the Pacific, even their sick and wounded fought to the death. In China, they were known to kill their sick and wounded before leaving them. During World War II, the U.S. Army suffered 234,874 battle deaths and 83,400 nonbattle deaths (a 3:1 ratio). A better comparison for the Japanese fighting the Philippine guerrillas: during the Spanish-American War, the U.S. Army suffered 369 combat deaths to 2,061 noncombat (about 1:5). Nese F. DeBruyne, *American War and Military Operations Casualties: Lists and Statistics* (Washington, D.C: Congressional Research Service, 26 April 2017), table 1, "Principal Wars or Conflicts in Which the United States Participated U.S. Military Personnel Serving and Casualties (1775–1991)," 1–2.
4. Phillip Jowett, *The Japanese Army 1931–1945*, vol. I (Oxford: Osprey Publishing, 2002), 7.
5. Japanese Monographs 2, 45–56.
6. Between 1942 and 1945, Thailand's payments and goods sent to Japan averaged 6 percent of gross domestic product (GDP) at wartime currency exchange rates and a little over 9 percent at 1937 rates. Payments by Indochina rose from 9.1 percent of GDP in 1932 to 25.4 percent in 1945. Indonesia rates fell from a high of 11.2 percent in 1943 as U.S Navy interdiction of sea lanes took effect. Gregg Huff and Shinobu Majima, *Financing Japan's World War II Occupation of Southeast Asia*, 6–9, http://eh.net/eha/wp-content/uploads/2013/11/Huffetal.pdf.
7. Dower, 230.
8. Tom Bennet, *World War II Wrecks, Philippines* (Milford Haven, Wales: Happy Fish Publications, 2010), 1–2.
9. Reel, 106.
10. See the Indian National Army and the Burma Independence Army in Christopher Bayly and Tim Harper, *Forgotten Armies: The Fall of British Asia, 1941–1945* (Cambridge, Mass.: The Belknap Press of Harvard University Press, 2004), 294.
11. Potter, *Nimitz*, 318.
12. Lofgren, 452. Some estimates hold that for every pound of supplies a Japanese soldier received, each American soldier received two tons.
13. Lofgren, 32.
14. Out of 381,550 total casualties, 255,795 died. Robert Ross Smith, *Triumph in the Philippines* (The United States Army in World War

II: The War in the Pacific) (Washington, D.C.: U.S. Army Center of Military History, 1993), 694.
15. Fertig diary, 29 May 1945.
16. Fertig heard I Corps planned to form four regiments from his organization with "the rest of the guerrillas to be thrown to the wolves," Fertig diary, 18 April 1945. See also Volckmann, 218. His USAFIP-NL became the 2nd Division of the Philippine Army. However, the Philippine civil affairs units planned to place their officers in command.
17. Blackburn interview, 79.
18. Guardia, *American Guerrilla*, 153.
19. Ramsey and Rivele, 333.
20. Ramsey and Rivele, 328.
21. C. Peter Chen, World War II Database, https://ww2db.com/country/Philippines. See also National World War II Museum, "Research Starters: World Wide Deaths in World War II," https://www.nationalww2museum.org/students-teachers/student-resources/research-starters/research-starters-worldwide-deaths-world-war.
22. Hartendorp, vol. II, 557.
23. Connaughton et al., 15.
24. Gross domestic product per capita fell by 60 percent (compared to Thailand's drop of 15 percent, Indochina's by 35 percent). "Between 1938 and 1946, income in the Philippines shrank by more than half. The combined income index of Philippines physical production fell by over three fifths." Huff and Majima, 13, table 4, 34.
25. Collingham.
26. MacArthur determined on 28 November 1944, "When our military forces have landed in Luzon, it shall be my firm purpose to run to earth every disloyal Filipino who has debased his country's cause so as to impede the services of USAFFE officers or men who have continued to resist," Abaya, 59.
27. McCoy, "Rent Seeking Families and the Philippine State," 474.
28. McCoy.
29. McCoy.
30. "Like most of the provincial political elite who cultivated allies on both sides of the battle lines, the Lopez faction had maintained contact with pro-American guerrillas through USAFFE intelligence officers, among them Captain Patricio Miguel, a prewar Lopez supporter in the city police, and Captain Alfredo Gestoso, who helped Fernando escape from the city at the war's end and later protected him from collaboration charges." McCoy, 475.
31. Fertig diary, 5 June 1945.

32. In early June, Judge Saguin complained to Fertig: "The people who had spent the war in the U.S. were very lenient in their treatment of collaborators." Fertig diary.
33. See Mao, 56. The Japanese killed Crisanto Evangelista, Pedro Abad Santos, Ramon de Santos, Guillermo Capadocia, and many others. Scaff, 4–7. See also Davis, 38.
34. Colleen Woods, "Bombs, Bureaucrats, and Rosary Beads: The United States, the Philippines, and the Making of Global Anti-Communism, 1945–1960," PhD dissertation, University of Michigan, 2012, 6.
35. Ramsey and Rivele, 132–33.
36. Carl von Clausewitz, *On War*, ed. and trans. Michael Howard and Peter Paret (New York: Alfred A. Knopf, 1993), 579–82.
37. Clausewitz, 16.
38. In 1941 the Philippine Islands were home to 16,356,000 people. U.S. Department of Commerce, Bureau of the Census, *Statistical Abstract of the United States*, Reports of the Sixteenth Census, 2, "Table No. 3, Area and Population of Continental United States and Outlying Territories and Possessions: 1930 and 1940," https://www2.census.gov/library/publications/1942/compendia/statab/63ed/1941-02.pdf.
39. Schmidt, 5.
40. This number comes from the Hunters' Colonel Eleuterio "Terry" Adevoso who became head of the Philippine Veterans Legion after the war. Hartendorp, vol. II, 610.
41. During the war, 16,112,566 U.S. citizens served in the armed forces. U.S. Department of Veteran's Affairs, "America's Wars," https://www.va.gov/opa/publications/factsheets/fs_americas_wars.pdf.

Selected Bibliography

ARCHIVAL SOURCES

Courtney Whitney Papers, Record Group 16, MacArthur Archives, Norfolk, Va.
Donald D. Blackburn Papers, U.S. Army Heritage and Education Center, Carlisle, Pa.
Japanese Monographs, Record Group 550, National Archives II, College Park, Md.
Philippines Archive Collection, Record Group 407, National Archives II, College Park, Md.
Wendell W. Fertig Papers, Center for Military History, Carlisle, Pa.

Online Archives

Australian War Memorial, Australia-Japan Research Project. http://ajrp.awm.gov.au/ajrp/AJRP2.nsf/530e35f7e2ae7707ca2571e3001a112d/e7daa03b9084ad56ca257209000a85f7?OpenDocument.
Basilio J. Valdes Digitized Collection, Presidential Museum and Library, Malacañan Palace, Manila, Philippines.
Chen, C. Peter. World War II Database. https://ww2db.com/country/philippines.
National World War II Museum. "Research Starters: World Wide Deaths in World War II." https://www.nationalww2museum.org/students-teachers/student-resources/research-starters/research-starters-worldwide-deaths-world-war.
Philippines Archive Collection, Philippines Veteran Affairs Office, Cubao, Quezon City. http://collections.pvao.mil.ph/.
U.S. Department of the Navy, Office of Naval Records and History, Ships' Histories Section.

U.S. Department of State, Office of the Historian. *Foreign Relations of the United States: Diplomatic Papers.* https://history.state.gov/historicaldocuments.

PRIMARY SOURCES

Abaya, Hernando J. *Betrayal in the Philippines.* New York: A. A. Wyn, 1946.

Agoncillo, Teodoro A. *The Fateful Years: Japan's Adventure in the Philippines, 1941–1945.* 2 vols. Quezon City: R. P. Garcia Publishing Company, 1965.

Chalek, William D. *Guest of the Emperor: 1941 to 1945 in the Philippines Surviving the War, and as a POW, Bataan Death March, Cabanatuan, Davao Penal Colony, the "Hell Ships."* Lincoln, Neb.: Writers Club Press, 2002.

Churchill, Winston. *The Second World War: Their Finest Hour.* Boston: Houghton Mifflin Company, 1949.

Cook, Haruko Taya, and Theodore F. Cook, eds. *Japan at War: An Oral History.* New York: The New Press, 1992.

Department of the Army. U.S. Army Field Manual 3-24/Marine Corps Warfighting Publication 3-33.5, *Counterinsurgency.* Washington, D.C.: Headquarters Department of the Army, 2006.

Gibney, Frank, ed., and Beth Cary, trans. *Senso: The Japanese Remember the Pacific War: Letters to the Editor of* Asahi Shimbun. London: M. E. Sharpe, 2007.

Hartendorp, A. V. H. *The Japanese Occupation of the Philippines.* 2 vols. Manila, Philippines Bookmark, 1967.

Henson, Maria Rosa. *Comfort Woman: A Filipina's Story of Prostitution and Slavery Under the Japanese Military.* New York: Rowman and Littlefield Publishers, 1999.

Holmes, Virginia Hansen. *Guerrilla Daughter.* Kent, Ohio: The Kent State University Press, 2009.

Ind, Allison W. *Secret War Against Japan: The Allied Intelligence Bureau in World War II.* Philadelphia: McKay Company, 1958.

Jennings, Isabel Yumol. *Changing Tides: World War II Occupation and Independence in the Philippines.* Buffalo Gap, Tex.: State House Press, 2016.

Lapham, Robert, and Bernard Norling. *Lapham's Raiders: Guerrillas in the Philippines 1942–1945.* Lexington: University Press of Kentucky, 1996.

Lichauco, Marcial P. *"Dear Mother Putnam": A Diary of the War in the Philippines.* Washington, D.C.: Publisher unknown, 1949.

MacArthur, Douglas. *Reminiscences*. New York: McGraw-Hill, 1964.
Marquez, Adalia. *Blood on the Sun: The Japanese Occupation of the Philippines*. Manila, Philippines: CreateSpace Independent, 2014.
Mellnik, Stephen M. *Philippine Diary, 1939–1945*. New York: Van Nostrand Reinhold Co., 1969.
Panlilio, Yay. *The Crucible: An Autobiography by Colonel Yay, Filipina American Guerrilla*. Denise Cruz, ed. New Brunswick, N.J.: Rutgers University Press, 2010.
Pestano-Jacinto, Pacita. *Living with the Enemy*. Pasig City, Philippines: Anvil Publishing, 1999.
Phillips, Claire, and Myron Goldsmith. *Agent High Pockets: A Woman's Fight Against the Japanese in the Philippines*. Place of publication not identified: American History Classics, 2017.
Quezon, Manuel. *The Good Fight*. New York: D. Appleton–Century Company, 1946.
Ramsey, Edwin Price, and Stephen J. Rivele. *Lieutenant Ramsey's War: From Horse Soldier to Guerrilla Commander*. Washington, D.C.: Brassey's Books, 1990.
Rodgers, Paul P. *The Good Years: MacArthur and Sutherland*. New York: Praeger Publishers, 1990.
Romulo, Carlos P. *I Saw the Fall of the Philippines*. New York: Doubleday, Doran, and Company, 1943.
Stahl, Bob. *Fugitives: Escaping and Evading the Japanese*. Lexington: University Press of Kentucky, 2001.
———. *You're No Good to Me Dead: Behind the Japanese Lines in the Philippines*. Annapolis, Md.: Naval Institute Press, 1997.
Supreme Commander for the Allied Powers. *Reports of General MacArthur*. Washington, D.C.: U.S. Army Center of Military History, 1994.
Taruc, Luis. *He Who Rides the Tiger: The Story of an Asian Guerrilla Leader*. New York: Frederick A. Praeger, 1967.
United States Army Forces, Pacific. *Intelligence Activities in the Philippines During the Japanese Occupation*, vol. II. Tokyo: General Headquarters Far East, 1948.
Villamor, Jesus with Gerald S. Snyder. *They Never Surrendered: A True Story of Resistance in World War II*. Quezon City, Philippines: Vera-Reyes, 1982.
Volckmann, Russell W. *We Remained: Three Years Behind the Enemy Lines in the Philippines*. New York: W. W. Norton and Company, 1954.
Whitney, Courtney. "MacArthur's Rendezvous with History." *LIFE*, 15 August 1955, 48–79.

Willis, Donald H., and Reyburn W. Myers. *The Sea Was My Last Chance: Memoir of an American Captured on Bataan in 1942 Who Escaped in 1944 and Led the Liberation of Western Mindanao.* Jefferson, N.C.: McFarland and Company, 1992.

SECONDARY SOURCES

Alden, John. *The Fleet Submarine in the U.S. Navy: A Design and Construction History.* Annapolis, Md.: Naval Institute Press, 1979.

Anderson, Charles Robert. *Leyte: The U.S. Army Campaigns of World War II.* Washington, D.C.: U.S. Army Center of Military History, 1994.

Andradé, Dale. *Luzon: The U.S. Army Campaigns of World War II.* Washington, D.C.: U.S. Army Center of Military History, 1996.

Andrus, E. C. et al., eds. *Advances in Military Medicine: Science in World War* II, vol. I. Boston: Little, Brown and Company, 1948.

Ara, Satoshi. "Food Supply Problem in Leyte, Philippines, During the Japanese Occupation (1942–44)." *Journal of Southeast Asian Studies* 39, no. 1 (February 2008).

Arcilla, Jose S. "Tomas Confesore's [sic] Letter to Fermin Caram." *Philippine Studies* 44, no. 2 (Second Quarter 1996): 250–56.

Baclagon, Uladarico S. *The Philippine Resistance Movement Against Japan, 10.12.1941–14.6.1945.* Quezon City, Philippines: Munoz Press, 1965.

Baer, George W. *One Hundred Years of Sea Power: The U.S. Navy, 1890–1990.* Stanford, Calif.: Stanford University Press, 1993.

Barrameda, Jose V., Jr. *In the Crucible of an Asymmetrical War in Camarines Sur 1942–1945 (The Story of the Tangcong Vaca Guerrilla Unit).* Manila, Philippines: National Historical Institute, 2007.

Barreveld, Dirk Jan. *Cushing's Coup: The True Story of How Lt. Col. James Cushing and His Filipino Guerrillas Captured Japan's Plan Z and Changed the Course of the Pacific War.* Havertown, Pa.: Casemate Publishers, 2015.

Bayly, Christopher, and Tim Harper. *Forgotten Armies: The Fall of British Asia, 1941–1945.* Cambridge, Mass.: The Belknap Press of Harvard University Press, 2004.

Bennet, Tom. *World War II Wrecks, Philippines.* Milford Haven, Wales: Happy Fish Publications, 2010.

Birtle, Andrew J. *U.S. Counterinsurgency and Contingency Doctrine 1860–1941.* Washington, D.C.: U.S. Army Center of Military History, 2001.

Black, Jonathan. "Jose P. Laurel and Jorge B. Vargas: Issues of Collaboration and Loyalty during the Japanese Occupation of the Philippines." Thesis, Claremont McKenna College, 2010.

Boot, Max. *The Savage Wars of Peace: Small Wars and the Rise of American Power.* New York: Basic Books, 2002.
Bradsher, Greg. "The Z Plan Story: Japan's 1944 Naval Battle Strategy Drifts into U.S. Hands." *Prologue Magazine* 37, no. 3 (Fall 2005).
Breuer, William B. *MacArthur's Undercover War: Spies, Saboteurs, Guerrillas, and Secret Missions.* New York: John Wiley and Sons, 1995.
Brown-Lamont, Raymond. *Kempeitai: Japan's Dreaded Military Police.* Gloucester, U.K.: Sutton Publishing, 1998.
Campbell, Douglas E. *Save Our Souls: Rescues Made by U.S. Submarines During World War II.* Morrisville, N.C.: Lulu Press, 2016.
Cannon, M. Hamlin. *Leyte, the Return to the Philippines* (U.S. Army in World War II, War in the Pacific). Washington, D.C.: U.S. Government Printing Office, 1954.
Castle, Alfred L. "President Roosevelt and General MacArthur at the Honolulu Conference of 1944." *The Hawaii Journal of History* 38 (2004): 165–73.
Centers for Disease Control and Prevention. "Malaria Information and Prophylaxis, by Country." *Health Information for International Travel 2016 (CDC's Yellow Book)*, http://www.cdc.gov/malaria/travelers/country_table/p.html.
Clausewitz, Carl von. *On War.* Edited and translated by Michael Howard and Peter Paret. New York: Alfred A. Knopf, 1993.
Coates, John Boyd, ed. *Preventive Medicine in World War II.* Vol. IV, *Communicable Diseases: Malaria.* Washington, D.C.: Department of the Army, 1963.
Collingham, Lizzie. *The Taste of War: World War II and the Battle for Food.* New York: Penguin Press, 2012.
Condon-Hall, Mary Ellen, and Albert E. Cowdrey. *The Medical Department: Medical Service in the War Against Japan* (United States Army in World War II: The Technical Services). Washington, D.C.: U.S. Army Center of Military History, 1998.
Connaughton, Richard, John Pimlott, and Duncan Anderson. *The Battle for Manila.* Novato, Calif.: Presidio Press, 1995.
Costello, John. *The Pacific War 1941–1945.* New York: Quill, 1982.
Cray, Ed. *General of the Army: George C. Marshall, Soldier and Statesman.* New York: Cooper Square Press, 1990.
Davis, Leonard. *Revolutionary Struggle in the Philippines.* New York: St. Martin's Press, 1989.
DeBruyne, Nese F. *American War and Military Operations Casualties: Lists and Statistics.* Washington, D.C.: Congressional Research Service, 26 April 2017.

Decker, Malcom. *From Bataan to Safety: The Rescue of 104 American Soldiers in the Philippines.* Jefferson, N.C.: McFarland and Company, 2008.

Donald, David, ed. *The Complete Encyclopedia of World Aircraft.* New York: Orbis Publishing, Ltd., 1997.

Dower, John W. *War Without Mercy: Race and Power in the Pacific War.* New York: Pantheon Books, 1986.

Drea, Edward J. *Japan's Imperial Army: Its Rise and Fall, 1853–1945.* Lawrence: University Press of Kansas, 2009.

Drea, Edward J., et al. *Researching Japanese War Crimes Records: Introductory Records.* Washington, D.C.: National Archives and Records Administration for the Nazi War Crimes and Japanese Imperial Government Records Interagency Working Group, 2006.

Edwards, Wallace. *Comfort Women: A History of Japanese Forced Prostitution During the Second World War.* North Charleston, S.C.: Absolute Crime Books, 2013.

Elshrec, Willard H. *Japan's Role in South-East Asia Nationalist Movements.* Cambridge, Mass.: Harvard University Press, 1953.

Escandor, Juan, Jr. "Village Won't Forget Guerrillas." *Inquirer Southern Luzon,* 14 March 2012.

Finnegan, John P. "U.S. Army Signals Intelligence in World War II: An Overview." In *U.S. Army Signals Intelligence in World War II: A Documentary History.* Edited by James L. Gilbert and John P. Finnegan. Washington, D.C.: U.S. Army Center of Military History, 1993.

Friedman, Norman. *U.S. Submarines Through 1945: An Illustrated Design History.* Annapolis, Md.: Naval Institute Press, 1995.

Fujitani, T. *Race for Empire: Koreans as Japanese and Japanese as Americans During World War II.* Berkeley: University of California Press, 2011.

Glusman, John A. *Conduct Under Fire: Four American Doctors and the Fight for Life as Prisoners of the Japanese, 1841–1945.* London: Penguin Books, 2005.

Goodman, Grant K. "'A Flood of Immigration': Japanese Immigration to the Philippines, 1900–1941." Lawrence: University of Kansas Center for Digital Scholarship, 2011.

Goto, Ken'ichi. *Tensions of Empire: Japan and Southeast Asia in the Colonial and Postcolonial World.* Athens: Ohio University, 2003.

Guardia, Mike. *American Guerrilla: The Forgotten Heroics of Russell W. Volckmann.* Philadelphia: Casemate, 2010.

———. *Shadow Commander: The Epic Story of Donald D. Blackburn, Guerrilla Leader and Special Forces Hero.* Philadelphia: Casemate, 2011.

Guevara, Che. *On Guerrilla Warfare.* New York: Frederick Praeger, 1961.

Hanyok, Robert J. "The Necessary Invention: The Cryptologic Effort by the Philippine Guerrilla Army, 1944–1945." *Cryptologic Almanac*, 13 September 2014. http://documents.theblackvault.com/documents/nsa/cryptoalmanac/The_Necessary_Invention.pdf.
Hardesty, Brian. "Japanese Counterinsurgency in the Philippines: 1942–45." *Small Wars Journal*, 29 April 2009, 1–7.
Harries, Meirion, and Susie Harries. *Soldier of the Sun: The Rise and Fall of the Imperial Japanese Army*. New York: Random House, 1991.
Hicks, George. *The Comfort Women: Japan's Brutal Regime of Enforced Prostitution in the Second World War*. New York: W. W. Norton and Company, 1995.
Huff, Gregg, and Shinobu Majima. *Financing Japan's World War II Occupation of Southeast Asia*. http://eh.net/eha/wp-content/uploads/2013/11/Huffetal.pdf.
Ienaga, Saburo. *The Pacific War 1931–1945*. New York: Random House, 1978.
Ingham, Travis. *Rendezvous by Submarine: The Story of Charles Parsons and the Guerrilla-Soldiers in the Philippines*. Garden City, N.Y.: Doubleday, Doran, and Company, 1945.
Iriye, Akira. *Power and Culture: The Japanese-American War 1941–1945*. Cambridge, Mass.: Harvard University Press, 1981.
Jerry, Grant E. "All Those Who Remained: The American-Led Guerrillas in the Philippines, 1942–1945." Master's thesis, Command and General Staff College, 4 December 2014.
Jose, Ricardo T. "Governments in Exile." *Asian and Pacific Migration Journal* 8, nos. 1–2 (1999): 178–93.
Jowett, Phillip. *The Japanese Army 1931–1945*, vol. I. Oxford: Osprey Publishing, 2002.
Kaminski, Theresa. *Angels of the Underground: The American Women Who Resisted the Japanese in the Philippines in World War II*. New York: Oxford University Press, 2016.
Keats, John. *They Fought Alone*. New York: Pocket Books, 1965.
Kerkvliet, Benedict J. *The Huk Rebellion: A Study of Peasant Revolt in the Philippines*. Berkeley: University of California Press, 1977.
Kessler, Richard J. *Rebellion and Repression in the Philippines*. New Haven, Conn.: Yale University Press, 1989.
Koehler, John E. "Review: *The Huks: Philippine Agrarian Society in Revolt* by Eduardo Lachia." *Economic Development and Cultural Change* 23, no. 1 (October 1974): 187–88.
Kou, Cheng-Tian. *Global Competitiveness and Industrial Growth in Taiwan and the Philippines*. Pittsburgh: University of Pittsburgh Press, 1995.

Kreidberg, Marvin A., and Merton G. Henry. *History of Military Mobilization in the United States Army, 1775–1945*. Washington, D.C.: Department of the Army, 1955.

Kumai, Toshimi. *The Blood and Mud in the Philippines: Anti-Guerrilla Warfare on Panay Island*. Trans. Yukako Ibuki, ed. Ma. Luisa Mabunay and Ricardo T. Jose. Iloilo City, Philippines: Malones Printing and Publishing, 2009.

Lanzona, Vina A. *Amazons of the Huk Rebellion: Gender, Sex, and Revolution in the Philippines*. Madison: University of Wisconsin Press, 2009.

Lawton, Lancelot. *Empires of the Far East: A Study of Japan and of her Colonial Possessions of China and Manchuria and the Political Questions of Eastern Asia and the Pacific*, vol. I. London: Grant Richards, Ltd., 1912.

Lear, Elmer N. "The Western Leyte Guerrilla Warfare Forces: A Case Study in the Non-Legitimation of a Guerrilla Organization." *Journal of Southeast Asian History* 9, no. 1 (March 1968): 69–94.

LeFeber, Walter. *The Clash: U.S.-Japanese Relations Throughout History*. New York: W. W. Norton and Company, 1990.

Levine, Alan J. *Captivity, Flight and Survival in World War II*. Westport, Conn.: Praeger Publishers, 2000.

Linn, Brian McAllister. *Guardians of Empire: The U.S. Army and the Pacific, 1902–1940*. Chapel Hill: University of North Carolina Press, 1997.

———. *The Philippine War, 1899–1902*. Lawrence: University Press of Kansas, 2000.

Lofgren, Stephen J. *Southern Philippines: The U.S. Army Campaigns of World War II*. Washington, D.C.: U.S. Army Center of Military History, 2008.

Lukacs, John D. *Escape from Davao: The Forgotten Story of the Most Daring Prison Escape of the Pacific War*. New York: NAL Caliber, 2011.

Malcolm, George A. *The Commonwealth of the Philippines*. New York: D. Appleton-Century Company, 1936.

Manchester, William. *American Caesar: Douglas MacArthur, 1880–1964*. Boston: Little, Brown and Co., 1978.

Mann, B. David. "Japanese Defense of Bataan, Luzon, Philippine Islands 16 December 1944–4 September 1945." *Journal of Military History* 67, no. 4 (2003): 1149–76.

Mateo, Florinda d. F. "The Philippine Guerrilla Movement and Counterpropaganda During World War II." *Plaride: A Philippine Journal of Communication, Media, and Society* 3, issue 2 (August 2006): 75–122.

Matsuda, Matt K. *Pacific Worlds: A History of Seas, Peoples, and Cultures*. Cambridge: Cambridge University Press, 2012.

Matthiessen, Sven. *Japanese Pan-Asianism and the Philippines From the Late 19th Century to the End of World War II*. Lieden, Netherlands: Koninklijkew Brill, 2016.

Mayuga, Sylvia L. "Wit at War." *Philippine Inquirer*. 27 February 2016.

McCoy, Alfred W., ed. *An Anarchy of Families: State and Family in the Philippines*. Madison: University of Wisconsin Center for Southeast Asian Studies, 1993.

McLean, Donald B., ed. *Japanese Infantry Weapons*, vol. I. Forest Grove, Ore.: Normount Armament Company, 1966.

McNaughton, James C. *Nisei Linguists: Japanese Americans in the Military Intelligence Service during World War II*. Washington, D.C.: Department of the Army, 2006.

Miller, Merle. *Ike the Soldier: As They Knew Him*. New York: G. P. Putnam's Sons, 1987.

Mills, Scott A. *Stranded in the Philippines: Professor Bell's Private War Against the Japanese*. Annapolis, Md.: Naval Institute Press, 2009.

Minch, Pat. "1LT Graft Jacob 'Spence or Budd' Spencer." http://www.findagrave.com/cgi-bin/fg.cgi?page=gr&GRid=56753681.

Morton, Louis. *The Fall of the Philippines, The War in the Pacific* (United States Army in World War II). Washington, D.C.: U.S. Army Center of Military History, 1989.

Motoe, Terami-Wada. "Lt. Shigenobu Mochizuki and the New Philippine Cultural Institute." *Journal of Southeast Asian Studies* 27, no. 1 (March 1996): 104–23.

Muyco-Tobin, Trish. "Her Name Means Light." In *Wells of Wisdom, Grandparents and Spiritual Journeys*. Edited by Andrew J. Weaver and Carolyn L. Stapleton. Eugene, Ore.: Resource Press, 2005.

Mydans, Seth. "Japanese Veteran Writes of Brutal Philippine War." *The New York Times*, 2 September 2001.

Nakano, Satoshi. "Captain Hitomi's 'Goodwill' Mission in Luzon and Panay, 1942–43: A Logic of Conciliation in the Japanese Propaganda in the Philippines." Draft paper prepared for 13th IAHA Conference, Sophia University, Tokyo, 5–9 September 1994.

Norling, Bernard. *The Intrepid Guerrillas of Northern Luzon*. Lexington: University Press of Kentucky, 1999.

Paine, S. C. M. *The Wars for Asia, 1911–1949*. Cambridge: Cambridge University Press, 2012.

Pogue, Forrest C. *George C. Marshall, Interviews and Reminiscences for Forrest C. Pogue*. Edited by Larry I. Bland. Lexington, Va.: George C. Marshall Research Foundation, 1991.

Potter, E. B. *Admiral Arleigh Burke*. Annapolis, Md.: Naval Institute Press, 1990.

———. *Nimitz.* Annapolis, Md.: Naval Institute Press, 1976.

Raines, Rebecca Robbins. *Getting the Message Through: A Branch History of the U.S. Army Signal Corps.* Washington, D.C.: U.S. Army Center of Military History, 1996.

Raposas, Al. "Japanese Involvement in the Philippines." *Filipino Historian International.* 16 December 2012.

Reel, A. Frank. *The Case of General Yamashita.* Chicago: University of Chicago Press, 1949.

Romulo, Carlos P., and Marvin M. Gray. *The Magsaysay Story.* New York: The John Day Company, 1956.

Roscoe, Theodore. *United States Submarine Operations in World War II.* Annapolis, Md.: United States Naval Institute, 1949.

Rundell Walter, Jr. *Military Money: A Fiscal History of the U.S. Army Overseas in World War II.* College Station: Texas A&M University Press, 1980.

Scaff, Alvin H. *The Philippine Answer to Communism.* Stanford, Calif.: Stanford University Press, 1955.

Schmidt, Larry S. "American Involvement in the Filipino Resistance Movement on Mindanao During the Japanese Occupation, 1942–1945." Master's thesis, Command and General Staff College, 1982.

Setsuho, Ikehata, and Ricardo Trota Jose, eds. *The Philippines Under Japan: Occupation Policy and Reaction.* Manila, Philippines: Ateneo De Manila University Press, 1999.

Shapiro, Steven, and Tina Forrester. *Hoodwinked: Outwitting the Enemy.* Buffalo, N.Y.: Annik Press, 2004.

Sides, Hampton. *Ghost Soldiers: The Epic Account of World War II's Greatest Rescue Mission.* New York: Doubleday, 2001.

Sinclair II, Peter T. "Men of Destiny: The American and Filipino Guerrillas During the Japanese Occupation of the Philippines." Master's thesis, Command and General Staff College, 20 December 2011.

Sloan, Bill. *Undefeated: America's Heroic Fight for Bataan and Corregidor.* New York: Simon and Schuster Paperbacks, 2012.

Smith, Robert Ross. *Triumph in the Philippines* (The United States Army in World War II: The War in the Pacific). Washington, D.C.: U.S. Army Center of Military History, 1993.

Snow, Edgar. *Red Star Over China.* New York: Grove Press, 1978.

Spector, Ronald H. *Eagle Against the Sun: The American War with Japan.* New York: Vintage Books, 1985.

Strong, Richard P. *Stitt's Diagnosis, Prevention, and Treatment of Tropical Diseases,* vols. I and II. Philadelphia: The Blakiston Company, 1944.

Sturma, Michael. *Fremantle's Submarines: How the Allied Submarines and Western Australia Helped to Win the War in the Pacific.* Annapolis, Md.: Naval Institute Press, 2015.

Tanaka, Yuki. *Hidden Horrors: Japanese War Crimes in World War II.* Boulder, Colo.: Westview Press, 1996.
Tarling, Nicholas. *A Sudden Rampage: The Japanese Occupation of Southeast Asia, 1941–1945.* Honolulu: University of Hawaii Press, 2001.
Toland, John. *The Rising Sun: The Decline and Fall of the Japanese Empire, 1936–1945.* New York: Random House, 1970.
Utley, Garrick. "Philippine Women Seek Apology and Retribution from the Japanese Years after World War II." *NBC Nightly News*, 3 April 1993.
Walker, Scott. *The Edge of Terror: The Heroic Story of American Families Trapped in the Japanese-Occupied Philippines.* New York: Thomas Dunne Books, 2009.
Warshaw, Leon I. *Malaria: The Biography of a Killer.* New York: Rhinehart and Co., 1949.
Westerfield, Hargis. "125th Infantry Regiment (Moro): The Sulu Guerrilla Story, Part I." *41st Division Filipino Infantry Jungleer*, March 1997.
Wilson, Joyce C. *Japan's Greater East Asian Co-Prosperity Sphere in World War II, Selected Readings and Documents.* London: Oxford University Press, 1975.
Wilson, Sandra. "The 'New Paradise': Japanese Emigration to Manchuria in the 1930s and 1940s." *The International History Review* 17, no. 2 (May 1995): 249–86.
Wise, William. *Secret Mission to the Philippines: The Story of "Spyron" and the American-Filipino Guerrillas of World War II.* Lincoln, Neb.: iUniverse.com, 2001.
Woods, Colleen. "Bombs, Bureaucrats, and Rosary Beads: The United States, the Philippines, and the Making of Global Anti-Communism, 1945–1960." PhD diss., University of Michigan, 2012.
Yu-Jose, Lydia N. *Japan Views the Philippines, 1900–1944.* Manila, Philippines: Ateneo de Manila University Press, 1992.
———. "The Koreans in Second World War Philippines: Rumor and History." *Journal of Southeast Asian Studies* 43, no. 2 (June 2012).
Yuk-Wai, Yung Li. *The Huaqiao Warriors: Chinese Resistance Movement in the Philippines 1942–45.* Hong Kong: Hong Kong University Press, 1995.

Index

Abad Santos, Jose (chief justice), 14, 20, 55, 79, 344n33
Abcede, Salvadore: crash documents and, 233; Cunanan and, 182; Fertig and, 140; Negros guerrillas and, 74, 88, 119–20, 125, 168–69; as Peralta agent, 181; SWPA approves as commander, 186; Villamor and, 135, 137, 207, 211, 212, 327n79
Ablan, Roques, 26, 32, 44–45, 55, 86, 115, 144, 223
Adevoso, Eleuterio "Terry," 27, 71, 90, 344n40
Agoncillo, Teodoro, 48–49, 79, 90, 103, 177, 236
Aguinaldo, Emilio, 1, 3, 179, 200
Allied Air Forces, weather posts for, 238
Allied Intelligence Bureau (AIB): Australia headquarters, 84; code for Praeger, 115; compartmentalized designs, 211–12; MacArthur on Parsons for, 98; Merle-Smith and, 58, 82; Philippine regional section (PRS), 83, 170–71, 172, 173; Philippine subsection, 113; Philippines missions and, 165; on Villamor's return to Negros, 135. *See also* radios
Alonto, Domocao and Madiki, 75
American Red Cross, 209
amnesty, 201, 216, 221
Anderson, Bernard: declining influence of, 250; financial accounting and, 175, 318n52; on Hua Zhi loyalties, 80; Hunters fighting with Marking and Huks, 221; on Lapus' troops as military, 251; Luzon Guerrilla Force and, 79; MacArthur's return and, 205; Marking and, 189–90; Ramsey and, 156, 226, 313n165; supplies for, 254; Thorp and, 109
Andrews, Edwin D., 66–67, 108, 166, 178, 207, 211, 233, 234
Anti-Japanese and Chinese-Protection Committee (AJCPC), 21
Aquino, Benigno, 28, 37, 73, 103, 123–24, 179, 237
Aquino, Corazon, 276
Arteche, Pedro and Melecio, 220
Augustin, Marcos V. (Marking), 22, 90, 140, 188, 189–90, 259, 299n131. *See also* Marking's guerrillas
Aureus, Leon S. A., 43, 89, 128, 133, 151, 180, 230–31, 319n98. *See also* TVGU
Ausejo, Placido, 95, 135, 137, 168, 169, 180, 186
Australia, 36, 41. *See also* MacArthur, Douglas

Baba, Kamekau, 130, 138–39, 236, 250, 308n228
Bagong Sirang Society assassination squad, 206
Baldwin, Rufino, 99, 115, 116, 169

357

Ball, Robert, 68, 88, 108, 214, 225, 253
baltik (Filipino weapon), 16
Barker, Joe: Bataan surrender and, 50; bodyguard captured, 133; bounty on, 103; execution, 215, 239; on guerrilla warfare, 102, 275; Huks and, 80, 109; illness, 53; Luzon Guerrilla Force and, 71, 79; Ramsey and, 129; on romantic attachments, 159; on the run, 133; in Thorp's camp, 60
Barnett, George, 101, 115, 192, 223
Barrameda, Jose V., Jr.: on comfort women, 23; on Japanese in Naga, 15, 16, 28; on Kuroda, 170; on living with the war, 230; on Miranda, 180, 212, 327n81; on Miranda's wife as *balato*, 151; on TVGU, 44, 104; on U.S. air raids, 265; on Vera's power, 128
Barros, Russell D., 51, 140, 190, 254–55
Bataan (Peninsula): Death March, 53, 55, 100; escapees from, 51, 53, 76, 91, 96–97; fall of, 60; Japanese airfield on, 11; Japanese shelling, 49–50; MacArthur and, 20, 40
Bautista, Antonio, 21, 176–77. *See also* Marquez, Adalia
Bell, Henry Roy, 74–75, 95, 108, 125, 142, 162, 168, 207
Beloncio, Esteban P., 191, 209–10, 227, 330n190
beriberi, 93
Bicol (southern Luzon), 18, 72, 158–59, 190, 212, 230
Blackburn, Donald, 14, 17, 89, 162–63, 204, 240; on Bell, 93; Connolly's Rangers and, 267; escapes Bataan, 51; guerrilla warfare and, 193; on the Huks, 49, 109; in Ifugao, 327n96; illnesses of, 161, 176, 216, 274; on Japanese, 116, 117, 120; on Land Communication Company, 70; post-war legal troubles, 338–39n232; on Praeger, 192–93. *See also* Volckmann, Russell

Boayes, Francisco "Turko," 15, 104, 150, 151, 179–80, 212, 230, 231, 281n27, 302n32
Bolo battalions, 66–67, 69, 70, 75, 87, 104, 227
Bowler, Robert V., 107, 131, 164, 166
Buenaventura Plantado guerrillas, 59
Bulacan Military Area guerrillas, 250
Bulkeley, John D., 36, 39, 40, 209
Burma, Japanese on independence for, 194

Cagayan guerrilla force, 19
Cagayan-Apayao guerrilla force, 79, 157
Calvert, Parker, 24, 26, 46, 69, 144, 169, 192
Camp Equip, 100
Camp Isarog guerrillas, 16, 128, 150
Camp Keithley, Mindanao, 75
Camp Liberty guerrillas, 70
Camp Manchuria guerrillas, 81, 103
Camp Tinawagan guerrillas, 18, 59, 150
Castañeda, Eulogio, 254–55
caste system, in Japan, 113
Catholic church, 1, 47, 101–2, 108, 150, 184, 247
Cebu, 54–55, 163, 292n115. *See also* Cushing, James
Centino, Ciriaco and Isabelo, 72, 155, 203
China, Japanese invasion of, 4
Chinese Anti-Japanese Guerrilla Force (*Feilubin huaqiao kangri zhidui*). *See* Hua Zhi
Chinese community, 21–22, 27–28, 48, 65–66, 75
Chinese Salvation Association, 66
Clark Field, Philippines, 11
Clausewitz, Carl von, 275
coast watching/watchers, 154, 214–15, 273
Cobb, Alfred and Paul, 69, 96, 181–82
coconut fuel, 154, 175, 197, 313n144
coconuts, versatility of, 175–76
codes, for communicating, 115, 118, 130, 138, 142, 310n39

collaborators with Japanese, 32, 152–53, 167, 177, 223, 257, 274–75, 318n70, 344n32
comfort women, 23, 45
command situations, 135, 142, 143
communication networks, 70–71. *See also* radios
Communist Party, 3, 33, 47–48. *See also* Huks
Confesor, Tomas, 65, 95–96, 127, 148–49, 162, 221
constabulary training academy, Japanese-supervised, 62
Cook, Haruko Taya and Theodore, 242
Corregidor, 40, 55, 60–61, 62–63
Cotabato Chinese Mutual Aid Society, 75
cotton, 85, 95, 141, 298n101, 310n68
couriers, 70. *See also* communication networks; radios
Crevalle, 233
currency. *See* money, issues with
Cushing, Charles, 29, 99, 115, 157
Cushing, James, 54, 162, 182–83, 191, 199, 205, 231, 232, 233, 234, 270, 322n186
Cushing, Walter, 26, 28–29, 69, 75–76, 91, 95, 100–101, 133
CVP (Chinese volunteers of the Philippines), 21, 22

Dangwa, Bado, 20, 100, 101, 204, 320n129
Davao, Mindanao, 17, 256, 270
Dawn of Freedom, The, filming of, 185
Deisher's camp, 68, 87
Dianela, Damaso O., 18, 59, 121–22, 133, 150, 312n125
Dizon, Herminia "Minang," 29, 109, 160, 290n34

East Central Luzon Guerrilla Area (ECLGA), 216, 220–21, 239, 247–48, 261, 268
East Coast Luzon Guerrilla Force (ECLGF), 109, 129, 130, 133

Emergency Action Committee, Chinese community and, 21
enemy estimates, guerrilla inflation of, 267–68
Enriquez, Manuel P., 24, 104, 115, 157, 216, 221, 222
Escoda, Tony and Josefa, 158
Escudero, Salvador C., 18, 72, 126, 151, 182, 190, 212

FAIT (Fil-American Irregular Troops), 30, 89, 90, 126, 188–89, 221
Fassoth, Bill and Martin, 53, 76, 81–82, 96–97, 102, 109, 133, 292n109, 296n36, 296n42
Federation of Filipino Retailer Associations, 85
Fenton, Harry, 54, 95, 162–63, 182–83, 191–92
Fertig, Wendell W.: Americans sailing to Australia and, 130; Cushing (J.) and, 199, 233; guerrilla operations, 107–8, 118, 119, 142, 147–48, 155, 164, 166, 202, 343n16; illness, 178; Jan. 1943 summary report, 131–32; on Japanese and prostitutes, 45; Japanese on Leyte and, 262; on Japanese promises, 141; Leyte guerrillas and, 203; MacArthur on, 142, 144, 276; on Manila destruction, 269; Manzano and Luzon intelligence for, 240; Mindanao and, 87, 106–7, 121, 185–86, 270–71; Morgan and, 164, 190–91, 198, 322n183, 323n230, 323n235; on Muslim-Christian conflict, 86; *Narwhal* rendezvous, 208–9, 326n48; on popular support, 126; post-war celebrations, 271; radioing Australia, 138, 216; Sharp's surrender and, 68; on shortages, 257; on Straughn's capture, 188; supplies for, 146–47, 197; SWPA to investigate authority of, 137; on tropical forest survival, 52; U.S. invasion and, 265
Fifty, Operation, 146
Filipinos: as Asians but not Asians, Japanese on, 30–31; Japanese invasion of

the Philippines and, 12; unemployed, PEC employment bureau and, 139
flag, Filipino, 194
Flier, sinking, crew saved from, 333–34n63
Flor, Faustino, 16, 58–59, 180, 250–51
food shortages, 48, 50, 51, 157, 174, 175–76, 189, 217, 218, 236, 257. *See also* rice
Formosan labor service corps, 77
Fort Santiago, 42–43, 244–45, 256
France, Japanese reaction to fall (1940) of, 4
Free Negros, 88
Free Philippines, 21, 22
French Indochina, Japan occupation of, 4
Furukawa Plantation Company, 46–47

Gador, Gabriel, 78, 95, 125, 135, 157–58, 164, 168, 169, 180, 186, 199
gambling, indigenous, Japanese military and, 45
Ganaps, 37, 44, 123, 194, 259. *See also* Sakdal political party of peasants
General Workers' Union (*Aguman ding Malding Talapagobra* [AMT]), 3, 7, 33, 279n44
Grayling, 187
Great Marianas Turkey Shoot, 244
Greater East Asia Co-Prosperity Sphere, 5, 30, 138
Greater East Asian War Inquiry Commission, 184–85
Greater Japan Islam Association, 229
Gudgeon, 129, 134–35, 164
Guerrero family, 52, 60, 76, 294n162
guerrilla warfare: Americans recruited for, 56; conventional warfighting and, 268; impending U.S. invasion and, 265; Japanese airfields construction plans and, 237; Japan's defeat and, 272–73; major units traced by SWPA G-2 (1943–44), 136; Ramsey on fighting for the people's values and, 226
guerrillas, status of, 201, 276, 344n40
guns. *See* weapons

Hamamoto, Masakatsu, 200, 224, 261, 324n243
Hamner, Jordan, 68, 87, 130–31, 138, 173–74, 178, 224–25
Harries, Meirion and Susie, 111
Hayashi, Yoshihide, 62
Hedges, Charlie, 68, 86, 87, 137–38
Hitomi, Junsuke and Hitomi Propaganda Platoon, 31–32, 55, 85–86, 117, 149–50, 230, 312n121
Homma, Masaharu: Bataan surrender and, 50; Cebu operations and, 54; insurgents and, 22, 43, 55; Japanese on, 30; Japanese residents in Davao and, 17; Manila occupation and, 19, 24, 76–77; Mindanao attack by, 61; Philippine campaign orders for, 8; reinforcements for, 49; removed from command, 90; Sharp's surrender and, 69
Hong Kong, 30
Horan, John P., 17, 18, 24, 26, 34, 46, 69, 285n122
Hua Zhi (Chinese Anti-Japanese Guerrilla Force), 21, 35, 79–81, 194, 206
Huks (People's Army to Fight the Japs): assault Japanese on Mount Arayat, 256; chasing Ramsey, 102; guerrilla resistance and, 275; Hua Zhi training and, 79–80; MacArthur's isolation of, 276; mixed feelings about, 109–10; names of, 291n68; organization of, 291n60; Philippine constitution and, 194; Ramsey's bombings in Manila and, 250; SWPA wanting information on, 263–64; USAFFE guerrillas and, 145; on using war to create communist state, 47–49
hunger. *See* food shortages
Hunters/Hunter's guerrillas, 72, 89, 90, 189, 206, 220–21, 268

Igorots, guerrilla warfare by, 15–16
illnesses, 51–52, 91–93, 174. *See also* malaria; *specific guerrillas*
Ind, Allison, 82, 83, 84, 113, 119

independence, Philippine: elements fueling, 1, 3; FDR's pledge for, 20–21, 25, 42; Japanese and, 141, 200; MacArthur's victory and, 273–74; Mindanao guerrilla unit after, 202; preparatory committee for, 188; Quezon's physician on, 211; Tojo on, 42, 179; Tydings-McDuffie Act on, 4
inflation, 185, 217–18, 222, 328n119
informers, 122. *See also* collaborators with Japanese
infrastructure, Philippine, 66, 77
Ingeniero, Ismael P., 78, 95, 120, 208–9, 210, 252
intelligence, military, 29–30, 243. *See also* Allied Intelligence Bureau; *specific guerrillas/guerrilla groups*
Inuzuka, Koreshige, 192, 261, 322n188
irregular resistance. *See* guerrilla warfare

Japan: Allied POWs as forced labor in, 94; battle/nonbattle casualty rate, 342n3; combat deaths, 273, 342n14; losses on Luzon, 271; military alliance with Vichy French Indochina and, 5; Philippines Operation as decisive not defensive, 256; planning for guerrilla fighting, 229; preparations for war, 6, 7–9; regional interests of Overseas Development Society, 3; Second Philippine Republic and economic exploitation rights in, 200; on Tydings-McDuffie Act, 4; wartime payments/goods sent from occupied countries to, 342n6. *See also specific detachments*
Japanese military administration (JMA): on battle with MacArthur as inevitable, 224; domestic production and, 46–47; on ending the resistance, 183–84; famine and, 222, 328n148; farming concerns, 141; on "Fertig's death," 138; general shortages effects and, 176; government training institute of, 62; imperial general headquarters on complacency of, 228; Manila neighborhood associations and, 91, 217; mines and, 94; money printing, 218; munition storage sites' construction by, 170; on Muslim-Christian conflict, 86; non-Japanese auxiliary units, 162; Philippine constitution drafting and, 179; Philippine economy and, 84–85; on Philippine women, 160–61; refocus on economic exploitation, 122; shifts troops away from Japan, 248, 335n108; Utsunomiya and, 101; Vargas on, 194, 200
Japanese soldiers: brutalities by, 22–23, 66, 73–74, 112–13, 117, 122; on Mindanao, 178; observations on, 110–12; in Philippines, 320n135; radio propaganda by, 26–27; regular and reserve roster counts (1940 vs. 1943), 304n80
Japanese Supreme Southern Army headquarters, 236–37
Japanese-Americans, 115, 305n121
jungle, tropical, survival in, 51–53
Jurado, Enrique, 120, 181, 191, 209–10, 227
Jurika, Blanche W., 14, 77, 198, 218, 256
Jurika, Tommy, 77, 186, 197, 198

KALIBAPI (Association for Service to the New Philippines [*Kapisanan ng Paglilingkod sa Bagong Pilipinas*]), 123–24, 141, 179, 194
kamikazes, 266, 267, 340n271
Kang Fan (Philippine Chinese Anti-Japanese and Anti-Puppets League), 35, 65–66
Kangleon, Ruperto K.: disrupting Japanese exploitation of mines, 95; Leyte guerrillas and, 154–55, 163, 203–4, 313n152, 315n232; MacArthur recognizes as Leyte area commander, 265, 276, 339n255; moving natives from invasion beaches and, 262–63; *Narwhal* delivering supplies and, 208–9; Parsons and Rawolle on moving natives off beaches and, 264–65; supply requests, 197
Kano detachment, 12

Kawaguchi, Kiyotake, 49, 54, 55, 61, 69, 292n115
Kawamura, Saburo, 49, 54, 56–57, 61, 69
KAZ radio, Darwin, Australia, 118, 125–26, 135
Kempeitai (Japanese military police), 33, 42, 47, 129, 177, 213, 223. *See also* Nagahama, Akira
KFS radio, near San Francisco, 82–83, 108, 118, 138, 142, 244, 306n144
KGEI radio, San Francisco, 76, 167
Kimura detachment, 14
kinship networks, 1, 37, 44, 47, 56, 108, 109, 117, 127
knives, tribal variations in blades, 16
Korea, as Japanese colony, 160
KZRH radio, Japanese-controlled, 34, 167

Lang-Jain group, 203
language barriers, Filipino, Japan detachment landings and, 14
Lapham, Robert, 56, 79, 104, 115, 269; activates all squadrons, 267; on Bataan as medical disaster, 37; Bataan escape, 51, 91; on civilian support, 126, 174–75; Escudero's eviction of, 238; on guerrillas, 81, 89, 127, 226; on the Huks, 48, 263–64; Huks and, 49, 80–81, 250; imposter and, 120–21; Japanese patrols and, 103, 111–12; liberating POWs, 268; on MacArthur, 169, 263; medical aid for, 158; on O'Day and collaborators, 223; on POWs, 127; on Putnam, 130; radio and supplies for, 253–55; on romantic attachments, 159; Second Military District and, 235–36; on Thorp, 29, 60, 109, 290n34; U.S. invasion and, 265; Volckmann and Blackburn and, 133; Volckmann's Reorganization Plan of 1943 and, 192; on volunteers as runners, 70
Lapus, Licerio P., 14, 18, 72, 126, 151, 180, 190, 212, 220, 250–51

Laurel, Jose P.: amnesty order of, 216; Catholic church and, 150; on Filipinos in Japanese army, 273; gratitude mission to Tokyo and, 237; on hunger, 218; international radio and, 205–6; Japanese and, 61, 179, 183, 206, 236, 261; on Makapili, 130; new Philippine government and, 28; Pérez on, 213–14; Quezon and, 14, 19; Roxas and, 79, 147, 223–24; Sakdals as informers and, 194; as Second Philippine Republic president, 200; shooting of, 177, 318n70; son of, in Japan, 170; on Straughn, 189; war declarations and, 194, 249, 259
law and order, guerrillas maintaining, 88–89
leeches, 52
Leyte, 72–73, 125, 265
Leyte Gulf, Battle of, 266
LGAF (Luzon Guerrilla Armed Forces), 49, 157
LGF (Luzon Guerrilla Force), 71, 79
Lofgren, Stephen, 270, 271, 273, 341n307
looting, guerrillas' punishments for, 89
Luzon: casualties and killed in action on, 271, 341n313. *See also* Marking's guerrillas; Ramsey, Ed; Thorp, Claude A.; USAFIP-NL; Volckmann, Russell

MACA radio, 214, 225, 241
MacArthur, Douglas: Australian theater and, 36; authorized to occupy Leyte, 258; craving information from Philippines, 82; on Cushing surrendering prisoners, 233; Cushing's Japanese crash documents and, 233–34; on disloyal Filipinos, 343n26; evacuation from Philippines, 39–40; evacuation to Corregidor, 19; FDR recalls to active duty in Philippines, 5; on FDR's pledge for Philippine independence, 25; on fighting to

complete destruction, 31; Filipino trust in, 56; as first field marshal in Philippines, 4; on friction between allied military in Negros, 157; G-2 on Fertig's guerrillas on Mindanao, 131; on guerrilla commanders, 142, 144; on guerrilla leaders to focus on intelligence not hostile contacts, 142; on guerrillas' intelligence acquisitions, 263; on Horan's units retreating from Lingayen Gulf, 17–18; on Japanese landings on the Philippines, 12; on killing POWs, 127; on liberation of Manila, 269; mobilizing in Philippines by, 6; Nakar message to, on not surrendering, 83–84, 298n81, 298n85; orders on Bataan defense, 50; Pacific theater divided between Nimitz and, 41; Parsons' SPYRON plan and, 197; on Peralta commanding in the Visayas, 126, 307n204; Philippine guerrillas and operations planning by, 262; preparations for guerrilla war by, 29, 30; Quezon inauguration ceremony and, 20; Quezon leaving Corregidor and, 36; Quezon on Corregidor and, 24; on Ramsey returning to Luzon to command resistance forces, 227; reorganizes forces for guerrilla resistance, 38; reports from the Philippines and, 170–71; restricting Peralta's guerrilla activities, 126–27; return, guerrillas' effect on, 273; return, landing on Leyte, 265, 266; return, making case for, 252–53; as Southwest Pacific Area commander in chief, 57–58; supplies for Fertig and, 146–47; SWPA preparations for return of, 204–5; U.S. air raids and, 265; on Wainwright orders' validity, 67; on Whitney on AIB's Philippine regional section, 171, 173

Magsaysay, Ramon, 82, 127, 206, 267, 276

Makapili (informants), 130, 259

malaria, 36–37, 92, 256

Malaya, 30

Manila: internment camp in, 25–26; invasion and disrupted life in, 27–29; Japanese in, 63, 73, 123, 236–37; Kempeitai headquarters, 42–43; large fires (Jan. 1942), 24; liberation of, 268–69; looting in, 20; MacArthur declaration as open city, 19; neighborhood associations, 91, 217; Roeder's pipe bomb explosions, 249–50; U.S. air attack on, 258–59

Manila Harbor, Danish ships applying for Panamanian registration in, 14

Manila Tribune, 45, 46, 141, 144, 188, 256, 310n65

Manzano, Narciso L., 22, 177, 240, 284n88

Mao Tse-Tung, 35, 80, 102, 126, 275

Marking's guerrillas: American officers join, 51; assassination list, 287n188; Fil-American Irregular Troops and, 89; freeing American POWs, 78–79; Hunters and, 220–21; Japanese attack, 161, 235; Japanese patrols and, 157; Manila liberation and, 268; pressure on, 139; resistance fighters under, 22; Roxas on killing Laurel and, 213; Straughn's capture and, 188; supplies and radio operators to, 250. *See also* Augustin, Marcos V.

Marquez, Adalia, 12, 152, 177, 194–97, 244–45, 246, 256, 259, 261

Mata, Ernesto S., 18, 74, 125, 169, 316n2

McClish, Ernest, 88, 146–47, 154, 224

McGuire, Ralph, 29, 79, 103, 129, 133

medicines, 52–53, 175, 205, 239–40

Mellnik, Steve, 52, 70, 71, 107, 151, 186, 246

Merle-Smith, Van Santvoord, 57–58, 82, 83

Merrill, Gyles, 81–82, 96–97, 109, 133, 148, 169

Merritt, Pedro, 214, 225–26, 262, 329n175

messengers, 71. *See also* communication networks; radios
mestizo *hacienderos* (landowners), 1
military districts and SWPA-appointed commanders (Feb. 1943), 143
Mindanao, 185–86, 257, 270–71
Mindoro, 69, 119
mines (floating), 242
mines (ore), 47, 70, 78, 94, 134, 162, 184, 248–49, 260, 273, 300n166. *See also* war resources in the Philippines
Miranda, Blas, 72, 125, 155, 181, 203–4, 240, 276
Miranda, Juan Q., 43, 58–59, 122, 128, 133, 151, 180, 212, 230–31. *See also* TVGU
Miura, Toshio, 17, 61, 69, 294n165
Molintas, Dennis, 101, 115, 192, 204
money, issues with, 107–8, 142, 147, 175, 181, 185, 194, 217, 218–19, 238, 328n119
Morgan, Luis: alternate names for, 302n42; becomes a warlord, 105–6; confiscating boats, 108; evacuation to Australia for, 199, 323n235; Fertig and, 190–91, 322n183; Fertig on Mindanao and, 121; on Fertig's embrace of Moros and Americans, 166; Hamner, Smith, and Smith sailing to Australia and, 130; Japanese on Mindanao and, 178; McClish fighting against Japanese and, 146–47; recruiting for Fertig, 131, 163–64
Moros, 66, 75, 86, 105, 137–38, 166, 178, 229, 276. *See also* Bolo battalions
Moses, Martin: bounty for, 103; capture of, 177; on central Luzon mines, 17; escapes Bataan, 51; execution of, 239; on Japanese, 169; as leader, 28–29, 101, 115, 133, 134, 148; Luzon Guerrilla Force and, 71; radios and, 145, 156; Volckmann and Blackburn and, 99, 100, 116
Murata, Shozo, 141, 200, 224, 261
Murphy, Arthur, 24, 46, 69, 144
Muslims. *See* Moros

Naga, bowing to Japanese sentries in, 25
Nagahama, Akira, 31, 79, 103, 130, 223–24
Nagano, Osami and Nagao detachment, 6, 7, 55, 69
Nakar, Guillermo, 24, 83–84, 91, 103–4, 133, 298n81, 298n85
Napa, scuttling of, 50
Narwhal: civilian evacuees aboard, 209; Parsons ashore on Mindoro and, 208, 326n44; preparing for MacArthur's return and, 205; supplies deliveries and evacuee pickups, 221, 224–25, 251, 254, 257–58, 336n138, 336n158; war patrols and deliveries by, 238–39, 333n37, 336n137
National Salvation Society (Chinese group), 66
Navy, U.S., 11, 154, 248, 257, 259–60, 265, 267
navy, USAFIP, 131
Negritos, 15, 110
Negros, 74–75, 88, 93, 135, 157–58, 186–87, 247, 270. *See also* Abcede, Salvadore; Villamor, Jesus
New Guinea, Japanese bomb Port Moresby in, 32–33
newsletters/newspapers: Chinese, 35, 66; *The Echo of the Free North*, 69; Japanese control of, 123; Lavilles,' on Bohol, 210; Ramsey's, 247; Roces,' 179; TVGU, 44; Visayan, 188; Volckmann's, 194. *See also Manila Tribune*
Nichols Field, Philippines, 12
Nimitz, Chester, 41, 234, 252–53, 258
Nishihara, Takamaro, 269
Noble, Arthur, 133, 134, 174, 177, 239. *See also* Moses, Martin

O'Day, Patrick, 91, 99, 223, 299n142
Olongapo detachment, 69
Osmeña, Sergio, Sr., 14, 254, 262, 265, 266, 276, 340n265
Ota Corporation (Development Company), 46–47

Ozámiz, Jose, 166–67, 178, 217, 218, 223, 316n250, 329n159

P-38 Lightning fighters, 258–59, 337n197
Padua, Lorenzo, 128, 150, 180, 212, 319n98
Panama, Parsons as honorary consul for, 14
Panay, 117, 134, 187, 213, 270. *See also* Peralta, Macario
Panlilio, Yay, 12, 34, 43, 159, 188, 189; on food shortages, 222, 328n148; on Japanese, 73, 112, 113, 157, 235, 245–46; Marking and, 90, 139, 175, 299n131
Parker, George M., Jr., 14, 222, 281n17
Parsons, Chick, 12, 14, 281n13; arrives New York City, 98; diplomatic immunity, 25; Fertig-Pendatun dispute and, 164, 166; flying to Kangleon, 264; intelligence contacts, 166–67, 316n250; invasion currency and, 217; Japanese and, 58, 77, 95, 178, 218; Japanese on, 198; Leyte guerrillas and, 203; MacArthur's return and, 205, 262–63; meets Peralta, 221; on Negritos, 110; Philippines mission, 145–46; Phillips' landing spot and, 227; plan to go to Peralta, 306n147; radios and, 153–54; Smith on Mindanao and, 151; SPYRON plan and, 197; supplies coordination and, 173, 254; on *Trout* to Brisbane, 186
PCPI (preparatory committee for Philippine independence), 179, 188
Pearl Harbor, Japanese attack and Filipino concerns after, 11
PEC (Philippine Executive Committee), 28, 37, 123–24, 156–57, 179
Pendatun, Salapida, 66–67, 87, 105, 131, 164, 166, 197
Peralta, Macario: Abcede and, 120; agents, equipment, and supplies delivered to, 187; on all Philippine guerrillas, 118–19; allied military

and, 157–58, 314n177; Beloncio and Ruffy and, 191; Bicol and, 190; intelligence network, 181, 228, 258, 319n101; Japanese raids and, 187; leadership disputes and, 142; Leyte guerrillas and, 203; MacArthur on, 126–27, 144; meets Parsons, 221; Mindoro guerrillas and, 209–10; Muyco and Garcia and, 205; Panay guerrillas and, 65, 95–96, 125–26, 220–21; on Quezon, 152; radio network, 117–18, 181, 306n143, 319–20n106; on Ramsey, 227; SWPA's intelligence priorities and, 208; TVGU infighting and, 151; VCJC radio on Panay and, 82–83; Villamor and, 137; Villamor on, 148
Pestano-Jacinto, Pacita, 20, 41, 43, 45, 73, 123, 177
Philippine Chinese Anti-Japanese Volunteer Corps, 21–22
Philippine Chinese United Workers' Union, 21
Philippine Civil Liberties Union, 21
Philippine Constabulary, 105, 125, 199–200, 215
Philippine Prime Commodities Distribution Control Association, 85
Philippine Scouts, 6, 26, 51, 105, 125. *See also* Vera, Gaudencio V.
Philippine Sea, Battle of, 244
Philippines: AIB's Philippine regional section and, 173; casualties and war damage to, 274, 341–42n2; economic effects of war, 343n24; FDR's pledge for independence of, 20; history of conflict in, 1; independence under Japanese, 200; Japanese and new government in, 28; Japanese occupation plans for, 9; Japanese projections on campaign to conquer, 8; Japan's island defense for, 248; map of islands and major ethnic groups, 2; map of Japanese invasion landings in (Dec. 1941), 13; population (1941), 344n38; treasury's gold removed to

safeguard, 33; U.S. attraction policy and political movements in, 3–4. *See also* Second Philippine Republic
Philippines Chinese Youth Wartime Special Services Corps, 21
Philippines Cotton Growers Association, 141
Phillips, Lawrence H., 208, 209–10, 219, 227, 326n61, 326n63
Planet, Operation, 113–14, 134–35, 152, 207
political parties, Japanese and, 123–24
Pony Express, 221
Praeger, Ralph: attacks after Wainwright's surrender by, 91; attacks Japanese airfield at Tuguegarao, 27; bounty on, 103; Cagayan guerrilla force and, 19; capture of, 192; death of, 193, 239; intelligence for Moses and, 134; Luzon Guerrilla Force and, 79; radio, 100, 115–16, 134, 155–56; USAFIP-NL and, 115–16
President Coolidge, 58
President Quezon's Own Guerrillas, 37, 89, 189
prisoners of war, Japanese: Allies attack ships transferring, 246–47; Bataan death march, 53, 55, 100; brutalities against, 245–46, 334n78, 334nn83–84; executions of, 268; Filipino, paroled, 77; guerrillas killing of, 127; internment camps, 25–26, 47; paraded through Manila, 63; Philippine mines and, 95, 184, 320n126; reimprisonment of, 93–94
propaganda, 31–32, 35, 45–46, 115, 117, 124, 284n88
PRS (Philippine regional section): AIB organizing and, 83; arms for guerrillas and, 181, 320n110; on competition among intelligence teams, 258; guerrillas grow in value for, 197; preparing agents for intelligence missions, 173, 317nn31–32; radio network expansion by, 221; regional sections missions (map), 172; submarines for MacArthur's return and, 205; supplies for Lapham and, 253–54; SWPA reorganization and, 242; transformed from subsection to regional section, 170–71
psychological challenges, guerrillas and, 174

Quezon, Manuel: Americans on exile location for, 55–56; on call-up of reservists, 6–7; on collaborators with Japanese, 32; on Corregidor, 24; Cruz as representative of, 187, 211; death of, 254; departs for United States, 58; evacuation from Corregidor, 36; evacuation of, 19; on FDR's pledge for Philippine independence, 20–21, 25; on Filipinas captured as comfort women, 23; as first president of Philippines, 4; on guerrilla warfare, 7; guerrilla-staffed Mindanao currency board and, 147; on issuing emergency notes, 44; Japanese landings and council of state for, 14–15; on joining U.S. if it enters the war, 6; MacArthur on protection of, 14; MacArthur's departing letter to, 40; radio broadcast from Australia to Filipinos, 49
Quezon's physician (Emigdio Cruz), 187, 211
Quinto, Emilio, 114–15, 129, 135, 140, 152, 305n115

racism, Villamor on, 211, 212
radios: AIB's search for, 294n146; Almendres, Bell, and Ball complete, 108; Almendres' infrastructure for, 108; alternate stations, Smith on, 240; Avendaño's, 179; Castandeda's, Ramsey and, 239; Fenton's WJE station, 163; guerrilla, intelligence procurement through, 197; guerrilla, Japanese on elimination of, 249; hand-crank, for Barros, 255; high humidity and, 51–52; Ingeniero's, 210; Japanese attacks on, 241; Kangleon's, 339n247; Laurel's, listening

to international broadcasts, 205–6; MacArthur's chain of command and, 126; on Mindanao for AIB, 173; Nakar's, Japanese capture, 103–4; Nakar's, MacArthur and, 83–84, 298n81, 298n85; Negros defense and, 75; Operation Planet on Negros, 135; on Panay trying to contact Australia, 117–18; Parsons conditions for Fertig on, 146; Peralta's, on Luzon, 181; Praeger's, 100, 115–16, 134, 155–56; Praeger's, Japanese interception of, 192; Praeger's, offline, 177–78; preparing for MacArthur's return and, 205; Ramos Island observation team and, 242; Ramsey's camp, 247; Rowe's, on Mindoro, 251–52; saturating the islands with, 263; Smith's, in Sorsogon, 238; Smith's coast watching team, 214–15; smuggling, 156; on Surigao Strait, 153–54; for Thorp, 46; U.S. Army, 26; USAFIP-NL and Ball-Smith-SWPA net, 253; for Villamor's mission, 114, 179, 305nn114–115; for Volckmann, 161, 204; Whitney's search for, 317n24

railroad bridges, TVGU and, 43

Ramos, Benigno, 3, 28, 37, 123, 141, 261

Ramsey, Ed: on America's failure to defend the Philippines, 41; appendicitis of, 261; on Barker's death, 239; Barker's update to, 129; communicating without radio, 156; composite sketch for Baba of, 130; enemy harassment techniques, 247–48; on Filipino natives, 71–72; on Filipinos after Japanese invasion, 12; on food shortages, 260; on guerrilla leaders being paraded after torture, 193; on Huks, 80; Huks' bounty on, 159, 314n197; illnesses of, 102, 176, 274; invitation to visit Lim in Manila, 212–13; on Japanese propaganda, 31; on joining Filipino guerrillas, 56; on killing POWs, 127; on Lapham commanding Second Military District, 236; liberation of Manila and, 268; Luzon Guerrilla Force and, 79; MacArthur return questions and, 169; on MacArthur's demands for intelligence, 263; on MacArthur's departure, 40; MacArthur's support for, 276; on Makapili (informants), 138–39; meets colonel from Wainwright's staff, 121; to Mindanao in search of radio, 219, 226–27; Mona Snyder and, 158; move to Thorp's camp by, 60; Nagahama's bounty on, 103; on orders to defend east coast with Filipino cavalrymen, 16–17; on Philippines losing hope, 36–37; on quinine dose for malaria, 53; Ramon Magsaysay, 50–51; Roeder's pipe bombs around Manila and, 249–50; on romantic attachments, 159; on shelling of Bataan, 49–50; on survival in tropical forests, 52; on teenaged executioner, 128; Thorp's organization and, 109; Volckmann and Blackburn and, 133; on will to live, 93

rape, 44–45, 89, 104. *See also* comfort women

Recto, Claro, 28, 62, 179, 218

Red Star over China (Snow), 35, 80

religion. *See* Catholic church

Relunia, Leopoldo, 65, 180, 208

resources. *See* cotton; mine (ore); rice; war resources in the Philippines

Ricarte, Artemio, 28, 44, 86, 200, 211, 219, 261

rice: famine and shortages, 189, 206; inflation and, 222, 329n149; Japanese rationing of, 85, 298n96; Japanese seizure of, 27; Makapili (Japanese informants) and power of, 139; monopoly on, 218; Philippine production (1944), 260; shipment from Saigon to Manila, 62; shortage, Japanese control and, 46; shortage, JMA's cotton harvest goal and, 141. *See also* food shortages

rifles, 66, 72, 107, 283n81

Romulo, Carlos, 12, 26–27, 40, 47, 110, 139

rondas (vigilantes), 230
Roosevelt, Franklin (FDR): Atlantic Charter by Churchill and, 80; French Indochina recognition and, 5; guerrillas' effect on MacArthur's return and, 273; MacArthur meeting with, 252–53; on MacArthur's departure from Philippines, 39–40; PEC telegram on Filipino independence to, 37; on the Philippines as lost, 19; pledge on Philippine independence by, 20; on protecting Philippines from foreign invasion, 4; Quezon in exile and, 57; refuses to recognize Second Philippine Republic, 200; on sending planes to Europe, 36
Roxas, Manuel: asks Marking to not shoot Laurel again, 213; asks to be intelligence coordinator for Luzon, 240; continued loyalty to Quezon, 211; Economic Planning Board and, 236, 332n12; as intelligence source for Fertig, 147; Mona Snyder and, 158; Nagahama demanding arrest of, 223–24; post-war Liberal Party and, 276; preparatory committee for Philippine independence and, 179; Quezon's council of state on Japanese landings and, 14; Quezon's departing instructions to, 36; Snyder and, 189; surrender of, 79
Ruffy, Ramon, 119, 191, 209–10, 226–27, 326n62, 330n190

Saipan, battle for, 242, 249
Sakdal political party of peasants, 3, 123, 130, 194. *See also* Ganaps
Samar guerrillas, 262
Sandico, Francisco, 18, 30, 72, 190, 212
Santo Tomás. *See* University of Santo Tomás, Manila
schools, Filipino, 62, 294n176
Seadragon, 50
Seawolf, 259, 338n205
Second Philippine Republic, 200
sharecropper peasants, 1
Sharp, William F., 17, 38, 66, 67, 78, 125

Shinyo Maru, sinking of, 246–47, 257–58, 335n95
Short, Albert, 46, 51, 63, 87, 103
Smith, Charles M.: alternate radio stations for, 240; coast watcher team and, 214–15; confrontation with Merritt and, 225–26, 329n175; diversionary landings on Samar and, 262, 339n236; Fertig on Mindanao and, 87; Lapus funding by, 230; MACA radio and, 225; mysteries involving, 151; on new commonwealth government, 273; Parsons' mission to Philippines and, 146; radio contact with Fertig using KFS, 138; sailing to Australia, 130–31; Sharp's surrender and, 68; weather reports and, 238
Snyder, Ramona "Mona," 158, 189, 213, 247, 335n100
Socialist Party, 3, 33
Spanish-American War (1898), 1, 3
Spearfish, 61
Spencer, Grafton "Budd," 24, 46, 169, 235
spies, 43, 127, 204. *See also* collaborators with Japanese; intelligence, military
Stahl, Bob: on AIB communications, 84; Barros' radio and, 255; Chapman's dispatch on Japanese fleet and, 244; on Japanese interference with radio stations, 241; on Japanese radio-direction-finding rigs, 249; on lethality of Igorots, 15–16; MACA radio and, 225; on *Narwhal* in Butuan Bay, 209; new radio station on Bondoc Peninsula and, 263; romantic attachments and, 160; seeking aid from Vera, 251, 336n132; Smith's alternate radio stations and, 240; Smith's coast watching team and, 214–15; on weather observations' risk, 239
Straughn, Hugh, 30, 46, 89, 90, 188, 215, 321n157
submarines, 115. *See also Narwhal*; *Seawolf*
supplies: for AIB's regional section, Parsons and, 173; for Fertig's

guerrillas, 146–47; for Japanese vs. American soldiers, 342n12; *Narwhal* deliveries of, 221, 224–25, 238–39, 251; *Nautilus* delivery of, 241–42; for Panay and Mindanao guerrillas, 164; preparing for MacArthur's return and, 204–5; *Seawolf* deliveries of personnel and, 259; SWPA, to Visayan compadre networks, 181; transported across jungles by *cargadores*, 70; for Volckmann, 253
Sutherland, Richard, 17, 171, 233, 234, 262, 263
Swick, Herb, 99, 100, 161, 193
Swordfish, 36

Taguchi, Yoshigoro, 5–6, 47, 101, 184
Taiwan, Japanese seizure (1895) of, 3
Tanaka, Yuki and Tanaka detachment, 12, 111, 112–13, 170, 199–200, 245
Taruc, Luis, 3, 33, 38, 48, 49, 80, 102
Texans in Cavit, 221
textile industry, 185. *See also* cotton
Thorp, Claude A.: Barker and Ramsey and, 102; bounty on, 103; capture of, 109; execution of, 215, 239; fall of Bataan and, 60; Huks and, 49, 80; Luzon Guerrilla Force and, 71, 79, 99; MacArthur's support for, 276; Merrill as challenge to, 81–82; organizing guerrillas by, 29, 53; in prison, 133; radio for, 46, 290n34; report for MacArthur from, 129; Volckmann and Blackburn and, 97
Thresher, 173, 187
Tojo, Hideki, 7–8, 9, 10, 30, 42, 61–62, 141, 179, 183, 206, 255
Tokyo, 58, 206, 237, 248
Trout, 33, 173
Tuguegarao, Praeger-led attack on Japanese airfield at, 27
Tular, 105
Turko. *See* Boayes, Francisco "Turko"
TVGU (Tangcong Vaca Guerrilla Unit), 43–44, 59, 89, 104, 128, 206, 212, 220, 230, 231
Tydings-McDuffie Act, 4

Underground Railroad, 221
Uniform Code of Military Justice, guerrillas on POWs and, 127
United States "attraction policy," 3
University of Santo Tomás, Manila, 25, 47, 58, 68, 77, 157, 259, 268
Untalan, Sofronio T., 120, 219, 328n138
USAFFE (United States Army Forces, Far East), 11, 12, 16–17, 34, 50, 239–40, 283n81. *See also* MacArthur, Douglas
USAFIP-NL (United States Army Forces in the Philippines, North Luzon), 115–16, 215, 239–40, 268, 343n16
US-CVP (Chinese volunteers of the Philippines), 21, 283n81
Utsunomiya, Naokata, 101, 122, 150, 179, 200, 260, 261

Vargas, Jorge B., 19, 34, 162, 179, 194; Japanese and, 22, 61–62, 167; on Marking's assassination list, 287n188; new Philippine government and, 28; Quezon's representative and, 187, 211; son of, 170
VCJC radio, 82–83
Vera, Gaudencio V., 37, 128, 241, 251, 336n132, 336n134
Villafuerte, Mariano, 15, 27–28, 59–60
Villamor, Jesus: Abcede's briefing and, 135, 137; allied military and, 157–58, 173; to Australia to debrief, 207; on collaborators, 152–53; Cushing (J.) appeals to, 191–92; on famine, 174; on FDR, 20; guerrilla politics and, 142, 148; on Ingeniero, 78; as intelligence agent, 113–14; on Japanese soldiers, 73, 110, 112, 123; on MacArthur, 40; Mindanao guerrilla units after independence and, 202; on morale, 187–88; on Morgan, 164; Negros command and, 168–69, 180, 186; Parsons and Smith landing on Mindanao and, 151; on Philippine economy, 84–85; Quezon and, 58; on Quezon denouncing Vargas, 152; radio network, 140, 179, 319n93;

regiment roster stolen, 221–22; romantic attachments and, 160, 170; on Straughn's capture, 321n157; on SWPA racism, 211; Young report for, 129. *See also* Planet, Operation

Vinzons, Wenceslao Q., 15, 16, 58–59, 82

Vinzons' Traveling Guerrillas (VTG), 15, 58–59, 104, 150, 151

Visayan-Mindanao force, 34, 54

Visayas, 69, 126, 207–8, 269–70, 307n204

Volckmann, Russell: *bacci* ceremony to protect camp of, 169–70; on Bataan escapees, 91; on Benget vs. Ifuago, 215–16, 327n96; on collaborators, 153; company-sized camps and, 193; on Dangwa, 101; escapes Bataan, 51; expansion plans, 215; on field hospitals, 239–40; on Filipino kinship networks, 109; on Filipino reservist training, 6–7; full-time guerrilla outfits and, 193–94; headquarters at Parker's camp in Benguet, 222; health recovery, 53, 96–98, 99, 100; illness, 52, 60, 76, 176, 274, 296n42, 318n68; inland airfields for MacArthur and, 267; Japanese counterattack and, 116–17; on Japanese informants, 122; Japanese seizing Lingayen Gulf and, 17; on Japanese torture, 334n83; at Kiangan-area camp, 124; on killing POWs, 127; Land Communication Company and, 70; MacArthur and, 20, 276; Moses and Noble capture and, 177–78; on North Luzon resistance, 18; post-war legal troubles, 338–39n232; on psychological challenges, 174; radio contact with SWPA, 204, 253, 255; Ramsey and Lapham and, 133; Reorganization Plan of 1943, 192, 322n190; on Second Military District, 235–36; Sixth Army in northern Luzon and, 268; USAFIP-NL and, 115. *See also* USAFIP-NL

Wa Chi (Chinese Squadron 48), 48

Wachi, Takaji, 79, 138, 179, 183, 260–61

Wainwright, Jonathan, 11, 29, 38, 50, 54, 60–61, 62–63

war resources in the Philippines, 5, 9, 47, 77, 94–95, 300n166. *See also* cotton; mine (floating) and (ore); rice

Warner, Everett, 24, 26, 69, 83

Wartime Service Corps, 21

weapons, 15–16, 128, 175. *See also* rifles; supplies

wearing-out policy, Filipino guerrillas and, 155, 313n159

weather stations, 238–39

Whitney, Courtney, Jr., 171, 173, 197, 265, 317n24; civilian evacuees and, 209; crash site documents and, 233, 234; on Cushing, 233; Parsons and, 264; on Peralta, 181; Rosenquist's POW assistance and, 246; on Villamor, 207

Willis, Donald, 37, 52, 66, 159, 160, 176, 245, 246, 334n88

Willoughby, Charles, 29, 83, 84, 211–12

WJE radio, Fenton's use of, 163

women: comfort women, 23, 45; failed rice harvest and famine and, 206; Ingeniero's Boforce auxiliary, 210; Japanese molestation of, 44–45, 89, 104, 250; JMA on reform of, 160–61; Parker's Benguet camp auxiliary, 222; resistance and, 158–59, 314nn186–187; as sex slaves, 20

World War II, 33, 36, 64, 65

Yamashita, Tomoyuki, 260–61, 266, 267, 268, 271

Yokoyama, Shizuo, 260, 267, 269

YuHico, Delfin, 114, 129, 152, 312n133

Yulo, Jose, 14, 28, 162, 179, 200, 211, 237

Yumol family, 11, 19, 22, 73, 91, 152, 258

Zabat, Montano, 18, 151, 180, 190, 212, 230, 231, 250–51, 331n215

Zambales guerrillas, 82

About the Author

Dr. James Kelly Morningstar is a retired U.S. Army armor officer and decorated combat veteran with degrees from West Point and Kansas State University, a master's degree from Georgetown University, and a PhD from the University of Maryland. He currently teaches military history at Georgetown. This is his second book.

The Naval Institute Press is the book-publishing arm of the U.S. Naval Institute, a private, nonprofit, membership society for sea service professionals and others who share an interest in naval and maritime affairs. Established in 1873 at the U.S. Naval Academy in Annapolis, Maryland, where its offices remain today, the Naval Institute has members worldwide.

Members of the Naval Institute support the education programs of the society and receive the influential monthly magazine *Proceedings* or the colorful bimonthly magazine *Naval History* and discounts on fine nautical prints and on ship and aircraft photos. They also have access to the transcripts of the Institute's Oral History Program and get discounted admission to any of the Institute-sponsored seminars offered around the country.

The Naval Institute's book-publishing program, begun in 1898 with basic guides to naval practices, has broadened its scope to include books of more general interest. Now the Naval Institute Press publishes about seventy titles each year, ranging from how-to books on boating and navigation to battle histories, biographies, ship and aircraft guides, and novels. Institute members receive significant discounts on the Press' more than eight hundred books in print.

Full-time students are eligible for special half-price membership rates. Life memberships are also available.

For more information about Naval Institute Press books that are currently available, visit www.usni.org/press/books. To learn about joining the U.S. Naval Institute, please write to:

Member Services
U.S. Naval Institute
291 Wood Road
Annapolis, MD 21402-5034
Telephone: (800) 233-8764
Fax: (410) 571-1703
Web address: www.usni.org

www.ingramcontent.com/pod-product-compliance
Lightning Source LLC
Chambersburg PA
CBHW030509080526
44586CB00011B/124